INDIA

WHAT CAN IT TEACH US?

INDIA
WHAT CAN IT TEACH US?

by

F. MAX MULLER, K.M.

GYAN

Published by

Gyan Publishing House
5, Ansari Road
Daryaganj, New Delhi-110002
Phone: 011-47034999, 9811692060
E-mail: books@gyanbooks.com

Distribution Network
gyanbooks.com
India, USA, Canada, UK, Australia, France

ISBN : 978-81-212-9972-5 (PB)
First Published, 1883

2nd Impression 2021

Printed at: Gyan Press, Delhi.

India
What Can it Teach us?
Author: F. Max Muller

INDIA

WHAT CAN IT TEACH US?

A Course of Lectures

DELIVERED BEFORE THE UNIVERSITY OF CAMBRIDGE

BY

F. MAX MÜLLER, K.M.

HON. DOCTOR OF LAW IN THE UNIVERSITY OF CAMBRIDGE;
MEMBER OF THE FRENCH INSTITUTE.

London:

LONGMANS, GREEN, AND CO.

1883.

DEDICATED

TO

E. B. COWELL, M.A. LL.D.

PROFESSOR OF SANSKRIT AND FELLOW OF CORPUS CHRISTI COLLEGE
IN THE UNIVERSITY OF CAMBRIDGE.

My dear Cowell,

As these Lectures would never have been written or delivered but for your hearty encouragement, I hope you will now allow me to dedicate them to you, not only as a token of my sincere admiration of your great achievements as an Oriental scholar, but also as a memorial of our friendship, now more than thirty years old, a friendship which has grown from year to year, has weathered many a storm, and will last, I trust, for what to both of us may remain of our short passage from shore to shore.

I must add, however, that in dedicating these Lectures to you, I do not wish to throw upon you any responsibility for the views which I have put forward in them. I know that you do not agree with some of my views on the ancient religion and literature of India, and I am well aware that with regard to the recent date which I have assigned to the whole of what is commonly called the Classical Sanskrit Literature, I stand almost alone. No, if friendship can claim any voice in the courts of science and literature, let me assure you that I shall consider your outspoken criticism of my Lectures as the very best proof of your true and honest friendship. I have through life considered it the greatest honour if real scholars, I mean men not only of learning, but of judgment and character, have considered my writings worthy of a severe and searching criticism, and I have cared far more for the production of one single new fact, though it spoke against me, than for any amount of empty praise or empty abuse. Sincere devotion to his studies and an unswerving love of truth ought to furnish the true scholar with an armour impermeable to flattery or abuse, and with a vizor that shuts out no ray of light, from whatever quarter it may come. More light, more truth, more facts, more combination of facts, these are his quest. And if in that quest he fails, as many have failed before him, he knows that in the search for truth failures are sometimes the condition of victory, and the true conquerors often those whom the world calls the vanquished.

You know better than anybody else the present state of Sanskrit scholarship. You know that at present and for some time to come Sanskrit scholarship means discovery and conquest. Every one of your own works marks a real advance, and a permanent occupation of new ground. But you know also how small a strip has as yet been explored of the vast continent of Sanskrit literature, and how much still remains *terra incognita*. No doubt this exploring work is troublesome, and often disappointing, but young students must learn the truth of a remark lately made by a distinguished member of the Indian Civil Service, whose death we all deplore, Dr. Burnell, 'that no trouble is thrown away which saves trouble to others.' We want men who will work hard, even at the risk of seeing their labours unrequited; we want strong and bold men who are not afraid of storms and shipwrecks. The worst sailors are not those who suffer shipwreck, but those who only dabble in puddles and are afraid of wetting their feet.

It is easy now to criticise the labours of Sir William Jones, Thomas Colebrooke, and Horace Hayman Wilson, but what would have become of Sanskrit scholarship if they had not rushed in where even now so many fear to tread? and what will become of Sanskrit scholarship if their conquests are for ever to mark the limits of our knowledge? You know best that there is more to be discovered in Sanskrit literature than Nalas and Sakuntalâs, and surely the young men who every year go out to India are not deficient in the spirit of enterprise, or even of adventure? Why then should it be said that the race of bold explorers, who once rendered the name of the Indian Civil Service illustrious over the whole world, has well-nigh become extinct, and that England, which offers the strongest incentives and the most brilliant opportunities for the study of the ancient language, literature, and history of India, is no longer in the van of Sanskrit scholarship?

If some of the young Candidates for the Indian Civil Service who listened to my Lectures, quietly made up their minds that such a reproach shall be wiped out, if a few of them at least determined to follow in the footsteps of Sir William Jones, and to show to the world that Englishmen who have been able to achieve by pluck, by perseverance, and by real political genius the material conquest of India, do not mean to leave the laurels of its intellectual conquest entirely to other countries, then I shall indeed rejoice, and feel that I have paid back, in however small a degree, the large debt of gratitude which I owe to my adopted country and to some of its greatest statesmen, who have given me the opportunity which I could find nowhere else of realising the dreams of my life,—the publication of the text and commentary of the Rig-veda, the most ancient book of Sanskrit, aye of Aryan literature, and now the edition of the translations of the 'Sacred Books of the East.'

I have left my Lectures very much as I delivered them at Cambridge. I am fond of the form of Lectures, because it seems to me the most natural form which in our age didactic composition ought to take. As in ancient Greece the dialogue reflected most truly the intellectual life of the people, and as in the Middle Ages learned literature naturally assumed with the recluse in his monastic cell the form of a long monologue, so with us the lecture places the writer most readily in that position in which he is accustomed to deal with his fellow-men, and to communicate his knowledge to others. It has no doubt certain disadvantages. In a lecture which is meant to be didactic we have, for the sake of completeness, to say and to repeat certain things which must be familiar to some of our readers, while we are also forced to leave out information which, even in its imperfect form, we should probably not hesitate to submit to our fellow-students, but which we feel we have not yet sufficiently mastered and matured to enable us to place it clearly and simply before a larger public.

But the advantages outweigh the disadvantages. A lecture, by keeping a critical audience constantly before our eyes, forces us to condense our subject, to discriminate between what is important and what is not, and often to deny ourselves the pleasure of displaying what may have cost us the greatest labour, but is of little consequence to other scholars. In lecturing we are constantly reminded of what students are so apt to forget, that their knowledge is meant not for themselves only, but for others, and that to know well means to be able to teach well. I confess I can never write unless I think of somebody for whom I write, and I should never wish for a better audience to have before my mind than the learned, brilliant, and kind-hearted assembly by which I was greeted in your University.

Still I must confess that I did not succeed in bringing all I wished to say, and more particularly the evidence on which some of my statements rested, up to the higher level of a lecture, and I have therefore added a number of notes containing the less organised matter which resisted as yet that treatment which is necessary before our studies can realise their highest purpose, that of feeding, invigorating, and inspiriting the minds of others.

Yours affectionately,

F. MAX MÜLLER.

OXFORD,

December 16, 1882.

CONTENTS.

WHAT CAN INDIA TEACH US?

LECTURE I.

When I received from the Board of Historical Studies at Cambridge the invitation to deliver a course of lectures, specially intended for the Candidates for the Indian Civil Service, I hesitated for some time, feeling extremely doubtful whether in a few public discourses I could say anything that would be of real use to them in passing their examinations. To enable young men to pass their examinations seems now to have become the chief, if not the only object of the Universities; and to no class of students is it of greater importance to pass their examinations, and to pass them well, than to the Candidates for the Indian Civil Service.

But although I was afraid that attendance on a few public lectures, such as I could give, would hardly benefit a Candidate who was not already fully prepared to pass through the fiery ordeal of the three London examinations, I could not on the other hand shut my eyes completely to the fact that, after all, Universities were not meant entirely, or even chiefly, as stepping-stones to an examination, but that there is something else which Universities can teach and ought to teach—nay, which I feel quite sure they were originally meant to teach—something that may not have a marketable value before a Board of Examiners, but which has a permanent value for the whole of our life, and that is a real interest in our work, and, more than that, a love of our work, and, more than that, a true joy and happiness in our work. If a University can teach that, if it can engraft that one small living germ in the minds of the young men who come here to study and to prepare themselves for the battle of life, and, for what is still more difficult to encounter, the daily dull drudgery of life, then, I feel convinced, a University has done more, and conferred a more lasting benefit on its pupils than by helping them to pass the most difficult examinations, and to take the highest place among Senior Wranglers or First-Class men.

Unfortunately that kind of work which is now required for passing one examination after another, that process of cramming and crowding which has of late been brought to the highest pitch of perfection, has often the very opposite effect, and instead of exciting an appetite for work, it is apt to produce an indifference, if not a kind of intellectual nausea, that may last for life.

And nowhere is this so much to be feared as in the case of Candidates for the Indian Civil Service. After they have passed their first examination for admission to the Indian Civil Service, and given proof that they have received the benefits of a liberal education, and acquired that general information in classics, history, and mathematics, which is provided at our Public Schools, and forms no doubt the best and surest foundation for all more special and professional studies in later life, they suddenly find themselves torn away from their old studies and their old friends, and compelled to take up new subjects which to many of them seem strange, outlandish, if not repulsive. Strange alphabets, strange languages, strange names, strange literatures and laws have to be faced, 'to be got up' as it is called, not from choice, but from dire necessity. The whole course of study during two years is determined for them, the subjects fixed, the books prescribed; the examinations regulated, and there is no time to look either right or left, if a candidate wishes to make sure of taking each successive fence in good style, and without an accident.

I know quite well that this cannot be helped. I am not speaking against the system of examinations in general, if only they are intelligently conducted; nay, as an old examiner myself, I feel bound to say that the amount of knowledge produced ready-made at these examinations is to my mind perfectly astounding. But while the answers are there on paper, strings of dates, lists of royal names and battles, irregular verbs, statistical figures and whatever else you like, how seldom do we find that the heart of the candidates is in the work which they have to do. The results produced are certainly most ample and voluminous, but they rarely contain a spark of original thought, or even a clever mistake. It is work done from necessity, or, let us be just, from a sense of duty, but it is seldom, or hardly ever, a labour of love.

Now why should that be? Why should a study of Greek and Latin,—of the poetry, the philosophy, the laws and the art of Greece and Italy,—seem congenial to us, why should it excite even a certain enthusiasm, and command general respect, while a study of Sanskrit, and of the ancient poetry, the philosophy, the laws, and the art of India is looked upon, in the best case, as curious, but is considered by most people as useless, tedious, if not absurd.

And, strange to say, this feeling exists in England more than in any other country. In France, Germany, and Italy, even in Denmark, Sweden, and Russia, there is a vague charm connected with the name of India. One of the most beautiful poems in the German language is the *Weisheit der Brahmanen*, the 'Wisdom of the Brahmans,' by Rückert, to my mind more rich in thought and more perfect in form than even Goethe's *West-östlicher Divan*. A scholar who studies Sanskrit in Germany is supposed to be initiated in the deep and dark mysteries of ancient wisdom, and a man who has travelled in India, even if he has only discovered Calcutta, or Bombay, or Madras, is listened to like another Marco Polo. In England a student of Sanskrit is generally considered a bore, and an old Indian Civil servant, if he begins to describe the marvels of Elephanta or the Towers of Silence, runs the risk of producing a count-out.

There are indeed a few Oriental scholars whose works are read, and who have acquired a certain celebrity in England, because they were really men of uncommon genius, and would have ranked among the great glories of the country, but for the misfortune that their energies were devoted to Indian literature—I mean Sir William Jones, 'one of the most enlightened of the sons of men,' as Dr. Johnson called him, and Thomas Colebrooke. But the names of others who have done good work in their day also, men such as Ballantyne, Buchanan, Carey, Crawfurd, Davis, Elliot, Ellis, Houghton,

Leyden, Mackenzie, Marsden, Muir, Prinsep, Rennell, Turnour, Upham, Wallich, Warren, Wilkins, Wilson, and many others, are hardly known beyond the small circle of Oriental scholars, and their works are looked for in vain in libraries which profess to represent with a certain completeness the principal branches of scholarship and science in England.

How many times when I advised young men, candidates for the Indian Civil Service, to devote themselves before all things to a study of Sanskrit, have I been told, 'What is the use of our studying Sanskrit? There are translations of Sakuntalâ, Manu, and the Hitopadesa, and what else is there in that literature that is worth reading? Kâlidâsa may be very pretty, and the Laws of Manu are very curious, and the fables of the Hitopadesa are very quaint; but you would not compare Sanskrit literature with Greek, or recommend us to waste our time in copying and editing Sanskrit texts which neither teach us nothing that we do not know already, or teach us something which we do not care to know?'

This seems to me a most unhappy misconception, and it will be the chief object of my lectures to try to remove it, or at all events to modify it, as much as possible. I shall not attempt to prove that Sanskrit literature is as good as Greek literature. Why should we always compare? A study of Greek literature has its own purpose, and a study of Sanskrit literature has its own purpose; but what I feel convinced of, and hope to convince you of, is that Sanskrit literature, if studied only in a right spirit, is full of human interests, full of lessons which even Greek could never teach us, a subject worthy to occupy the leisure, and more than the leisure, of every Indian Civil servant;

and certainly the best means of making any young man who has to spend five-and-twenty years of his life in India, feel at home among the Indians, as a fellow-worker among fellow-workers, and not as an alien among aliens. There will be abundance of useful and most interesting work for him to do, if only he cares to do it, work such as he would look for in vain, whether in Italy or in Greece, or even among the pyramids of Egypt or the palaces of Babylon.

You will now understand why I have chosen as the title of my lectures, *What can India teach us?* True, there are many things which India has to learn from us; but there are other things, and, in one sense, very important things, which we too may learn from India.

If I were to look over the whole world to find out the country most richly endowed with all the wealth, power, and beauty that nature can bestow—in some parts a very paradise on earth—I should point to India. If I were asked under what sky the human mind has most fully developed some of its choicest gifts, has most deeply pondered on the greatest problems of life, and has found solutions of some of them which well deserve the attention even of those who have studied Plato and Kant—I should point to India. And if I were to ask myself from what literature we, here in Europe, we who have been nurtured almost exclusively on the thoughts of Greeks and Romans, and of one Semitic race, the Jewish, may draw that corrective which is most wanted in order to make our inner life more perfect, more comprehensive, more universal, in fact more truly human, a life, not for this life only, but a transfigured and eternal life—again I should point to India.

I know you will be surprised to hear me say this. I know that more particularly those who have spent many years of active life in Calcutta, or Bombay, or Madras, will be horror-struck at the idea that the humanity they meet with there, whether in the bazaars or in the courts of justice, or in so-called native society, should be able to teach *us* any lessons.

Let me therefore explain at once to my friends who may have lived in India for years, as civil servants, or officers, or missionaries, or merchants, and who ought to know a great deal more of that country than one who has never set foot on the soil of Âryâvarta, that we are speaking of two very different Indias. I am thinking chiefly of India, such as it was a thousand, two thousand, it may be three thousand years ago; they think of the India of to-day. And again, when thinking of the India of to-day, they remember chiefly the India of Calcutta, Bombay, or Madras, the India of the towns. I look to the India of the village communities, the true India of the Indians.

What I wish to show to you, I mean more especially the candidates for the Indian Civil Service, is that this India of a thousand, or two thousand, or three thousand years ago, aye the India of to-day also, if only you know where to look for it, is full of problems the solution of which concerns all of us, even us in this Europe of the nineteenth century.

If you have acquired any special tastes here in England, you will find plenty to satisfy them in India; and whoever has learnt to take an interest in any of the great problems that occupy the best thinkers and workers at home, need certainly not be afraid of India proving to him an intellectual exile.

If you care for geology, there is work for you from the Himâlayas to Ceylon

If you are fond of botany, there is a flora rich enough for many Hookers.

If you are a zoologist, think of Haeckel, who is just now rushing through Indian forests and dredging in Indian seas, and to whom his stay in India is like the realisation of the brightest dream of his life.

If you are interested in Ethnology, why India is like a living ethnological museum.

If you are fond of Archæology, if you have ever assisted at the opening of a barrow in England, and know the delight of finding a fibula, or a knife, or a flint in a heap of rubbish, read only 'General Cunningham's Annual Reports of the Archæological Survey of India,' and you will be impatient for the time when you can take your spade and bring to light the ancient Vihâras or Colleges built by the Buddhist monarchs of India.

If ever you amused yourselves with collecting coins, why the soil of India teems with coins, Persian, Carian, Thracian, Parthian, Greek, Macedonian, Scythian, Roman[1], and Mohammedan. When Warren Hastings was Governor-General, an earthen pot was found on the bank of a river in the province of Benares, containing 172 gold Darics[2]. Warren Hastings considered himself as making the most munificent present to his masters that he might

---

[1] Pliny (VI. 26) tells us that in his day the annual drain of bullion into India, in return for her valuable produce, reached the immense amount of 'five hundred and fifty millions of sesterces.' See E. Thomas, The Indian Balhará, p. 13.

[2] Cunningham, in the Journal of the Asiatic Society of Bengal, 1881, p. 184.

ever have it in his power to send them, by presenting those ancient coins to the Court of Directors. The story is that they were sent to the melting pot. At all events they had disappeared when Warren Hastings returned to England. It rests with you to prevent the revival of such Vandalism.

In one of the last numbers of the 'Asiatic Journal of Bengal' you may read of the discovery of a treasure as rich in gold almost as some of the tombs opened by Dr. Schliemann at Mykenæ, nay I should add, perhaps not quite unconnected with some of the treasures found at Mykenæ; yet hardly any one has taken notice of it in England[1]!

The study of Mythology has assumed an entirely new character, chiefly owing to the light that has been thrown on it by the ancient Vedic Mythology of India. But though the foundation of a true Science of Mythology has been laid, all the detail has still to be worked out, and could be worked out nowhere better than in India.

Even the study of fables owes its new life to India, from whence the various migrations of fables have been traced at various times and through various channels from East to West[2]. Buddhism is now known to have been the principal source of our legends and parables. But here too, many problems still wait for their solution. Think, for instance, of the allusion[3] to the fable of the donkey in the lion's skin,

---

[1] See note A.

[2] See Selected Essays, vol. I, p. 500, 'The Migration of Fables.'

[3] Cratylus 411 A. 'Still, as I have put on the lion's skin, I must not be faint-hearted.' Possibly, however, this may refer to Hercules, and not to the fable of the donkey in the lion's or the tiger's skin. In the Hitopadesa, a donkey, being nearly starved, is

which occurs in Plato's Cratylus. Was that borrowed from the East? Or take the fable of the weasel changed by Aphrodite into a woman who, when she saw a mouse, could not refrain from making a spring at it. This, too, is very like a Sanskrit fable, but how then could it have been brought into Greece early enough to appear in one of the comedies of Strattis, about 400 B.C.[1]? Here, too, there is still plenty of work to do.

We may go back even further into antiquity, and still find strange coincidences between the legends of India and the legends of the West, without as yet being able to say how they travelled, whether from East to West, or from West to East. That at the time of Solomon, there was a channel of communication open between India and Syria and Palestine is established beyond doubt, I believe, by certain Sanskrit words which occur in the Bible as names of articles of export from Ophir, articles such as ivory, apes, peacocks, and sandalwood, which, taken together, could not have been exported from any country but India[2]. Nor is there any reason to suppose that the commercial intercourse between India, the Persian Gulf, the Red Sea and the Mediterranean was ever completely interrupted, even at the time when the Book of Kings is supposed to have been written.

---

sent by his master into a cornfield to feed. In order to shield him he puts a tiger's skin on him. All goes well till a watchman approaches, hiding himself under his grey coat, and trying to shoot the tiger. The donkey thinks it is a grey female donkey, begins to bray, and is killed. On a similar fable in Æsop, see Benfey, Pantschatantra, vol. I, p. 463; M. M., Selected Essays, vol. I, p. 513.

[1] See Fragmenta Comic. (Didot) p. 302; Benfey, l. c. vol. I, p. 374.

[2] Lectures on the Science of Language, vol. I, p. 231.

Now you remember the judgment of Solomon, which has always been admired as a proof of great legal wisdom among the Jews[1]. I must confess that, not having a legal mind, I never could suppress a certain shudder when reading the decision of Solomon: 'Divide the living child in two, and give half to the one, and half to the other.'

Let me now tell you the same story as it is told by the Buddhists, whose sacred Canon is full of such legends and parables. In the Kanjur, which is the Tibetan translation of the Buddhist Tripi*t*aka, we likewise read of two women who claimed each to be the mother of the same child. The king, after listening to their quarrels for a long time, gave it up as hopeless to settle who was the real mother. Upon this Visâkhâ stepped forward and said: 'What is the use of examining and cross-examining these women. Let them take the boy and settle it among themselves.' Thereupon both women fell on the child, and when the fight became violent, the child was hurt and began to cry. Then one of them let him go, because she could not bear to hear the child cry.

That settled the question. The king gave the child to the true mother, and had the other beaten with a rod.

This seems to me, if not the more primitive, yet the more natural form of the story—showing a deeper knowledge of human nature, and more wisdom than even the wisdom of Solomon[2].

---

[1] 1 Kings iii. 25.

[2] See some excellent remarks on this subject in Rhys Davids, Buddhist Birth Stories, vol. I, pp. xiii and xliv. The learned scholar gives another version of the story from a Singhalese trans-

Many of you may have studied not only languages, but also the Science of Language, and is there any country in which some of the most important problems of that science, say only the growth and decay of dialects, or the possible mixture of languages, with regard not only to words, but to grammatical elements also, can be studied to greater advantage than among the Aryan, the Dravidian and the Mu*nd*a inhabitants of India, when brought in contact with their various invaders and conquerors, the Greeks, the Yue-tchi, the Arabs, the Persians, the Moguls, and lastly the English.

Again, if you are a student of Jurisprudence, there is a history of law to be explored in India, very different from what is known of the history of law in Greece, in Rome, and in Germany, yet both by its contrasts and by its similarities full of suggestions to the student of Comparative Jurisprudence. New materials are being discovered every year, as, for instance, the so-called Dharma or Samayâ*k*ârika Sûtras, which have supplied the materials for the later metrical law-books, such as the famous Laws of Manu. What was once called 'The Code of Laws of Manu,' and confidently referred to 1200, or at least 500 B.C., is now hesitatingly referred to perhaps the fourth century A.D., and called neither a Code, nor a Code of Laws, least of all, the Code of Laws of Manu.

If you have learnt to appreciate the value of recent researches into the antecedents of all law, namely the foundation and growth of the simplest political communities—and nowhere could you have had better opportunities for it than here at Cambridge—you

lation of the *G*âtaka, dating from the fourteenth century, and he expresses a hope that Dr. Fausböll will soon publish the Pâli original.

will find a field of observation opened before you in the still existing village estates in India that will amply repay careful research.

And take that which, after all, whether we confess or deny it, we care for more in this life than for anything else—nay, which is often far more cared for by those who deny than by those who confess—take that which supports, pervades, and directs all our acts and thoughts and hopes—without which there can be neither village community nor empire, neither custom nor law, neither right nor wrong—take that which, next to language, has most firmly fixed the specific and permanent barrier between man and beast—which alone has made life possible and bearable, and which, as it is the deepest, though often hidden spring of individual life, is also the foundation of all national life,—the history of all histories, and yet the mystery of all mysteries—take religion, and where can you study its true origin, its natural growth, and its inevitable decay better than in India, the home of Brahmanism, the birthplace of Buddhism, and the refuge of Zoroastrianism, even now the mother of new superstitions—and why not, in the future, the regenerate child of the purest faith, if only purified from the dust of nineteen centuries?

You will find yourselves everywhere in India between an immense past and an immense future, with opportunities such as the old world could but seldom, if ever, offer you. Take any of the burning questions of the day—popular education, higher education, parliamentary representation, codification of laws, finance, emigration, poor-law, and whether you have anything to teach and to try, or anything to observe and to learn, India will supply you with a laboratory such as exists nowhere else. That very Sanskrit, the study of which may at first seem so tedious to you and so useless, if only you will carry it on, as you may carry it on here at Cambridge better than anywhere else, will open before you large layers of literature, as yet almost unknown and unexplored, and allow you an insight into strata of thought deeper than any you have known before, and rich in lessons that appeal to the deepest sympathies of the human heart.

Depend upon it, if only you can make leisure, you will find plenty of work in India for your leisure hours.

India is not, as you may imagine, a distant, strange, or, at the very utmost, a curious country. India for the future belongs to Europe, it has its place in the Indo-European world, it has its place in our own history, and in what is the very life of history, the history of the human mind.

You know how some of the best talent and the noblest genius of our age has been devoted to the study of the development of the outward or material world, the growth of the earth, the first appearance of living cells, their combination and differentiation, leading up to the beginning of organic life, and its steady progress from the lowest to the highest stages. Is there not an inward and intellectual world also which has to be studied in its historical development, from the first appearance of predicative and demonstrative roots, their combination and differentiation, leading up to the beginning of rational thought in its steady progress from the lowest to the highest stages? And in that study of the history of the human mind, in that study of ourselves, of our true selves, India occupies a place second to no other country. Whatever sphere of the human mind you may select for your special study, whether it be language, or religion, or mythology, or philosophy, whether it be laws or customs, primitive art or primitive science, everywhere, you have to go to India, whether you like it or not, because some of the most valuable and most instructive materials in the history of man are treasured up in India, and in India only.

And while thus trying to explain to those whose lot will soon be cast in India the true position which that wonderful country holds or ought to hold in universal history, I may perhaps be able at the same time to appeal to the sympathies of other members of this University, by showing them how imperfect our knowledge of universal history, our insight into the development of the human intellect, must always remain, if we narrow our horizon to the history of Greeks and Romans, Saxons and Celts, with a dim background of Palestine, Egypt, and Babylon, and leave out of sight our nearest intellectual relatives, the Aryans of India, the framers of the most wonderful language, the Sanskrit, the fellow-workers in the construction of our fundamental concepts, the fathers of the most natural of natural religions, the makers of the most transparent of mythologies, the inventors of the most subtle philosophy, and the givers of the most elaborate laws.

There are many things which we think essential in a liberal education, whole chapters of history which we teach in our schools and universities, that cannot for one moment compare with the chapter relating to India, if only properly understood and freely interpreted.

In our time, when the study of history threatens to become almost an impossibility—such is the mass of details which historians collect in archives and pour out before us in monographs—it seems to me more than ever the duty of the true historian to find out the real proportion of things, to arrange his materials according to the strictest rules of artistic perspective, and to keep completely out of sight all that may be rightly ignored by us in our own passage across the historical stage of the world. It is this power of discovering what is really important that distinguishes the true historian from the mere chronicler, in whose eyes everything is important, particularly if he has discovered it himself. I think it was Frederick the Great who, when sighing for a true historian of his reign, complained bitterly that those who wrote the history of Prussia never forgot to describe the buttons on his uniform. And it is probably of such historical works that Carlyle was thinking when he said that he had waded through them all, but that nothing should ever induce him to hand even their names and titles down to posterity. And yet how much is there even in Carlyle's histories that might safely be consigned to oblivion!

Why do we want to know history? Why does history form a recognized part of our liberal education? Simply because all of us, and every one of us, ought to know how we have come to be what we are, so that each generation need not start again from the same point, and toil over the same ground, but, profiting by the experience of those who came before, may advance towards higher points and nobler aims. As a child when growing up, might ask his father or grandfather, *who* had built the house they lived in, or who had cleared the field that yielded them their food, we ask the historian whence we came, and how we came into possession of what we call our own. History may tell us afterwards many useful and amusing things, gossip, such as a child might like to hear from his mother or grandmother; but what history has to teach us before all and everything, is our own antecedents, our own ancestors, our own descent.

Now our principal intellectual ancestors are, no doubt, the *Jews*, the *Greeks*, the *Romans*, and the *Saxons*, and we, here in Europe, should not call a man educated or enlightened who was ignorant of the debt which he owes to his intellectual ancestors in Palestine, Greece, Rome, and Germany. The whole past history of the world would be darkness to him, and not knowing what those who came before him had done for him, he would probably care little to do anything for those who are to come after him. Life would be to him a chain of sand, while it ought to be a kind of electric chain that makes our hearts tremble and vibrate with the most ancient thoughts of the past, as well as with the most distant hopes of the future.

Let us begin with our religion. No one can understand even the historical possibility of the Christian religion without knowing something of the Jewish race, which must be studied chiefly in the pages of the Old Testament. And in order to appreciate the true relation of the Jews to the rest of the ancient world, and to understand what ideas were peculiarly their own, and what ideas they shared in common with the other members of the Semitic stock, or what moral and religious impulses they received from their historical contact with other nations of antiquity, it is absolutely necessary that we should pay some attention to the history of Babylon, Nineveh, Phœnicia, and Persia. These may seem distant countries and forgotten people, and many might feel inclined to say, 'Let the dead bury their dead; what are those mummies to us?' Still, such is the marvellous continuity of history, that I could easily show you many things which we, even we who are here assembled, owe to Babylon, to Nineveh, to Egypt, Phœnicia, and Persia.

Every one who carries a watch, owes to the Babylonians the division of the hour into sixty minutes. It may be a very bad division, yet such as it is, it has come to us from the Greeks and Romans, and it came to them from Babylon. The sexagesimal division is peculiarly Babylonian. Hipparchos, 150 B.C., adopted it from Babylon, Ptolemy, 150 A.D., gave it wider currency, and the French, when they decimated everything else, respected the dial plates of our watches, and left them with their sixty Babylonian minutes.

Everyone who writes a letter, owes his alphabet to the Romans and Greeks; the Greeks owed their alphabet to the Phœnicians, and the Phœnicians learnt it in Egypt. It may be a very imperfect alphabet—as all the students of phonetics will tell you; yet, such as it is, and has been, we owe it to the old Phœnicians and Egyptians, and in every letter we trace, there lies imbedded the mummy of an ancient Egyptian hieroglyphic.

What do we owe to the Persians? It does not seem to be much, for they were not a very inventive race, and what they knew, they had chiefly learnt from their neighbours, the Babylonians and Assyrians.

Still, we owe them something. First of all, we owe them a large debt of gratitude for having allowed themselves to be beaten by the Greeks; for think what the world would have been, if the Persians had beaten the Greeks at Marathon, and had enslaved, that means, annihilated, the genius of ancient Greece. However, this may be called rather an involuntary contribution to the progress of humanity, and I mention it only in order to show, how narrowly, not only Greeks and Romans, but Saxons and Anglo-Saxons too, escaped becoming Parsis or Fire-worshippers.

But I can mention at least one voluntary gift which came to us from Persia, and that is the relation of silver to gold in our bi-metallic currency. That relation was, no doubt, first determined in Babylonia, but it assumed its practical and historical importance in the Persian empire, and spread from there to the Greek colonies in Asia, and thence to Europe, where it has maintained itself with slight variation to the present day.

A *talent*[1] was divided into sixty *minæ*, a mina into sixty *shekels*. Here we have again the Babylonian sexagesimal system, a system which owes its origin and popularity, I believe, to the fact that *sixty* has the greatest number of divisors. Shekel was translated into Greek by *Stater*, and an Athenian gold stater, like the Persian gold stater, down to the times of Crœsus, Darius, and Alexander, was the sixtieth part of a mina of gold, not very far therefore from our sovereign. The proportion of silver to gold was fixed as 13 or 13⅓ to 1; and if the weight of a

[1] See Cunningham, Journal of the Asiatic Society of Bengal, 1881, pp. 162–168.

silver shekel was made as 13 to 10, such a coin would correspond very nearly to our florin [1]. Half a silver shekel was a *drachma*, and this was therefore the true ancestor of our shilling.

Again you may say that any attempt at fixing the relative value of silver and gold is, and always has been, a great mistake. Still it shows how closely the world is held together, and how, for good or for evil, we are what we are, not so much by ourselves as by the toil and moil of those who came before us, our true intellectual ancestors, whatever the blood may have been composed of that ran through their veins, or the bones which formed the rafters of their skulls.

And if it is true, with regard to religion, that no one could understand it and appreciate its full purport without knowing its origin and growth, that is, without knowing something of what the cuneiform inscriptions of Mesopotamia, the hieroglyphic and hieratic texts of Egypt, and the historical monuments of Phœnicia and Persia can alone reveal to us, it is equally true, with regard to all the other elements that constitute the whole of our intellectual life. If we are Jewish or Semitic in our religion, we are *Greek* in our philosophy, *Roman* in our politics, and *Saxon* in our morality, and it follows that a knowledge of the history of the Greeks, Romans, and Saxons, or of the flow of civilization from Greece to Italy, and through Germany to these isles, forms an essential element in what is called a liberal, that is, an historical and rational education.

But then it might be said, Let this be enough. Let us know by all means all that deserves to be

---

[1] *Sîm*, the Persian word for silver, has also the meaning of one-thirteenth; see Cunningham, l. c. p. 165.

known about our real spiritual ancestors in the great historical kingdoms of the world; let us be grateful for all we have inherited from Egyptians, Babylonians, Phœnicians, Jews, Greeks, Romans, and Saxons. But why bring in India? Why add a new burden to what every man has to bear already, before he can call himself fairly educated? What have we inherited from the dark dwellers on the Indus and the Ganges, that we should have to add their royal names and dates and deeds to the archives of our already overburdened memory?

There is some justice in this complaint. The ancient inhabitants of India are not our intellectual ancestors in the same direct way as Jews, Greeks, Romans, and Saxons are; but they represent, nevertheless, a collateral branch of that family to which we belong by language, that is, by thought, and their historical records extend in some respects so far beyond all other records and have been preserved to us in such perfect and such legible documents, that we can learn from them lessons which we can learn nowhere else, and supply missing links in our intellectual ancestry far more important than that missing link (which we can well afford to miss), the link between Ape and Man.

I am not speaking as yet of the literature of India as it is, but of something far more ancient, the language of India, or Sanskrit. No one supposes any longer that Sanskrit was the common source of Greek, Latin, and Anglo-Saxon. This used to be said, but it has long been shown that Sanskrit is only a collateral branch of the same stem from which spring Greek, Latin, and Anglo-Saxon; and not only these, but all the Teutonic, all the Celtic, all the

Slavonic languages, nay, the languages of Persia and Armenia also.

What, then, is it that gives to Sanskrit its claim on our attention, and its supreme importance in the eyes of the historian?

First of all, its antiquity,—for we know Sanskrit at an earlier period than Greek. But what is far more important than its merely chronological antiquity is the antique state of preservation in which that Aryan language has been handed down to us. The world had known Latin and Greek for centuries, and it was felt, no doubt, that there was some kind of similarity between the two. But how was that similarity to be explained? Sometimes Latin was supposed to give the key to the formation of a Greek word, sometimes Greek seemed to betray the secret of the origin of a Latin word. Afterwards, when the ancient Teutonic languages, such as Gothic and Anglo-Saxon, and the ancient Celtic and Slavonic languages too, came to be studied, no one could help seeing a certain family likeness among them all. But how such a likeness between these languages came to be, and how, what is far more difficult to explain, such striking differences too between these languages came to be, remained a mystery, and gave rise to the most gratuitous theories, most of them, as you know, devoid of all scientific foundation. As soon, however, as Sanskrit stepped into the midst of these languages, there came light and warmth and mutual recognition. They all ceased to be strangers, and each fell of its own accord into its right place. Sanskrit was the eldest sister of them all, and could tell of many things which the other members of the family had quite forgotten. Still, the other languages too had each their own tale to tell; and it is out of all their tales together that a chapter in the human mind has been put together which, in some respects, is more important to us than any of the other chapters, the Jewish, the Greek, the Latin, or the Saxon.

The process by which that ancient chapter of history was recovered is very simple. Take the words which occur in the same form and with the same meaning in all the seven branches of the Aryan family, and you have in them the most genuine and trustworthy records in which to read the thoughts of our true ancestors, before they had become Hindus, or Persians, or Greeks, or Romans, or Celts, or Teutons, or Slaves. Of course, some of these ancient charters may have been lost in one or other of these seven branches of the Aryan family, but even then, if they are found in six, or five, or four, or three, or even two only of its original branches, the probability remains, unless we can prove a later historical contact between these languages, that these words existed before the great *Aryan Separation.* If we find *agni*, meaning fire, in Sanskrit, and *ignis*, meaning fire, in Latin, we may safely conclude that *fire* was known to the undivided Aryans, even if no trace of the same name of fire occurred anywhere else. And why? Because there is no indication that Latin remained longer united with Sanskrit than any of the other Aryan languages, or that Latin could have borrowed such a word from Sanskrit, after these two languages had once become distinct. We have, however, the Lithuanian *ugnis*, and the Scottish *ingle*, to show that the Slavonic and possibly the Teutonic languages also, knew the same word for fire, though they replaced it in time by other words. Words, like all other things, will die, and why they should live on in one soil and wither away and perish in another, is not always easy to say. What has become of *ignis*, for instance, in all the Romance languages? It has withered away and perished, probably because, after losing its final unaccentuated syllable, it became awkward to pronounce; and another word *focus*, which in Latin meant fire-place, hearth, altar, has taken its place.

Suppose we wanted to know whether the ancient Aryans before their separation knew the mouse: we should only have to consult the principal Aryan dictionaries, and we should find in Sanskrit *mûsh*, in Greek *μῦς*, in Latin *mus*, in Old Slavonic *mўse*, in Old High German *mûs*, enabling us to say that, at a time so distant from us that we feel inclined to measure it by Indian rather than by our own chronology, the mouse was known, that is, was named, was conceived and recognised as a species of its own, not to be confounded with any other vermin.

And if we were to ask whether the enemy of the mouse, the *cat*, was known at the same distant time, we should feel justified in saying decidedly, No. The cat is called in Sanskrit mâr*g*âra and vi*d*âla. In Greek and Latin the words usually given as names of the cat, *γαλέη* and *αἴλουρος*, *mustella* and *feles*, did not originally signify the tame cat, but the weasel or marten. The name for the real cat in Greek was *κάττα*, in Latin *catus*, and these words have supplied the names for cat in all the Teutonic, Slavonic, and Celtic languages. The animal itself, so far as we know at present, came to Europe from Egypt, where it had been worshipped for centuries and tamed; and as this arrival probably dates from the fourth century A.D., we can well understand that no common name for it could have existed when the Aryan nations separated[1].

In this way a more or less complete picture of the state of civilization, previous to the Aryan Separation, can be and has been reconstructed, like a mosaic put together with the fragments of ancient stones; and I doubt whether, in tracing the history of the human mind, we shall ever reach to a lower stratum than that which is revealed to us by the converging rays of the different Aryan languages.

Nor is that all; for even that Proto-Aryan language, as it has been reconstructed from the ruins scattered about in India, Greece, Italy, and Germany, is clearly the result of a long, long process of thought. One shrinks from chronological limitations when looking into such distant periods of life. But if we find Sanskrit as a perfect literary language, totally different from Greek and Latin, 1500 B.C., where can those streams of Sanskrit, Greek, and Latin meet, as we trace them back to their common source? And then, when we have followed these mighty national streams back to their common meeting point, even then that common language looks like a rock washed down and smoothed for ages by the ebb and flow of thought. We find in that language such a compound, for instance, as *asmi*, I am, Greek ἐσμι. What would other languages give for such a pure concept as *I am*? They may say, *I stand*, or *I live*, or *I grow*, or *I turn*, but it is given to few languages only to be able to say *I am*. To us nothing seems more natural

---

[1] See note B.

than the auxiliary verb *I am:* but, in reality, no work of art has required greater efforts than this little word *I am.* And all those efforts lie beneath the level of the common Proto-Aryan speech. Many different ways were open, were tried, too, in order to arrive at such a compound as *asmi*, and such a concept as *I am.* But all were given up, and this one alone remained, and was preserved for ever in all the languages and all the dialects of the Aryan family. In *as-mi, as* is the root, and in the compound *as-mi*, the predicative root *as*, to be, is predicated of *mi*, I. But no language could ever produce at once so empty, or, if you like, so general a root as *as*, to be. *As* meant originally *to breathe*, and from it we have *asu*, breath, spirit, life, also *âs* the mouth, Latin *ôs, ôris.* By constant wear and tear this root *as*, to breathe, had first to lose all signs of its original material character, before it could convey that purely abstract meaning of existence, without any qualification, which has rendered to the higher operations of thought the same service which the nought, likewise the invention of Indian genius, has to render in arithmetic. Who will say how long the friction lasted which changed *as*, to breathe, into *as*, to be? And even a root *as*, to breathe, was an Aryan root, not Semitic, not Turanian. It possessed an historical individuality—it was the work of our forefathers, and represents a thread which unites us in our thoughts and words with those who first thought for us, with those who first spoke for us, and whose thoughts and words men are still thinking and speaking, though divided from them by thousands, it may be by hundreds of thousands of years.

This is what I call *history* in the true sense of the word, something really worth knowing, far more so than the scandals of courts, or the butcheries of nations, which fill so many pages of our Manuals of History. And all this work is only beginning, and whoever likes to labour in these the most ancient of historical archives will find plenty of discoveries to make—and yet people ask, what is the use of learning Sanskrit?

We get accustomed to everything, and cease to wonder at what would have startled our fathers and upset all their stratified notions, like a sudden earthquake. Every child now learns at school that English is an Aryan or Indo-European language, that it belongs to the Teutonic branch, and that this branch, together with the Italic, Greek, Celtic, Slavonic, Iranic, and Indic branches, all spring from the same stock, and form together the great Aryan or Indo-European family of speech.

But this, though it is taught now in our elementary schools, was really, but fifty years ago, like the opening of a new horizon of the world of the intellect, and the extension of a feeling of closest fraternity that made us feel at home where before we had been strangers, and changed millions of so-called barbarians into our own kith and kin. To speak the same language constitutes a closer union than to have drunk the same milk; and Sanskrit, the ancient language of India, is substantially the same language as Greek, Latin, and Anglo-Saxon. This is a lesson which we should never have learnt but from a study of Indian language and literature, and if India had taught us nothing else, it would have taught us more than almost any other language ever did.

It is quite amusing, though instructive also, to read what was written by scholars and philosophers when this new light first dawned on the world. They would not have it, they would not believe that there could be any community of origin between the people of Athens and Rome, and the so-called Niggers of India. The classical scholars scouted the idea, and I myself still remember the time, when I was a student at Leipzig and began to study Sanskrit, with what contempt any remarks on Sanskrit or comparative grammar were treated by my teachers, men such as Gottfried Hermann, Haupt, Westermann, Stallbaum, and others. No one ever was for a time so completely laughed down as Professor Bopp, when he first published his Comparative Grammar of Sanskrit, Zend, Greek, Latin, and Gothic. All hands were against him; and if in comparing Greek and Latin with Sanskrit, Gothic, Celtic, Slavonic, or Persian, he happened to have placed one single accent wrong, the shouts of those who knew nothing but Greek and Latin, and probably looked in their Greek Dictionaries to be quite sure of their accents, would never end. Dugald Stewart, rather than admit a relationship between Hindus and Scots, would rather believe that the whole Sanskrit language and the whole of Sanskrit literature—mind, a literature extending over three thousand years and larger than the ancient literature of either Greece or Rome,—was a forgery of those wily priests, the Brahmans. I remember too how, when I was at school at Leipzig, (and a very good school it was, with such masters as Nobbe, Forbiger, Funkhaenel, and Palm,—an old school too, which could boast of Leibniz among its former pupils) I remember, I say, one of our masters (Dr. Klee) telling us one afternoon, when it was too hot to do any serious work, that there was a language spoken in India, which was much the same as Greek and Latin, nay, as German and Russian. At first we thought it was a joke, but when one saw the parallel columns of Numerals, Pronouns, and Verbs in Sanskrit, Greek, and Latin written on the black board, one felt in the presence of facts, before which one had to bow. All one's ideas of Adam and Eve, and the Paradise, and the tower of Babel, and Shem, Ham, and Japhet, with Homer and Æneas and Virgil too, seemed to be whirling round and round, till at last one picked up the fragments and tried to build up a new world, and to live with a new historical consciousness.

Here you will see why I consider a certain knowledge of India an essential portion of a liberal or an historical education. The concept of the European man has been changed and widely extended by our acquaintance with India, and we know now that we are something different from what we thought we were. Suppose the Americans, owing to some cataclysmal events, had forgotten their English origin, and after two or three thousand years found themselves in possession of a language and of ideas which they could trace back historically to a certain date, but which, at that date, seemed, as it were, fallen from the sky, without any explanation of their origin and previous growth, what would they say if suddenly the existence of an English language and literature were revealed to them, such as they existed in the eighteenth century—explaining all that seemed before almost miraculous, and solving almost every question that could be asked! Well, this is much the same as what the discovery of Sanskrit has done for us. It has added a new period to our historical consciousness, and revived the recollections of our childhood, which seemed to have vanished for ever.

Whatever else we may have been, it is quite clear now that, many thousands of years ago, we were something that had not yet developed into an Englishman, or a Saxon, or a Greek, or a Hindu either, yet contained in itself the germs of all these characters. A strange being, you may say. Yes, but for all that a very real being, and an ancestor too of whom we must learn to be proud, far more than of any such modern ancestors, as Normans, Saxons, Celts, and all the rest.

And this is not all yet that a study of Sanskrit and the other Aryan languages has done for us. It has not only widened our views of man, and taught us to embrace millions of strangers and barbarians as members of one family, but it has imparted to the whole ancient history of man a reality which it never possessed before.

We speak and write a great deal about antiquities, and if we can lay hold of a Greek statue or an Egyptian Sphinx or a Babylonian Bull, our heart rejoices, and we build museums grander than any Royal palaces to receive the treasures of the past. This is quite right. But are you aware that every one of us possesses what may be called the richest and most wonderful Museum of Antiquities, older than any statues, sphinxes, or bulls? And where? Why, in our own language. When I use such words as *father* or *mother*, *heart* or *tear*, *one*, *two*, *three*, *here* and *there*, I am handling coins or counters that were current before there was one single Greek statue, one single Babylonian Bull, one single Egyptian Sphinx. Yes, each of us carries about with him the richest and most wonderful Museum of Antiquities; and if he only knows how to treat those treasures, how to rub and polish them till they become translucent again, how to arrange them and read them, they will tell him marvels more marvellous than all hieroglyphics and cuneiform inscriptions put together. The stories they have told us are beginning to be old stories now. Many of you have heard them before. But do not let them cease to be marvels, like so many things which cease to be marvels because they happen every day. And do not think that there is nothing left for you to do. There are more marvels still to be discovered in language than have ever been revealed to us; nay, there is no word, however common, if only you know how to take it to pieces, like a cunningly contrived work of art, fitted together thousands of years ago by the most cunning of artists, the human mind, that will not make you listen and marvel more than any chapter of the Arabian Nights.

But I must not allow myself to be carried away from my proper subject. All I wish to impress on you by way of introduction is that the results of the Science of Language, which, without the aid of Sanskrit, would never have been obtained, form an essential element of what we call a liberal, that is an historical education,—an education which will enable a man to do what the French call *s'orienter*, that is, 'to find his East,' 'his true East,' and thus to determine his real place in the world; to know, in fact, the port whence man started, the course he has followed, and the port towards which he has to steer.

We all come from the East—all that we value

most has come to us from the East, and in going to the East, not only those who have received a special Oriental training, but everybody who has enjoyed the advantages of a liberal, that is, of a truly historical education, ought to feel that he is going to his 'old home,' full of memories, if only he can read them. Instead of feeling your hearts sink within you, when next year you approach the shores of India, I wish that every one of you could feel what Sir William Jones felt, when, just one hundred years ago, he came to the end of his long voyage from England, and saw the shores of India rising on the horizon. At that time young men going to the wonderland of India, were not ashamed of dreaming dreams, and seeing visions: and this was the dream dreamt and the vision seen by Sir William Jones, then simple Mr. Jones:—

'When I was at sea last August (that is in August 1783), on my voyage to this country (India) I had long and ardently desired to visit, I found one evening, on inspecting the observations of the day, that *India* lay before us, *Persia* on our left, whilst a breeze from *Arabia* blew nearly on our stern. A situation so pleasing in itself and to me so new, could not fail to awaken a train of reflections in a mind, which had early been accustomed to contemplate with delight the eventful histories and agreeable fictions of this Eastern world. It gave me inexpressible pleasure to find myself in the midst of so noble an amphitheatre, almost encircled by the vast regions of Asia, which has ever been esteemed the nurse of sciences, the inventress of delightful and useful arts, the scene of glorious actions, fertile in the productions of human genius, and infinitely diversified in the forms of religion and government, in the laws, manners, customs, and languages, as well as in the features and complexions of men. I could not help remarking how important and extensive a field was yet unexplored, and how many solid advantages unimproved.'

India wants more such dreamers as that young Mr. Jones, standing alone on the deck of his vessel and watching the sun diving into the sea—with the memories of England behind and the hopes of India before him, feeling the presence of Persia and its ancient monarchs, and breathing the breezes of Arabia and its glowing poetry. Such dreamers know how to make their dreams come true, and how to change their visions into realities.

And as it was a hundred years ago, so it is now; or at least, so it may be now. There are many bright dreams to be dreamt about India, and many bright deeds to be done in India, if only you will do them. Though many great and glorious conquests have been made in the history and literature of the East, since the days when Sir William Jones landed at Calcutta, depend upon it, no young Alexander here need despair because there are no kingdoms left for him to conquer on the ancient shores of the Indus and the Ganges.

TRUTHFUL CHARACTER OF THE HINDUS.

LECTURE II.

In my first Lecture I endeavoured to remove the prejudice that everything in India is strange, and so different from the intellectual life which we are accustomed to in England that the twenty or twenty-five years which a Civil servant has to spend in the East seem often to him a kind of exile that he must bear as well as he can, but that severs him completely from all those higher pursuits by which life is made enjoyable at home. This need not be so and ought not to be so, if only it is clearly seen how almost every one of the higher interests that make life worth living here in England, may find as ample scope in India as in England.

To-day I shall have to grapple with another prejudice which is even more mischievous, because it forms a kind of icy barrier between the Hindus and their rulers, and makes anything like a feeling of true fellowship between the two utterly impossible.

That prejudice consists in looking upon our stay in India as a kind of *moral* exile, and in regarding the Hindus as an inferior race, totally different from ourselves in their moral character, and, more particularly in what forms the very foundation of the English character, respect for truth.

I believe there is nothing more disheartening to any high-minded young man than the idea that he will have to spend his life among human beings whom he can never respect or love—natives, as they are called, not to use even more offensive names—men whom he is taught to consider as not amenable to the recognised principles of self-respect, uprightness, and veracity, and with whom therefore any community of interests and action, much more any real friendship, is supposed to be out of the question.

So often has that charge of untruthfulness been repeated, and so generally is it now accepted, that it seems almost Quixotic to try to fight against it.

Nor should I venture to fight this almost hopeless battle, if I were not convinced that such a charge, like all charges brought against a whole nation, rests on the most flimsy induction, and that it has done, is doing, and will continue to do more mischief than anything that even the bitterest enemy of English dominion in India could have invented. If a young man who goes to India as a Civil servant or as a military officer, goes there fully convinced that the people whom he is to meet with are all liars, liars by nature or by national instinct, never restrained in their dealings by any regard for truth, never to be trusted on their word, need we wonder at the feelings of disgust with which he thinks of the Hindus, even before he has seen them; the feelings of distrust with which he approaches them, and the contemptuous way in which he treats them when brought into contact with them for the transaction of public or private business? When such tares have once been sown by the enemy, it will be difficult to gather them up. It has become almost an article of faith with every

Indian Civil servant that all Indians are liars; nay, I know I shall never be forgiven for my heresy in venturing to doubt it.

Now, quite apart from India, I feel most strongly that every one of these international condemnations is to be deprecated, not only for the sake of the self-conceited and uncharitable state of mind from which they spring, and which they serve to strengthen and confirm, but for purely logical reasons also, namely for the reckless and slovenly character of the induction on which such conclusions rest. Because a man has travelled in Greece and has been cheated by his dragoman, or been carried off by brigands, does it follow that all Greeks, ancient as well as modern, are cheats and robbers, or that they approve of cheating and robbery? And because in Calcutta, or Bombay, or Madras, Indians who are brought before judges, or who hang about the law courts and the bazaars, are not distinguished by an unreasoning and uncompromising love of truth, is it not a very vicious induction to say, in these days of careful reasoning, that all Hindus are liars—particularly if you bear in mind that, according to the latest census, the number of inhabitants of that vast country amounts to 253 millions. Are all these 253 millions of human beings to be set down as liars, because some hundreds, say even some thousands of Indians, when they are brought to an English court of law, on suspicion of having committed a theft or a murder, do not speak the truth, the whole truth, and nothing but the truth? Would an English sailor, if brought before a dark-skinned judge, who spoke English with a strange accent, bow down before him and confess at once any misdeed that he may have committed; and would all his mates rush forward and eagerly bear witness against him, when he had got himself into trouble?

The rules of induction are general, but they depend on the subjects to which they are applied. We may, to follow an Indian proverb, judge of a whole field of rice by tasting one or two grains only, but if we apply this rule to human beings, we are sure to fall into the same mistake as the English chaplain who had once, on board an English vessel, christened a French child, and who remained fully convinced for the rest of his life that all French babies had very long noses.

I can hardly think of anything that you could safely predicate of *all* the inhabitants of India, and I confess to a little nervous tremor whenever I see a sentence beginning with 'The people of India,' or even with 'All the Brahmans,' or 'All the Buddhists.' What follows is almost invariably wrong. There is a greater difference between an Afghan, a Sikh, a Hindustani, a Bengalese, and a Dravidian than between an Englishman, a Frenchman, a German, and a Russian—yet all are classed as Hindus, and all are supposed to fall under the same sweeping condemnation.

Let me read you what Sir John Malcolm says about the diversity of character to be observed by any one who has eyes to observe, among the different races whom we promiscuously call Hindus, and whom we promiscuously condemn as Hindus. After describing the people of Bengal as weak in body and timid in mind, and those below Calcutta as the lowest of our Hindu subjects, both in character and appearance, he continues: 'But from the moment you enter the district of Behar, the Hindu inhabitants are a race of men, generally speaking, not more distinguished by their lofty stature and robust frame than they are for some of the finest qualities of the mind. They are brave, generous, humane, and their truth is as remarkable as their courage.'

But because I feel bound to protest against the indiscriminating abuse that has been heaped on the people of India from the Himâlaya to Ceylon, do not suppose that it is my wish or intention to draw an ideal picture of India, leaving out all the dark shades, and giving you nothing but 'sweetness and light.' Having never been in India myself, I can only claim for myself the right and duty of every historian, namely, the right of collecting as much information as possible, and the duty to sift it according to the recognised rules of historical criticism. My chief sources of information with regard to the national character of the Indians in ancient times will be the works of Greek writers and the literature of the ancient Indians themselves. For later times we must depend on the statements of the various conquerors of India, who are not always the most lenient judges of those whom they may find it more difficult to rule than to conquer. For the last century to the present day, I shall have to appeal, partly to the authority of those who, after spending an active life in India and among the Indians, have given us the benefit of their experience in published works, partly to the testimony of a number of distinguished Civil servants and of Indian gentlemen also, whose personal acquaintance I have enjoyed in England, in France, and in Germany.

As I have chiefly to address myself to those who will themselves be the rulers and administrators of

India in the future, allow me to begin with the opinions which some of the most eminent, and, I believe, the most judicious among the Indian Civil servants of the past have formed and deliberately expressed on the point which we are to-day discussing, namely, the veracity or want of veracity among the Hindus.

And here I must begin with a remark which has been made by others also, namely, that the Civil servants who went to India in the beginning of this century, and under the auspices of the old East-India-Company, many of whom I had the honour and pleasure of knowing when I first came to England, seemed to have seen a great deal more of native life, native manners, and native character than those whom I had to examine five-and-twenty years ago, and who are now, after a distinguished career, coming back to England. India is no longer the distant island which it was, where each Crusoe had to make a home for himself as best he could. With the short and easy voyages from England to India and from India to England, with the frequent mails, and the telegrams, and the Anglo-Indian newspapers, official life in India has assumed the character of a temporary exile rather, which even English ladies are now more ready to share than fifty years ago. This is a difficulty which cannot be removed, but must be met, and which, I believe, can best be met by inspiring the new Civil servants with new and higher interests during their stay in India.

I knew the late Professor Wilson, our Boden Professor of Sanskrit at Oxford, for many years, and often listened with deep interest to his Indian reminiscences.

Let me read you what he, Professor Wilson, says of his native friends, associates, and servants[1]:

'I lived, both from necessity and choice, very much amongst the Hindus, and had opportunities of becoming acquainted with them in a greater variety of situations than those in which they usually come under the observation of Europeans. In the Calcutta mint, for instance, I was in daily personal communication with a numerous body of artificers, mechanics, and labourers, and always found amongst them cheerful and unwearied industry, good-humoured compliance with the will of their superiors, and a readiness to make whatever exertions were demanded from them: there was among them no drunkenness, no disorderly conduct, no insubordination. It would not be true to say that there was *no* dishonesty, but it was comparatively rare, invariably petty, and much less formidable than, I believe, it is necessary to guard against in other mints in other countries. There was considerable skill and ready docility. So far from there being any servility, there was extreme frankness, and I should say that where there is confidence without fear, frankness is one of the most universal features in the Indian character. Let the people feel sure of the temper and good-will of their superiors, and there is an end of reserve and timidity, without the slightest departure from respect . . . .'

Then, speaking of the much-abused Indian Pandits, he says: 'The studies which engaged my leisure brought me into connection with the men of learning, and in them I found the similar merits of industry,

[1] Mill's History of British India, ed. Wilson, vol. i. p. 375.

intelligence, cheerfulness, frankness, with others peculiar to their avocation. A very common characteristic of these men, and of the Hindus especially, was a simplicity truly childish, and a total unacquaintance with the business and manners of life. Where that feature was lost, it was chiefly by those who had been long familiar with Europeans. Amongst the Pandits, or the learned Hindus, there prevailed great ignorance and great dread of the European character. There is, indeed, very little intercourse between any class of Europeans and Hindu scholars, and it is not wonderful, therefore, that mutual misapprehension should prevail.'

Speaking, lastly, of the higher classes in Calcutta and elsewhere, Professor Wilson says that he witnessed among them 'polished manners, clearness and comprehensiveness of understanding, liberality of feeling and independence of principle that would have stamped them gentlemen in any country in the world.' 'With some of this class,' he adds, 'I formed friendships which I trust to enjoy through life.'

I have often heard Professor Wilson speak in the same, and in even stronger terms of his old friends in India, and his correspondence with Ram Comul Sen, the grandfather of Keshub Chunder Sen, a most orthodox, not to say bigoted, Hindu, which has lately been published, shows on what intimate terms Englishmen and Hindus may be, if only the advances are made on the English side.

There is another Professor of Sanskrit, of whom your University may well be proud, and who could speak on this subject with far greater authority than I can. He too will tell you, and I have no doubt has often told you, that if only you look out for friends among the Hindus, you will find them, and you may trust them.

There is one book which for many years I have been in the habit of recommending, and another against which I have always been warning those of the candidates for the Indian Civil Service whom I happened to see at Oxford; and I believe both the advice and the warning have in several cases borne the very best fruit. The book which I consider most mischievous, nay, which I hold responsible for some of the greatest misfortunes that have happened to India, is Mill's History of British India, even with the antidote against its poison, which is supplied by Professor Wilson's notes. The book which I recommend, and which I wish might be published again in a cheaper form, so as to make it more generally accessible, is Colonel Sleeman's Rambles and Recollections of an Indian Official, published in 1844, but written originally in 1835–1836.

Mill's History, no doubt, you all know, particularly the Candidates for the Indian Civil Service, who, I am sorry to say, are recommended to read it and are examined in it. Still, in order to substantiate my strong condemnation of the book, I shall have to give a few proofs:—

Mill in his estimate of the Hindu character is chiefly guided by Dubois, a French missionary, and by Orme and Buchanan, Tennant, and Ward, all of them neither very competent nor very unprejudiced judges. Mill[1], however, picks out all that is most unfavourable from their works, and omits the qualifications which even these writers felt bound to give to their wholesale

[1] Mill's History, ed. Wilson, vol. i. p. 368.

condemnation of the Hindus. He quotes as serious, for instance, what was said in joke[1], namely, that 'a Brahman is an ant's nest of lies and impostures.' Next to the charge of untruthfulness, Mill upbraids the Hindus for what he calls their litigiousness. He writes[2]: 'As often as courage fails them in seeking more daring gratification to their hatred and revenge, their malignity finds a vent in the channel of litigation.' Without imputing dishonourable motives, as Mill does, the same fact might be stated in a different way, by saying, 'As often as their conscience and respect of law keep them from seeking more daring gratification to their hatred and revenge, say by murder or poisoning, their trust in English justice leads them to appeal to our Courts of Law.' Dr. Robertson, in his 'Historical Disquisitions concerning India[3],' seems to have considered the litigious subtlety of the Hindus as a sign of high civilisation rather than of barbarism, but he is sharply corrected by Mr. Mill, who tells him that 'nowhere is this subtlety carried higher than among the wildest of the Irish.' That courts of justice, like the English, in which a verdict was not to be obtained, as formerly in Mohammedan courts, by bribes and corruption, should at first have proved very attractive to the Hindus, need not surprise us. But is it really true that the Hindus are more fond of litigation than other nations? If we consult Sir Thomas Munro, the eminent Governor of Madras, and the powerful advocate of the Ryotwar settlements, he tells us in so many words[4]: 'I have had ample opportunity of observing the Hindus in

---

[1] Mill's History, ed. Wilson, vol. i. p. 325. [2] L. c. vol. i. p. 329.
[3] P. 217. [4] Mill's History, vol. i. p. 329.

every situation, and I can affirm, that they are not litigious[1].'

But Mill goes further still, and in one place he actually assures his readers[2] that a 'Brahman may put a man to death when he lists.' In fact, he represents the Hindus as such a monstrous mass of all vices that, as Colonel Vans Kennedy[3] remarked, society could not have held together, if it had really consisted of such reprobates only. Nor does he seem to see the full bearing of his remarks. Surely, if a Brahman might, as he says, put a man to death whenever he lists, it would be the strongest testimony in their favour that you hardly ever hear of their availing themselves of such a privilege, to say nothing of the fact—and a fact it is—that, according to statistics, the number of capital sentences was one in every 10,000 in England, but only one in every million in Bengal[4].

Colonel Sleeman's Rambles are less known than they deserve to be. To give you an idea of the man, I must read you some extracts from the book.

His sketches being originally addressed to his sister, this is how he writes to her :—

'My dear Sister,

'Were anyone to ask your countrymen in India, what had been their greatest source of pleasure while there, perhaps, nine in ten would say, the letters which they receive from their sisters at

---

[1] Manu, VIII. 43, says: 'Neither a King himself nor his officers must ever promote litigation; nor ever neglect a lawsuit instituted by others.'

[2] Mill's History, vol. i. p. 327. [3] L. c. p. 368.

[4] See Elphinstone, History of India, ed. Cowell, p. 219 note. 'Of the 232 sentences of death 64 only were carried out in England, while the 59 sentences of death in Bengal were all carried out.'

home . . . . And while thus contributing so much to our happiness, they no doubt tend to make us better citizens of the world, and servants of government, than we should otherwise be; for in our "struggles through life" in India, we have all, more or less, an eye to the approbation of those circles which our kind sisters represent,—who may therefore be considered in the exalted light of a valuable species of *unpaid magistracy* to the government of India.'

There is a touch of the old English chivalry even in these few words addressed to a sister whose approbation he values, and with whom he hoped to spend the winter of his days. Having been, as he confesses, idle in answering letters, or rather, too busy to find time for long letters, he made use of his enforced leisure, while on his way from the Nerbuddah river to the Himmaleh mountains, in search of health, to give to his sister a full account of his impressions and experiences in India. Though what he wrote was intended at first 'to interest and amuse his sister only and the other members of his family at home,' he adds in a more serious tone: 'Of one thing I must beg you to be assured, that I have nowhere indulged in fiction, either in the narrative, the recollections, or the conversations. What I relate on the testimony of others, I believe to be true; and what I relate on my own, you may rely upon as being so.'

When placing his volumes before the public at large in 1844, he expresses a hope that they may 'tend to make the people of India better understood by those of our countrymen whose destinies are cast among them, and inspire more kindly feelings towards them.'

You may ask why I consider Colonel Sleeman so trustworthy an authority on the Indian character, more trustworthy, for instance, than even so accurate and unprejudiced an observer as Professor Wilson. My answer is—because Wilson lived chiefly in Calcutta, while Colonel Sleeman saw India, where alone the true India can be seen, namely, in the village-communities. For many years he was employed as Commissioner for the suppression of Thuggee. The Thuggs were professional assassins, who committed their murders under a kind of religious sanction. They were originally 'all Mohammedans, but for a long time past Mohammedans and Hindus had been indiscriminately associated in the gangs, the former class, however, still predominating[1].'

In order to hunt up these gangs, Colonel Sleeman had constantly to live among the people in the country, to gain their confidence, and to watch the good as well as the bad features in their character.

Now what Colonel Sleeman continually insists on is that no one knows the Indians who does not know them in their village-communities—what we should now call their *communes*. It is that village-life which in India has given its peculiar impress to the Indian character, more so than in any other country we know. When in Indian history we hear so much of kings and emperors, of râjahs and mahârâjahs, we are apt to think of India as an Eastern monarchy, ruled by a central power, and without any trace of that self-government which forms the pride of England. But those who have most carefully studied the political life of India tell you the very opposite.

---

[1] Sir Ch. Trevelyan, Christianity and Hinduism, 1882, p. 42.

The political unit, or the social cell in India has always been, and, in spite of repeated foreign conquests, is still the village-community. Some of these political units will occasionally combine or be combined for common purposes (such a confederacy being called a grâma*g*âla), but each is perfect in itself. When we read in the laws of Manu [1] of officers appointed to rule over ten, twenty, a hundred, or a thousand of these villages, that means no more than that they were responsible for the collection of taxes, and generally for the good behaviour of these villages. And when, in later times, we hear of circles of 84 villages, the so-called Chourasees (*K*aturasîti [2]), and of 360 villages, this too seems to refer to fiscal arrangements only. To the ordinary Hindu, I mean to ninety-nine in every hundred, the village was his world, and the sphere of public opinion, with its beneficial influences on individuals, seldom extended beyond the horizon of his village [3].

Colonel Sleeman was one of the first who called attention to the existence of these village-communities in India, and their importance in the social fabric

---

[1] Manu VII. 115.

[2] H. M. Elliot, Supplement to the Glossary of Indian Terms, p. 151.

[3] I see from Dr. Hunter's latest statistical tables that the whole number of towns and villages in British India amounts to 493,429. Out of this number 448,320 have less than 1000 inhabitants, and may be called villages. In Bengal, where the growth of towns has been most encouraged through Government establishments, the total number of homesteads is 117,042, and more than half of these contain less than 200 inhabitants. Only 10,077 towns in Bengal have more than 1000 inhabitants; that is, no more than about a seventeenth part of all the settlements are anything but what we should call substantial villages. In the North-Western Provinces the last census gives us 105,124 villages, against 297 towns. See Times, 14th Aug. 1882.

of the whole country both in ancient and in modern times; and though they have since become far better known and celebrated through the writings of Sir Henry Maine, it is still both interesting and instructive to read Colonel Sleeman's account. He writes as a mere observer, and uninfluenced as yet by any theories on the development of early social and political life among the Aryan nations in general.

I do not mean to say that Colonel Sleeman was the first who pointed out the palpable fact that the whole of India is parcelled out into estates of villages. Even so early an observer as Megasthenes[1] seems to have been struck by the same fact when he says that 'in India the husbandmen with their wives and children live in the country, and entirely avoid going into town.' What Colonel Sleeman was the first to point out was that all the native virtues of the Hindus are intimately connected with their village-life.

That village-life, however, is naturally the least known to English officials, nay, the very presence of an English official is often said to be sufficient to drive away those native virtues which distinguish both the private life and the public administration of justice and equity in an Indian village[2]. Take a man out of his village-community, and you remove him from all the restraints of society. He is out of

---

[1] Ancient India as described by Megasthenes and Arrian, by McCrindle, p. 42.

[2] 'Perjury seems to be committed by the meanest and encouraged by some of the better sort among the Hindus and Mussulmans, with as little remorse as if it were a proof of ingenuity, or even a merit.' Sir W. Jones, Address to Grand Jury at Calcutta, in Mill's History of India, vol. i. p. 324. 'The longer we possess a province, the more common and grave does perjury become.' Sir G. Campbell, quoted by S. Johnson, Oriental Religions, India, p. 288.

his element, and, under temptation, is more likely to go wrong than to remain true to the traditions of his home-life. Even between village and village the usual restraints of public morality are not always recognised. What would be called theft or robbery at home, is called a successful raid or conquest if directed against distant villages; and what would be falsehood or trickery in private life is honoured by the name of policy and diplomacy if successful against strangers. On the other hand, the rules of hospitality applied only to people of other villages, and a man of the same village could never claim the right of an *Atithi*, or guest[1].

Let us hear now what Colonel Sleeman tells us about the moral character of the members of these village-communities[2], and let us not forget that the Commissioner for the suppression of Thuggee had ample opportunities of seeing the dark as well as the bright ideas of the Indian character.

He assures us that falsehood or lying between members of the same village is almost unknown. Speaking of some of the most savage tribes, the Gonds, for instance, he maintains that nothing would induce them to tell a lie, though they would think nothing of lifting a herd of cattle from a neighbouring plain.

Of these men it might perhaps be said that they have not yet learned the value of a lie; yet even such blissful ignorance ought to count in a nation's character. But I am not pleading here for Gonds, or Bhils, or Santhals, and other non-Aryan tribes. I am speaking of the Aryan and more or less civilized in-

---

[1] Vasish*th*a, translated by Bühler, VIII. 8. [2] See Note C.

habitants of India. Now among them, where rights, duties, and interests begin to clash in one and the same village, public opinion, in its limited sphere, seems strong enough to deter even an evil-disposed person from telling a falsehood. The fear of the gods also has not yet lost its power[1]. In most villages there is a sacred tree, a pipal-tree (Ficus Indica), and the gods are supposed to delight to sit among its leaves, and listen to the music of their rustling. The deponent takes one of these leaves in his hand, and invokes the god, who sits above him, to crush him, or those dear to him, as he crushes the leaf in his hand, if he speaks anything but the truth. He then plucks and crushes the leaf, and states what he has to say.

The pipal-tree is generally supposed to be occupied by one of the Hindu deities, while the large cotton-tree, particularly among the wilder tribes, is supposed to be the abode of local gods, all the more terrible, because entrusted with the police of a small settlement only. In their puncháyets, Sleeman tells us, men adhere habitually and religiously to the truth, and 'I have had before me hundreds of cases,' he says, 'in which a man's property, liberty, and life has depended upon his telling a lie, and he has refused to tell it.'

Could many an English judge say the same?

In their own tribunals under the pipal-tree or cotton-tree, imagination commonly did what the deities, who were supposed to preside, had the credit of doing. If the deponent told a lie, he believed that the god who sat on his sylvan throne above

[1] Sleeman, vol. ii. p. 111.

him, and searched the heart of man, must know it; and from that moment he knew no rest, he was always in dread of his vengeance. If any accident happened to him, or to those dear to him, it was attributed to this offended deity; and if no accident happened, some evil was brought about by his own disordered imagination [1]. It was an excellent superstition, inculcated in the ancient law-books, that the ancestors watched the answer of a witness, because, according as it was true or false, they themselves would go to heaven or to hell [2].

Allow me to read you the abstract of a conversation between an English official and a native law-officer as reported by Colonel Sleeman. The native lawyer was asked what he thought would be the effect of an act to dispense with oaths on the Koran and Ganges-water, and to substitute a solemn declaration made in the name of God, and under the same penal liabilities as if the Koran or Ganges-water had been in the deponent's hand.

'I have practised in the courts,' the native said, 'for thirty years, and during that time I have found only three kinds of witnesses—two of whom would, by such an act, be left precisely where they were, while the third would be released by it from a very salutary check.'

'And, pray, what are the three classes into which you divide the witnesses in our courts?'

'First, Sir, are those who will always tell the truth, whether they are required to state what they know in the form of an oath or not.'

'Do you think this a large class?'

---

[1] Sleeman, vol. ii. p. 116.

[2] Vasish*th*a XVI. 32.

'Yes, I think it is; and I have found among them many whom nothing on earth could make to swerve from the truth. Do what you please, you could never frighten or bribe them into a deliberate falsehood.

'The second are those who will not hesitate to tell a lie when they have a motive for it, and are not restrained by an oath. In taking an oath, they are afraid of two things, the anger of God, and the odium of men.

'Only three days ago,' he continued, 'I required a power of attorney from a lady of rank, to enable me to act for her in a case pending before the court in this town. It was given to me by her brother, and two witnesses came to declare that she had given it. "Now," said I, "this lady is known to live under the curtain, and you will be asked by the judge whether you saw her give this paper: what will you say?" They both replied—"If the judge asks us the question without an oath we will say '*Yes*'—it will save much trouble, and we know that she *did* give the paper, though we did not really *see* her give it; but if he puts the Koran into our hands, we must say '*No*,' for we should otherwise be pointed at by all the town as perjured wretches—our enemies would soon tell everybody that we had taken a false oath."

'Now,' the native lawyer went on, 'the form of an oath is a great check on this sort of persons.

'The third class consists of men who will tell lies whenever they have a sufficient motive, whether they have the Koran or Ganges-water in their hand or not. Nothing will ever prevent their doing so; and the declaration which you propose would be just as well as any other for them.'

'Which class do you consider the most numerous of the three?'

'I consider the second the most numerous, and wish the oath to be retained for them.'

'That is, of all the men you see examined in our courts, you think the most come under the class of those who will, under the influence of strong motives, tell lies, if they have not the Koran or Ganges-water in their hands?'

'Yes.'

'But do not a great many of those whom you consider to be included among the second class come from the village-communities,—the peasantry of the country?'

'Yes.'

'And do you not think that the greatest part of those men who will tell lies in the court, under the influence of strong motives, unless they have the Koran or Ganges-water in their hands, would refuse to tell lies, if questioned before the people of their villages, among the circle in which they live?'

'Of course I do; three-fourths of those who do not scruple to lie in the courts, would be ashamed to lie before their neighbours, or the elders of their village.'

'You think that the people of the village-communities are more ashamed to tell lies before their neighbours than the people of towns?'

'Much more—there is no comparison.'

'And the people of towns and cities bear in India but a small proportion to the people of the village-communities?'

'I should think a very small proportion indeed.'

'Then you think that in the mass of the population of India, *out of our courts*, the first class, or those who speak truth, whether they have the Koran or Ganges-water in their hands or not, would be found more numerous than the other two?'

'Certainly I do; if they were always to be questioned before their neighbours or elders, so that they could feel that their neighbours and elders could know what they say.'

It was from a simple sense of justice that I felt bound to quote this testimony of Colonel Sleeman as to the truthful character of the natives of India, when *left to themselves*. My interest lies altogether with the people of India, *when left to themselves*, and historically I should like to draw a line after the year one thousand after Christ. When you read the atrocities committed by the Mohammedan conquerors of India from that time to the time when England stepped in and, whatever may be said by her envious critics, made, at all events, the broad principles of our common humanity respected once more in India, the wonder, to my mind, is how any nation could have survived such an *Inferno* without being turned into devils themselves.

Now, it is quite true that during the two thousand years which precede the time of Mahmud of Gazni, India has had but few foreign visitors, and few foreign critics; still it is surely extremely strange that whenever, either in Greek, or in Chinese, or in Persian, or in Arab writings, we meet with any attempts at describing the distinguishing features in the national character of the Indians, regard for truth and justice should always be mentioned first.

Ktesias, the famous Greek physician of Artaxerxes Mnemon (present at the battle of Cunaxa, 404 B.C.), the first Greek writer who tells us anything about the character of the Indians, such as he heard it described at the Persian court, has a special chapter 'On the justice of the Indians[1].'

Megasthenes[2], the ambassador of Seleucus Nicator at the court of Sandrocottus in Palibothra (Pâtaliputra, the modern Patna), states that thefts were extremely rare, and that they honoured truth and virtue[3].

Arrian (in the second century, the pupil of Epictetus), when speaking of the public overseers or superintendents in India, says[4]: 'They oversee what goes on in the country or towns, and report everything to the king, where the people have a king, and to the magistrates, where the people are self-governed, and it is against use and wont for these to give in a false report; *but indeed no Indian is accused of lying*[5].

The Chinese, who come next in order of time, bear the same, I believe, unanimous testimony in favour of the honesty and veracity of the Hindus. Let me quote Hiouen-thsang, the most famous of the Chinese Buddhist pilgrims, who visited India in the seventh century[6]. 'Though the Indians,' he writes, 'are of a light temperament, they are distinguished by the straightforwardness and honesty of their character. With regard to riches, they never take anything unjustly; with regard to justice, they make even excessive concessions . . . . Straightforwardness is the distinguishing feature of their administration.'

---

[1] Ktesiae Fragmenta (ed. Didot), p. 81.

[2] See Indian Antiquary, 1876, p. 333.

[3] Megasthenis Fragmenta (ed. Didot) in Fragm. Histor. Graec. vol. ii. p. 426 b: Ἀλήθειάν τε ὁμοίως καὶ ἀρετὴν ἀποδέχονται.

[4] Indica, cap. xii. 6.

[5] See McCrindle in Indian Antiquary, 1876, p. 92.

[6] Vol. ii. p. 83.

If we turn to the accounts given by the Mohammedan conquerors of India, we find Idrisi, in his Geography (written in the 11th century), summing up their opinion of the Indians in the following words[1]:

'The Indians are naturally inclined to justice, and never depart from it in their actions. Their good faith, honesty, and fidelity to their engagements are well known, and they are so famous for these qualities that people flock to their country from every side.'

In the thirteenth century we have the testimony of Marco Polo[2], who thus speaks of the *Abraiaman*, a name by which he seems to mean the Brahmans who, though not traders by profession, might well have been employed for great commercial transactions by the king. This was particularly the case during times which the Brahmans would call times of distress, when many things were allowed which at other times were forbidden by the laws. 'You must know,' Marco Polo says, 'that these Abraiaman are the best merchants in the world, and the most truthful, for they would not tell a lie for anything on earth.'

In the fourteenth century we have Friar Jordanus, who goes out of his way to tell us that the people of Lesser India (South and Western India) are true in speech and eminent in justice[3].

In the fifteenth century Kamal-eddin Abd-errazak Samarkandi (1413–1482), who went as ambassador of the Khakan to the prince of Kalikut and to the King of Vidyânagara (about 1440–1445), bears testimony to the perfect security which merchants enjoy in that country[4].

---

[1] Elliot, History of India, vol. i. p. 88.

[2] Marco Polo, ed. H. Yule, vol. ii. p. 350. [3] Ib. p. 354.

[4] Notices des Manuscrits, tom. xiv. p. 436. He seems to have

In the sixteenth century, Abu Fazl, the minister of the Emperor Akbar, says in his Ayin Akbari: 'The Hindus are religious, affable, cheerful, lovers of justice, given to retirement, able in business, admirers of truth, grateful and of unbounded fidelity; and their soldiers know not what it is to fly from the field of battle[1].'

And even in quite modern times the Mohammedans seem willing to admit that the Hindus, at all events in their dealings with Hindus, are more straightforward than Mohammedans in their dealings with Mohammedans.

Thus Meer Sulamut Ali, a venerable old Mussulman, and, as Colonel Sleeman says, a most valuable public servant, was obliged to admit that 'a Hindu may feel himself authorised to take in a Mussulman, and might even think it meritorious to do so; but he would never think it meritorious to take in one of his own religion. There are no less than seventy-two sects of Mohammedans; and every one of these sects would not only take in the followers of every other religion on earth, but every member of every one of the other seventy-one sects; and the nearer that sect is to his own, the greater the merit of taking in its members[2].'

So I could go on quoting from book after book, and again and again we should see how it was love of truth that struck all the people who came in contact with India, as the prominent feature in the national character of its inhabitants. No one ever accused them of falsehood. There must surely be

been one of the first to state that the Persian text of the Kalilah and Dimna was derived from the wise people of India.

[1] Samuel Johnson, India, p. 294.

[2] Sleeman, Rambles, vol. i. p. 63.

some ground for this, for it is not a remark that is frequently made by travellers in foreign countries, even in our time, that their inhabitants invariably speak the truth. Read the accounts of English travellers in France, and you will find very little said about French honesty and veracity, while French accounts of England are seldom without a fling at *Perfide Albion!*

But if all this is true, how is it, you may well ask, that public opinion in England is so decidedly unfriendly to the people of India; at the utmost tolerates and patronizes them, but will never trust them, never treat them on terms of equality?

I have already hinted at some of the reasons. Public opinion with regard to India is made up in England chiefly by those who have spent their lives in Calcutta, Bombay, Madras, or some other of the principal towns in India. The native element in such towns contains mostly the most unfavourable specimens of the Indian population. An insight into the domestic life of the more respectable classes, even in towns, is difficult to obtain; and, when it is obtained, it is extremely difficult to judge of their manners according to our standard of what is proper, respectable, or gentlemanlike. The misunderstandings are frequent and often most grotesque; and such, we must confess, is human nature, that when we hear the different and often most conflicting accounts of the character of the Hindus, we are naturally sceptical with regard to unsuspected virtues among them, while we are quite disposed to accept unfavourable accounts of their character.

Lest I should seem to be pleading too much on the native side of the question, and to exaggerate the difficulty of forming a correct estimate of the character of the Hindus, let me appeal to one of the most distinguished, learned, and judicious members of the Indian Civil Service, the author of the History of India, Mountstuart Elphinstone. 'Englishmen in India[1],' he says, 'have less opportunity than might be expected of forming opinions of the native character. Even in England, few know much of the people beyond their own class, and what they do know, they learn from newspapers and publications of a description which does not exist in India. In that country also, religion and manners put bars to our intimacy with the natives, and limit the number of transactions as well as the free communication of opinions. We know nothing of the interior of families but by report, and have no share in those numerous occurrences of life in which the amiable parts of character are most exhibited.' 'Missionaries of a different religion, judges, police-magistrates, officers of revenue or customs, and even diplomatists, do not see the most virtuous portion of a nation, nor any portion, unless when influenced by passion, or occupied by some personal interest. What we *do* see we judge by our own standard. We conclude that a man who cries like a child on slight occasions, must always be incapable of acting or suffering with dignity; and that one who allows himself to be called a liar would not be ashamed of any baseness. Our writers also confound the distinctions of time and place; they combine in one character the Maratta and the Bengalese; and tax the present generation with the crimes of the heroes of the Mahâbhârata. It might be argued, in oppo-

[1] Elphinstone's History of India, ed. Cowell, p. 213.

sition to many unfavourable testimonies, that those who have known the Indians longest have always the best opinion of them; but this is rather a compliment to human nature than to them, since it is true of every other people. It is more in point, that all persons who have retired from India think better of the people they have left, after comparing them with others, even of the most justly admired nations.'

But what is still more extraordinary than the ready acceptance of judgments unfavourable to the character of the Hindus, is the determined way in which public opinion, swayed by the statements of certain unfavourable critics, has persistently ignored the evidence which members of the Civil Service, officers and statesmen—men of the highest authority—have given again and again, in direct opposition to these unfavourable opinions. Here, too, I must ask to be allowed to quote at least a few of these witnesses on the other side.

Warren Hastings thus speaks of the Hindus in general: 'They are gentle and benevolent, more susceptible of gratitude for kindness shown them, and less prompted to vengeance for wrongs inflicted than any people on the face of the earth; faithful, affectionate, submissive to legal authority.'

Bishop Heber said: 'The Hindus are brave, courteous, intelligent, most eager for knowledge and improvement; sober, industrious, dutiful to parents, affectionate to their children, uniformly gentle and patient, and more easily affected by kindness and attention to their wants and feelings than any people I ever met with [1].'

---

[1] Samuel Johnson, l. c. p. 293.

Elphinstone states: 'No set of people among the Hindus are so depraved as the dregs of our own great towns. The villagers are everywhere amiable, affectionate to their families, kind to their neighbours, and towards all but the government honest and sincere. Including the Thugs and Dacoits, the mass of crime is less in India than in England. The Thugs are almost a separate nation, and the Dacoits are desperate ruffians in gangs. The Hindus are mild and gentle people, more merciful to prisoners than any other Asiatics. Their freedom from gross debauchery is the point in which they appear to most advantage; and their superiority in purity of manners is not flattering to our self-esteem[1].'

Yet Elphinstone can be most severe on the real faults of the people of India. He states that, at present, want of veracity is one of their prominent vices, but he adds[2] 'that such deceit is most common in people connected with government, a class which spreads far in India, as, from the nature of the land-revenue, the lowest villager is often obliged to resist force by fraud[3].'

Sir John Malcolm writes[4]: 'I have hardly ever known where a person did understand the language, or where a calm communication was made to a native of India, through a well-informed and trustworthy medium, that the result did not prove, that what had at first been stated as falsehood, had either proceeded from fear, or from misapprehension. I by no means wish to state that our Indian subjects are more free from this vice than other nations that occupy a nearly

[1] See History of India, pp. 375–381.

[2] L. c. p. 215.

[3] L. c. p. 218.

[4] Mill's History of India, ed. Wilson, vol. i. p. 370.

equal position in society, but I am positive that they are not more addicted to untruth.'

Sir Thomas Munro bears even stronger testimony. He writes[1]: 'If a good system of agriculture, unrivalled manufacturing skill, a capacity to produce whatever can contribute to either convenience or luxury, schools established in every village for teaching reading, writing, and arithmetic[2], the general practice of hospitality and charity amongst each other, and above all, a treatment of the female sex full of confidence, respect, and delicacy, are among the signs which denote a civilised people—then the Hindus are not inferior to the nations of Europe, and if civilisation is to become an article of trade between England and India, I am convinced that England will gain by the import cargo.'

My own experience with regard to the native character has been, of course, very limited. Those Hindus whom I have had the pleasure to know personally in Europe may be looked upon as exceptional, as the best specimens, it may be, that India could produce. Also, my intercourse with them has natu-

---

[1] Mill's History, vol. i. p. 371.

[2] Sir Thomas Munro estimated the children educated at public schools in the Madras presidency as less than one in three. But low as it was, it was, as he justly remarked, a higher rate than existed till very lately in most countries of Europe. Elphinstone, Hist. of India, p. 205.

In Bengal there existed no less than 80,000 native schools, though, doubtless, for the most part, of a poor quality. According to a Government Report of 1835, there was a village school for every 400 persons. Missionary Intelligencer, IX. 183–193.

Ludlow (British India, I. 62) writes: 'In every Hindu village which has retained its old form I am assured that the children generally are able to read, write, and cipher; but where we have swept away the village system, as in Bengal, there the village school has also disappeared.'

rally been such that it could hardly have brought out the darker sides of human nature. During the last twenty years, however, I have had some excellent opportunities of watching a number of native scholars under circumstances where it is not difficult to detect a man's true character, I mean in literary work and, more particularly, in literary controversy. I have watched them carrying on such controversies both among themselves and with certain European scholars, and I feel bound to say that, with hardly one exception, they have displayed a far greater respect for truth, and a far more manly and generous spirit than we are accustomed to even in Europe and America. They have shown strength, but no rudeness; nay I know that nothing has surprised them so much as the coarse invective to which certain Sanskrit scholars have condescended, rudeness of speech being, according to their view of human nature, a safe sign not only of bad breeding, but of want of knowledge. When they were wrong, they have readily admitted their mistakes; when they were right, they have never sneered at their European adversaries. There has been, with few exceptions, no quibbling, no special pleading, no untruthfulness on their part, and certainly none of that low cunning of the scholar who writes down and publishes what he knows perfectly well to be false, and snaps his fingers at those who still value truth and self-respect more highly than victory or applause at any price. Here, too, we might possibly gain by the import cargo.

Let me add that I have been repeatedly told by English merchants that commercial honour stands higher in India than in any other country, and that a dishonoured bill is hardly known there.

I have left to the last the witnesses who might otherwise have been suspected—I mean the Hindus themselves. The whole of their literature from one end to the other is pervaded by expressions of love and reverence for truth. Their very word for truth is full of meaning. It is sat or satya, sat being the participle of the verb as, to be. True, therefore, was with them simply *that which is.* The English *sooth* is connected with sat, also the Greek ὄν for ἔσον, and the Latin *sens*, in *præsens.*

We are all very apt to consider truth to be what is trowed by others, or believed in by large majorities. That kind of truth is easy to accept. But whoever has once stood alone, surrounded by noisy assertions, and overwhelmed by the clamour of those who ought to know better, or perhaps who did know better—call him Galileo or Darwin, Colenso or Stanley, or any other name—he knows what a real delight it is to feel in his heart of hearts, this is true—this is—this is sat—whatever daily, weekly, or quarterly papers, whatever bishops, archbishops, or popes, may say to the contrary.

Another name for truth is the Sanskrit *ri*ta, which originally seems to have meant *straight, direct,* while an*ri*ta is untrue, false.

Now one of the highest praises bestowed upon the gods in the Veda is that they are satya, true, truthful, trustworthy[1]; and it is well known that both in modern and ancient times, men always ascribe to God or to their gods those qualities which they value most in themselves.

Other words applied to the gods as truthful beings,

---

[1] Rig-veda I. 87, 4; 145, 5; 174, 1; V. 23, 2.

are adrogha, lit. not deceiving[1]. Adrogha-vâk means, he whose word is never broken. Thus Indra, the Vedic Jupiter, is said to have been praised by the fathers[2] 'as reaching the enemy, overcoming him, standing on the summit, *true of speech*, most powerful in thought.'

Droghavâk[3], on the contrary, is used for deceitful men. Thus Vasish*th*a, one of the great Vedic poets, says: 'If I had worshipped false gods, or if I believed in the gods vainly—but why art thou angry with us, O *G*âtavedas? May liars go to destruction!'

Satyam, as a neuter, is often used as an abstract, and is then rightly translated by truth. But it also means that which is, the true, the real; and there are several passages in the Rig-veda where, instead of *truth*, I think we ought simply to translate satyam by the true, that is, the real, τὸ ὄντως ὄν. It sounds, no doubt, very well to translate Satyena uttabhitâ bhûmi*h* by 'the earth is founded on truth;' and I believe every translator has taken satya in that sense here. Ludwig translates, 'Von der Wahrheit ist die Erde gestützt.' But such an idea, if it conveys any tangible meaning at all, is far too abstract for those early poets and philosophers. They meant to say 'the earth, such as we see it, is held up, that is, rests on something real, though we may not see it, on something which they called the Real[4], and to which, in

---

[1] Rig-veda III. 32, 9; VI. 5, 1.

[2] Rig-veda VI. 22, 2.

[3] Rig-veda III. 14, 6.

[4] Sometimes they trace even this Satya or *R*ita, the Real or Right, to a still higher cause and say (Rig-veda X. 190, 1):

'The Right and Real was born from the Lighted Heat; from thence was born Night, and thence the billowy sea. From the sea was born Sa*m*vatsara, the year, he who ordereth day and night, the Lord of all that moves (winks). The Maker (dhât*ri*) shaped Sun

course of time, they gave many more names, such as *Ri*ta, the right, Brahman,' &c.

Of course where there is that strong reverence for truth, there must also be the sense of guilt arising from untruth. And thus we hear one poet pray that the waters may wash him clean, and carry off all his sins and all untruth:

'Carry away, ye waters[1], whatever evil there is in me, wherever I may have deceived, or may have cursed, and also all untruth (an*ri*tam[2]).'

Or again, in the Atharva-veda IV. 16:

'May all thy fatal snares, which stand spread out seven by seven and threefold, catch the man who tells a lie, may they pass by him who tells the truth!'

From the Brâhma*n*as, or theological treatises of the Brahmans, I shall quote a few passages only:

'Whosoever[3] speaks the truth, makes the fire on his own altar blaze up, as if he poured butter into the lighted fire. His own light grows larger, and from to-morrow to to-morrow he becomes better. But whosoever speaks untruth, he quenches the fire on his altar, as if he poured water into the lighted fire; his own light grows smaller and smaller, and from to-morrow to to-morrow he becomes more wicked. Let man therefore speak truth only[4].'

And again[5]: 'A man becomes impure by uttering falsehood.'

And again[6]: 'As a man who steps on the edge

---

and Moon in order; he shaped the sky, the earth, the welkin, and the highest heaven.'

[1] Rig-veda I. 23, 22.

[2] Or it may mean, 'Wherever I may have deceived, or sworn false.'

[3] *S*atapatha Brâhma*n*a II. 2, 2, 19.

[4] Cf. Muir, Metrical Translations, p. 268.

[5] *S*at. Br. III. 1, 2, 10.

[6] Taitt. Âra*n*yaka X. 9.

of a sword placed over a pit cries out, I shall slip, I shall slip into the pit, so let a man guard himself from falsehood (or sin').

In later times we see the respect for truth carried to such an extreme, that even a promise, unwittingly made, is considered to be binding.

In the Ka*th*a-Upanishad, for instance, a father is introduced offering what is called an *All*-sacrifice, where everything is supposed to be given up. His son, who is standing by, taunts his father with not having altogether fulfilled his vow, because he has not sacrificed his son. Upon this, the father, though angry and against his will, is obliged to sacrifice his son. Again, when the son arrives in the lower world, he is allowed by the Judge of the Dead to ask for three favours. He then asks to be restored to life, to be taught some sacrificial mysteries, and, as the third boon, he asks to know what becomes of man after he is dead. Yama, the lord of the Departed, tries in vain to be let off from answering this last question. But he, too, is bound by his promise, and then follows a discourse on life after death, or immortal life, which forms one of the most beautiful chapters in the ancient literature of India.

The whole plot of one of the great Epic poems, the Râmâya*n*a, rests on a rash promise given by Dasaratha, king of Ayodhyâ, to his second wife, Kaikeyî, that he would grant her two boons. In order to secure the succession to her own son, she asks that Râma, the eldest son by the king's other wife, should be banished for fourteen years. Much as the king repents his promise, Râma, his eldest son, would on no account let his father break his word, and he leaves his kingdom to wander in the forest with his wife Sîtâ and his brother Lakshma*n*a. After the father's death, the son of the second wife declines the throne, and comes to Râma to persuade him to accept the kingdom of his father. But all in vain. Râma will keep his exile for fourteen years, and never disown his father's promise. Here follows a curious dialogue between a Brâhman *G*âbâli and Prince Râma, of which I shall give some extracts[1]:

'The Brâhman, who is a priest and courtier, says, "Well, descendant of Raghu, do not thou, so noble in sentiments, and austere in character, entertain, like a common man, this useless thought. What man is a kinsman of any other? What relationship has anyone with another? A man is born alone and dies alone. Hence he who is attached to anyone as his father or his mother, is to be regarded as if he were insane, for no one belongs to another. Thou oughtest not to abandon thy father's kingdom and stay here in a sad and miserable abode, attended with many trials. Let thyself be inaugurated king in the wealthy Ayodhyâ. Dasaratha, thy father is nothing to thee, or thou to him; the king is one, and thou another, do therefore what is said . . . Then offer oblations to the departed spirits (of thy forefathers) on prescribed days; but see what a waste of food! For what can a dead man eat? If what is eaten by one here enters into the body of another (viz., of the departed), let *S*râddhas be offered to those who are travelling; they need not then get food to eat on their journey. These books (the Vedas), (which enjoin men to) sacrifice, give, consecrate themselves, practise austerities, and forsake

[1] Muir, Metrical Translations, p. 218.

the world, are composed by clever men to induce others to bestow gifts. Authoritative words do not fall from heaven. Let me, and others like yourselves, embrace whatever assertion is supported by reason. Adhere to what is apparent to the senses, and reject what is invisible. . . . *This world is the next world;* do thou therefore enjoy pleasure, for every virtuous man does not gain it. Virtuous men are greatly distressed, while the unrighteous are seen to be happy."'

These positivist sentiments sound strange, particularly from the mouth of a Brâhman. But the poet evidently wishes to represent a Brâhman living at court, who has an argument ready for anything and everything that is likely to please his king.

But what does Râma answer? 'The words,' he says, 'which you have addressed to me, though they recommend what *seems* to be right and salutary, advise, in fact, the contrary. The sinful transgressor, who lives according to the rules of heretical systems, obtains no esteem from good men. It is good conduct that marks a man to be noble or ignoble, heroic or a pretender to manliness, pure or impure. Truth and mercy are immemorial characteristics of a king's conduct. Hence royal rule is in its essence *truth*. On truth the world is based. Both sages and gods have esteemed truth. The man who speaks truth in this world attains the highest imperishable state. Men shrink with fear and horror from a liar as from a serpent. In this world the chief element in virtue is truth; it is called the basis of everything. Truth is lord in the world; virtue always rests on truth. All things are founded on truth; nothing is higher than it. Why, then, should I not be true to my promise, and faithfully observe the truthful injunction given by my father? Neither through covetousness, nor delusion, nor ignorance, will I, overpowered by darkness, break through the barrier of truth, but remain true to my promise to my father. How shall I, having promised to him that I would thus reside in the forest, transgress his injunction, and do what Bharata recommends?'

The other epic poem too, the Mahâbhârata, is full of episodes showing a profound regard for truth and an almost slavish submission to a pledge once given. The death of Bhîshma, one of the most important events in the story of the Mahâbhârata, is due to his vow never to hurt a woman. He is thus killed by Sikhandin, whom he takes to be a woman[1].

Were I to quote from all the law-books, and from still later works, everywhere you would hear the same keynote of truthfulness vibrating through them all.

We must not, however, suppress the fact that, under certain circumstances, a lie was allowed, or, at all events, excused by Indian lawgivers. Thus Gautama says[2]: 'An untruth spoken by people under the influence of anger, excessive joy, fear, pain, or grief, by infants, by very old men, by persons labouring under a delusion, being under the influence of drink, or by mad men, does not cause the speaker to fall, or, as we should say, is a venial, not a mortal sin[3].'

This is a large admission, yet even in that open admission there is a certain amount of honesty. Again and again in the Mahâbhârata is this excuse pleaded[4].

---

[1] Holtzmann, Das alte indische Epos, p. 21, note 83.

[2] V. 24.

[3] See Note D.

[4] I. 3412; III. 13844; VII. 8742; VIII. 3436, 3464.

Nay there is in the Mahâbhârata[1] the well-known story of Kausika, called Satyavâdin, the Truth-speaker, who goes to hell for having spoken the truth. He once saw men flying into the forest before robbers (dasyu). The robbers came up soon after them, and asked Kausika, which way the fugitives had taken. He told them the truth, and the men were caught by the robbers and killed. But Kausika, we are told, went to hell for having spoken the truth.

The Hindus may seem to have been a priest-ridden race, and their devotion to sacrifice and ceremonial is well known. Yet this is what the poet of the Mahâbhârata dares to say:

'Let a thousand sacrifices (of a horse) and truth be weighed in the balance—truth will exceed the thousand sacrifices[2].'

These are words addressed by Sakuntalâ, the deserted wife, to King Dushyanta, when he declined to recognise her and his son. And when he refuses to listen to her appeal, what does she appeal to as the highest authority?—*The voice of conscience.*

'If you think I am alone,' she says to the king, 'you do not know that wise man within your heart. He knows of your evil deed—in *his* sight you commit sin. A man who has committed sin may think that no one knows it. The gods know it and the old man within[3].'

This must suffice. I say once more that I do not wish to represent the people of India as 253 millions of angels, but I do wish it to be understood and to be

---

[1] Mahâbhârata VIII. 3448.

[2] Muir, l. c. p. 268; Mahâbhârata I. 3095.

[3] Mahâbhârata I. 3015–16.

accepted as a fact, that the damaging charge of untruthfulness brought against that people is utterly unfounded with regard to ancient times. It is not only not true, but the very opposite of the truth. As to modern times, and I date them from about 1000 after Christ, I can only say that, after reading the accounts of the terrors and horrors of Mohammedan rule, my wonder is that so much of native virtue and truthfulness should have survived. You might as well expect a mouse to speak the truth before a cat, as a Hindu before a Mohammedan judge. If you frighten a child, that child will tell a lie—if you terrorise millions, you must not be surprised if they try to escape from your fangs. Truthfulness is a luxury, perhaps the greatest, and let me assure you, the most expensive luxury in our life—and happy the man who has been able to enjoy it from his very childhood. It may be easy enough in our days and in a free country, like England, never to tell a lie—but the older we grow, the harder we find it to be always true, to speak the truth, the whole truth and nothing but the truth. The Hindus too had made that discovery. They too knew how hard, nay how impossible it is, always to speak the truth, the whole truth, and nothing but the truth. There is a short story in the *S*atapatha Brâhma*n*a, to my mind full of deep meaning, and pervaded by the real sense of truth, the real sense of the difficulty of truth. His kinsman said to Aru*n*a Aupavesi, 'Thou art advanced in years, establish thou the sacrificial fires.' He replied: 'Thereby you tell me henceforth to keep silence. For he who has established the fires must not speak an untruth, and only by not speaking at all, one speaks no untruth. To that extent the service of the sacrificial fires consists in truth[1].'

I doubt whether in any other of the ancient literatures of the world you will find traces of that extreme sensitiveness of conscience which despairs of our ever speaking the truth, and which declares silence gold, and speech silver, though in a much higher sense than our proverb.

What I should wish to impress on those who will soon find themselves the rulers of millions of human beings in India, is the duty to shake off national prejudices, which are apt to degenerate into a kind of madness. I have known people with a brown skin whom I could look up to as my betters. Look for them in India, and you will find them, and if you meet with disappointments, as, no doubt you will, think of the people with white skins whom you have trusted, and whom you can trust no more. We are all apt to be Pharisees in international judgments. I read only a few days ago in a pamphlet written by an enlightened politician, the following words:—

'Experience only can teach that nothing is so truly astonishing to a morally depraved people as the phenomenon of a race of men in whose word perfect confidence may be placed[2] .... The natives are conscious of their inferiority in nothing so much as in this. They require to be taught rectitude of conduct much more than literature and science.'

If you approach the Hindus with such feelings, you will teach them neither rectitude, nor science, nor literature. Nay, they might appeal to their

[1] *Satapatha Brâhmana*, translated by Eggeling, Sacred Books of the East, vol. xii. p. 313, § 20.

[2] Sir Charles Trevelyan, Christianity and Hinduism, p. 81.

own literature, even to their law-books, to teach us at least one lesson of truthfulness, truthfulness to ourselves, or, in other words,—humility.

What does Yâ*gñ*avalkya say[1]?

'It is not our hermitage,' he says—our religion we might say—'still less the colour of our skin, that produces virtue; virtue must be practised. Therefore let no one do to others what he would not have done to himself.'

And the Laws of the Mânavas, which were so much abused by Mill, what do they teach[2]?

'Evil doers think indeed that no one sees them; but the gods see them, and the old man within.'

'Self is the witness of Self, Self is the refuge of Self. Do not despise thy own Self, the highest witness of men[3].'

'If, friend, thou thinkest thou art self-alone, remember there is the silent thinker (the Highest Self) always within thy heart, and *he* sees what is good, and what is evil[4].'

'O friend, whatever good thou mayest have done from thy very birth, all will go to the dogs, if thou speak an untruth.'

Or in Vasish*th*a, XXX. 1:

'Practise righteousness, not unrighteousness; speak truth, not untruth; look far, not near; look up towards the Highest, not towards anything low.'

No doubt, there is moral depravity in India, and where is there no moral depravity in this world? But to appeal to international statistics would be, I believe, a dangerous game. Nor must we forget that our standards of morality differ, and, on some

---

[1] IV. 65. [2] VIII. 85. [3] VIII. 90. [4] VIII. 92.

points, differ considerably from those recognised in India; and we must not wonder, if sons do not at once condemn as criminal what their fathers and grandfathers considered right. Let us hold by all means to *our* sense of what is right and what is wrong; but in judging others, whether in public or in private life, whether as historians or politicians, let us not forget that a kindly spirit will never do any harm. Certainly I can imagine nothing more mischievous, more dangerous, more fatal to the permanence of English rule in India, than for the young Civil Servants to go to that country with the idea that it is a sink of moral depravity, an ant's nest of lies; for no one is so sure to go wrong, whether in public or in private life, as he who says in his haste: 'All men are liars.'

HUMAN INTEREST OF SANSKRIT LITERATURE.

LECTURE III.

My first Lecture was intended to remove the prejudice that India is and always must be a strange country to us, and that those who have to live there will find themselves stranded, and far away from that living stream of thoughts and interests which carries us along in England and in other countries of Europe.

My second Lecture was directed against another prejudice, namely, that the people of India with whom the young Civil Servants will have to pass the best years of their life are a race so depraved morally, and more particularly so devoid of any regard for truth, that they *must* always remain strangers to us, and that any real fellowship or friendship with them is quite out of the question.

To-day I shall have to grapple with a third prejudice, namely, that the literature of India, and more especially the classical Sanskrit literature, whatever may be its interest to the scholar and the antiquarian, has little to teach us which we cannot learn better from other sources, and that at all events it is of little practical use to young civilians. If only they learn to express themselves in Hindustani or Tamil, that is considered quite enough; nay, as they have to deal with men and with the ordinary affairs of life, and as, before everything else, they are to be men of the world and men of business, it is even supposed to be dangerous, if they allowed themselves to become absorbed in questions of abstruse scholarship or in researches on ancient religion, mythology, and philosophy.

I take the very opposite opinion, and I should advise every young man who wishes to enjoy his life in India, and to spend his years there with profit to himself and to others, to learn Sanskrit, and to learn it well.

I know it will be said, What can be the use of Sanskrit at the present day? Is not Sanskrit a dead language? And are not the Hindus themselves ashamed of their ancient literature? Do they not learn English, and do they not prefer Locke, and Hume, and Mill to their ancient poets and philosophers?

No doubt Sanskrit, in one sense, is a dead language. It was, I believe, a dead language more than two thousand years ago. Buddha, about 500 B.C., commanded his disciples to preach in the dialects of the people; and King Asoka, in the third century B.C., when he put up his Edicts, which were intended to be read or, at least, to be understood by the people, had them engraved on rocks and pillars in the various local dialects from Cabul[1] in the North to Ballabhi in the South, from the sources of the Ganges and the Jumnah to Allahabad and Patna, nay even down to Orissa. These various dialects are as different from Sanskrit as Italian is from Latin, and we have therefore good

[1] See Cunningham, Corpus Inscriptionum Indicarum, vol. i, 1877.

reason to suppose that, in the third century B.C., if not earlier, Sanskrit had ceased to be the spoken language of the people at large.

There is an interesting passage in the *K*ullavagga, where we are told that, even during Buddha's lifetime, some of his pupils, who were Brâhmans by birth, complained that people spoiled the words of Buddha by every one repeating them in his own dialect (nirutti). They proposed to translate his words into Sanskrit; but he declined, and commanded that each man should learn his doctrine in his own language [1].

And there is another passage, quoted by Hardy in his Manual of Buddhism, p. 186, where we read that at the time of Buddha's first preaching each of the countless listeners thought that the sage was looking towards him, and was speaking to him in his own tongue, though the language used was Mâgadhi [2].

Sanskrit, therefore, as a language spoken by the people at large, had ceased to exist in the third century B.C.

Yet such is the marvellous continuity between the past and the present in India, that in spite of repeated social convulsions, religious reforms, and foreign invasions, Sanskrit may be said to be still the only language that is spoken over the whole extent of that vast country.

Though the Buddhist sovereigns published their edicts in the vernaculars, public inscriptions and private official documents continued to be composed

---

[1] *K*ullavagga V. 33, 1. The expression used is *Kh*andaso âropemâ 'ti.

[2] See Rhys Davids, Buddhist Suttas, Sacred Books of the East, vol. xi. p. 142.

in Sanskrit during the last two thousand years. And though the language of the sacred writings of Buddhists and *G*ainas was borrowed from the vulgar dialects, the literature of India never ceased to be written in Pâ*n*inean Sanskrit, while the few exceptions, as, for instance, the use of Prâkrit by women and inferior characters in the plays of Kâlidâsa and others, are themselves not without an important historical significance.

Even at the present moment, after a century of English rule and English teaching, I believe that Sanskrit is more widely understood in India than Latin was in Europe at the time of Dante.

Whenever I receive a letter from a learned man in India, it is written in Sanskrit. Whenever there is a controversy on questions of law and religion, the pamphlets published in India are written in Sanskrit. There are Journals written in Sanskrit which must entirely depend for their support on readers who prefer that classical language to the vulgar dialects. There is *The Pandit*, published at Benares, containing not only editions of ancient texts, but treatises on modern subjects, reviews of books published in England, and controversial articles, all in Sanskrit.

Another paper of the same kind is the *Pratna-Kamra-nandinî*, 'the Delight of lovers of old things,' published likewise at Benares, and full of valuable materials.

There is also the *Vidyodaya*, 'the Rise of Knowledge,' a Sanskrit journal published at Calcutta, which sometimes contains important articles. There are probably others, which I do not know.

There is a Monthly Serial published at Bombay,

by M. Moreshwar Kunte, called the *Shad-darshana-Chintanikâ*, or 'Studies in Indian Philosophy,' giving the text of the ancient systems of philosophy, with commentaries and treatises, written in Sanskrit, though in this case accompanied by a Marathi and an English translation.

Of the Rig-veda, the most ancient of Sanskrit books, two editions are now coming out in monthly numbers, the one published at Bombay, by what may be called the liberal party, the other at Prayâga (Allahabad) by Dayânanda Sarasvatî, the representative of Indian orthodoxy. The former gives a paraphrase in Sanskrit, and a Marathi and an English translation; the latter a full explanation in Sanskrit, followed by a vernacular commentary. These books are published by subscription, and the list of subscribers among the natives of India is very considerable.

There are other journals, which are chiefly written in the spoken dialects, such as Bengali, Marathi, or Hindi; but they contain occasional articles in Sanskrit, as, for instance, the Hari*s*kandra*k*andrikâ, published at Benares, the *Tattvabodhinî*, published at Calcutta, and several more.

It was only the other day that I saw in the *Liberal*, the journal of Keshub Chunder Sen's party, an account of a meeting between Brahmavrata Samadhyayi, a Vedic scholar of Nuddea, and Kashinath Trimbak Telang, a M.A. of the University of Bombay. The one came from the east, the other from the west, yet both could converse fluently in Sanskrit[1].

Still more extraordinary is the number of Sanskrit texts, issuing from native presses, for which there

---

[1] The *Liberal*, March 12, 1882.

seems to be a large demand, for if we write for copies to be sent to England, we often find that, after a year or two, all the copies have been bought up in India itself. That would not be the case with Anglo-Saxon texts in England, or with Latin texts in Italy!

But more than this, we are told that the ancient epic poems of the Mahâbhârata and Râmâya*n*a are still recited in the temples for the benefit of visitors, and that in the villages large crowds assemble around the Kâthaka, the reader of these ancient Sanskrit poems, often interrupting his recitations with tears and sighs, when the hero of the poem is sent into banishment, while when he returns to his kingdom, the houses of the village are adorned with lamps and garlands. Such a recitation of the whole of the Mahâbhârata is said to occupy ninety days, or sometimes half a year[1]. The people at large require, no doubt, that the Brahman narrator (Kâthaka) should interpret the old poem, but there must be some few people present who understand, or imagine they understand, the old poetry of Vyâsa and Vâlmîki.

There are thousands of Brahmans[2] even now, when so little inducement exists for Vedic studies, who know the whole of the Rig-veda by heart and can repeat it; and what applies to the Rig-veda applies to many other books.

But even if Sanskrit were more of a dead language than it really is, all the living languages of India,

[1] See R. G. Bhandarkar, Consideration of the date of the Mahâbhârata, Journal of the R. A. S. of Bombay, 1872; Talboys Wheeler, History of India, ii. 365, 572; Holtzmann, Über das alte indische Epos, 1881, p. 1; Phear, The Aryan Village in India and Ceylon, p. 19.

[2] Hibbert Lectures, p. 157.

both Aryan and Dravidian, draw their very life and soul from Sanskrit[1]. On this point, and on the great help that even a limited knowledge of Sanskrit would render in the acquisition of the vernaculars, I, and others better qualified than I am, have spoken so often, though without any practical effect, that I need not speak again. Any Candidate who knows but the elements of Sanskrit grammar will well understand what I mean, whether his special vernacular may be Bengali, Hindustani, or even Tamil. To a classical scholar I can only say that between a Civil Servant who knows Sanskrit and Hindustani, and another who knows Hindustani only, there is about the same difference in their power of forming an intelligent appreciation of India and its inhabitants, as there is between a traveller who visits Italy with a knowledge of Latin, and a party personally conducted to Rome by Messrs. Cook and Co.

Let us examine, however, the objection that Sanskrit literature is a dead or an artificial literature, a little more carefully, in order to see whether there is not some kind of truth in it. Some people hold that the literary works which we possess in Sanskrit never had any real life at all, that they were altogether scholastic productions, and that therefore they can teach us nothing of what we really care for, namely

[1] 'Every person acquainted with the spoken speech of India knows perfectly well that its elevation to the dignity and usefulness of written speech has depended, and must still depend, upon its borrowing largely from its parent or kindred source; that no man who is ignorant of Arabic or Sanskrit can write Hindustani or Bengali with elegance, or purity, or precision, and that the condemnation of the classical languages to oblivion would consign the dialects to utter helplessness and irretrievable barbarism.' H. H. Wilson, Asiatic Journal, Jan. 1836; vol. xix. p. 15.

the historical growth of the Hindu mind. Others maintain that at the present moment, at all events, and after a century of English rule, Sanskrit literature has ceased to be a motive power in India, and that it can teach us nothing of what is passing now through the Hindu mind and influencing it for good or for evil.

Let us look at the facts. Sanskrit literature is a wide and a vague term. If the Vedas, such as we now have them, were composed about 1500 B.C., and if it is a fact that considerable works continue to be written in Sanskrit even now, we have before us a stream of literary activity extending over three thousand four hundred years. With the exception of China there is nothing like this in the whole world.

It is difficult to give an idea of the enormous extent and variety of that literature. We are only gradually becoming acquainted with the untold treasures which still exist in manuscripts, and with the titles of that still larger number of works which must have existed formerly, some of them being still quoted by writers of the last three or four centuries[1].

The Indian Government has of late years ordered a kind of bibliographical survey of India to be made, and has sent some learned Sanskrit scholars, both European and native, to places where collections of Sanskrit MSS. are known to exist, in order to examine and catalogue them. Some of these catalogues have been published, and we learn from them

[1] It would be a most useful work for any young scholar to draw up a list of Sanskrit books which are quoted by later writers, but have not yet been met with in Indian libraries.

that the number of separate works in Sanskrit, of which MSS. are still in existence, amounts to about 10,000[1]. This is more, I believe, than the whole classical literature of Greece and Italy put together. Much of it, no doubt, will be called mere rubbish; but then you know that even in our days the writings of a very eminent philosopher have been called 'mere rubbish.' What I wish you to see is this, that there runs through the whole history of India, through its three or four thousand years, a high road, or, it is perhaps more accurate to say, a high mountain-path of literature. It may be remote from the turmoil of the plain, hardly visible perhaps to the millions of human beings in their daily struggle of life. It may have been trodden by a few solitary wanderers only. But to the historian of the human race, to the student of the development of the human mind, those few solitary wanderers are after all the true representatives of India from age to age. Do not let us be deceived. The true history of the world must always be the history of the few; and as we measure the Himâlaya by the height of Mount Everest, we must take the true measure of India from the poets of the Veda, the sages of the Upanishads, the founders of the Vedânta and Sânkhya philosophies, and the authors of the oldest law-books, and not from the millions who are born and die in their villages, and who have never for one moment been roused out of their drowsy dream of life.

To large multitudes in India, no doubt, Sanskrit literature was not merely a dead literature, it was

---

[1] Hibbert Lectures, p. 133.

simply non-existent; but the same might be said of almost every literature, and more particularly of the literatures of the ancient world.

Still, even beyond this, I am quite prepared to acknowledge to a certain extent the truth of the statement, that a great portion of Sanskrit literature has never been living and national, in the same sense in which the Greek and Roman literatures reflected at times the life of a whole nation; and it is quite true besides, that the Sanskrit books which are best known to the public at large, belong to what might correctly be called the Renaissance period of Indian literature, when those who wrote Sanskrit had themselves to learn the language, as we learn Latin, and were conscious that they were writing for a learned and cultivated public only, and not for the people at large.

This will require a fuller explanation.

We may divide the whole of Sanskrit literature, beginning with the Rig-veda and ending with Dayânanda's Introduction to his edition of the Rig-veda, his by no means uninteresting Rig-veda-bhûmikâ, into two great periods: that preceding the great Turanian invasion, and that following it.

The former comprises the Vedic literature and the ancient literature of Buddhism, the latter all the rest.

If I call the invasion which is generally called the invasion of the Sakas, or the Scythians, or Indo-Scythians, or Turushkas, the *Turanian invasion*, it is simply because I do not as yet wish to commit myself more than I can help as to the nationality of the tribes who took possession of India, or, at least, of the government of India, from about the first century B.C. to the third century A.D.

They are best known by the name of *Yueh-chi*, this being the name by which they are called in Chinese chronicles. These Chinese chronicles form the principal source from which we derive our knowledge of these tribes, both before and after their invasion of India. Many theories have been started as to their relationship with other races. They are described as of pink and white complexion and as shooting from horseback; and as there was some similarity between their Chinese name *Yueh-chi* and the *Gothi* or *Goths*, they were identified by Remusat[1] with those German tribes, and by others with the *Getae*, the neighbours of the Goths. Tod went even a step further, and traced the *Gâts* in India and the Rajputs back to the *Yueh-chi* and *Getae*[2]. Some light may come in time out of all this darkness, but for the present we must be satisfied with the fact that, between the first century before and the third century after our era, the greatest political revolution took place in India owing to the repeated inroads of Turanian, or, to use a still less objectionable term, of Northern tribes. Their presence in India, recorded by Chinese historians, is fully confirmed by coins, by inscriptions, and by the traditional history of the country, such as it is; but to my mind nothing attests the presence of these foreign invaders more clearly than the break, or, I could almost say, the blank in the Brahmanical literature of India from the first century before to the third century after our era[3].

---

[1] Recherches sur les langues Tartares, 1820, vol. i. p. 327; Lassen, I. A., vol. ii. p. 359.

[2] Lassen, who at first rejected the identification of *Gâts* and Yueh-chi, was afterwards inclined to accept it.

[3] See Note E.

If we consider the political and social state of that country, we can easily understand what would happen in a case of invasion and conquest by a warlike race. The invaders would take possession of the strongholds or castles, and either remove the old Rajahs, or make them their vassals and agents. Everything else would then go on exactly as before. The rents would be paid, the taxes collected, and the life of the villagers, that is, of the great majority of the people of India, would go on almost undisturbed by the change of government. The only people who might suffer would be, or, at all events, might be the priestly caste, unless they should come to terms with the new conquerors. The priestly caste, however, was also to a great extent the literary caste, and the absence of their old patrons, the native Rajahs, might well produce for a time a complete cessation of literary activity. The rise of Buddhism and its formal adoption by King Asoka had already considerably shaken the power and influence of the old Brahmanic hierarchy. The Northern conquerors, whatever their religion may have been, were certainly not believers in the Veda. They seem to have made a kind of compromise with Buddhism, and it is probably due to that compromise, or to an amalgamation of Saka legends with Buddhist doctrines, that we owe the so-called Mahâyâna form of Buddhism,—and more particularly the Amitâbha worship,—which was finally settled at the Council under Kanishka, one of the Turanian rulers of India in the first century A. D.

If then we divide the whole of Sanskrit literature into these two periods, the one anterior to the great Turanian invasion, the other posterior to it, we may call the literature of the former period *ancient* and *natural*, that of the latter *modern* and *artificial*.

Of the former period we possess, *first*, what has been called the *Veda*, i. e. Knowledge, in the widest sense of the word—a considerable mass of literature, yet evidently a wreck only, saved out of a general deluge; *secondly*, the works collected in the Buddhist Tripi*t*aka, now known to us chiefly in what is called the Pâli dialect, the Gâthâ dialects, and Sanskrit, and probably much added to in later times.

The second period of Sanskrit literature comprehends everything else. Both periods may be subdivided again, but this does not concern us at present.

Now I am quite willing to admit that the literature of the second period, the modern Sanskrit literature, never was a living or national literature. It here and there contains remnants of earlier times, adapted to the literary, religious, and moral tastes of a later period; and whenever we are able to disentangle those ancient elements, they may serve to throw light on the past, and, to a certain extent, supplement what has been lost in the literature of the Vedic times. The metrical Law-books, for instance, contain old materials which existed during the Vedic period, partly in prose, as Sûtras, partly in more ancient metres, as Gâthâs. The Epic poems, the Mahâbhârata and Râmâya*n*a, have taken the place of the old Itihâsas and Âkhyânas. The Purâ*n*as, even, may contain materials, though much altered, of what was called in Vedic literature the Purâ*n*a[1].

But the great mass of that later literature is artificial or scholastic, full of interesting compositions,

[1] Hibbert Lectures, p. 154, note.

and by no means devoid of originality and occasional beauty; yet, with all that, curious only, and appealing to the interests of the Oriental scholar far more than the broad human sympathies of the historian and the philosopher.

It is different with the ancient literature of India, the literature dominated by the Vedic and the Buddhistic religions. That literature opens to us a chapter in what has been called the Education of the Human Race, to which we can find no parallel anywhere else. Whoever cares for the historical growth of our language, that is, of our thoughts; whoever cares for the first intelligible development of religion and mythology; whoever cares for the first foundation of what in later times we call the sciences of astronomy, metronomy, grammar, and etymology; whoever cares for the first intimations of philosophical thought, for the first attempts at regulating family life, village life, and state life, as founded on religion, ceremonial, tradition and contract (samaya)—must in future pay the same attention to the literature of the Vedic period as to the literatures of Greece and Rome and Germany.

As to the lessons which the early literature of Buddhism may teach us, I need not dwell on them at present. If I may judge from the numerous questions that are addressed to me with regard to that religion and its striking coincidences with Christianity, Buddhism has already become a subject of general interest, and will and ought to become so more and more[1]. On that whole class of literature, however, it is not my intention to dwell in this short course of Lectures, which can hardly suffice even for

[1] Note F.

a general survey of Vedic literature, and for an elucidation of the principal lessons which, I think, we may learn from the Hymns, the Brâhma*n*as, the Upanishads, and the Sûtras.

It was a real misfortune that Sanskrit literature became first known to the learned public in Europe through specimens belonging to the second, or, what I called, the Renaissance period. The Bhagavadgîtâ, the plays of Kâlidâsa, such as *S*akuntalâ or Urvasî, a few episodes from the Mahâbhârata and Râmâya*n*a, such as those of Nala and the Ya*gñ*adattabadha, the fables of the Hitopadesa, and the sentences of Bhart*ri*hari are, no doubt, extremely curious; and as, at the time when they first became known in Europe, they were represented to be of extreme antiquity, and the work of a people formerly supposed to be quite incapable of high literary efforts, they naturally attracted the attention of men such as Sir William Jones in England, Herder and Goethe in Germany, who were pleased to speak of them in terms of highest admiration. It was the fashion at that time to speak of Kâlidâsa, as, for instance, Alexander von Humboldt did even in so recent a work as his Kosmos, as 'the great contemporary of Virgil and Horace, who lived at the splendid Court of Vikramâditya,' this Vikramâditya being supposed to be the founder of the Samvat era, 56 B.C. But all this is now changed. Whoever the Vikramâditya was who is supposed to have defeated the *S*akas, and to have founded another era, the Samvat era, 56 B.C., he certainly did not live in the first century B.C. Nor are the Indians looked upon any longer as an illiterate race, and their poetry as popular and artless. On the contrary, they are judged now by the same standards as Persians and Arabs,

Italians or French; and, measured by that standard, such works as Kâlidâsa's plays are not superior to many plays that have long been allowed to rest in dust and peace on the shelves of our libraries. Their antiquity is no longer believed in by any critical Sanskrit scholar. Kâlidâsa is mentioned with Bhâravi as a famous poet in an inscription[1] dated A.D. 585–6 (507 *S*aka era), and for the present I see no reason to place him much earlier. As to the Laws of Manu, which used to be assigned to a fabulous antiquity[2], and are so still sometimes by those who write at random or at second-hand, I doubt whether, in their present form, they can be older than the fourth century of our era, nay I am quite prepared to see an even later date assigned to them. I know this will seem heresy to many Sanskrit scholars, but we must try to be honest to ourselves. Is there any evidence to constrain us to assign the Mânava-dharma-sâstra, such as we now possess it, written in continuous *S*lokas, to any date anterior to 300 A.D.? And if there is not, why should we not openly state it, challenge opposition, and feel grateful if our doubts can be removed?

That Manu was a name of high legal authority before that time, and that Manu and the Mânavam are frequently quoted in the ancient legal Sûtras, is quite true; but this serves only to confirm the conviction that the literature which succeeded the Turanian

---

[1] Published by Fleet in the Indian Antiquary, 1876, pp. 68–73, and first mentioned by Dr. Bhao Daji, Journal Asiatic Society, Bombay Branch, vol. ix.

[2] Sir William Jones fixed their date at 1280 B.C.; Elphinstone as 900 B.C. It has recently been stated that they could not reasonably be placed later than the fifth century B.C.

invasion is full of wrecks saved from the intervening deluge. If what we call the *Laws of Manu* had really existed as a Code of Laws, like the Code of Justinian, during previous centuries, is it likely that it should nowhere have been quoted and appealed to?

Varâhamihira (who died 587 A.D.) refers to Manu several times, but not to a Mânava-dharma-sâstra; and the only time where he seems actually to quote a number of verses from Manu, these verses are not to be met with in our text[1].

---

[1] A very useful indication of the age of the Dharma-sûtras, as compared with the metrical Dharma-sâstras or Sa*m*hitâs, is to be found in the presence or absence in them of any reference to written documents. Such written documents, if they existed, could hardly be passed over in silence in law-books, particularly when the nature of witnesses is discussed in support of loans, pledges, etc. Now we see that in treating of the law of debt and debtors *, the Dharma-sûtras of Gautama, Baudhâyana, and Âpastamba never mention evidence in writing. Vasish*th*a only refers to written evidence, but in a passage which may be interpolated †, considering that in other respects his treatment of the law of debt is very crude. Manu's metrical code shows here again its usual character. It is evidently based on ancient originals, and when it simply reproduces them, gives us the impression of great antiquity. But it freely admits more modern ingredients, and does so in our case. It speaks of witnesses, fixes their minimum number at three, and discusses very minutely their qualifications and disqualifications, without saying a word about written documents. But in one place (VIII. 168) it speaks of the valuelessness of written agreements obtained by force, thus recognising the practical employment of writing for commercial transactions. Professor Jolly ‡, it is true, suggests that this verse may be a later addition, particularly as it occurs *totidem verbis* in Nârada (IV. 55); but the final composition of Manu's Sa*m*hitâ, such as we possess it, can hardly be referred to a period when writing was not yet used, at all events for commercial purposes. Manu's Law-book is older than Yâ*gñ*a-

---

* Über das Indische Schuldrecht von J. Jolly, p. 291.

† Jolly, l. c. p. 322. ‡ L. c. p. 290.

I believe it will be found that the century in which Varâhamihara lived and wrote was the age of the literary Renaissance in India. That Kâlidâsa and Bhâravi were famous at that time, we know from the evidence of inscriptions. We also know that during that century the fame of Indian literature had reached Persia, and that the King of Persia, Khosru Nushirvan, sent his physician, Barzôî, to India, in order to translate the fables of the Pa*ñk*atantra, or rather their original, from Sanskrit into Pahlavi. The famous 'Nine Gems,' or 'the nine classics,' as we should say, have been referred, at least in part, to the same age [1], and I doubt whether we shall be able to assign a much earlier date to anything we possess of Sanskrit literature, excepting always the Vedic and Buddhistic writings.

Although the specimens of this modern Sanskrit literature, when they first became known, served to arouse a general interest, and serve even now to keep alive a certain superficial sympathy for Indian literature, more serious students had soon disposed of these compositions, and while gladly admitting their claim to be called pretty and attractive, could not think of allowing to Sanskrit literature a place among

---

valkya's, in which writing has become a familiar subject. Vish*n*u often agrees literally with Yâ*gñ*avalkya, while Nârada, as showing the fullest development of the law of debt, is most likely the latest *.

See B*ri*hatsa*m*hitâ, ed. Kern, pref. p. 43; Journal of the R. A. S., 1875, p. 106.

[1] Kern, Preface to B*ri*hatsa*m*hitâ, p. 20.

---

* Jolly, l. c. p. 322. He places Kâtyâyana and B*ri*haspati after Nârada, possibly Vyâsa and Hârîta also. See also Stenzler, Z. d. D. M. G. ix. 664.

the world-literatures, a place by the side of Greek and Latin, Italian, French, English or German.

There was indeed a time when people began to imagine that all that was worth knowing about Indian literature was known, and that the only ground on which Sanskrit could claim a place among the recognised branches of learning in a University was its usefulness for the study of the Science of Language.

At that very time, however, now about forty years ago, a new start was made, which has given to Sanskrit scholarship an entirely new character. The chief author of that movement was Burnouf, then Professor at the *Collège de France* in Paris, an excellent scholar, but at the same time a man of wide views and true historical instincts, and the last man to waste his life on mere Nalas and Sakuntalâs. Being brought up in the old traditions of the classical school in France (his father was the author of the well-known Greek Grammar), then for a time a promising young barrister, with influential friends such as Guizot, Thiers, Mignet, Villemain, at his side, and with a brilliant future before him, he was not likely to spend his life on pretty Sanskrit ditties. What he wanted when he threw himself on Sanskrit was history, human history, world-history, and with an unerring grasp he laid hold of Vedic literature and Buddhist literature, as the two stepping-stones in the slough of Indian literature. He died young, and has left a few arches only of the building he wished to rear. But his spirit lived on in his pupils and his friends, and few would deny that the first impulse, directly or indirectly, to all that has been accomplished since by the students of Vedic and

Buddhist literature, was given by Burnouf and his lectures at the *Collège de France*.

What then, you may ask, do we find in that ancient Sanskrit literature and cannot find anywhere else? My answer is, We find there the Aryan man, whom we know in his various characters, as Greek, Roman, German, Celt, and Slave, in an entirely new character. Whereas in his migrations northward his active and political energies are called out and brought to their highest perfection, we find the other side of the human character, the passive and meditative, carried to its fullest growth in India. In some of the hymns of the Rig-veda we can still watch an earlier phase. We see the Aryan tribes taking possession of the land, and under the guidance of such warlike gods as Indra and the Maruts, defending their new homes against the assaults of the black-skinned aborigines as well as against the inroads of later Aryan colonists. But that period of war soon came to an end, and when the great mass of the people had once settled down in their homesteads, the military and political duties seem to have been monopolised by what we call a *caste*[1], that is

---

[1] During times of conquest and migration, such as are represented to us in the hymns of the Rig-veda, the system of castes, as it is described, for instance, in the Laws of Manu, would have been a simple impossibility. It is doubtful whether such a system was ever more than a social ideal, but even for such an ideal the materials would have been wanting during the period when the Âryas were first taking possession of the land of the Seven Rivers. On the other hand, even during that early period, there must have been a division of labour, and hence we expect to find and do find in the grâmas of the Five Nations, *warriors*, sometimes called nobles, leaders, kings; *counsellors*, sometimes called priests, prophets, judges; and *working men*, whether ploughers, or builders, or

by a small aristocracy, while the great majority of the people were satisfied with spending their days within the narrow spheres of their villages, little concerned about the outside world, and content with the gifts that nature bestowed on them, without much labour. We read in the Mahâbhârata (XIII. 22):

'There is fruit on the trees in every forest, which every one who likes may pluck without trouble. There is cool and sweet water in the pure rivers here and there. There is a soft bed made of the twigs of beautiful creepers. And yet wretched people suffer pain at the door of the rich!'

At first sight we may feel inclined to call this quiet enjoyment of life, this mere looking on, a degeneracy rather than a growth. It seems so different from what *we* think life ought to be. Yet, from a higher point of view it may appear that those Southern Aryans have chosen the good part, or at least the part good for them, while we, Northern Aryans, have been careful and troubled about many things.

It is at all events a problem worth considering whether, as there is in nature a South and a North, there are not two hemispheres also in human nature, both worth developing—the active, combative, and political on one side, the passive, meditative, and philosophical on the other; and for the solution of that problem no literature furnishes such ample materials as that of the Veda, beginning with the Hymns and ending with the Upanishads. We enter

---

road-makers. These three divisions we can clearly perceive even in the early hymns of the Rig-veda.

into a new world—not always an attractive one, least of all to us; but it possesses one charm, it is real, it is of natural growth, and like everything of natural growth, I believe it had a hidden purpose, and was intended to teach us some kind of lesson that is worth learning, and that certainly we could learn nowhere else. We are not called upon either to admire or to despise that ancient Vedic literature; we have simply to study and to try to understand it.

There have been silly persons who have represented the development of the Indian mind as superior to any other, nay, who would make us go back to the Veda or to the sacred writings of the Buddhists in order to find there a truer religion, a purer morality, and a more sublime philosophy than our own. I shall not even mention the names of these writers or the titles of their works. But I feel equally impatient when I see other scholars criticising the ancient literature of India as if it were the work of the nineteenth century, as if it represented an enemy that must be defeated, and that can claim no mercy at our hands. That the Veda is full of childish, silly, even to our minds monstrous conceptions, who would deny? But even these monstrosities are interesting and instructive; nay, many of them, if we can but make allowance for different ways of thought and language, contain germs of truth and rays of light, all the more striking, because breaking upon us through the veil of the darkest night.

Here lies the general, the truly human interest which the *ancient* literature of India possesses, and which gives it a claim on the attention, not only of Oriental scholars or of students of ancient history, but of every educated man and woman.

There are problems which we may put aside for a time, aye, which we must put aside while engaged each in our own hard struggle for life, but which will recur for all that, and which, whenever they do recur, will stir us more deeply than we like to confess to others, or even to ourselves. It is true that with us one day only out of seven is set apart for rest and meditation, and for the consideration of what the Greeks called τὰ μέγιστα—'the greatest things.' It is true that that seventh day also is passed by many of us either in mere church-going routine or in thoughtless rest. But whether on week-days or on Sundays, whether in youth or in old age, there are moments, rare though they be, yet for all that the most critical moments of our life, when the old simple questions of humanity return to us in all their intensity, and we ask ourselves, What are we? What is this life on earth meant for? Are we to have no rest here, but to be always toiling and building up our own happiness out of the ruins of the happiness of our neighbours? And when we have made our home on earth as comfortable as it can be made with steam and gas and electricity, are we really so much happier than the Hindu in his primitive homestead?

With us, as I said just now, in these Northern climates, where life is and always must be a struggle, and a hard struggle too, and where accumulation of wealth has become almost a necessity to guard against the uncertainties of old age or the accidents inevitable in our complicated social life, with us, I say, and in our society, hours of rest and meditation are but few and far between. It was the same as long as we know the history of the Teutonic races; it was the same even with Romans and Greeks. The European climate with its long cold winters, in many places also the difficulty of cultivating the soil, the conflict of interests between small communities, has developed the instinct of self-preservation (not to say, self-indulgence) to such an extent that most of the virtues and most of the vices of European society can be traced back to that source. Our own character was formed under these influences, by inheritance, by education, by necessity. We all lead a fighting-life; our highest ideal of life is a fighting-life. We work till we can work no longer, and are proud, like old horses, to die in harness. We point with inward satisfaction to what we and our ancestors have achieved by hard work, in founding a family, or a business, a town or a state. We point to the marvels of what we call civilisation—our splendid cities, our high-roads and bridges, our ships, our railways, our telegraphs, our electric light, our pictures, our statues, our music, our theatres. We imagine we have made life on earth quite perfect; in some cases so perfect that we are almost sorry to leave it again. But the lesson which both Brahmans and Buddhists are never tired of teaching is that this life is but a journey from one village to another, and not a resting-place. Thus we read[1]:

'As a man journeying to another village may enjoy a night's rest in the open air, but, after leaving his resting-place, proceeds again on his journey the next day, thus father, mother, wife, and wealth are all but like a night's rest to us—wise people do not cling to them for ever.'

Instead of simply despising this Indian view of life, might we not pause for a moment and consider

[1] Boehtlingk, Sprüche, 5101.

whether their philosophy of life is entirely wrong, and ours entirely right; whether this earth was really meant for work only (for with us pleasure also has been changed into work), for constant hurry and flurry; or whether we, sturdy Northern Aryans, might not have been satisfied with a little less of work, and a little less of so-called pleasure, but with a little more of thought, and a little more of rest. For, short as our life is, we are not mere Mayflies that are born in the morning to die at night. We have a past to look back to and a future to look forward to, and it may be that some of the riddles of the future find their solution in the wisdom of the past.

Then why should we always fix our eyes on the present only? Why should we always be racing, whether for wealth or for power or for fame? Why should we never rest and be thankful?

I do not deny that the manly vigour, the silent endurance, the public spirit, and the private virtues too of the citizens of European states represent one side, it may be a very important side, of the destiny which man has to fulfil on earth.

But there is surely another side of our nature, and possibly another destiny open to man in his journey across this life, which should not be entirely ignored. If we turn our eyes to the East, and particularly to India, where life is, or at all events was, no very severe struggle, where the climate was mild, the soil fertile, where vegetable food in small quantities sufficed to keep the body in health and strength, where the simplest hut or cave in a forest was all the shelter required, and where social life never assumed the gigantic, aye monstrous proportions of a London or Paris, but fulfilled itself within the narrow boundaries of village communities,—was it not, I say, natural there, or, if you like, was it not *intended* there, that another side of human nature should be developed—not the active, the combative and acquisitive, but the passive, the meditative and reflective? Can we wonder that the Aryans who stepped as strangers into some of the happy fields and valleys along the Indus or the Ganges should have looked upon life as a perpetual Sunday or Holyday, or a kind of Long Vacation, delightful so long as it lasts, but which must come to an end sooner or later? Why should they have accumulated wealth? why should they have built palaces? why should they have toiled day and night? After having provided from day to day for the small necessities of the body, they thought they had the right, it may be the duty, to look round upon this strange exile, to look inward upon themselves, upward to something not themselves, and to see whether they could not understand a little of the true purport of that mystery which we call life on earth.

Of course *we* should call such notions of life dreamy, unreal, unpractical, but may not *they* look upon our notions of life as short-sighted, fussy, and, in the end, most unpractical, because involving a sacrifice of life for the sake of life?

No doubt these are both extreme views, and they have hardly ever been held or realised in that extreme form by any nation, whether in the East or in the West. We are not always plodding—we sometimes allow ourselves an hour of rest and peace and thought—nor were the ancient people of India always dreaming and meditating on τὰ μέγιστα, on the great problems of life, but, when called upon, we know that they too could fight like heroes, and that, without machinery, they could by patient toil raise even the meanest handiwork into a work of art, a real joy to the maker and to the buyer.

All then that I wish to put clearly before you is this, that the Aryan man, who had to fulfil his mission in India, might naturally be deficient in many of the practical and fighting virtues, which were developed in the Northern Aryans by the very struggle without which they could not have survived, but that his life on earth had not therefore been entirely wasted. His very view of life, though we cannot adopt it in this Northern climate, may yet act as a lesson and a warning to us, not, for the sake of life, to sacrifice the highest objects of life.

The greatest conqueror of antiquity stood in silent wonderment before the Indian Gymnosophists, regretting that he could not communicate with them in their own language, and that their wisdom could not reach him except through the contaminating channels of sundry interpreters.

That need not be so at present. Sanskrit is no longer a difficult language, and I can assure every young Indian Civil Servant that if he will but go to the fountain-head of Indian wisdom, he will find there, among much that is strange and useless, some lessons of life which are worth learning, and which we in our haste are too apt to forget or to despise.

Let me read you a few sayings only, which you may still hear repeated in India when, after the heat of the day, the old and the young assemble together under the shadow of their village tree—sayings which to them seem truth, to us, I fear, mere truism!

'As all have to sleep together laid low in the

earth, why do foolish people wish to injure one another[1]?

'A man seeking for eternal happiness (moksha) might obtain it by a hundredth part of the sufferings which a foolish man endures in the pursuit of riches[2].

'Poor men eat more excellent bread than the rich: for hunger gives it sweetness[3].

'Our body is like the foam of the sea, our life like a bird, our company with those whom we love does not last for ever; why then sleepest thou, my son[4]?

'As two logs of wood meet upon the ocean and then separate again, thus do living creatures meet[5].

'Our meeting with wives, relations, and friends occurs on our journey. Let a man therefore see clearly where he is, whither he will go, what he is, why tarrying here, and why grieving for anything[6].

'Family, wife, children, our very body and our wealth, they all pass away. They do not belong to us. What then is ours? Our good and our evil deeds[7].

'When thou goest away from here, no one will follow thee. Only thy good and thy evil deeds, they will follow thee wherever thou goest[8].

'Whatever act, good or bad, a man performs, of that by necessity he receives the recompense[9].

'According to the Veda[10] the soul (life) is eternal, but the body of all creatures is perishable. When the body is destroyed, the soul departs elsewhere, fettered by the bonds of our works.

---

[1] Mahâbh. XI. 121.
[2] Pañkat. II. 127 (117).
[3] Mahâbh. V. 1144.
[4] Mahâbh. XII. 12050.
[5] L. c. XII. 869.
[6] L. c. XII. 872.
[7] L. c. XII. 12453.
[8] L. c. XII. 12456.
[9] L. c. III. 13846 (239).
[10] L. c. III. 13864.

'If I know that my own body is not mine, and yet that the whole earth is mine, and again that it is both mine and thine, no harm can happen then[1].

'As a man puts on new garments in this world, throwing aside those which he formerly wore, even so the Self of man puts on new bodies which are in accordance with his acts[2].

'No weapons will hurt the Self of man, no fire will burn it, no water moisten it, no wind will dry it up.

'It is not to be hurt, not to be burnt, not to be moistened, not to be dried up. It is imperishable, unchanging, immoveable, without beginning.

'It is said to be immaterial, passing all understanding, and unchangeable. If you know the Self of man to be all this, grieve not.

'There is nothing higher than the attainment of the knowledge of the Self[3].

'All living creatures are the dwelling of the Self who lies enveloped in matter, who is immortal, and spotless. Those who worship the Self, the immoveable, living in a moveable dwelling, become immortal.

'Despising everything else, a wise man should strive after the knowledge of the Self.'

We shall have to return to this subject again, for this knowledge of the Self is really the *Vedânta*, that is, the end, the highest goal of the Veda. The highest wisdom of Greece was 'to know ourselves;' the highest wisdom of India is 'to know our Self.'

If I were asked to indicate by one word the distinguishing feature of the Indian character, as I have

---

[1] Kâm. Nîtis, 1, 23 (Boehtlingk, 918).
[2] Vish*n*u-sûtras XX. 50–53.
[3] Âpastamba Dharma-sûtras I. 8, 22.

here tried to sketch it, I should say it was *transcendent*, using that word, not in its strict technical sense, as fixed by Kant, but in its more general acceptation, as denoting a mind bent on transcending the limits of empirical knowledge. There are minds perfectly satisfied with empirical knowledge, a knowledge of facts, well ascertained, well classified, and well labelled. Such knowledge may assume very vast proportions, and, if knowledge is power, it may impart great power, real intellectual power to the man who can wield and utilise it. Our own age is proud of that kind of knowledge, and to be content with it, and never to attempt to look beyond it, is, I believe, one of the happiest states of mind to be in.

But, for all that, there is a Beyond, and he who has once caught a glance of it, is like a man who has gazed at the sun—wherever he looks, everywhere he sees the image of the sun. Speak to him of finite things, and he will tell you that the Finite is impossible and meaningless without the Infinite. Speak to him of death, and he will call it birth; speak to him of time, and he will call it the mere shadow of eternity. To us the senses seem to be the organs, the tools, the most powerful engines of knowledge; to him they are, if not actually deceivers, at all events heavy fetters, checking the flight of the spirit. To us this earth, this life, all that we see, and hear, and touch is certain. Here, we feel, is our home, here lie our duties, here our pleasures. To him this earth is a thing that once was not, and that again will cease to be; this life is a short dream from which we shall soon awake. Of nothing he professes greater ignorance than of what to others seems to be most certain, namely what we see, and hear, and touch; and as to our home, wherever that may be, he knows that certainly it is not here.

Do not suppose that such men are mere dreamers. Far from it! And if we can only bring ourselves to be quite honest to ourselves, we shall have to confess that at times we all have been visited by these transcendental aspirations, and have been able to understand what Wordsworth meant when he spoke of those

> 'Obstinate questionings
> Of sense and outward things,
> Fallings from us, vanishings;
> Blank misgivings of a creature
> Moving about in worlds not realised.'

The transcendent temperament acquired no doubt a more complete supremacy in the Indian character than anywhere else: but no nation, and no individual, is entirely without that 'yearning beyond;' indeed we all know it under a more familiar name—namely, *Religion*.

It is necessary, however, to distinguish between religion and *a* religion, quite as much as in another branch of philosophy we have to distinguish between language and *a* language or many languages. A man may accept *a* religion, he may be converted to the Christian religion, and he may change his own particular religion from time to time, just as he may speak different languages. But in order to have *a* religion, a man must have religion. He must once *at least* in his life have looked beyond the horizon of this world, and carried away in his mind an impression of the Infinite, which will never leave him again. A being satisfied with the world of sense, unconscious of its finite nature, undisturbed by the limited or negative character of all perceptions of the senses, would be incapable of any religious concepts. Only when the finite character of all human knowledge has been perceived is it possible for the human mind to conceive that which is beyond the Finite, call it what you like, the Beyond, the Unseen, the Infinite, the Supernatural, or the Divine. That step must have been taken before religion of any kind becomes possible. What kind of religion it will be, depends on the character of the race which elaborates it, its surroundings in nature, and its experience in history.

Now we may seem to know a great many religions —I speak here, of course, of ancient religions only, of what are sometimes called national or autochthonous religions—not of those founded in later times by individual prophets or reformers.

Yet, among those ancient religions we seldom know, what after all is the most important point, their origin and their gradual growth. The Jewish religion is represented to us as perfect and complete from the very first, and it is with great difficulty that we can discover its real beginnings and its historical growth. And take the Greek and the Roman religions, take the religions of the Teutonic, Slavonic or Celtic tribes, and you will find that their period of growth has always passed, long before we know them, and that from the time we know them, all their changes are purely *metamorphic*—changes in form of substances ready at hand.

Now let us look to the ancient inhabitants of India. With them, first of all, religion was not only *one* interest by the side of many. It was the all-absorbing interest; it embraced not only worship and prayer, but what we call philosophy, morality, law, and government,—all was pervaded by religion.

Their whole life was to them a religion—everything else was, as it were, a mere concession made to the ephemeral requirements of this life.

What then can we learn from the ancient religious literature of India—or from the Veda?

It requires no very profound knowledge of Greek religion and Greek language to discover in the Greek deities the original outlines of certain physical phenomena. Every schoolboy knows that in *Zeus* there is something of the sky, in *Poseidon* of the sea, in *Hades* of the lower world, in *Apollo* of the sun, in *Artemis* of the moon, in *Hephæstos* of the fire. But for all that, there is, from a Greek point of view, a very considerable difference between *Zeus* and the sky, between *Poseidon* and the sea, between *Apollo* and the sun, between *Artemis* and the moon.

Now what do we find in the Veda? No doubt here and there a few philosophical hymns which have been quoted so often that people have begun to imagine that the Veda is a kind of collection of Orphic hymns. We also find some purely mythological hymns, in which the Devas or gods have assumed nearly as much dramatic personality as in the Homeric hymns.

But the great majority of Vedic hymns consists in simple invocations of the fire, the water, the sky, the sun, and the storms, often under the same names which afterwards became the proper names of Hindu deities, but as yet nearly free from all that can be called irrational or mythological. There is nothing irrational, nothing I mean we cannot enter into or sympathise with, in people imploring the storms to cease, or the sky to rain, or the sun to shine. I say there is nothing irrational in it, though perhaps it might be more accurate to say that there is nothing in it that would surprise anybody who is acquainted with the growth of human reason, or, at all events, of childish reason. It does not matter how we call the tendency of the childish mind to confound the manifestation with that which manifests itself, effect with cause, act with agent. Call it Animism, Personification, Metaphor, or Poetry, we all know what is meant by it, in the most general sense of all these names; we all know that it exists, and the youngest child who beats the chair against which he has fallen, or who scolds his dog, or who sings, 'Rain, rain, go to Spain,' can teach us that, however irrational all this may seem to us, it is perfectly rational, natural, aye inevitable in the first periods, or the childish age of the human mind.

Now it is exactly this period in the growth of ancient religion, which was always presupposed, or postulated, but was absent everywhere else, that is clearly put before us in the hymns of the Rig-veda. It is this ancient chapter in the history of the human mind which has been preserved to us in Indian literature, while we look for it in vain in Greece or Rome or elsewhere.

It has been a favourite idea of those who call themselves 'students of man,' or anthropologists, that in order to know the earliest or so-called prehistoric phases in the growth of man, we should study the life of savage nations, as we may watch it still in some parts of Asia, Africa, Polynesia and America.

There is much truth in this, and nothing can be more useful than the observations which we find collected in the works of such students as Waitz, Tylor, Lubbock, and many others. But let us be honest, and confess, first of all, that the materials on which we have here to depend are often extremely untrustworthy.

Nor is this all. What do we know of savage tribes beyond the last chapter of their history? Do we ever get an insight into their antecedents? Can we understand, what after all is everywhere the most important and the most instructive lesson to learn, how they have come to be what they are? There is indeed their language, and in it we see traces of growth that point to distant ages, quite as much as the Greek of Homer, or the Sanskrit of the Vedas. Their language proves indeed that these so-called heathens, with their complicated systems of mythology, their artificial customs, their unintelligible whims and savageries, are not the creatures of to-day or yesterday. Unless we admit a special creation for these savages, they must be as old as the Hindus, the Greeks and Romans, as old as we ourselves. We may assume, of course, if we like, that their life has been stationary, and that they are to-day what the Hindus were no longer 3000 years ago. But that is a mere guess, and is contradicted by the facts of their language. They may have passed through ever so many vicissitudes, and what we consider as primitive may be, for all we know, a relapse into savagery, or a corruption of something that was more rational and intelligible in former stages. Think only of the rules that determine marriage among the lowest of savage tribes. Their complication passes all understanding, all seems a chaos of prejudice, superstition, pride, vanity and stupidity. And yet we catch a glimpse here and there that there was some reason in most of that unreason; we see how sense dwindled away into nonsense, custom into ceremony, ceremony into farce. Why then should this surface of savage life represent to us the lowest stratum of human life, the very beginnings of civilization, simply because we cannot dig beyond that surface?

Now, I do not wish to be misunderstood. I do not claim for the ancient Indian literature any more than I should willingly concede to the fables and traditions and songs of savage nations, such as we can study at present in what we call a state of nature. Both are important documents to the student of the Science of Man. I simply say that in the Veda we have a nearer approach to a beginning, and an intelligible beginning, than in the wild invocations of Hottentots or Bushmen. But when I speak of a beginning, I do not mean an absolute beginning, a beginning of all things. Again and again the question has been asked whether we could bring ourselves to believe that man, as soon as he could stand on his legs, instead of crawling on all fours, as he is supposed to have done, burst forth into singing Vedic hymns? But who has ever maintained this? Surely whoever has eyes to see can see in every Vedic hymn, aye, in every Vedic word, as many rings within rings as is in the oldest tree that was ever hewn down in the forest.

I shall say even more, and I have said it before, namely, that supposing that the Vedic hymns were composed between 1500 and 1000 B.C., we can hardly understand how, at so early a date, the Indians had developed ideas which to us sound decidedly modern. I should give anything if I could escape from the conclusion that the collection of the Vedic Hymns, a collection in ten books, existed at least 1000 B.C., that is about 500 years before the rise of Buddhism. I do not mean to say that something may not be discovered hereafter to enable us to refer that collection to a later date. All I say is that, so far as we know *at present*, so far as all honest Sanskrit scholars know *at present*, we cannot well bring our pre-Buddhistic literature into narrower limits than five hundred years.

What then is to be done? We must simply keep our pre-conceived notions of what people call primitive humanity in abeyance for a time, and if we find that people three thousand years ago were familiar with ideas that seem novel and nineteenth-century-like to us, well, we must somewhat modify our conceptions of the primitive savage, and remember that things hid from the wise and prudent have sometimes been revealed to babes.

I maintain then that for a study of man, or, if you like, for a study of Aryan humanity, there is nothing in the world equal in importance with the Veda. I maintain that to everybody who cares for himself, for his ancestors, for his history, or for his intellectual development, a study of Vedic literature is indispensable; and that, as an element of liberal education, it is far more important and far more improving than the reigns of Babylonian and Persian kings, aye even than the dates and deeds of many of the kings of Judah and Israel.

It is curious to observe the reluctance with which these facts are accepted, particularly by those to whom they ought to be most welcome, I mean the students of anthropology. Instead of devoting all their energy to the study of these documents, which have come upon us like a miracle, they seem only bent on inventing excuses why they need not be studied. Let it not be supposed that, because there are several translations of the Rig-veda in English, French and German, therefore all that the Veda can teach us has been learned. Far from it. Every one of these translations has been put forward as tentative only. I myself, though during the last thirty years I have given translations of a number of the more important hymns, have only ventured to publish a specimen of what I think a translation of the Veda ought to be; and that translation, that *traduction raisonnée* as I ventured to call it, of twelve hymns only, fills a whole volume. We are still on the mere surface of Vedic literature, and yet our critics are ready with ever so many arguments why the Veda can teach us nothing as to a primitive state of man. If they mean by primitive that which came absolutely first, then they ask for something which they will never get, not even if they discovered the private correspondence of Adam and Eve, or of the first *Homo* and *Femina sapiens*. We mean by primitive the earliest state of man of which, from the nature of the case, we can hope to gain any knowledge; and here, next to the archives hidden away in the secret drawers of language, in the treasury of words common to all the Aryan tribes, and in the radical elements of which each word is compounded, there is no literary relic more full of lessons to the true anthropologist, to the true student of mankind, than the Rig-veda.

OBJECTIONS.

LECTURE IV.

It may be quite true that controversy often does more harm than good, that it encourages the worst of all talents, that of plausibility, not to say dishonesty, and generally leaves the world at large worse confounded than it was before. It has been said that no clever lawyer would shrink from taking a brief to prove that the earth forms the centre of the world, and, with all respect for English Juries, it is not impossible that even in our days he might gain a verdict against Galileo. Nor do I deny that there is a power and vitality in truth which in the end overcomes and survives all opposition, as shown by the very doctrine of Galileo which at present is held by hundreds and thousands who would find it extremely difficult to advance one single argument in its support. I am ready to admit also that those who have done the best work, and have contributed most largely toward the advancement of knowledge and the progress of truth, have seldom wasted their time in controversy, but have marched on straight, little concerned either about applause on the right or abuse on the left. All this is true, perfectly true, and yet I feel that I cannot escape from devoting the whole of a lecture to the answering of certain objections which have been raised against the views which I have put forward with regard to the character and the historical importance of Vedic literature. We must not forget that the whole subject is new, the number of competent judges small, and mistakes not only possible, but almost inevitable. Besides, there are mistakes and mistakes, and the errors of able men are often instructive, nay one might say sometimes almost indispensable for the discovery of truth. There are criticisms which may be safely ignored, criticisms for the sake of criticism, if not inspired by meaner motives. But there are doubts and difficulties which suggest themselves naturally, objections which have a right to be heard, and the very removal of which forms the best approach to the stronghold of truth. Nowhere has this principle been so fully recognised and been acted on as in Indian literature. Whatever subject is started, the rule is that the argument should begin with the pûrvapaksha, with all that can be said against a certain opinion. Every possible objection is welcome, if only it is not altogether frivolous and absurd, and then only follows the uttarapaksha, with all that can be said against these objections and in support of the original opinion. Only when this process has been fully gone through is it allowed to represent an opinion as siddhânta, or established.

Therefore, before opening the pages of the Veda, and giving you a description of the poetry, the religion, and philosophy of the ancient inhabitants of India, I thought it right and necessary to establish, first of all, certain points without which it would be impossible to form a right appreciation of the historical value of the Vedic hymns, and of their importance even to us who live at so great a distance from those early poets.

The *first* point was purely preliminary, namely that the Hindus in ancient, and in modern times also, are a nation deserving of our interest and sympathy, worthy also of our confidence, and by no means guilty of the charge so recklessly brought against them—the charge of an habitual disregard of truth.

Secondly, that the ancient literature of India is not to be considered simply as a curiosity and to be handed over to the good pleasure of Oriental scholars, but that, both by its language, the Sanskrit, and by its most ancient literary documents, the Vedas, it can teach us lessons which nothing else can teach, as to the origin of our own language, the first formation of our own concepts, and the true natural germs of all that is comprehended under the name of civilisation, at least the civilisation of the Aryan race, that race to which we and all the greatest nations of the world—the Hindus, the Persians, the Greeks and Romans, the Slaves, the Celts, and last, not least, the Teutons, belong. A man may be a good and useful ploughman without being a geologist, without knowing the stratum on which he takes his stand, or the strata beneath that give support to the soil on which he lives and works, and from which he draws his nourishment. And a man may be a good and useful citizen, without being an historian, without knowing how the world in which he lives came about, and how many phases mankind had to pass through in language, religion, and philosophy, before it could supply him with that intellectual soil on which he lives and works, and from which he draws his best nourishment.

But there must always be an aristocracy of those who know, and who can trace back the best which we possess, not merely to a Norman Count, or a Scandinavian Viking, or a Saxon Earl, but to far older ancestors and benefactors, who thousands of years ago were toiling for us in the sweat of their face, and without whom we should never be what we are,—the ancestors of the whole Aryan race, the first framers of our words, the first poets of our thoughts, the first givers of our laws, the first prophets of our gods, and of Him who is God above all gods.

That aristocracy of those who know,—*di color che sanno*,—or try to know, is open to all who are willing to enter, to all who have a feeling for the past, an interest in the genealogy of our thoughts, and a reverence for the ancestry of our intellect, who are in fact historians in the true sense of the word, i.e. inquirers into that which is past, but not lost.

Thirdly, having explained to you why the ancient literature of India, the really ancient literature of that country, I mean that of the Vedic period, deserves the careful attention, not of Oriental scholars only, but of every educated man and woman who wishes to know how we, even we here in England and in this nineteenth century of ours, came to be what we are, I tried to explain to you the difference, and the natural and inevitable difference, between the development of the human character in such different climates as those of India and Europe. And while admitting that the Hindus were deficient in many of those manly virtues and practical achievements which we value most, I wished to point out that there was another sphere of intellectual activity in which the Hindus excelled—the meditative and transcendent—and that here we might learn from them some lessons of life which we ourselves are but too apt to ignore or to despise.

Fourthly, fearing that I might have raised too high expectations of the ancient wisdom, the religion and philosophy of the Vedic Indians, I felt it my duty to state that, though primitive in one sense, we must not expect the Vedic religion to be primitive in the anthropological sense of the word, as containing the utterances of beings who had just broken their shells, and were wonderingly looking out for the first time upon this strange world. The Veda may be called primitive, because there is no other literary document more primitive than it: but the language, the mythology, the religion and philosophy that meet us in the Veda open vistas of the past which no one would venture to measure in years. Nay, they contain, by the side of simple, natural, childish thoughts, many ideas which to us sound modern, or secondary and tertiary, as I called them, but which nevertheless are older than any other literary document, and give us trustworthy information of a period in the history of human thought of which we knew absolutely nothing before the discovery of the Vedas [1].

But even thus our path is not yet clear. Other objections have been raised against the Veda as an historical document. Some of them are important; and I have at times shared them myself. Others are at least instructive, and will give us an opportunity of testing the foundation on which we stand.

---

[1] If we applied the name of literature to the cylinders of Babylon and the papyri of Egypt, we should have to admit that some of these documents are more ancient than any date we dare as yet assign to the hymns collected in the ten books of the Rig-veda.

The first objection then against our treating the Veda as an historical document is that it is not truly national in its character, and does not represent the thoughts of the whole of the population of India, but only of a small minority, namely of the Brahmans, and not even of the whole class of Brahmans, but only of a small minority of them, namely of the professional priests.

Objections should not be based on demands which, from the nature of the case, are unreasonable. Have those who maintain that the Vedic hymns do not represent the whole of India, that is the whole of its ancient population, in the same manner as they say that the Bible represents the Jews or Homer the Greeks, considered what they are asking for? So far from denying that the Vedic hymns represent only a small and, it may be, a priestly minority of the ancient population of India, the true historian would probably feel inclined to urge the same cautions against the Old Testament and the Homeric poems also.

No doubt, after the books which compose the Old Testament had been collected as a Sacred Canon, they were known to the majority of the Jews. But when we speak of the primitive state of the Jews, of their moral, intellectual, and religious status while in Mesopotamia or Canaan or Egypt, we should find that the different books of the Old Testament teach us as little of the whole Jewish race, with all its local characteristics and social distinctions, as the Homeric poems do of all the Greek tribes, or the Vedic hymns of all the inhabitants of India. Surely, even when we speak of the history of the Greeks or the Romans, we know that we shall not find there a complete picture of the social, intellectual, and religious life of a whole nation. We know very little of the intellectual life of a whole nation, even during the Middle Ages, aye even at the present day. We may know something of the generals, of the commanders-in-chief, but of the privates, of the millions, we know next to nothing. And what we do know of kings or generals or ministers is mostly no more than what was thought of them by a few Greek poets or Jewish prophets, men who were one in a million among their contemporaries.

But it might be said that though the writers were few, the readers were many. Is that so? I believe you would be surprised to hear how small the number of readers is even in modern times, while in ancient times reading was restricted to the very smallest class of privileged persons. There may have been listeners at public and private festivals, at sacrifices, and later on in theatres, but readers, in our sense of the word, are a very modern invention.

There never has been so much reading, reading spread over so large an area, as in our times. But if you asked publishers as to the number of copies sold of books which are supposed to have been read by everybody, say Macaulay's History of England, the Life of the Prince Consort, or Darwin's Origin of Species, you would find that out of a population of thirty-two millions not one million has possessed itself of a copy of these works. The book which of late has probably had the largest sale is the Revised Version of the New Testament; and yet the whole number of copies sold among the eighty millions of English-speaking people is probably not more than four millions. Of ordinary books which are called books of the season, and which are supposed to have had a great success, an edition of three or four thousand copies is not considered unsatisfactory by publishers or authors in England. But if you look to other countries, such, for instance, as Russia, it would be very difficult indeed to name books that could be considered as representative of the whole nation, or as even known by more than a very small minority.

And if we turn our thoughts back to the ancient nations of Greece and Italy, or of Persia and Babylonia, what book is there, with the exception perhaps of the Homeric poems, of which we could say that it had been read or even heard of by more than a few thousand people? We think of Greeks and Romans as literary people, and so no doubt they were, but in a very different sense from what we mean by this. What we call Greeks and Romans are chiefly the citizens of Athens and Rome, and here again those who could produce or who could read such works as the Dialogues of Plato or the Epistles of Horace constituted a very small intellectual aristocracy indeed. What we call history—the memory of the past—has always been the work of minorities. Millions and millions pass away unheeded, and the few only to whom has been given the gift of fusing speech and thought into forms of beauty remain as witnesses of the past.

If then we speak of times so distant as those represented by the Rig-veda, and of a country so disintegrated, or rather as yet so little integrated as India was three thousand years ago, surely it requires but little reflection to know that what we see in the Vedic poems are but a few snow-clad peaks, representing to us, from a far distance, the whole mountain-range of a nation, completely lost beyond the horizon of history. When we speak of the Vedic hymns as representing the religion, the thoughts and customs of India three thousand years ago, we cannot mean by India more than some unknown quantity of which the poets of the Veda are the only spokesmen left. When we now speak of India, we think of 250 millions, a sixth part of the whole human race, peopling the vast peninsula from the Himalayan mountains between the arms of the Indus and the Ganges, down to Cape Comorin and Ceylon, an extent of country nearly as large as Europe. In the Veda the stage on which the life of the ancient kings and poets is acted, is the valley of the Indus and the Punjab, as it is now called, the Sapta Sindhasa*h*, the Seven Rivers of the Vedic poets. The land watered by the Ganges is hardly known, and the whole of the Dekkan seems not yet to have been discovered.

Then again, when these Vedic hymns are called the lucubrations of a few priests, not the outpourings of the genius of a whole nation, what does that mean? We may no doubt call these ancient Vedic poets priests, if we like, and no one would deny that their poetry is pervaded not only by religious, mythological, and philosophical, but likewise by sacrificial and ceremonial conceits. Still a priest, if we trace him back far enough, is only a *presbyteros* or an elder, and, as such, those Vedic poets had a perfect right to speak in the name of a whole class, or of the village community to which they belonged. Call Vasish*th*a a priest by all means, only do not let us imagine that he was therefore very like Cardinal Manning.

After we have made every possible concession to

arguments, most of which are purely hypothetical, there remains this great fact that here, in the Rig-veda, we have poems, composed in perfect language, in elaborate metre, telling us about gods and men, about sacrifices and battles, about the varying aspects of nature and the changing conditions of society, about duty and pleasure, philosophy and morality—articulate voices reaching us from a distance from which we never heard before the faintest whisper; and instead of thrilling with delight at this almost miraculous discovery, some critics stand aloof and can do nothing but find fault, because these songs do not represent to us primitive men exactly as they think they ought to have been; not like Papúas or Bushmen, with arboraceous habits and half-animal clicks, not as worshipping stocks or stones, or believing in fetishes, as according to Comte's inner consciousness they ought to have done, but rather, I must confess, as beings whom we can understand, with whom to a certain extent we can sympathise, and to whom, in the historical progress of the human intellect, we may assign a place, not very far behind the ancient Jews and Greeks.

Once more then, if we mean by primitive, people who inhabited this earth as soon as the vanishing of the glacial period made this earth inhabitable, the Vedic poets were certainly not primitive. If we mean by primitive, people who were without a knowledge of fire, who used unpolished flints, and ate raw flesh, the Vedic poets were not primitive. If we mean by primitive, people who did not cultivate the soil, had no fixed abodes, no kings, no sacrifices, no laws, again, I say, the Vedic poets were not primitive. But if we mean by primitive the people who have been the first of the Aryan race to leave behind literary relics of their existence on earth, then I say the Vedic poets are primitive, the Vedic language is primitive, the Vedic religion is primitive, and, taken as a whole, more primitive than anything else that we are ever likely to recover in the whole history of our race.

When all these objections had failed, a last trump was played. The ancient Vedic poetry was said to be, if not of foreign origin, at least very much infected by foreign, and more particularly by Semitic influences. It had always been urged by Sanskrit scholars as one of the chief attractions of Vedic literature that it not only allowed us an insight into a very early phase of religious thought, but that the Vedic religion was the only one the development of which took place without any extraneous influences, and could be watched through a longer series of centuries than any other religion. Now with regard to the first point, we know how perplexing it is in the religion of ancient Rome to distinguish between Italian and Greek ingredients, to say nothing of Etruscan and Phœnician influences. We know the difficulty of finding out in the religion of the Greeks what is purely home-grown, and what is taken over from Egypt, Phœnicia, it may be, from Scythia; or at all events, slightly coloured by those foreign rays of thought. Even in the religion of the Hebrews, Babylonian, Phœnician, and at a later time Persian influences have been discovered, and the more we advance towards modern times, the more extensive becomes the mixture of thought, and the more difficult the task of assigning to each nation the share which it contributed to the common intellectual currency of the world. In India alone, and more particularly in Vedic India, we see a plant entirely grown on native soil, and entirely nurtured by native air. For this reason, because the religion of the Veda was so completely guarded from all strange infections, it is full of lessons which the student of religion could learn nowhere else.

Now what have the critics of the Veda to say against this? They say that the Vedic poems show clear traces of *Babylonian* influences.

I must enter into some details, because, small as they seem, you can see that they involve very wide consequences.

There is one verse in the Rig-veda, VIII. 78, 2[1], which has been translated as follows: 'O Indra, bring to us a brilliant jewel, a cow, a horse, an ornament, together with a golden Manâ[2].'

Now what is a golden Manâ? The word does not occur again by itself, either in the Veda or anywhere else, and it has been identified by Vedic scholars with the Latin *mina*, the Greek *μνᾶ*, the Phœnician *manah* (מָנֶה)[3], the well-known weight which we actually possess now among the treasures brought from Babylon and Nineveh to the British Museum[4].

---

[1] Â na*h* bhara vyá*ñg*anam gấm ásvam abhyá*ñg*anam Sá*k*â manấ hira*n*yáyâ.

[2] Grassman translates, 'Zugleich mit goldenem Geräth;' Ludwig, 'Zusammt mit goldenem Zierrath;' Zimmer, 'Und eine Manâ gold.' The Petersburg Dictionary explains manâ by 'ein bestimmtes Geräth oder Gewicht' (Gold).

[3] According to Dr. Haupt, Die Sumerisch-akkadische Sprache, p. 272, mana is an Accadian word.

[4] According to the weights of the lions and ducks preserved in the British Museum, an Assryian mina was=7,747 grains. The same difference is still preserved to the present day, as the *man* of

If this were so, it would be irrefragable evidence of at all events a commercial intercourse between Babylon and India at a very early time, though it would in no way prove a real influence of Semitic on Indian thought. But is it so? If we translate sa*k*â manâ hira*n*yayâ by 'with a mina of gold,' we must take manâ hira*n*yayâ as instrumental cases. But sa*k*â never governs an instrumental case. This translation therefore is impossible, and although the passage is difficult, because manâ does not occur again in the Rig-veda, I should think we might take manâ hira*n*yayâ for a dual, and translate, 'Give us also two golden armlets.' To suppose that the Vedic poets should have borrowed this one word and this one measure from the Babylonians, would be against all the rules of historical criticism. The word manâ never occurs again in the whole of Sanskrit literature, no other Babylonian weight occurs again in the whole of Sanskrit literature, and it is not likely that a poet who asks for a cow and a horse, would ask in the same breath for a foreign weight of gold, that is, for about sixty sovereigns.

But this is not the only loan that India has been supposed to have negotiated in Babylon. The twenty-seven Nakshatras, or the twenty-seven constellations, which were chosen in India as a kind of lunar Zodiac, were supposed to have come from Babylon. Now the Babylonian Zodiac was solar, and, in spite of repeated researches, no trace of a lunar Zodiac has been found, where so many things have been found, in

Shiraz and Bagdâd is just double that of Tabraz and Bushir, the average of the former being 14.0 and that of the latter only 6.985. See Cunningham, Journal of the Asiatic Society, Calcutta, 1881, p. 163.

the cuneiform inscriptions. But supposing even that a lunar Zodiac had been discovered in Babylon, no one acquainted with Vedic literature and with the ancient Vedic ceremonial would easily allow himself to be persuaded that the Hindus had borrowed that simple division of the sky from the Babylonians. It is well known that most of the Vedic sacrifices depend on the moon, far more than on the sun[1]. As the Psalmist says, 'He appointed the moon for seasons; the sun knoweth his going down,' we read in the Rig-veda X. 85, 18, in a verse addressed to sun and moon, 'They walk by their own power, one after the other (or from east to west), as playing children they go round the sacrifice. The one looks upon all the worlds, the other is born again and again, determining the seasons.

'He becomes new and new, when he is born; as the herald of the days, he goes before the dawns. By his approach he determines their share for the gods, the moon increases a long life.'

The moon, then, determines the seasons, the *ri*tus, the moon fixes the share, that is, the sacrificial oblation for all the gods. The seasons and the sacrifices were in fact so intimately connected together in the thoughts of the ancient Hindus, that one of the commonest names for priest was *ri*tv-i*g*, literally, the season-sacrificer.

Besides the rites which have to be performed every day, such as the five Mahâya*gñ*as, and the Agnihotra in the morning and the evening, the important sacrifices in Vedic times were the Full and New-moon sacrifices (darsapûr*n*amâsa); the Season-sacrifices (*k*âturmâsya), each season consisting of four months[2];

[1] Preface to the fourth volume of my edition of the Rig-veda, p. li.

[2] Vais*v*adevam on the full-moon of Phalguna, Varu*n*apraghâsâ*h*

and the Half-yearly sacrifices, at the two solstices. There are other sacrifices (Âgrayana, &c.) to be performed in autumn and summer, others in winter and spring, whenever rice and barley are ripening [1].

The regulation of the seasons, as one of the fundamental conditions of an incipient society, seems in fact to have been so intimately connected with the worship of the gods, as the guardians of the seasons and the protectors of law and order, that it is sometimes difficult to say whether in their stated sacrifices the maintenance of the calendar or the maintenance of the worship of the gods was more prominent in the minds of the old Vedic priests.

The twenty-seven Nakshatras then were clearly suggested by the moon's passage [2]. Nothing was more natural for the sake of counting days, months, or seasons than to observe the twenty-seven places which the moon occupied in her passage from any point of the sky back to the same point. It was far easier than to determine the sun's position either from day to day, or from month to month; for the stars, being hardly visible at the actual rising and setting of the sun, the idea of the sun's conjunction with certain stars could not suggest itself to a listless observer. The moon, on the contrary, progressing from night to night, and coming successively in contact with certain stars, was like the finger of a clock, moving round a circle, and coming in contact with one figure after another on the dial-plate of the sky. Nor would the portion of about one-third of a

---

on the full-moon of Ashâdha, Sâkamedhâh on the full-moon of Krittikâ; see Boehtlingk, Dictionary, s. v.

[1] See Vishnu-smriti, ed. Jolly, LIX. 4; Âryabhata, Introduction.

[2] See Preface to vol. iv of Rig-veda, p. li (1862).

lunation in addition to the twenty-seven stars from new moon to new moon, create much confusion in the minds of the rough-and-ready reckoners of those early times. All they were concerned with were the twenty-seven celestial stations which, after being once traced out by the moon, were fixed, like so many mile-stones, for determining the course of all the celestial travellers that could be of any interest for signs and for seasons, and for days and for years. A circle divided into twenty-seven sections, or any twenty-seven poles planted in a circle at equal distances round a house, would answer the purpose of a primitive Vedic observatory. All that was wanted to be known was between which pair of poles the moon, or afterwards the sun also, was visible at their rising or setting, the observer occupying the same central position on every day.

Our notions of astronomy cannot in fact be too crude and too imperfect if we wish to understand the first beginnings in the reckoning of days and seasons and years. We cannot expect in those days more than what any shepherd would know at present of the sun and moon, the stars and seasons. Nor can we expect any observations of heavenly phenomena unless they had some bearing on the practical wants of primitive society.

If then we can watch in India the natural, nay inevitable, growth of the division of the heaven into twenty-seven equal divisions, each division marked by stars, which may have been observed and named long before they were used for this new purpose—if, on the other hand, we could hardly understand the growth and development of the Indian ceremonial except as determined by a knowledge of the lunar asterisms, the lunar months, and the lunar seasons, surely it would be a senseless hypothesis to imagine that the Vedic shepherds or priests went to Babylonia in search of a knowledge which every shepherd might have acquired on the banks of the Indus, and that, after their return from that country only, where a language was spoken which no Hindu could understand, they set to work to compose their sacred hymns, and arrange their simple ceremonial. We must never forget that what is natural in one place is natural in other places also, and we may sum up without fear of serious contradiction, that no case has been made out in favour of a foreign origin of the elementary astronomical notions of the Hindus as found or presupposed in the Vedic hymns[1].

The Arabs, as is well known, have twenty-eight lunar stations, the *Manzil*, and I can see no reason why Mohammed and his Bedouins in the desert should not have made the same observation as the Vedic poets in India, though I must admit at the same time that Colebrooke has brought forward very cogent arguments to prove that, in their scientific employment at least, the Arabic Manzil were really borrowed from an Indian source[2].

The Chinese, too, have their famous lunar stations, *the Sieu*, originally twenty-four in number, and afterwards raised to twenty-eight[3]. But here again there is no necessity whatever for admitting, with Biot, Lassen and others, that the Hindus went to China to gain their simplest elementary notions of lunar chrononomy. First of all, the Chinese began with

---

[1] See Zimmer, Altindisches Leben, pp. 352–357.

[2] L. c. p. lxx.

[3] L. c. p. xlvii.

twenty-four, and raised them to twenty-eight; the Hindus began with twenty-seven, and raised them to twenty-eight. Secondly, out of these twenty-eight asterisms, there are seventeen only which can really be identified with the Hindu stars (târâs). Now if a scientific system is borrowed, it is borrowed complete. But, in our case, I see really no possible channel through which Chinese astronomical knowledge could have been conducted to India so early as 1000 before our era. In Chinese literature India is never mentioned before the middle of the second century before Christ; and if the *K*înas in the later Sanskrit literature are meant for Chinese, which is doubtful, it is important to observe that that name never occurs in Vedic literature[1].

---

[1] In the Mahâbhârata and elsewhere the *K*înas are mentioned among the Dasyus or non-Aryan races in the North and in the East of India. King Bhagadatta is said to have had an army of *K*înas and Kirâtas*, and the Pâ*nd*avas are said to reach the town of the King of the Kulindas, after having passed through the countries of *K*înas, Tukhâras, and Daradas. All this is as vague as ethnological indications generally are in the late epic poetry of India. The only possibly real element is that Kirâta and *K*îna soldiers are called kâ*ñk*ana, gold or yellow coloured†, and compared to a forest of Kar*n*ikâras, which were trees with yellow flowers‡. In Mahâbh. VI. 9, v. 373, vol. ii. p. 344, the *K*înas occur in company with Kambo*g*as and Yavanas, which again conveys nothing definite.

Chinese scholars tell us that the name of China is of modern origin, and only dates from the Thsin dynasty or from the famous Emperor Shi-hoang-ti, 247 B.C. But the name itself, though in a more restricted sense, occurs in earlier documents, and may, as Lassen thinks §, have become known to the Western neighbours of

---

* Lassen, i. p. 1029; Mahâbh. III. 117, v. 12350; vol. i. p. 619.
† Mahâbh. V. 18, v. 584; vol. ii. p. 106.
‡ See Vâ*k*aspatya s. v.; Ka*sk*it Kar*n*ikâragaura*h*.
§ Lassen, vol. i. p. 1029, n. 2.

When therefore the impossibility of so early a communication between China and India had at last been recognised, a new theory was formed, namely 'that the knowledge of Chinese astronomy was not imported straight from China to India, but was carried, together with the Chinese system of division of the heavens into twenty-eight mansions, into Western Asia, at a period not much later than 1100 B.C., and was then adopted by some Western people, either Semitic or Iranian. In their hands it was supposed to have received a new form, such as adapted it to a ruder and less scientific method of observation, the limiting stars of the mansions being converted into zodiacal groups or constellations, and in some instances altered in position, so as to be brought nearer to the general planetary path of the ecliptic. In this changed form, having become a means of roughly determining and describing the places and movements of the planets, it was believed to have passed into the keeping of the Hindus, very probably along with the first knowledge of the planets themselves, and entered upon an independent career of history in India. It still maintained itself in its old seat, leaving its traces later in the Bundahash; and made its way so far westward as finally to become known and adopted by the Arabs.' With due respect for the astronomical knowledge of those who hold this view, all I can say is that this is a novel, and nothing but a novel, without any facts to support it, and that the few facts which are known to us do not enable a

China. It is certainly strange that the *Sinim* too, mentioned in Isaiah xlix. 12, have been taken by the old commentators for people of China, visiting Babylon as merchants and travellers.

careful reasoner to go beyond the conclusions stated many years ago by Colebrooke, that the 'Hindus had undoubtedly made some progress at an early period in the astronomy cultivated by them for the regulation of time. Their calendar, both civil and religious, was governed chiefly, not exclusively, by the moon and the sun: and the motions of these luminaries were carefully observed by them, and with such success, that their determination of the moon's synodical revolution, which was what they were principally concerned with, is a much more correct one than the Greeks ever achieved. They had a division of the ecliptic into twenty-seven and twenty-eight parts, suggested evidently by the moon's period in days, and seemingly their own; it was certainly borrowed by the Arabians.'

There is one more argument which has been adduced in support of a Babylonian, or, at all events, a Semitic influence to be discovered in Vedic literature which we must shortly examine. It refers to the story of the *Deluge*.

That story, as you know, has been traced in the traditions of many races, which could not well have borrowed it from one another; and it was rather a surprise that no allusion even to a local deluge should occur in any of the Vedic hymns, particularly as very elaborate accounts of different kinds of deluges are found in the later Epic poems, and in the still later Purâ*n*as, and form in fact a very familiar subject in the religious traditions of the people of India.

Three of the *Avatâras* or incarnations of Vish*n*u are connected with a deluge, that of the *Fish*, that of the *Tortoise*, and that of the *Boar*, Vish*n*u in each case rescuing mankind from destruction by water, by assuming the form of a fish, or a tortoise, or a boar.

This being so, it seemed a very natural conclusion to make that, as there was no mention of a deluge in the most ancient literature of India, that legend had penetrated into India from without at a later time.

When, however, the Vedic literature became more generally known, stories of a deluge were discovered, if not in the hymns, at least in the prose writings, belonging to the second period, commonly called the Brâhmana period. Not only the story of Manu and the *Fish*, but the stories of the *Tortoise* and of the *Boar* also, were met with there in a more or less complete form, and with this discovery the idea of a foreign importation lost much of its plausibility. I shall read you at least one of these accounts of a Deluge which is found in the Satapatha Brâhmana, and you can then judge for yourselves whether the similarities between it and the account in Genesis are really such as to require, nay as to admit, the hypothesis that the Hindus borrowed their account of the Deluge from their nearest Semitic neighbours.

We read in the Satapatha Brâhmana I. 8, 1:

'In the morning they brought water to Manu for washing, as they bring it even now for washing our hands.

'While he was thus washing, a fish came into his hands.

'2. The fish spoke this word to Manu: "Keep me, and I shall save thee."

'Manu said: "From what wilt thou save me?"

'The fish said: "A flood will carry away all these creatures, and I shall save thee from it."

'Manu said: "How canst thou be kept?"

'3. The fish said: "So long as we are small, there is much destruction for us, for fish swallows fish. Keep me therefore first in a jar. When I outgrow that, dig a hole and keep me in it. When I outgrow that, take me to the sea, and I shall then be beyond the reach of destruction."

'4. He became soon a large fish (*gh*asha), for such a fish grows largest. The fish said: "In such and such a year the flood will come. Therefore when thou hast built a ship, thou shalt meditate on me. And when the flood has risen, thou shalt enter into the ship, and I will save thee from the flood."

'5. Having thus kept the fish, Manu took him to the sea. Then in the same year which the fish had pointed out, Manu, having built the ship, meditated on the fish. And when the flood had risen, Manu entered into the ship. Then the fish swam towards him, and Manu fastened the rope of the ship to the fish's horn, and he thus hastened towards[1] the Northern Mountain.

'6. The fish said: "I have saved thee; bind the ship to a tree. May the water not cut thee off, while thou art on the mountain. As the water subsides, do thou gradually slide down with it." Manu then slid down gradually with the water, and therefore this is called "the Slope of Manu" on the Northern Mountain. Now the flood had carried away all these creatures, and thus Manu was left there alone.

'7. Then Manu went about singing praises and

[1] I prefer now the reading of the Kâ*n*va-sâkhâ, abhidudrâva, instead of atidudrâva or adhidudrâva of the other MSS. See Weber, Ind. Streifen, i. p. 11.

toiling, wishing for offspring. And he sacrificed there also with a Pâka-sacrifice. He poured clarified butter, thickened milk, whey, and curds in the water as a libation. In one year a woman arose from it. She came forth as if dripping, and clarified butter gathered on her step. Mitra and Varu*n*a came to meet her.

'8. They said to her: "Who art thou?" She said: "The daughter of Manu." They rejoined: "Say that thou art ours." "No," she said, "he who has begotten me, his I am."

'Then they wished her to be their sister, and she half agreed and half did not agree, but went away, and came to Manu.

'9. Manu said to her: "Who art thou?" She said: "I am thy daughter." "How, lady, art thou my daughter?" he asked.

'She replied: "The libations which thou hast poured into the water, clarified butter, thickened milk, whey and curds, by them thou hast begotten me. I am a benediction—perform (me) this benediction at the sacrifices. If thou perform (me) it at the sacrifice, thou wilt be rich in offspring and cattle. And whatever blessing thou wilt ask by me, will always accrue to thee." He therefore performed that benediction in the middle of the sacrifice, for the middle of the sacrifice is that which comes between the introductory and the final offerings.

'10. Then Manu went about with her, singing praises and toiling, wishing for offspring. And with her he begat that offspring which is called the offspring of Manu; and whatever blessing he asked with her, always accrued to him. She is indeed I*d*â, and whosoever, knowing this, goes about (sacrifices) with *Idâ*, begets the same offspring which Manu begat, and whatever blessing he asks with her, always accrues to him.'

This, no doubt, is the account of a deluge, and Manu acts in some respects the same part which is assigned to Noah in the Old Testament. But if there are similarities, think of the dissimilarities, and how they are to be explained. It is quite clear that, if this story was borrowed from a Semitic source, it was not borrowed from the Old Testament, for in that case it would really seem impossible to account for the differences between the two stories. That it may have been borrowed from some unknown Semitic source cannot, of course, be disproved, because no tangible proof has ever been produced that would admit of being disproved. But if it were, it would be the only Semitic loan in ancient Sanskrit literature—and that alone ought to make us pause!

The story of the boar and the tortoise too, can be traced back to the Vedic literature. For we read in the Taittirîya Sa*m*hitâ[1]:

'At first this was water, fluid. Pra*g*âpati, the lord of creatures, having become wind, moved on it. He saw this earth, and becoming a boar, he took it up. Becoming Vi*s*vakarman, the maker of all things, he cleaned it. It spread and became the wide-spread Earth, and this is why the Earth is called P*ri*thivî, the wide-spread[2].'

And we find in the *S*atapatha Brâhma*n*a[3] the following slight allusion at least to the tortoise myth:

---

[1] VII. 1, 5, 1 seq.; Muir, i. p. 52; Colebrooke, Essays, i. 75.
[2] See Note H.
[3] VII. 5, 1, 5; Muir, Original Sanskrit Texts, i. p. 54.

'Pra*g*âpati, assuming the form of a tortoise (Kûrma), brought forth all creatures. In so far as he brought them forth, he made them (akarot), and because he made them he was (called) tortoise (Kûrma). A tortoise is (called) Kâsyapa, and therefore all creatures are called Kâsyapa, tortoise-like. He who was this tortoise (Kûrma) was really Âditya, (the sun).'

One other allusion to something like a deluge[1], important chiefly on account of the name of Manu occurring in it, has been pointed out in the Kâ*th*aka (XI. 2), where this short sentence occurs: 'The waters cleaned this, Manu alone remained.'

All this shows that ideas of a deluge, that is, of a submersion of the earth by water and of its rescue through divine aid, were not altogether unknown in the early traditions of India, while in later times they were embodied in several of the Avâtaras of Vish*n*u.

When we examine the numerous accounts of a deluge among different nations in almost every part of the world, we can easily perceive that they do not refer to one single historical event, but to a natural phenomenon repeated every year, namely the deluge or flood of the rainy season or the winter[2].

This is nowhere clearer than in Babylon. Sir Henry Rawlinson was the first to point out that the twelve cantos of the poem of Izdubar or Nimrod refer to the twelve months of the year and the twelve representative signs of the Zodiac. Dr. Haupt afterwards pointed out that Êabânî, the wise bull-man in the second canto, corresponds to the second month, Ijjar, April–May, represented in the Zodiac by the bull; that the union between Êabânî

---

[1] Weber, Indische Streifen, i. p. 11.

[2] See Lecture V, p. 152.

and Nimrod in the third canto corresponds to the third month, Sivan, May–June, represented in the Zodiac by the twins; that the sickness of Nimrod in the seventh canto corresponds to the seventh month, Tishri, September–October, when the sun begins to wane; and that the flood in the eleventh canto corresponds to the eleventh month, Shabaṭu, dedicated to the storm-god Rimmôn, represented in the Zodiac by the waterman[1].

If that is so, we have surely a right to claim the same natural origin for the story of the Deluge in India which we are bound to admit in other countries. And even if it could be proved that in the form in which these legends have reached us in India they show traces of foreign influences[2], the fact would still remain that such influences have been perceived in comparatively modern treatises only, and not in the ancient hymns of the Rig-veda.

Other conjectures have been made with even less foundation than that which would place the ancient poets of India under the influence of Babylon. China has been appealed to, nay even Persia, Parthia, and Bactria, countries beyond the reach of India at that early time of which we are here speaking, and probably not even then consolidated into independent nations or kingdoms. I only wonder that traces of the lost Jewish tribes have not been discovered in the Vedas, considering that Afghanistan has so often been pointed out as one of their favourite retreats.

After having thus carefully examined all the traces of supposed foreign influences that have been brought

---

[1] See Haupt, Der Keilinschriftliche Sintfluthbericht, 1881, p. 10.

[2] See M. M., Genesis and Avesta (German translation), i. p. 148.

forward by various scholars, I think I may say that there really is no trace whatever of any foreign influence in the language, the religion, or the ceremonial of the ancient Vedic literature of India. As it stands before us now, so it has grown up, protected by the mountain ramparts in the North, the Indus and the Desert in the West, the Indus or what was called the sea in the South, and the Ganges in the East. It presents us with a home-grown poetry, and a home-grown religion; and history has preserved to us at least this one relic, in order to teach us what the human mind can achieve if left to itself, surrounded by a scenery and by conditions of life that might have made man's life on earth a paradise, if man did not possess the strange art of turning even a paradise into a place of misery.

THE LESSONS OF THE VEDA.

LECTURE V.

ALTHOUGH there is hardly any department of learning which has not received new light and new life from the ancient literature of India, yet nowhere is the light that comes to us from India so important, so novel, and so rich as in the study of religion and mythology. It is to this subject therefore that I mean to devote the remaining lectures of this course. I do so, partly because I feel myself most at home in that ancient world of Vedic literature in which the germs of Aryan religion have to be studied, partly because I believe that for a proper understanding of the deepest convictions, or, if you like, the strongest prejudices of the modern Hindus, nothing is so useful as a knowledge of the Veda. It is perfectly true that nothing would give a falser impression of the actual Brahmanical religion than the ancient Vedic literature, supposing we were to imagine that three thousand years could have passed over India without producing any change. Such a mistake would be nearly as absurd as to deny any difference between the Vedic Sanskrit and the spoken Bengali. But no one will gain a scholarlike knowledge or a true insight into the secret springs of Bengali who is ignorant of the grammar of Sanskrit; and no one will ever understand the present religious, philosophical, legal, and social opinions of the Hindus who is unable to trace them back to their true sources in the Veda.

I still remember how, many years ago, when I began to publish for the first time the text and the commentary of the Rig-veda, it was argued by a certain, perhaps not quite disinterested party, that the Veda was perfectly useless, that no man in India, however learned, could read it, and that it was of no use either for missionaries or for any one else who wished to study and to influence the native mind. It was said that we ought to study the later Sanskrit, the Laws of Manu, the epic poems, and, more particularly, the Purâ*n*as. The Veda might do very well for German students, but not for Englishmen.

There was no excuse for such ignorant assertions even thirty years ago, for in these very books, in the Laws of Manu, in the Mahâbhârata, and in the Purâ*n*as, the Veda is everywhere proclaimed as the highest authority in all matters of religion[1]. 'A Brahman,' says Manu, 'unlearned in holy writ, is extinguished in an instant like dry grass on fire.' 'A twice-born man (that is a Brâhma*n*a, a Kshatriya, and a Vaisya) not having studied the Veda, soon falls, even when living, to the condition of a *S*ûdra, and his descendants after him.'

How far this license of ignorant assertion may be carried is shown by the same authorities who denied the importance of the Veda for a historical study of Indian thought, boldly charging those wily priests, the Brahmans, with having withheld their sacred literature from any but their own caste. Now so far from withholding it, the Brahmans have always been

---

[1] Wilson, Lectures, p. 9.

striving, and often striving in vain, to make the study of their sacred literature obligatory on all castes, except the *S*ûdras, and the passages just quoted from Manu show what penalties were threatened, if children of the second and third castes, the Kshatriyas and Vaisyas, were not instructed in the sacred literature of the Brahmans.

At present the Brahmans themselves have spoken, and the reception they have accorded to my edition of the Rig-veda[1] and its native commentary, the zeal with which they have themselves taken up the study of Vedic literature, and the earnestness with which different sects are still discussing the proper use that should be made of their ancient religious writings, show abundantly that a Sanskrit scholar ignorant of, or, I should rather say, determined to ignore the Veda, would be not much better than a Hebrew scholar ignorant of the Old Testament.

I shall now proceed to give you some characteristic specimens of the religion and poetry of the Rig-veda. They can only be few, and as there is nothing like system or unity of plan in that collec-

---

[1] As it has been doubted, and even denied, that the publication of the Rig-veda and its native commentary has had some important bearing on the resuscitation of the religious life of India, I feel bound to give at least one from the many testimonials which I have received from India. It comes from the Âdi Brahma Samâj, founded by Ram Mohun Roy, and now represented by its three branches, the Âdi Brahma Samâj, the Brahma Samâj of India, and the Sadhârano Brahma Samâj. 'The Committee of the Âdi Brahma Samâj beg to offer you their hearty congratulations on the completion of the gigantic task which has occupied you for the last quarter of a century. By publishing the Rig-veda at a time when Vedic learning has by some sad fatality become almost extinct in the land of its birth, you have conferred a boon upon us Hindus, for which we cannot but be eternally grateful.'

tion of 1017 hymns, which we call the Sa*m*hitâ of the Rig-veda, I cannot promise that they will give you a complete panoramic view of that intellectual world in which our Vedic ancestors passed their life on earth.

I could not even answer the question, if you were to ask it, whether the religion of the Veda was *polytheistic*, or *monotheistic*. Monotheistic, in the usual sense of that word, it is decidedly not, though there are hymns that assert the unity of the Divine as fearlessly as any passage of the Old Testament, or the New Testament, or the Koran. Thus one poet says (Rig-veda I. 164, 46): 'That which is *one*, sages name it in various ways—they call it Agni, Yama, Mâtarisvan.'

Another poet says: 'The wise poets represent by their words Him who is one with beautiful wings, in many ways[1].'

And again we hear of a being called Hira*n*yagarbha, the golden germ (whatever the original of that name may have been), of whom the poet says[2]: 'In the beginning there arose Hira*n*yagarbha; he was the one born lord of all this. He established the earth and this sky. Who is the god to whom we shall offer our sacrifice?' That Hira*n*yagarbha, the poet says, 'is alone God above all gods' (ya*h* deveshu adhi deva*h* eka*h* âsît)—an assertion of the unity of the Divine which could hardly be exceeded in strength by any passage from the Old Testament.

But by the side of such passages, which are few in number, there are thousands in which ever so many divine beings are praised and prayed to. Even their number is sometimes given as 'thrice eleven[3]'

---

[1] Rig-veda X. 114, 5. [2] Rig-veda X. 121. [3] Muir, iv. 9.

or thirty-three, and one poet assigns eleven gods to the sky, eleven to the earth, and eleven to the waters[1], the waters here intended being those of the atmosphere and the clouds. These thirty-three gods have even wives apportioned to them[2], though few of these only have as yet attained to the honour of a name[3].

These thirty-three gods, however, by no means include all the Vedic gods, for such important deities as Agni, the fire, Soma, the rain, the Maruts or Storm-gods, the Asvins, the gods of Morning and Evening, the Waters, the Dawn, the Sun are mentioned separately; and there are not wanting passages in which the poet is carried away into exaggerations, till he proclaims the number of his gods to be, not only thirty-three, but three thousand three hundred and thirty-nine[4].

If therefore there must be a name for the religion of the Rig-veda, polytheism would seem at first sight the most appropriate. Polytheism, however, has assumed with us a meaning which renders it totally inapplicable to the Vedic religion.

Our ideas of polytheism being chiefly derived from Greece and Rome, we understand by it a certain more or less organised system of gods, different in power and rank, and all subordinate to a supreme God, a

---

[1] Rig-veda I. 139, 11.

[2] Rig-veda III. 6, 9.

[3] The following names of Devapatnîs or wives of the gods are given in the Vaitâna Sûtra XV. 3 (ed. Garbe): P*ri*thivî, the wife of Agni, Vâ*k* of Vâta, Senâ of Indra, Dhenâ of B*ri*haspati, Pathyâ of Pûshan, Gâyatrî of Vasu, Trish*t*ubh of Rudra, *G*agati of Âditya, Anush*t*ubh of Mitra, Virâ*g* of Varu*n*a, Pa*n*kti of Vish*n*u, Dîkshâ of Soma.

[4] Rig-veda III. 9, 9.

Zeus or Jupiter. The Vedic polytheism differs from the Greek and Roman polytheism, and, I may add, likewise from the polytheism of the Ural-Altaic, the Polynesian, the American, and most of the African races, in the same manner as a confederacy of village communities differs from a monarchy. There are traces of an earlier stage of village-community life to be discovered in the later republican and monarchical constitutions, and in the same manner nothing can be clearer, particularly in Greece, than that the monarchy of Zeus was preceded by what may be called the septarchy of several of the great gods of Greece. The same remark applies to the mythology of the Teutonic nations also[1]. In the Veda, however, the gods worshipped as supreme by each sept stand still side by side. No one is first always, no one is last always. Even gods of a decidedly inferior and limited character assume occasionally in the eyes of a devoted poet a supreme place above all other gods[2]. It was necessary, therefore, for the purpose of accurate reasoning to have a name, different from *polytheism*, to signify this worship of single gods, each occupying for a time a supreme position, and I pro-

---

[1] Grimm showed that Thôrr is sometimes the supreme god, while at other times he is the son of Ôdinn. This, as Professor Zimmer truly remarks, need not be regarded as the result of a revolution, or even of gradual decay, as in the case of Dyaus and Týr, but simply as inherent in the character of a nascent polytheism. See Zeitschrift für D. A., vol. xii. p. 174.

[2] 'Among not yet civilised races prayers are addressed to a god with a special object, and to that god who is supposed to be most powerful in a special domain. He becomes for the moment the highest god to whom all others must give place. He may be invoked as the highest and the only god, without any slight being intended for the other gods.' Zimmer, l. c. p. 175.

posed for it the name of *Kathenotheism*, that is a worship of one god after another, or of *Henotheism*, the worship of single gods. This shorter name of *Henotheism* has found more general acceptance, as conveying more definitely the opposition between *Monotheism*, the worship of one only God, and *Henotheism*, the worship of single gods; and, if but properly defined, it will answer its purpose very well. However, in researches of this kind we cannot be too much on our guard against technical terms. They are inevitable, I know; but they are almost always misleading. There is, for instance, a hymn addressed to the *Indus* and the rivers that fall into it, of which I hope to read you a translation, because it determines very accurately the geographical scene on which the poets of the Veda passed their life. Now native scholars call these rivers devatâs or deities, and European translators too speak of them as gods and goddesses. But in the language used by the poet with regard to the Indus and the other rivers, there is nothing to justify us in saying that he considered these rivers as *gods* and *goddesses*, unless we mean by *gods* and *goddesses* something very different from what the Greeks called River-gods and River-goddesses, Nymphs, Najades, or even Muses.

And what applies to these rivers, applies more or less to all the objects of Vedic worship. They all are still oscillating between what is seen by the senses, what is created by fancy, and what is postulated by the understanding; they are things, persons, causes, according to the varying disposition of the poets: and if we call them gods or goddesses, we must remember the remark of an ancient native theologian, who reminds us that by devatâ or deity he means no more than the object celebrated in a hymn, while *Ri*shi or seer means no more than the subject or the author of a hymn.

It is difficult to treat of the so-called gods celebrated in the Veda according to any system, for the simple reason that the concepts of these gods and the hymns addressed to them sprang up spontaneously and without any pre-established plan. It is best perhaps for our purpose to follow an ancient Brahmanical writer, who is supposed to have lived about 400 B.C. He tells us of students of the Veda, before his time, who admitted three deities only, viz. Agni or fire, whose place is on the earth; Vâyu or Indra, the wind and the god of the thunderstorm, whose place is in the air; and Sûrya, the sun, whose place is in the sky. These deities, they maintained, received severally many appellations, in consequence of their greatness, or of the diversity of their functions, just as a priest, according to the functions which he performs at various sacrifices, receives various names.

This is *one* view of the Vedic gods, and, though too narrow, it cannot be denied that there is some truth in it. A very useful division of the Vedic gods might be made, and has been made by Yâska, into *terrestrial*, *aerial*, and *celestial*, and if the old Hindu theologians meant no more than that all the manifestations of divine power in nature might be traced back to three centres of force, one in the sky, one in the air, and one on the earth, he deserves great credit for his sagacity.

But he himself perceived evidently that this generalisation was not quite applicable to all the gods, and he goes on to say, 'Or, it may be, these gods are all distinct beings, for the praises addressed to them are distinct, and their appellations also.' This is quite right. It is the very object of most of these divine names to impart distinct individuality to the manifestations of the powers of nature; and though the philosopher or the inspired poet might perceive that these numerous names were but names, while that which was named was *one* and *one* only, this was certainly not the idea of most of the Vedic *Ri*shis themselves, still less of the people who listened to their songs at fairs and festivals. It is the peculiar character of that phase of religious thought which we have to study in the Veda, that in it the Divine is conceived and represented as manifold, and that many functions are shared in common by various gods, no attempt having yet been made at organising the whole body of the gods, sharply separating one from the other, and subordinating all of them to several or, in the end, to one supreme head.

Availing ourselves of the division of the Vedic gods into terrestrial, aerial, and celestial, as proposed by some of the earliest Indian theologians, we should have to begin with the gods connected with the earth.

Before we examine them, however, we have first to consider one of the earliest objects of worship and adoration, namely *Earth and Heaven*, or *Heaven and Earth*, conceived as a divine couple. Not only in India, but among many other nations, both savage, half-savage, or civilised, we meet with Heaven and Earth as one of the earliest objects, pondered on, transfigured, and animated by the early poets, and more or less clearly conceived by early philosophers. It is surprising that it should be so, for the conception of the Earth as an independent being, and of Heaven as an independent being, and then of both together as a divine couple embracing the whole universe, requires a considerable effort of abstraction, far more than the concepts of other divine powers, such as the Fire, the Rain, the Lightning, or the Sun.

Still so it is, and as it may help us to understand the ideas about Heaven and Earth, as we find them in the Veda, and show us at the same time the strong contrast between the mythology of the Aryans and that of real savages (a contrast of great importance, though I admit very difficult to explain), I shall read you first some extracts from a book, published by a friend of mine, the Rev. William Wyatt Gill, for many years an active and most successful missionary in Mangaia, one of those Polynesian islands that form a girdle round one quarter of our globe[1], and all share in the same language, the same religion, the same mythology, and the same customs. The book is called 'Myths and Songs from the South Pacific[2],' and it is full of interest to the student of mythology and religion.

The story, as told him by the natives of Mangaia, runs as follows[3]:

'The sky is built of solid blue stone. At one time it almost touched the earth; resting upon the stout broad leaves of the teve (which attains the height of

---

[1] 'Es handelt sich hier nicht um amerikanische oder afrikanische Zersplitterung, sondern eine überraschende Gleichartigkeit dehnt sich durch die Weite und Breite des Stillen Oceans, und wenn wir Oceanien in der vollen Auffassung nehmen mit Einschluss Mikro- und Mela-nesiens (bis Malaya), selbst weiter. Es lässt sich sagen, dass ein einheitlicher Gedankenbau, in etwa 120 Längen und 70 Breitegraden, ein Viertel unsers Erdglobus überwölbt.' Bastian, Die Heilige Sage der Polynesier, p. 57.

[2] Henry S. King & Co., London, 1876.

[3] P. 58.

about six feet) and the delicate indigenous arrow-root (whose slender stem rarely exceeds three feet)..... In this narrow space between earth and sky the inhabitants of this world were pent up. Ru, whose usual residence was in Avaiki, or the shades, had come up for a time to this world of ours. Pitying the wretched confined residence of the inhabitants, he employed himself in endeavouring to raise the sky a little. For this purpose he cut a number of strong stakes of different kinds of trees, and firmly planted them in the ground at Rangimotia, the centre of the island, and with him the centre of the world. This was a considerable improvement, as mortals were thereby enabled to stand erect and to walk about without inconvenience. Hence Ru was named "The sky-supporter." Wherefore Teka sings (1794):

> "Force up the sky, O Ru,
> And let the space be clear!"

'One day when the old man was surveying his work, his graceless son Mâui contemptuously asked him what he was doing there. Ru replied, "Who told youngsters to talk? Take care of yourself, or I will hurl you out of existence."

'"Do it, then," shouted Mâui.

'Ru was as good as his word, and forthwith seized Mâui, who was small of stature, and threw him to a great height. In falling Mâui assumed the form of a bird, and lightly touched the ground, perfectly unharmed. Mâui, now thirsting for revenge, in a moment resumed his natural form, but exaggerated to gigantic proportions, and ran to his father, saying:

> "Ru, who supportest the many heavens,
> The third, even to the highest, ascend!"

Inserting his head between the old man's legs, he

exerted all his prodigious strength, and hurled poor Ru, sky and all, to a tremendous height,—so high, indeed, that the blue sky could never get back again. Unluckily, however, for the sky-supporting Ru, his head and shoulders got entangled among the stars. He struggled hard, but fruitlessly, to extricate himself. Mâui walked off well pleased with having raised the sky to its present height, but left half his father's body and both his legs ingloriously suspended between heaven and earth. Thus perished Ru. His body rotted away, and his bones came tumbling down from time to time, and were shivered on the earth into countless fragments. These shivered bones of Ru are scattered over every hill and valley of Mangaia, to the very edge of the sea.'

What the natives call 'the bones of Ru' (te ivi o Ru) are pieces of pumice-stone.

Now let us consider, first of all, whether this story, which with slight variations is told all over the Polynesian islands[1], is pure non-sense, or whether there was originally some sense in it. My conviction is that non-sense is everywhere the child of sense, only that unfortunately many children, like that youngster Mâui, consider themselves much wiser than their fathers, and occasionally succeed in hurling them out of existence.

It is a peculiarity of many of the ancient myths that they represent events which happen every day, or every year, as having happened once upon a time[2]. The daily battle between day and night, the yearly battle between winter and spring, are represented

[1] There is a second version of the story even in the small island of Mangaia; see Myths and Songs, p. 71.

[2] See before, p. 138.

almost like historical events, and some of the episodes and touches belonging originally to these constant battles of nature, have certainly been transferred into and mixed up with battles that took place at a certain time, such as, for instance, the siege of Troy. When historical recollections failed, legendary accounts of the ancient battles between Night and Morning, Winter and Spring, were always at hand; and, as in modern times we constantly hear 'good stories,' which we have known from our childhood, told again and again of any man whom they seem to fit, in the same manner, in ancient times, any act of prowess, or daring, or mischief, originally told of the sun, 'the orient Conqueror of gloomy Night,' was readily transferred to and believed of any local hero who might seem to be a second Jupiter, or Mars, or Hercules.

I have little doubt therefore that as the accounts of a deluge, for instance, which we find almost everywhere, are originally recollections of the annual torrents of rain or snow that covered the little worlds within the ken of the ancient village-bards, this tearing asunder of heaven and earth too was originally no more than a description of what might be seen every morning. During a dark night the sky seemed to cover the earth; the two seemed to be one, and could not be distinguished one from the other. Then came the Dawn, which with its bright rays lifted the covering of the dark night to a certain point, till at last Mâui appeared, small in stature, a mere child, that is, the sun of the morning—thrown up suddenly, as it were, when his first rays shot through the sky from beneath the horizon, then falling back to the earth, like a bird, and rising in gigantic form on the morning sky. The dawn now was hurled away, and the sky was seen lifted high above the earth; and Mâui, the sun, marched on well pleased with having raised the sky to its present height.

Why pumice-stone should be called the bones of Ru, we cannot tell, without knowing a great deal more of the language of Mangaia than we do at present. It is most likely an independent saying, and was afterwards united with the story of Ru and Mâui.

Now I must quote at least a few extracts from a Maori legend as written down by Judge Manning[1]:

'This is the Genesis of the New Zealanders:

'The Heavens which are above us, and the Earth which lies beneath us, are the progenitors of men, and the origin of all things.

'Formerly the Heaven lay upon the Earth, and all was darkness. . . .

'And the children of Heaven and Earth sought to discover the difference between light and darkness, between day and night. . . .

'So the sons of Rangi (Heaven) and of Papa (Earth) consulted together, and said: "Let us seek means whereby to destroy Heaven and Earth, or to separate them from each other."

'Then said Tumatauenga (the God of War), "Let us destroy them both."

'Then said Tane-Mahuta (the Forest God), "Not so; let them be separated. Let one of them go upwards and become a stranger to us; let the other remain below and be a parent for us."

'Then four of the gods tried to separate Heaven

[1] Bastian, Heilige Sage der Polynesier, p. 36.

and Earth, but did not succeed, while the fifth, Tane, succeeded.

'After Heaven and Earth had been separated, great storms arose, or, as the poet expresses it, one of their sons, Tawhiri-Matea, the god of the winds, tried to revenge the outrage committed on his parents by his brothers. Then follow dismal dusky days, and dripping chilly skies, and arid scorching blasts. All the gods fight, till at last Tu only remains, the god of war, who had devoured all his brothers, except the Storm. More fights follow, in which the greater part of the earth was overwhelmed by the waters, and but a small portion remained dry. After that, light continued to increase, and as the light increased, so also the people who had been hidden between Heaven and Earth increased. . . . And so generation was added to generation down to the time of Mâui-Potiki, he who brought death into the world.

'Now in these latter days Heaven remains far removed from his wife, the Earth; but the love of the wife rises upward in sighs towards her husband. These are the mists which fly upwards from the mountain-tops; and the tears of Heaven fall downwards on his wife; behold the dew-drops!'

So far the Maori Genesis.

Let us now return to the Veda, and compare these crude and somewhat grotesque legends with the language of the ancient Aryan poets. In the hymns of the Rig-veda the separating and keeping apart of Heaven and Earth is several times alluded to, and here too it is represented as the work of the most valiant gods. In I. 67, 3 it is Agni, fire, who holds the earth and supports the heaven; in X. 89, 4 it is Indra who keeps them apart; in IX. 101, 15 Soma is celebrated for the same deed, and in III. 31, 12 other gods too share the same honour[1].

In the Aitareya Brâhma*n*a we read[2]: 'These two worlds (Heaven and Earth) were once joined together. They went asunder. Then it did not rain, nor did the sun shine. And the five tribes did not agree with one another. The gods then brought the two (Heaven and Earth) together, and when they came together, they performed a wedding of the gods.'

Here we have in a shorter form the same fundamental ideas; first, that formerly Heaven and Earth were together; that afterwards they were separated; that when they were thus separated there was war throughout nature, and neither rain nor sunshine; that, lastly, Heaven and Earth were conciliated, and that then a great wedding took place.

Now I need hardly remind those who are acquainted with Greek and Roman literature, how familiar these and similar conceptions about a marriage between Heaven and Earth were in Greece and Italy. They seem to possess there a more special reference to the annual reconciliation between Heaven and Earth, which takes place in spring, and to their former estrangement during winter. But the first cosmological separation of the two always points to the want of light and the impossibility of distinction during the night, and the gradual lifting up of the blue sky through the rising of the sun[3].

In the Homeric hymns[4] the Earth is addressed as

'Mother of Gods, the wife of the starry Heaven[5];'

---

[1] Bergaigne, La Religion Védique, p. 240.

[2] Ait. Br. IV. 27; Muir, iv. p. 23.

[3] See Muir, iv. p. 24.

[4] Homer, Hymn xxx. 17.

[5] Χαῖρε θεῶν μήτηρ, ἄλοχ' Οὐρανοῦ ἀστερόεντος.

and the Heaven or Æther is often called the father. Their marriage too is described, as, for instance, by Euripides, when he says:

'There is the mighty Earth, Jove's Æther:
He (the Æther) is the creator of men and gods;
The earth receiving the moist drops of rain,
Bears mortals,
Bears food, and the tribes of animals.
Hence she is not unjustly regarded
As the mother of all[1].'

And what is more curious still is that we have evidence that Euripides received this doctrine from his teacher, the philosopher Anaxagoras. For Dionysius of Halicarnassus[2] tells us that Euripides frequented the lectures of Anaxagoras. Now, it was the theory of that philosopher that originally all things were in all things, but that afterwards they became separated. Euripides later in life associated with Sokrates, and became doubtful regarding that theory. He accordingly propounds the ancient doctrine by the mouth of another, namely Melanippe, who says:

'This saying (myth) is not mine, but came from my mother, that formerly Heaven and Earth were one shape; but when they were separated from each other, they gave birth and brought all things into the light, trees, birds, beasts, and the fishes whom the sea feeds, and the race of mortals.'

---

[1] Euripides, Chrysippus, fragm. 6 (edit. Didot, p. 824):—

Γαῖα μεγίστη καὶ Διὸς αἰθήρ,
ὁ μὲν ἀνθρώπων καὶ θεῶν γενέτωρ,
ἡ δ' ὑγροβόλους σταγόνας νοτίους
παραδεξαμένη τίκτει θνατούς,
τίκτει δὲ βορὰν, φῦλά τε θηρῶν,
ὅθεν οὐκ ἀδίκως
μήτηρ πάντων νενόμισται.

[2] Dionysius Halic. vol. v. p. 355; Muir, v. p. 27.

Thus we have met with the same idea of the original union, of a separation, and of a subsequent re-union of Heaven and Earth in Greece, in India, and in the Polynesian islands.

Let us now see how the poets of the Veda address these two beings, Heaven and Earth.

They are mostly addressed in the dual, as two beings forming but one concept. We meet, however, with verses which are addressed to the Earth by herself, and which speak of her as 'kind, without thorns, and pleasant to dwell on[1],' while there are clear traces in some of the hymns that at one time Dyaus, the sky, was the supreme deity[2]. When invoked together they are called Dyâvâp*ri*thivyau, from dyu, the sky, and p*ri*thivî, the broad earth.

If we examine their epithets, we find that many of them reflect simply the physical aspects of Heaven and Earth. Thus they are called uru, wide, uruvya*k*as, widely expanded, dûre-ante, with limits far apart, gabhîra, deep, gh*ri*tavat, giving fat, madhudugha, yielding honey or dew, payasvat, full of milk, bhûri-retas, rich in seed.

Another class of epithets represents them already as endowed with certain human and superhuman qualities, such as asas*k*at, never tiring, a*g*ara, not decaying, which brings us very near to immortal; adruh, not injuring, or not deceiving, pra*k*etas, provident, and then pitâ-mâtâ, father and mother, devaputra, having the gods for their sons, *ri*tav*ri*dh and *ri*tavat, protectors of the *Ri*ta, of what is right, guardians of eternal laws.

Here you see what is so interesting in the Veda,

[1] Rig-veda I. 22, 15.

[2] See Lectures on the Science of Language, vol. ii. p. 468.

the gradual advance from the material to the spiritual, from the sensuous to the supersensuous, from the human to the superhuman and the divine. Heaven and Earth were seen, and, according to our notions, they might simply be classed as visible and finite beings. But the ancient poets were more honest to themselves. They could see Heaven and Earth, but they never saw them in their entirety. They felt that there was something beyond the purely finite aspect of these beings, and therefore they thought of them, not as they would think of a stone, or a tree, or a dog, but as something not-finite, not altogether visible or knowable, yet as something important to themselves, powerful, strong to bless, but also strong to hurt. Whatever was between Heaven and Earth seemed to be theirs, their property, their realm, their dominion. They held and embraced all; they seemed to have produced all. The Devas or bright beings, the sun, the dawn, the fire, the wind, the rain, were all theirs, and were called therefore the offspring of Heaven and Earth. Thus Heaven and Earth became the Universal Father and Mother.

Then we ask at once, 'Were then these Heaven and Earth gods? But gods in what sense? In our sense of God? Why, in our sense, God is altogether incapable of a plural. Then in the Greek sense of the word? No, certainly not, for what the Greeks called gods was the result of an intellectual growth totally independent of the Veda or of India. We must never forget that what we call gods in ancient mythologies are not substantial, living, individual beings, of whom we can predicate this or that. Deva, which we translate by god, is nothing but an adjective, expressive of a quality shared by heaven and earth, by the sun and the stars and the dawn and the sea, namely *brightness;* and the idea of god, at that early time, contains neither more nor less than what is shared in common by all these bright beings. That is to say, the idea of god is not an idea ready-made, which could be applied in its abstract purity to heaven and earth and other such like beings; but it is an idea, growing out of the concepts of heaven and earth and of the other bright beings, slowly separating itself from them, but never containing more than what was contained, though confusedly, in the objects to which it was successively applied.

Nor must it be supposed that heaven and earth, having once been raised to the rank of undecaying or immortal beings, of divine parents, of guardians of the laws, were thus permanently settled in the religious consciousness of the people. Far from it. When the ideas of other gods, and of more active and more distinctly personal gods had been elaborated, the Vedic *Ri*shis asked without hesitation, Who then has made heaven and earth? not exactly Heaven and Earth, as conceived before, but heaven and earth as seen every day, as a part of what began to be called Nature or the Universe.

Thus one poet says[1]:

'He was indeed among the gods the cleverest workman who produced the two brilliant ones (heaven and earth), that gladden all things; he who measured out the two bright ones (heaven and earth) by his wisdom, and established them on everlasting supports.'

---

[1] Rig-veda I. 160, 4.

And again[1]: 'He was a good workman who produced heaven and earth; the wise, who by his might brought together these two (heaven and earth), the wide, the deep, the well-fashioned in the bottomless space.'

Very soon this great work of making heaven and earth was ascribed, like other mighty works, to the mightiest of their gods, to Indra. At first we read that Indra, originally only a kind of *Jupiter pluvius*, or god of rain, stretched out heaven and earth, like a hide[2]; that he held them in his hand[3], that he upholds heaven and earth[4], and that he grants heaven and earth to his worshippers[5]. But very soon Indra is praised for having made Heaven and Earth[6]; and then, when the poet remembers that Heaven and Earth had been praised elsewhere as the parents of the gods, and more especially as the parents of Indra, he does not hesitate for a moment, but says[7]: 'What poets living before us have reached the end of all thy greatness? for thou hast indeed begotten thy father and thy mother together[8] from thy own body!'

That is a strong measure, and a god who once could do that, was no doubt capable of anything afterwards. The same idea, namely that Indra is greater than heaven and earth, is expressed in a less outrageous way by another poet, who says[9] that Indra is greater than heaven and earth, and that

---

[1] Rig-veda IV. 56, 3. [2] L. c. VIII. 6, 5.
[3] L. c. III. 30, 5. [4] L. c. III. 32, 8.
[5] L. c. III. 34, 8. [6] L. c. VIII. 36, 4. [7] L. c. X. 54, 3.
[8] Cf. IV. 17, 4, where Dyaus is the father of Indra; see however Muir, iv. 31, note.
[9] Rig-veda VI. 30, 1.

both together are only a half of Indra. Or again[1]: 'The divine Dyaus bowed before Indra, before Indra the great Earth bowed with her wide spaces.' 'At the birth of thy splendour Dyaus trembled, the Earth trembled for fear of thy anger[2].'

Thus, from one point of view, Heaven and Earth were the greatest gods, they were the parents of everything, and therefore of the gods also, such as Indra and others.

But, from another point of view, every god that was considered as supreme at one time or other, must necessarily have made heaven and earth, must at all events be greater than heaven and earth, and thus the child became greater than the father, aye, became the father of his father. Indra was not the only god that created heaven and earth. In one hymn[3] that creation is ascribed to Soma and Pûshan, by no means very prominent characters; in another[4] to Hira*n*yagarbha (the golden germ); in another again to a god who is simply called Dhât*ri*, the Creator[5], or Visvakarman[6], the maker of all things. Other gods, such as Mitra and Savit*ri*, names of the sun, are praised for upholding Heaven and Earth, and the same task is sometimes performed by the old god Varu*n*a[7] also.

What I wish you to observe in all this is the perfect freedom with which these so-called gods or Devas are handled, and particularly the ease and naturalness with which now the one, now the other emerges as supreme out of this chaotic theogony.

---

[1] Rig-veda I. 131, 1.
[2] L. c. IV. 17, 2.
[3] L. c. II. 40, 1.
[4] L. c. X. 121, 9.
[5] L. c. X. 190, 3.
[6] L. c. X. 81, 2.
[7] L. c. VI. 70, 1.

This is the peculiar character of the ancient Vedic religion, totally different both from the Polytheism and from the Monotheism as we see it in the Greek and the Jewish religions; and if the Veda had taught us nothing else but this *henotheistic* phase, which must everywhere have preceded the more highly organised phase of Polytheism which we see in Greece, in Rome, and elsewhere, the study of the Veda would not have been in vain.

It may be quite true that the poetry of the Veda is neither beautiful, in our sense of the word, nor very profound; but it is instructive. When we see those two giant spectres of Heaven and Earth on the background of the Vedic religion, exerting their influence for a time, and then vanishing before the light of younger and more active gods, we learn a lesson which it is well to learn, and which we can hardly learn anywhere else—the lesson *how gods were made and unmade*—how the Beyond or the Infinite was named by different names in order to bring it near to the mind of man, to make it for a time comprehensible, until, when name after name had proved of no avail, a nameless God was felt to answer best the restless cravings of the human heart.

I shall next translate to you the hymn to which I referred before as addressed to the Rivers. If the Rivers are to be called deities at all, they belong to the class of terrestrial deities. But the reason why I single out this hymn is not so much because it throws new light on the theogonic process, but because it may help to impart some reality to the vague conceptions which we form to ourselves of the ancient Vedic poets and their surroundings. The rivers invoked are, as we shall see, the real rivers of the Punjâb, and the poem shows a much wider geographical horizon than we should expect from a mere village bard[1].

1. 'Let the poet declare, O Waters, your exceeding greatness, here in the seat of Vivasvat[2]. By seven and seven they have come forth in three courses, but the Sindhu (the Indus) exceeds all the other wandering rivers by her strength.

2. 'Varu*n*a dug out paths for thee to walk on, when thou rannest to the race[3]. Thou proceedest

---

[1] Rig-veda X. 75. See Hibbert Lectures, Lect. iv.

[2] Vivasvat is a name of the sun, and the seat or home of Vivasvat can hardly be anything but the earth, as the home of the sun, or, in a more special sense, the place where a sacrifice is offered.

[3] I formerly translated yát vấ*g*ân abhí ádrava*h* tvám by 'when thou rannest for the prizes.' Grassman had translated similarly, 'When thou, O Sindhu, rannest to the prize of the battle,' while Ludwig wrote, 'When thou, O Sindhu, wast flowing on to greater powers.' Vâ*g*a, connected with vegeo, vigeo, vigil, wacker (see Curtius, Grundzüge, No. 159), is one of the many difficult words in the Veda the general meaning of which may be guessed, but in many places cannot yet be determined with certainty. Vâ*g*a occurs very frequently, both in the singular and the plural, and some of its meanings are clear enough. The Petersburg Dictionary gives the following list of them—swiftness, race, prize of race, gain, treasure, race-horse, etc. Here we perceive at once the difficulty of tracing all these meanings back to a common source, though it might be possible to begin with the meanings of strength, strife, contest, race, whether friendly or warlike, then to proceed to what is won in a race or in war, viz. booty, treasure, and lastly to take vâ*g*â*h* in the more general sense of acquisitions, goods, even goods bestowed as gifts. We have a similar transition of meaning in the Greek ἆθλος, contest, contest for a prize, and ἆθλον, the prize of contest, reward, gift, while in the plural τὰ ἆθλα stands again for contest, or even the place of combat. The Vedic vâ*g*ambhara may in fact be rendered by ἀθλοφόρος, vâ*g*asâti by ἀθλοσύνη.

The transition from fight to prize is seen in passages such as: Rig-veda VI. 45, 12, vấ*g*ân indra *s*ravấyyân tváyâ *g*eshma hitám

on a precipitous ridge of the earth, when thou art lord in the van of all the moving streams.

3. 'The sound rises up to heaven above the earth; she stirs up with splendour her endless power[1]. As from a cloud, the showers thunder forth, when the Sindhu comes, roaring like a bull.

4. 'To thee, O Sindhu, they (the other rivers) come as lowing mother-cows (run) to their young with their milk[2]. Like a king in battle thou leadest the two wings, when thou reachest the front of these down-rushing rivers.

5. 'Accept, O Gaṅgâ (Ganges), Yamunâ (Jumna), Sarasvatî (Sursûti), *S*utudri (Sutlej), Parush*n*î (Irâvatî, Ravi), my praise[3]! With the Asiknî (Akesines) listen, O Marudv*ri*dhâ[4], and with the Vitastâ (Hy-

---

dhánam, 'May we with thy help, O Indra, win the glorious fights, the offered prize' (cf. ἀθλοθέτης).

Rig-veda VIII. 19, 18, té ít vấ*g*ebhi*h* *g*igyu*h* mahát dhánam, 'They won great wealth by battles.'

What we want for a proper understanding of our verse, are passages where we have, as here, a movement towards vâ*g*as in the plural. Such passages are few; for instance: X. 53, 8, átra *g*ahâma yé ásan ásevâ*h* sivấn vayám út tarema abhí vâ*g*ân, 'Let us leave here those who were unlucky (the dead), and let us get up to lucky toils.' No more is probably meant here when the Sindhu is said to run towards her vâ*g*as, that is, her struggles, her fights, her race across the mountains with the other rivers.

[1] On *s*ushma, strength, see Rig-veda, translation, vol. i. p. 105. We find *s*ubhrám *s*úshmam II. 11, 4; and iyarti with *s*úshmam IV. 17, 12.

[2] See Muir, Sanskrit Texts, v. p. 344.

[3] 'O Marudv*ri*dhâ with Asiknî, Vitastâ; O Âr*g*îkîyâ, listen with the Sushomâ,' *Ludwig*. 'Asiknî and Vitastâ and Marudv*ri*dhâ, with the Sushomâ, hear us, O Âr*g*îkîyâ,' *Grassmann*.

[4] Marudv*ri*dhâ, a general name for river. According to Roth the combined course of the Akesines and Hydaspes, *before* the junction with the Hydraotes: according to Ludwig, the river *after*

daspes, Behat); O Ârgîkîyâ[1], listen with the Sushomâ[2].

6. 'First thou goest united with the Trishtâmâ on thy journey, with the Susartu, the Rasâ (Ramhâ, Araxes[3]?), and the Svetî,—O Sindhu, with the Kubhâ (Kophen, Cabul river) to the Gomatî (Gomal), with the Mehatnu to the Krumu (Kurum)—with whom thou proceedest together.

7 'Sparkling, bright, with mighty splendour she carries the waters across the plains—the unconquered Sindhu, the quickest of the quick, like a beautiful mare—a sight to see.

8. 'Rich in horses, in chariots, in garments, in gold, in booty[4], in wool[5], and in straw[6], the Sindhu,

---

the junction with Hydraotes. Zimmer (Altindisches Leben, p. 12) adopts Roth's, Kiepert in his maps follows Ludwig's opinion.

[1] According to Yâska the Ârgîkîyâ is the Vipâs. Vivien de Saint-Martin takes it for the country watered by the Suwan, the Soanos of Megasthenes.

[2] According to Yâska the Sushomâ is the Indus. Vivien de Saint-Martin identifies it with the Suwan. Zimmer (l. c. p. 14) points out that in Arrian, Indica, iv. 12, there is a various reading Soamos for Soanos.

[3] Chips from a German Workshop, vol. i. p. 157.

[4] Vâginîvatî is by no means an easy word. Hence all translators vary, and none settles the meaning. Muir translates, 'yielding nutriment;' Zimmer, 'having plenty of quick horses;' Ludwig, 'like a strong mare.' Vagin, no doubt, means a strong horse, a racer, but vaginî never occurs in the Rig-veda in the sense of a mare, and the text is not vaginîvat, but vaginîvatî. If vâginî meant mare, we might translate rich in mares, but that would be a mere repetition after svasvâ, possessed of good horses. Vaginîvatî is chiefly applied to Ushas, Sarasvatî, and here to the river Sindhu. It is joined with vagebhih, Rig-veda I. 3. 10, which, if vâginî meant mare, would mean 'rich in mares through horses.' We also read, Rig-veda I. 48, 16, sám (nah mimikshvá) vấgaih vâginîvati, which we can hardly translate by 'give us horses, thou who art possessed of mares;' nor, Rig-veda I. 92, 15, yúkshva hí vâginîvati ásvân,

handsome and young, clothes herself in sweet flowers[7].

9. 'The Sindhu has yoked her easy chariot with horses; may she conquer prizes for us in the race.

'harness the horses, thou who art rich in mares.' In most of the passages where vâginîvatî occurs, the goddess thus addressed is represented as rich, and asked to bestow wealth, and I should therefore prefer to take vâgínî, as a collective abstract noun, like tretínî, in the sense of wealth, originally booty, and to translate vâginîvatî simply by rich, a meaning well adapted to every passage where the word occurs.

[5] Ûrnâvatî, rich in wool, probably refers to the flocks of sheep for which the North-West of India was famous. See Rig-veda I. 126, 7.

[6] Sîlamâvatî does not occur again in the Rig-veda. Muir translates, 'rich in plants;' Zimmer, 'rich in water;' Ludwig takes it as a proper name. Sâyana states that sîlamâ is a plant which is made into ropes. That the meaning of sîlamâvatî was forgotten at an early time we see by the Atharva-veda III. 12, 2, substituting sûnritâvatî for sîlamâvatî, as preserved in the Sânkhâyana Grihya-sûtras, 3, 3. I think sîlamâ means straw, from whatever plant it may be taken, and this would be equally applicable to a sâlâ, a house, a sthûnâ, a post, and to the river Indus. It may have been, as Ludwig conjectures, an old local name, and in that case it may possibly account for the name given in later times to the Suleiman range.

[7] Madhuvridh is likewise a word which does not occur again in the Rig-veda. Sâyana explains it by nirgundi and similar plants, but it is doubtful what plant is meant. Gunda is the name of a grass, madhuvridh therefore may have been a plant such as sugar-cane, that yielded a sweet juice, the Upper Indus being famous for sugar-cane; see Hiouen-thsang, II, p. 105. I take adhivaste with Roth in the sense 'she dresses herself,' as we might say 'the river is dressed in heather.' Muir translates, 'she traverses a land yielding sweetness;' Zimmer, 'she clothes herself in Madhuvridh;' Ludwig, 'the Sîlamâvatî throws herself into the increaser of the honey-sweet dew.' All this shows how little progress can be made in Vedic scholarship by merely translating either words or verses, without giving at the same time a full justification of the meaning assigned to every single word.

The greatness of her chariot is praised as truly great—that chariot which is irresistible, which has its own glory, and abundant strength[1].'

This hymn does not sound perhaps very poetical, in our sense of the word; yet if you will try to realise the thoughts of the poet who composed it, you will perceive that it is not without some bold and powerful conceptions.

Take the modern peasants, living in their villages by the side of the Thames, and you must admit that he would be a remarkable man who could bring himself to look on the Thames as a kind of general, riding at the head of many English rivers, and leading them on to a race or a battle. Yet it is easier to travel in England, and to gain a commanding view of the river-system of the country, than it was three thousand years ago to travel over India, even over that part of India which the poet of our hymn commands. He takes in at one swoop three great river-systems, or, as he calls them, three great armies of rivers—those flowing from the North-West into the Indus, those joining it from the North-East, and, in the distance, the Ganges and the Jumnah with their tributaries. Look on the map and you will see how well these three armies are determined; but our poet had no map—he had nothing but high mountains and sharp eyes to carry out his trigonometrical survey. Now I call a man, who for the first time could *see* those three marching armies of rivers, a poet.

The next thing that strikes one in that hymn—if hymn we must call it—is the fact that all these rivers, large and small, have their own proper names.

---

[1] See Petersburg Dictionary, s.v. virapsin.

That shows a considerable advance in civilised life, and it proves no small degree of coherence, or what the French call *solidarity*, between the tribes who had taken possession of Northern India. Most settlers call the river on whose banks they settle '*the river*.' Of course there are many names for river. It may be called the runner[1], the fertiliser, the roarer—or, with a little poetical metaphor, the arrow, the horse, the cow, the father, the mother, the watchman, the child of the mountains. Many rivers had many names in different parts of their course, and it was only when communication between different settlements became more frequent, and a fixed terminology was felt to be a matter of necessity, that the rivers of a country were properly baptised and registered. All this had been gone through in India before our hymn became possible.

And now we have to consider another, to my mind most startling fact. We here have a number of names of the rivers of India, as they were known to one single poet, say about 1000 B.C. We then hear nothing of India till we come to the days of Alexander, and when we look at the names of the Indian rivers, represented as well as they could be by Alexander's companions, mere strangers in India, and by means of a strange language and a strange alphabet, we recognise, without much difficulty, nearly all of the old Vedic names.

In this respect the names of rivers have a great advantage over the names of towns in India. What

---

[1] 'Among the Hottentots, the Kunene, Okavango and Orange rivers, all have the name of Garib, i. e. the Runner.' Dr. Theoph. Hahn, Cape Times, July 11, 1882.

we now call *Dilli* or *Delhi* was in ancient times called Indraprastha, in later times *Shahjahânabâd*. *Oude* is Ayodhyâ, but the old name of Saketa is forgotten. The town of Pa*t*aliputra, known to the Greeks as *Palimbothra*, is now called *Patna*[1].

Now I can assure you this persistency of the Vedic river names was to my mind something so startling that I often said to myself, This cannot be—there must be something wrong here. I do not wonder so much at the names of the *Indus* and the *Ganges* being the same. The Indus was known to early traders, whether by sea or by land. Skylax sailed from the country of the Paktys, i. e. the Pushtus, as the Afghans still call themselves, down to the mouth of the Indus. That was under Darius Hystaspes (521–486). Even before that time India and the Indians were known by their name, which was derived from *Sindhu*, the name of their frontier river. The neighbouring tribes who spoke Iranic languages all pronounced, like the Persian, the *s* as an *h*[2]. Thus Sindhu became Hindhu (Hidhu), and, as h's were dropped even at that early time, Hindhu became Indu. Thus the river was called *Indos*, the people *Indoi* by the Greeks, who first heard of India from the Persians.

Sindhu probably meant originally the divider, keeper, and defender, from sidh, to keep off. It was a masculine, before it became a feminine. No more telling name could have been given to a broad river, which guarded peaceful settlers both against the inroads of hostile tribes and the attacks of wild

---

[1] Cunningham, Archæological Survey of India, vol. xii. p. 113.

[2] Pliny, Hist. Nat. vi. 20, 71: 'Indus incolis Sindus appellatus.'

animals. A common name for the ancient settlements of the Aryans in India was 'the Seven Rivers,' 'Sapta Sindhava*h*.' But though sindhu was used as an appellative noun for river in general (cf. Rig-veda VI. 19, 5, samudré ná síndhava*h* yấdamânâ*h*, 'like rivers longing for the sea'), it remained throughout the whole history of India the name of its powerful guardian river, the Indus.

In some passages of the Rig-veda it has been pointed out that sindhu might better be translated by 'sea,' a change of meaning, if so it can be called, fully explained by the geographical conditions of the country. There are places where people could swim across the Indus, there are others where no eye could tell whether the boundless expanse of water should be called river or sea. The two run into each other, as every sailor knows, and naturally the meaning of sindhu, river, runs into the meaning of sindhu, sea.

But besides the two great rivers, the Indus and the Ganges,—in Sanskrit the Gaṅgâ, literally the Go-go,—we have the smaller rivers, and many of their names also agree with the names preserved to us by the companions of Alexander[1].

The Yamunâ, the Jumna, was known to Ptolemy as *Διάμουνα*[2], to Pliny as Jomanes, to Arrian, somewhat corrupted, as Jôbares[3].

The *S*utudrî, or, as it was afterwards called, *S*atadru, meaning 'running in a hundred streams,' was

---

[1] The history of these names has been treated by Professor Lassen, in his 'Indische Alterthumskunde,' and more lately by Professor Kaegi, in his very careful essay, 'Der Rig-veda,' pp. 146, 147.

[2] Ptol. vii. 1, 29.

[3] Arrian, Iudica, viii. 5.

known to Ptolemy as Ζαδάρδης or Ζάραδρος; Pliny called it Sydrus; and Megasthenes, too, was probably acquainted with it as Ζαδάρδης. In the Veda[1] it formed with the Vipâs the frontier of the Punjâb, and we hear of fierce battles fought at that time, it may be on the same spot where in 1846 the battle of the Sutledge was fought by Sir Hugh Gough and Sir Henry Hardinge. It was probably on the Vipâs (later Vipâsâ), a north-western tributary of the Sutledge, that Alexander's army turned back. The river was then called Hyphasis; Pliny calls it Hypasis[2], a very fair approximation to the Vedic Vipâs, which means 'unfettered.' Its modern name is Bias or Bejah.

The next river on the west is the Vedic Parush*n*î, better known as Irâvatî[3], which Strabo calls Hyarotis, while Arrian gives it a more Greek appearance by calling it Hydraotes. It is the modern Rawi. It was this river which the Ten Kings when attacking the T*ri*tsus under Sudâs tried to cross from the west by cutting off its water. But their stratagem failed, and they perished in the river (Rig-veda VII. 18, 8–9).

We then come to the Asiknî, which means 'black.'

---

[1] Rig-veda III. 33, 1: 'From the lap of the mountains Vipâs and *S*utudrî rush forth with their water like two lusty mares neighing, freed from their tethers, like two bright mother-cows licking (their calf).

'Ordered by Indra and waiting his bidding you run toward the sea like two charioteers; running together, as your waters rise, the one goes into the other, you bright ones.'

[2] Other classical names are Hypanis, Bipasis, and Bibasis. Yâska identifies it with the Âr*g*îkîyâ.

[3] Cf. Nirukta IX. 26.

That river had another name also, *K*andrabhâga, which means 'streak of the moon.' The Greeks, however, pronounced that name Σανδαροφάγος, and this had the unlucky meaning of 'the devourer of Alexander.' Hesychius tells us that in order to avert the bad omen Alexander changed the name of that river into Ἀκεσίνης, which would mean 'the Healer;' but he does not tell, what the Veda tells us, that this name Ἀκεσίνης was a Greek adaptation of another name of the same river, namely Asiknî, which had evidently supplied to Alexander the idea of calling the Asiknî Ἀκεσίνης. It is the modern Chinâb.

Next to the Akesines we have the Vedic Vitastâ, the last of the rivers of the Punjâb, changed in Greek into Hydaspes. It was to this river that Alexander retired, before sending his fleet down the Indus and leading his army back to Babylon. It is the modern Behat or Jilam.

I could identify still more of these Vedic rivers, such as, for instance, the Kubhâ, the Greek Cophen, the modern Kâbul river[1]; but the names which I have

---

[1] 'The first tributaries which join the Indus before its meeting with the Kubhâ or the Kabul river cannot be determined. All travellers in these northern countries complain of the continual changes in the names of the rivers, and we can hardly hope to find traces of the Vedic names in existence there after the lapse of three or four thousand years. The rivers intended may be the Shauyook, Ladak, Abba Seen, and Burrindu, and one of the four rivers, the Rasâ, has assumed an almost fabulous character in the Veda. After the Indus has joined the Kubhâ or the Kabul river, two names occur, the Gomatî and Krumu, which I believe I was the first to identify with the modern rivers the Gomal and Kurrum. (Roth, Nirukta, Erläuterungen, p. 43, Anm.) The Gomal falls into the Indus, between Dera Ismael Khan and Paharpore, and although Elphinstone calls it a river only during the rainy season,

traced from the Veda to Alexander, and in many cases from Alexander again to our own time, seem to me sufficient to impress upon us the real and historical character of the Veda. Suppose the Veda were a forgery—suppose at least that it had been put together after the time of Alexander—how could we explain these names? They are names that have mostly a meaning in Sanskrit, they are names corresponding very closely to their Greek corruptions, as pronounced and written down by people who did not know Sanskrit. How is a forgery possible here?

I selected this hymn for two reasons. First, because it shows us the widest geographical horizon of the Vedic poets, confined by the snowy mountains in the North, the Indus and the range of the Suleiman mountains in the West, the Indus or the sea in the South, and the valley of the Jumna and Ganges in the East. Beyond that, the world, though open, was unknown to the Vedic poets. Secondly, because the same hymn gives us also a kind of historical background

---

Klaproth (Foe-koue-ki, p. 23) describes its upper course as far more considerable, and adds: "Un peu à l'est de Sirmágha, le Gomal traverse la chaîne de montagnes de Solimán, passe devant Raghzi, et fertilise le pays habité par les tribus de Dauletkhail et de Gandehpour. Il se dessèche au défilé de Pezou, et son lit ne se remplit plus d'eau que dans la saison des pluies; alors seulement il rejoint la droite de l'Indus, au sud-est du bourg de Paharpour." The Kurrum falls into the Indus North of the Gomal, while, according to the poet, we should expect it South. It might be urged that poets are not bound by the same rules as geographers, as we see, for instance, in the verse immediately preceding. But if it should be taken as a serious objection, it will be better to give up the Gomatî than the Krumu, the latter being the larger of the two, and we might then take Gomatî, "rich in cattle," as an adjective belonging to Krumu.'—From a review of General Cunningham's 'Ancient Geography of India,' in *Nature*, 1871, Sept. 14.

to the Vedic age. These rivers, as we may see them to-day, as they were seen by Alexander and his Macedonians, were seen also by the Vedic poets. Here we have an historical continuity—almost living witnesses, to tell us that the people whose songs have been so strangely, aye, you may almost say, so miraculously preserved to us, were real people, lairds with their clans, priests, or rather, servants of their gods, shepherds with their flocks, dotted about on the hills and valleys, with enclosures or palisades here and there, with a few strongholds, too, in case of need—living their short life on earth, as at that time life might be lived by men, without much pushing and crowding and trampling on each other—spring, summer, and winter leading them on from year to year, and the sun in his rising and setting lifting up their thoughts from their meadows and groves which they loved, to a world in the East, from which they had come, or to a world in the West, to which they were gladly hastening on. They had what I call religion, though it was very simple, and hardly reduced as yet to the form of a creed. 'There is a Beyond,' that was all they felt and knew, though they tried, as well as they could, to give names to that Beyond, and thus to change religion into *a* religion. They had not as yet a name for God—certainly not in our sense of the word—or even a general name for the gods; but they invented name after name to enable them to grasp and comprehend by some outward and visible tokens powers whose presence they felt in nature, though their true and full essence was to them, as it is to us, invisible and incomprehensible.

VEDIC DEITIES.

LECTURE VI.

THE next important phenomenon of nature which was represented in the Veda as a terrestrial deity is Fire, in Sanskrit Agni, in Latin *ignis*. In the worship which is paid to the Fire and in the high praises bestowed on Agni we can clearly perceive the traces of a period in the history of man in which not only the most essential comforts of life, but life itself, depended on the knowledge of producing fire. To us fire has become so familiar that we can hardly form an idea of what life would be without it. But how did the ancient dwellers on earth get command and possession of fire? The Vedic poets tell us that fire first came to them from the sky, in the form of lightning, but that it disappeared again, and that then Mâtarisvan, a being to a certain extent like Prometheus, brought it back and confided it to the safe keeping of the clan of the Bh*ri*gus (Phlegyas)[1]. In other poems we hear of the mystery of fire being produced by rubbing pieces of wood; and here it is a curious fact that the name of the wood thus used for rubbing is in Sanskrit Pramantha, a word which, as Kuhn has shown, would in Greek come very near to the name of Prometheus. The possession of fire, whether by preserving it as sacred on

[1] Muir, iv. p. 209.

the hearth, or by producing it at pleasure with the fire-drill, represents an enormous step in early civilisation. It enabled people to cook their meat instead of eating it raw; it gave them the power of carrying on their work by night; and in colder climates it really preserved them from being frozen to death. No wonder, therefore, that the fire should have been praised and worshipped as the best and kindest of gods, the only god who had come down from heaven to live on earth, the friend of man, the messenger of the gods, the mediator between gods and men, the immortal among mortals. He, it is said, protects the settlements of the Aryans, and frightens away the black-skinned enemies.

Soon, however, fire was conceived by the Vedic poets under the more general character of light and warmth, and then the presence of Agni was perceived, not only on the hearth and the altar, but in the Dawn, in the Sun, and in the world beyond the Sun, while at the same time his power was recognised as ripening, or as they called it, as cooking, the fruits of the earth, and as supporting also the warmth and the life of the human body. From that point of view Agni, like other powers, rose to the rank of a Supreme God[1]. He is said to have stretched out heaven and earth—naturally, because without his light heaven and earth would have been invisible and undistinguishable. The next poet says that Agni held heaven aloft by his light, that he kept the two worlds asunder; and in the end Agni is said to be the progenitor and father of heaven and earth, and the maker of all that flies, or walks, or stands, or moves on earth.

[1] Muir, iv. p. 214.

Here we have once more the same process before our eyes. The human mind begins with being startled by a single or repeated event, such as the lightning, striking a tree and devouring a whole forest, or a spark of fire breaking forth from wood being rubbed against wood, whether in a forest, or in the wheel of a carriage, or at last in a fire-drill, devised on purpose. Man then begins to wonder at what to him is a miracle, none the less so because it is a fact, a simple, natural fact. He sees the effects of a power, but he can only guess at its cause, and if he is to speak of it, he can only do so by speaking of it as an agent, or as something like a human agent, and, if in some respects not quite human, in others more than human or super-human. Thus the concept of Fire grew, and while it became more and more generalised, it also became more sublime, more incomprehensible, more divine. Without Agni, without fire, light, and warmth, life would have been impossible. Hence he became the author and giver of life, of the life of plants and animals and of men; and his favour having once been implored for 'light and life and all things,' what wonder that in the minds of some poets, and in the traditions of this or that village community, he should have been raised to the rank of a supreme ruler, a god above all gods, their own true god!

We now proceed to consider the powers which the ancient poets might have discovered in the air, in the clouds, and, more particularly, in those meteoric conflicts which by thunder, lightning, darkness, storms, and showers of rain must have taught man that very important lesson that he was not alone in this world. Many philosophers, as you know, believe that all religion arose from fear or terror, and that without thunder and lightning to teach us, we should never have believed in any gods or god. This is a one-sided and exaggerated view. Thunderstorms, no doubt, had a large share in arousing feelings of awe and terror, and in making man conscious of his weakness and dependence. Even in the Veda Indra is introduced as saying: 'Yes, when I send thunder and lightning, then you believe in me.' But what we call religion would never have sprung from fear and terror alone. *Religion is trust*, and that trust arose in the beginning from the impressions made on the mind and heart of man by the order and wisdom of nature, and more particularly, by those regularly recurring events, the return of the sun, the revival of the moon, the order of the seasons, the law of cause and effect, gradually discovered in all things, and traced back in the end to a cause of all causes, by whatever name we choose to call it.

Still, the meteoric phenomena had, no doubt, their important share in the production of ancient deities; and in the poems of the Vedic Rishis they naturally occupy a very prominent place. If we were asked who was the principal god of the Vedic period, we should probably, judging from the remains of that poetry which we possess, say it was Indra, the god of the blue sky, the Indian Zeus, the gatherer of the clouds, the giver of rain, the wielder of the thunderbolt, the conqueror of darkness and of all the powers of darkness, the bringer of light, the source of freshness, vigour, and life, the ruler and lord of the whole world. Indra is this, and much more in the Veda. He is supreme in the hymns of many poets, and may have been so in the prayers addressed to him by many of the ancient septs or village communities in India. Compared with him the other gods are said to be decrepit old men. Heaven, the old Heaven or Dyaus, formerly the father of all the gods, nay the father of Indra himself, bows before him, and the Earth trembles at his approach. Yet Indra never commanded the permanent allegiance of all the other gods, like Zeus and Jupiter; nay, we know from the Veda itself that there were sceptics, even at that early time, who denied that there was any such thing as Indra[1].

By the side of Indra, and associated with him in his battles, and sometimes hardly distinguishable from him, we find the representatives of the wind, called Vâta or Vâyu, and the more terrible Storm-gods, the Maruts, literally the Smashers.

When speaking of the Wind, a poet says[2]: 'Where was he born? Whence did he spring? the life of the gods, the germ of the world! That god moves about where he listeth, his voices are heard, but he is not to be seen.'

The Maruts are more terrible than Vâta, the wind. They are clearly the representatives of such storms as are known in India, when the air is darkened by dust and clouds, when in a moment the trees are stripped of their foliage, their branches shivered, their stems snapped, when the earth seems to reel and the mountains to shake, and the rivers are lashed into foam and fury. Then the poet sees the Maruts approaching with golden helmets, with spotted skins on their shoulders, brandishing golden spears, whirling their axes, shooting fiery arrows, and cracking their whips amidst thunder and lightning. They are the comrades

---

[1] Hibbert Lectures, p. 307.

[2] X. 168, 3, 4.

of Indra, sometimes, like Indra, the sons of Dyaus or the sky, but also the sons of another terrible god, called Rudra, or the Howler, a fighting god, to whom many hymns are addressed. In him a new character is evolved, that of a healer and saviour,—a very natural transition in India, where nothing is so powerful for dispelling miasmas, restoring health, and imparting fresh vigour to man and beast, as a thunderstorm, following after weeks of heat and drought.

All these and several others, such as Par*g*anya and the *Ri*bhus, are the gods of mid-air, the most active and dramatic gods, ever present to the fancy of the ancient poets, and in several cases the prototypes of later heroes, celebrated in the epic poems of India. In battles, more particularly, these fighting gods of the sky were constantly invoked[1]. Indra is the leader in battles, the protector of the bright Aryans, the destroyer of the black aboriginal inhabitants of India. 'He has thrown down fifty thousand black fellows,' the poet says, 'and their strongholds crumbled away like an old rag.' Strange to say, Indra is praised for having saved his people from their enemies, much as Jehovah was praised by the Jewish prophets. Thus we read in one hymn that when Sudâs, the pious king of the T*ri*tsus, was pressed hard in his battle with the ten kings, Indra changed the flood into an easy ford, and thus saved Sudâs.

In another hymn we read[2]; 'Thou hast restrained the great river for the sake of Turvîti Vâyya: the flood moved in obedience to thee, and thou madest the rivers easy to cross.' This is not very different from the Psalmist (lxxviii. 13): 'He divided the

[1] See Kaegi, Rig-veda, p. 61.

[2] Rig-veda II. 13, 12; IV. 19, 6.

sea, and caused them to pass through; and he made the waters to stand as an heap.'

And there are other passages which have reminded some students of the Veda of Joshua's battle[1], when the sun stood still and the moon stayed, until the people had avenged themselves upon their enemies. For we read in the Veda also, as Professor Kaegi has pointed out (l.c. p. 63), that 'Indra lengthened the days into the night,' and that 'the Sun unharnessed its chariot in the middle of the day[2].'

In some of the hymns addressed to Indra his original connection with the sky and the thunderstorm seems quite forgotten. He has become a spiritual god, the only king of all worlds and all people[3], who sees and hears everything[4], nay, who inspires men with their best thoughts. No one is equal to him, no one excels him.

The name of Indra is peculiar to India, and must have been formed after the separation of the great Aryan family had taken place, for we find it neither in Greek, nor in Latin, nor in German. There are Vedic gods, as I mentioned before, whose names must have been framed before that separation, and which occur therefore, though greatly modified in character, sometimes in Greek, sometimes in Latin, sometimes in the Celtic, Teutonic, and Slavonic dialects. Dyaus, for instance, is the same word as Zeus or Ju-piter, Ushas is Eos, Naktâ is Nyx, Sûrya is Helios, Agni is ignis, Bhaga is Baga in Old Persian, Bogŭ in Old Slavonic, Varu*n*a is Uranos, Vâta is Wotan, Vâ*k* is vox, and in the name of the *Maruts*, or the storm-gods, the germs of the Italic god of war, Mars, have been dis-

[1] Joshua x. 13.
[2] Rig-veda IV. 30, 3; X. 138, 3.
[3] L. c. VIII. 37, 3.
[4] L. c. VIII. 78, 5.

covered. Besides these direct coincidences, some indirect relations have been established between Hermes and Sârameya, Dionysos and Dyunisya, Prometheus and pramantha, Orpheus and *Ri*bhu, Erinnys and Sara*n*yu, Pân and Pavana.

But while the name of Indra as the god of the sky, also as the god of the thunderstorm, and the giver of rain, is unknown among the North-western members of the Aryan family, the name of another god who sometimes acts the part of Indra (Indra*h* Par*g*anyâtmâ), but is much less prominent in the Veda, I mean Par*g*anya, must have existed before that of Indra, because two at least of the Aryan languages have carried it, as we shall see, to Germany, and to the very shores of the Baltic.

Sometimes this Par*g*anya stands in the place of Dyaus, the sky. Thus we read in the Atharva-veda, XII. 1, 12[1]: 'The Earth is the mother, and I am the son of the Earth. Par*g*anya is the father; may he help us!'

In another place (XII. 1, 42) the Earth, instead of being the wife of Heaven or Dyaus, is called the wife of Par*g*anya.

Now who or what is this Par*g*anya? There have been long controversies about him[2], as to whether he is the same as Dyaus, Heaven, or the same as Indra, the successor of Dyaus, whether he is the god of the sky, of the cloud, or of the rain.

To me it seems that this very expression, god of the sky, god of the cloud, is so entire an anachronism that we could not even translate it into Vedic Sanskrit without committing a solecism. It is true,

---

[1] Muir, iv. p. 23.

[2] Ibid. p. 142. An excellent paper on Par*g*anya was published by Bühler in 1862, 'Orient und Occident,' vol. i. p. 214.

no doubt, we must use our modern ways of speaking when we wish to represent the thoughts of the ancient world; but we cannot be too much on our guard against accepting the dictionary representative of an ancient word for its real counterpart. Deva, no doubt, means 'gods' and 'god,' and Par*g*anya means 'cloud,' but no one could say in Sanskrit par*g*anyasya deva*h*, 'the god of the cloud.' The god, or the divine or transcendental element, does not come from without, to be added to the cloud or to the sky or to the earth, but it springs from the cloud and the sky and the earth, and is slowly elaborated into an independent concept. As many words in ancient languages have an undefined meaning, and lend themselves to various purposes according to the various intentions of the speakers, the names of the gods also share in this elastic and plastic character of ancient speech. There are passages where Par*g*anya means cloud, there are passages where it means rain. There are passages where Par*g*anya takes the place which elsewhere is filled by Dyaus, the sky, or by Indra, the active god of the atmosphere. This may seem very wrong and very unscientific to the scientific mythologist. But it cannot be helped. It is the nature of ancient thought and ancient language to be unscientific, and we must learn to master it as well as we can, instead of finding fault with it, and complaining that our forefathers did not reason exactly as we do.

There are passages in the Vedic hymns where Par*g*anya appears as a supreme god. He is called father, like Dyaus, the sky. He is called asura, the living or life-giving god, a name peculiar to the oldest and the greatest gods. One poet says[1], 'He rules

[1] Rig-veda VII. 101, 6.

as god over the whole world; all creatures rest in him; he is the life (âtmâ) of all that moves and rests.'

Surely it is difficult to say more of a supreme god than what is here said of Par*g*anya. Yet in other hymns he is represented as performing his office, namely that of sending rain upon the earth, under the control of Mitra and Varu*n*a, who are then considered as the highest lords, the mightiest rulers of heaven and earth [1].

There are other verses, again, where par*g*anya occurs with hardly any traces of personality, but simply as a name of cloud or rain.

Thus we read [2]: 'Even by day the Maruts (the storm-gods) produce darkness with the cloud that carries water, when they moisten the earth.' Here cloud is par*g*anya, and it is evidently used as an appellative, and not as a proper name. The same word occurs in the plural also, and we read of many par*g*anyas or clouds vivifying the earth [3].

When Devâpi prays for rain in favour of his brother, he says [4]: 'O lord of my prayer (B*ri*haspati), whether thou be Mitra or Varu*n*a or Pûshan, come to my sacrifice! Whether thou be together with the Âdityas, the Vasus or the Maruts, let the cloud (par*g*anya) rain for *S*antanu.'

And again: 'Stir up the rainy cloud' (par*g*anya).

In several places it makes no difference whether we translate par*g*anya by cloud or by rain, for those who pray for rain, pray for the cloud, and whatever may be the benefits of the rain, they may nearly all be called

---

[1] Rig-veda V. 63, 3–6.
[2] L. c. I. 38, 9.
[3] L. c. I. 164, 51.
[4] L. c. X. 98, 1.

the benefits of the cloud. There is a curious hymn, for instance, addressed to the frogs who, at the beginning of the rains, come forth from the dry ponds, and embrace each other and chatter together, and whom the poet compares to priests singing at a sacrifice, a not very complimentary remark from a poet who is himself supposed to have been a priest. Their voice is said to have been revived by par*g*anya, which we shall naturally translate 'by rain,' though, no doubt, the poet may have meant, for all we know, either a cloud, or even the god Par*g*anya himself.

I shall try to translate one of the hymns addressed to Par*g*anya, when conceived as a god, or at least as so much of a god as it was possible to be at that stage in the intellectual growth of the human race[1].

1. 'Invoke the strong god with these songs! praise Par*g*anya, worship him with veneration! for he, the roaring bull, scattering drops, gives seed-fruit to plants.

2. 'He cuts the trees asunder, he kills evil spirits; the whole world trembles before his mighty weapon. Even the guiltless flees before the powerful, when Par*g*anya thundering strikes down the evil-doers.

3. 'Like a charioteer, striking his horses with a whip, he puts forth his messengers of rain. From afar arise the roarings of the lion, when Par*g*anya makes the sky full of rain.

4. 'The winds blow, the lightnings[2] fly, plants spring up, the sky pours. Food is produced for the

---

[1] Rig-veda V. 83. See Bühler, Orient und Occident, vol. i. p. 214; Zimmer, Altindisches Leben, p. 43.

[2] Both Bühler (Orient und Occident, vol. i. p. 224) and Zimmer (Z. f. D. A. vii. p. 169) say that the lightning is represented as the son of Par*g*anya in Rig-veda VII. 101, 1. This seems doubtful.

whole world, when Par*g*anya blesses the earth with his seed.

5. 'O Par*g*anya, thou at whose work the earth bows down, thou at whose work hoofed animals are scattered, thou at whose work the plants assume all forms, grant thou to us thy great protection!

6. 'O Maruts, give us the rain of heaven, make the streams of the strong horse run down! And come thou hither with thy thunder, pouring out water, for thou (O Par*g*anya) art the living god, thou art our father.

7. 'Do thou roar, and thunder, and give fruitfulness! Fly around us with thy chariot full of water! Draw forth thy water-skin, when it has been opened and turned downward, and let the high and the low places become level!

8. 'Draw up the large bucket, and pour it out; let the streams pour forth freely! Soak heaven and earth with fatness! and let there be a good draught for the cows!

9. 'O Par*g*anya, when roaring and thundering thou killest the evildoers, then everything rejoices, whatever lives on earth.

10. 'Thou hast sent rain, stop now! Thou hast made the deserts passable, thou hast made plants grow for food, and thou hast obtained praise from men.'

This is a Vedic hymn, and a very fair specimen of what these ancient hymns are. There is nothing very grand and poetical about them, and yet, I say, take thousands and thousands of people living in our villages, and depending on rain for their very life, and not many of them will be able to compose such a prayer for rain, even though three thousand years have passed over our heads since Par*g*anya was first invoked in India. Nor are these verses entirely without poetical conceptions and descriptions. Whoever has watched a real thunderstorm in a hot climate, will recognise the truth of those quick sentences, 'the winds blow, the lightnings fly, plants spring up, the hoofed cattle are scattered.' Nor is the idea without a certain drastic reality, that Par*g*anya draws a bucket of water from his well in heaven, and pours out skin after skin (in which water was then carried) down upon the earth.

There is even a moral sentiment perceptible in this hymn. 'When the storms roar and the lightnings flash and the rain pours down, even the guiltless trembles, and evildoers are struck down.' Here we clearly see that the poet did not look upon the storm simply as an outbreak of the violence of nature, but that he had a presentiment of a higher will and power which even the guiltless fears; for who, he seems to say, is entirely free from guilt?

If now we ask again, Who is Par*g*anya? or What is Par*g*anya? we can answer that par*g*anya was meant originally for the cloud, so far as it gives rain; but as soon as the idea of a giver arose, the visible cloud became the outward appearance only, or the body of that giver, and the giver himself was somewhere else, we know not where. In some verses Par*g*anya seems to step into the place of Dyaus, the sky, and P*ri*thivî, the earth, is his wife. In other places[1], however, he is the son of Dyaus or the sky, though no thought is given in that early stage to the fact that thus Par*g*anya might seem to be the husband of his

[1] Rig-veda VII. 102, 1.

mother. We saw that even the idea of Indra being the father of his own father did not startle the ancient poets beyond an exclamation that it was a very wonderful thing indeed.

Sometimes Par*g*anya does the work of Indra[1], the Jupiter Pluvius of the Veda; sometimes of Vâyu, the wind, sometimes of Soma, the giver of rain. Yet with all this he is not Dyaus, nor Indra, nor the Maruts, nor Vâyu, nor Soma. He stands by himself, a separate person, a separate god, as we should say—nay, one of the oldest of all the Aryan gods.

His name, par*g*anya, is derived from a root par*g*, which, like its parallel forms par*s* and parsh, must (I think) have had the meaning of sprinkling, irrigating, moistening. An interchange between final *g*, *s*, and sh may, no doubt, seem unusual, but it is not without parallel in Sanskrit. We have, for instance, the roots pi*ñg*, pingere; pish, to rub; pi*s*, to adorn (as in pe*s*as, ποικίλος, &c.); m*ri**g*, to rub, m*r*ish, to rub out, to forget; m*ris*, mulcere.

This very root m*rig* forms its participle as m*r*ish-*t*a, like ya*g*, ish*t*a, and vi*s*, vish*t*a; nay there are roots, such as druh, which optionally take a final lingual or guttural, such as dhru*t* and dhruk[2].

We may therefore compare par*g* in par*g*anya with such words as p*r*ishata, p*r*ishatî, speckled, drop of water[3]; also par*s*u, cloud, p*r*i*s*ni, speckled, cloud, earth; and in Greek πρόξ(ω), περκνός, etc.[4]

---

[1] Rig-veda VIII. 6, 1.

[2] See Max Müller, Sanskrit Grammar, § 174, 10.

[3] Cf. Gobh. G*r*ihya S. III. 3, 15, vidyut—stanayitnu—p*r*ishiteshu.

[4] U*gg*valadatta, in his commentary on the U*n*âdi-sûtras, iii. 103, admits the same transition of sh into *g* in the verb p*r*ish, as the etymon of par*g*anya.

If derived from parg, to sprinkle, Parganya would have meant originally 'he who irrigates or gives rain [1].'

When the different members of the Aryan family dispersed, they might all of them, Hindus as well as Greeks and Celts, and Teutons and Slaves, have carried that name for cloud with them. But you know that it happened very often that out of the common wealth of their ancient language, one and the same word was preserved, as the case might be, not by all, but by only six, or five, or four, or three, or two, or even by one only of the seven principal heirs; and yet, as we know that there was no historical contact between them, after they had once parted from each other, long before the beginning of what we call history, the fact that two of the Aryan languages have preserved the same finished word with the same finished meaning, is proof sufficient that it belonged to the most ancient treasure of Aryan thought.

Now there is no trace, at least no very clear trace, of Parganya, in Greek or Latin or Celtic, or even in Teutonic. In Slavonic, too, we look in vain, till we come to that almost forgotten side-branch called the *Lettic*, comprising the spoken *Lituanian* and *Lettish*, and the now extinct *Old Prussian*. Lituania is no longer an independent state, but it was once, not more than six centuries ago, a Grand Duchy, independent both of Russia and Poland. Its first Grand Duke was Ringold, who ruled from 1235, and his successors made successful conquests against the

[1] For different etymologies, see Bühler, Orient und Occident, i. p. 214; Muir, Original Sanskrit Texts, v. p. 140; Grassmann, in his Dictionary to the Rig-veda, s.v.; Zimmer, Zeitschrift für Deutsches Alterthum, Neue Folge, vii. p. 164.

Russians. In 1368 these grand dukes became kings of Poland, and in 1569 the two countries were united. When Poland was divided between Russia and Prussia, part of Lituania fell to the former, part to the latter. There are still about one million and a half of people who speak Lituanian in Russia and Prussia, while Lettish is spoken by about one million in Curland and Livonia.

The Lituanian language, even as it is now spoken by the common people, contains some extremely primitive grammatical forms—in some cases almost identical with Sanskrit. These forms are all the more curious, because they are but few in number, and the rest of the language has suffered much from the wear and tear of centuries.

Now in that remote Lituanian language we find that our old friend Par*g*anya has taken refuge. There he lives to the present day, while even in India he is almost forgotten, at least in the spoken languages; and there, in Lituania, not many centuries back might be heard among a Christianised or nearly Christianised people, prayers for rain, not very different from that which I translated to you from the Rig-veda. In Lituanian the god of thunder was called *Perkúnas*[1], and the same word is still used in the sense of thunder. In Old Prussian, thunder was *percunos*, and in Lettish to the present day *pérkons* is thunder, god of thunder[2].

---

[1] In order to identify Perkunas with par*g*anya, we must go another step backward, and look upon *g* or g, in the root parg, as a weakening of an original k in park. This, however, is a frequent phonetic process. See Bühler, in Benfey's Orient und Occident, ii. p. 717.

[2] Lituanian perkun-kulke, thunder-bolt, perkuno gaisis, storm. See Voelkel, Die lettischen Sprachreste, 1879, p. 23.

It was, I believe, Grimm who for the first time identified the Vedic Par*g*anya with the Old Slavonic Perûn, the Polish Piorun, the Bohemian Peraun. These words had formerly been derived by Dobrowsky and others from the root peru, I strike. Grimm (Teutonic Mythology, Engl. transl., p. 171) showed that the fuller forms Perkunas, Pehrkons, and Perkunos existed in Lituanian, Lettish, Old Prussian, and that even the Mordvinians had adopted the name Porguini as that of their thunder-god.

Simon Grunau, who finished his chronicle in 1521, speaks of three gods, as worshipped by the Old Prussians, Patollo, Patrimpo, and Perkuno, and he states that Perkuno was invoked 'for storm's sake, that they might have rain and fair weather at the proper time, and thunder and lightning should not injure them [1].'

The following Lituanian prayer has been preserved to us by Lasitzki [2]:

'Check thyself, O Percuna, and do not send misfortune on my field! and I shall give thee this flitch.'

Among the neighbours of the Lets, the Esthonians, who, though un-Aryan in language, have evidently learnt much from their Aryan neighbours, the following prayer was heard [3], addressed by an old peasant

---

[1] 'Perkuno, war der dritte Abgot und man in anruffte umbs gewitters willen, domit sie Regen hatten und schon wetter zu seiner Zeit, und in der Donner und blix kein schaden thett.' Cf. 'Gottesides bei den alten Preussen,' Berlin, 1870, p. 23. The triad of the gods is called Triburti, Tryboze; l. c. p. 29.

[2] Grimm, Teutonic Mythology, p. 175; and Lasitzki (Lasicius) Joannes, De Russorum, Moscovitarum et Tartarorum religione, sacrificiis, nuptiarum et funerum ritu, Spiræ Nemetum, 1582; idem, De Diis Samagitarum.

[3] Grimm, l.c. p. 176, quoting from Joh. Gutslaff, Kurzer Bericht und Unterricht von der falsch heilig genandten bäche in Liefland Wöhhanda, Dorpat, 1644, pp. 362–364.

to their god *Picker* or *Picken*, the god of thunder and rain, as late as the seventeenth century[1]:

'Dear Thunder (woda Picker), we offer to thee an ox that has two horns and four cloven hoofs; we would pray thee for our ploughing and sowing, that our straw be copper-red, our grain golden-yellow. Push elsewhere all the thick black clouds, over great fens, high forests, and wildernesses. But unto us, ploughers and sowers, give a fruitful season and sweet rain. Holy Thunder (pöha Picken), guard our seed-field, that it bear good straw below, good ears above, and good grain within[2].'

Now, I say again, I do not wish you to admire this primitive poetry, primitive, whether it is repeated in the Esthonian fens in the seventeenth century of our era, or sung in the valley of the Indus in the seventeenth century before our era. Let æsthetic critics say what they like about these uncouth poems. I only ask you, Is it not worth a great many poems, to have established this fact, that the same god Par*g*anya, the god of clouds and thunder and lightning and rain, who was invoked in India a thousand years before India was discovered by Alexander, should have been remembered and believed in by Lituanian peasants on the frontier between East Prussia and Russia, not more than two hundred years ago, and should have retained its old name Par*g*anya, which in Sanskrit meant 'showering,' under the form of *Perkuna*, which in Lituanian is a name and a name only, without any etymological meaning at all; nay, should live on, as some scholars assure us,

[1] In modern Esthonian Pitkne, the Finnish Pitcainen (?).

[2] On foreign influences in Esthonian stories, see Ehstnische Märchen, von T. Kreutzwald, 1869, Vorwort (by Schiefner), p. iv.

in an abbreviated form in most Slavonic dialects, namely, in Old Slavonic as *Perun*, in Polish as *Piorun*, in Bohemian as *Peraun*, all meaning thunder or thunder-storm[1]?

Such facts strike me as if we saw the blood suddenly beginning to flow again through the veins of old mummies; or as if the Egyptian statues of black granite were suddenly to begin to speak again. Touched by the rays of modern science the old words—call them mummies or statues—begin indeed to live again, the old names of gods and heroes begin indeed to speak again. All that is old becomes new, all that is new becomes old, and that one word, Par*g*anya, seems, like a charm, to open before our eyes the cave or cottage in which the fathers of the Aryan race, our own fathers,—whether we live on the Baltic or on the Indian Ocean,—are seen gathered together, taking refuge from the buckets of Par*g*anya, and saying: 'Stop now, Par*g*anya; thou hast sent rain; thou hast made the deserts passable, and hast made the plants to grow; and thou hast obtained praise from man.'

We have still to consider the third class of gods, in addition to the gods of the earth and the sky, namely the gods of the highest heaven, more serene in their character than the active and fighting gods of the air and the clouds, and more remote from the eyes of man, and therefore more mysterious in the exercise of their power than the gods of the earth or the air.

The principal deity is here no doubt the bright sky itself, the old *Dyaus*, worshipped as we know by the Aryans before they broke up into separate people and languages, and surviving in Greece as

[1] Note I.

Zeus, in Italy as Jupiter, Heaven-father, and among the Teutonic tribes as *Tŷr* and *Tiu*. In the Veda we saw him chiefly invoked in connection with the earth, as Dyâvâ-prithivî, Heaven and Earth. He is invoked by himself also, but he is a vanishing god, and his place is taken in most of the Vedic poems by the younger and more active god, *Indra*.

Another representative of the highest heaven, as covering, embracing, and shielding all things, is Varuna, a name derived from the root var, to cover, and identical with the Greek *Ouranos*. This god is one of the most interesting creations of the Hindu mind, because though we can still perceive the physical background from which he rises, the vast, starry, brilliant expanse above, his features, more than those of any of the Vedic gods, have become completely transfigured, and he stands before us as a god who watches over the world, punishes the evil-doer, and even forgives the sins of those who implore his pardon.

I shall read you one of the hymns addressed to him[1]:

'Let us be blessed in thy service, O Varuna, for we always think of thee and praise thee, greeting thee day by day, like the fires lighted on the altar, at the approach of the rich dawns.' 2.

'O Varuna, our guide, let us stand in thy keeping, thou who art rich in heroes and praised far and wide! And you, unconquered sons of Aditi, deign to accept us as your friends, O gods!' 3.

'Âditya, the ruler, sent forth these rivers; they follow the law of Varuna. They tire not, they cease not; like birds they fly quickly everywhere.' 4.

---

[1] Rig-veda II. 28.

'Take from me my sin, like a fetter, and we shall increase, O Varu*n*a, the spring of thy law. Let not the thread be cut while I weave my song! Let not the form of the workman break before the time!' 5.

'Take far away from me this terror, O Varu*n*a! Thou, O righteous king, have mercy on me! Like as a rope from a calf, remove from me my sin; for away from thee I am not master even of the twinkling of an eye.' 6.

'Do not strike us, Varu*n*a, with weapons which at thy will hurt the evil-doer. Let us not go where the light has vanished! Scatter our enemies, that we may live.' 7.

'We did formerly, O Varu*n*a, and do now, and shall in future also, sing praises to thee, O mighty one! For on thee, unconquerable hero, rest all statutes, immovable, as if established on a rock.' 8.

'Move far away from me all self-committed guilt, and may I not, O king, suffer for what others have committed! Many dawns have not yet dawned; grant us to live in them, O Varu*n*a.' 9.

You may have observed that in several verses of this hymn Varu*n*a was called Âditya, or son of Aditi. Now Aditi means *infinitude*, from *dita*, bound, and *a*, not, that is, not bound, not limited, absolute, infinite. Aditi itself is now and then invoked in the Veda, as the Beyond, as what is beyond the earth and the sky, and the sun and the dawn—a most surprising conception in that early period of religious thought. More frequently, however, than Aditi, we meet with the Âdityas, literally the sons of Aditi, or the gods beyond the visible earth and sky,—in one sense, the infinite gods. One of them is Varu*n*a, others Mitra and Aryaman (Bhaga, Daksha, A*m*sa), most of them abstract names, though pointing to heaven and the solar light of heaven as their first, though almost forgotten source.

When Mitra and Varu*n*a are invoked together, we can still perceive dimly that they were meant originally for day and night, light and darkness. But in their more personal and so to say dramatic aspect, day and night appear in the Vedic mythology as the two Asvins, the two horsemen.

Aditi, too, the infinite, still shows a few traces of her being originally connected with the boundless Dawn; but again, in her more personal and dramatic character, the Dawn is praised by the Vedic poets as Ushas, the Greek Eos, the beautiful maid of the morning, loved by the Asvins, loved by the sun, but vanishing before him at the very moment when he tries to embrace her with his golden rays. The sun himself, whom we saw reflected several times before in some of the divine personifications of the air and the sky and even of the earth, appears once more in his full personality, as the sun of the sky, under the names of Sûrya (Helios), Savit*ri*, Pûshan, and Vish*n*u, and many more.

You see from all this how great a mistake it would be to attempt to reduce the whole of Aryan mythology to solar concepts, and to solar concepts only. We have seen how largely the earth, the air, and the sky have each contributed their share to the earliest religious and mythological treasury of the Vedic Aryans. Nevertheless, the Sun occupied in that ancient collection of Aryan thought, which we call Mythology, the same central and commanding position which, under different names, it still holds in our own thoughts.

What we call the Morning, the ancient Aryans called the Sun or the Dawn; 'and there is no solemnity so deep to a rightly thinking creature as that of the Dawn.' (These are not my words, but the words of one of our greatest poets, one of the truest worshippers of Nature—John Ruskin.) What we call Noon, and Evening, and Night, what we call Spring and Winter, what we call Year, and Time, and Life, and Eternity—all this the ancient Aryans called *Sun*. And yet wise people wonder and say, how curious that the ancient Aryans should have had so many solar myths. Why, every time we say 'Good Morning,' we commit a solar myth. Every poet who sings about 'the May driving the Winter from the field again' commits a solar myth. Every 'Christmas Number' of our newspapers—ringing out the old year and ringing in the new—is brimfull of solar myths. Be not afraid of solar myths, but whenever in ancient mythology you meet with a name that, according to the strictest phonetic rules (for this is a *sine qua non*), can be traced back to a word meaning sun, or dawn, or morning, or night, or spring or winter, accept it for what it was meant to be, and do not be greatly surprised, if a story told of a solar eponymos was originally a solar myth.

No one has more strongly protested against the extravagances of Comparative Mythologists in changing everything into solar legends, than I have; but if I read some of the arguments brought forward against this new science, I confess they remind me of nothing so much as of the arguments brought forward, centuries ago, against the existence of Antipodes! People then appealed to what is called Common Sense, which ought to teach everybody that Antipodes could not possibly exist, because they would tumble off. The best answer that astronomers could give, was, 'Go and see.' And I can give no better answer to those learned sceptics who try to ridicule the Science of Comparative Mythology—'Go and see!' that is, go and read the Veda, and before you have finished the first Ma*nd*ala, I can promise you, you will no longer shake your wise heads at solar myths, whether in India, or in Greece, or in Italy, or even in England, where we see so little of the sun, and talk all the more about the weather—that is, about a solar myth.

We have thus seen from the hymns and prayers preserved to us in the Rig-veda, how a large number of so-called Devas, bright and sunny beings, or gods, were called into existence, how the whole world was peopled with them, and every act of nature, whether on the earth or in the air or in the highest heaven, ascribed to their agency. When we say, *it* thunders, they said Indra thunders; when we say, *it* rains, they said Par*g*anya pours out his buckets; when we say, *it* dawns, they said the beautiful Ushas appears like a dancer, displaying her splendour; when we say, *it* grows dark, they said Sûrya unharnesses his steeds. The whole of nature was alive to the poets of the Veda, the presence of the gods was felt everywhere, and in that sentiment of the presence of the gods there was a germ of religious morality, sufficiently strong, it would seem, to restrain people from committing as it were before the eyes of their gods what they were ashamed to commit before the eyes of men. When speaking of Varu*n*a, the old god of the sky, one poet says[1]:

'Varu*n*a, the great lord of these worlds, sees as

[1] Atharva-veda IV. 16.

if he were near. If a man stands or walks or hides, if he goes to lie down or to get up, what two people sitting together whisper to each other, King Varu*n*a knows it, he is there as the third[1]. This earth, too, belongs to Varu*n*a, the King, and this wide sky with its ends far apart. The two seas (the sky and the ocean) are Varu*n*a's loins; he is also contained in this small drop of water. He who should flee far beyond the sky, even he would not be rid of Varu*n*a, the King[2]. His spies proceed from heaven towards this world; with thousand eyes they overlook this earth. King Varu*n*a sees all this, what is between heaven and earth, and what is beyond. He has counted the twinklings of the eyes of men. As a player throws down the dice, he settles all things (irrevocably). May all thy fatal snares which stand spread out seven by seven and threefold, catch the man who tells a lie, may they pass by him who speaks the truth.'

You see this is as beautiful, and in some respects as true, as anything in the Psalms. And yet we know that there never was such a Deva, or god, or such a thing as Varu*n*a. We know it is a mere name, meaning originally 'covering or all-embracing,' which was applied to the visible starry sky, and afterwards, by a process perfectly intelligible, developed into the name of a Being, endowed with human and superhuman qualities.

---

[1] Psalm cxxxix. 1, 2, 'O Lord, thou hast searched me and known me. Thou knowest my downsitting and mine uprising, thou understandest my thought afar off.'

[2] Psalm cxxxix. 9, 'If I take the wings of the morning, and dwell in the uttermost parts of the sea; even there shall thy hand lead me, and thy right hand shall hold me.'

And what applies to Varu*n*a applies to all the other gods of the Veda and the Vedic religion, whether three in number, or thirty-three, or, as one poet said, 'three thousand three hundred and thirty-nine gods[1].' They are all but names, quite as much as Jupiter and Apollo and Minerva; in fact, quite as much as all the gods of every religion who are called by such appellative titles.

Possibly, if any one had said this during the Vedic age in India, or even during the Periklean age in Greece, he would have been called, like Sokrates, a blasphemer or an atheist. And yet nothing can be clearer or truer, and we shall see that some of the poets of the Veda too, and, still more, the later Vedântic philosopher, had a clear insight that it was so.

Only let us be careful in the use of that phrase 'it is a mere name.' No name is a mere name. Every name was originally meant for something; only it often failed to express what it was meant to express, and then became a weak or an empty name, or what we then call 'a mere name.' So it was with these names of the Vedic gods. They were all meant to express the *Beyond*, the Invisible behind the Visible, the Infinite within the Finite, the Supernatural above the Natural, the Divine, omnipresent, and omnipotent. They failed in expressing what, by its very nature, must always remain inexpressible. But that Inexpressible itself remained, and in spite of all these failures, it never succumbed, or vanished from the mind of the ancient thinkers and poets, but always called for new and better names, nay calls for them even now, and will call for them to the very end of man's existence upon earth.

---

[1] Rig-veda III. 9, 9; X. 52, 6.

VEDA AND VEDÂNTA.

LECTURE VII.

I DO not wonder that I should have been asked by some of my hearers to devote part of my last lecture to answering the question, how the Vedic literature could have been composed and preserved, if writing was unknown in India before 500 B.C., while the hymns of the Rig-veda are said to date from 1500 B.C. Classical scholars naturally ask what is the date of our oldest MSS. of the Rig-veda, and what is the evidence on which so high an antiquity is assigned to its contents. I shall try to answer this question as well as I can, and I shall begin with a humble confession that the oldest MSS. of the Rig-veda, known to us at present, date not from 1500 B.C. but from about 1500 A.D.

We have therefore a gap of three thousand years, which it will require a strong arch of argument to bridge over.

But that is not all.

You may know how, in the beginning of this century, when the age of the Homeric poems was discussed, a German scholar, Frederick August Wolf, asked two momentous questions :—

1. At what time did the Greeks first become acquainted with the alphabet and use it for inscrip-

tions on public monuments, coins, shields, and for contracts, both public and private[1]?

2. At what time did the Greeks first think of using writing for literary purposes, and what materials did they employ for that purpose?

These two questions and the answers they elicited threw quite a new light on the nebulous periods of Greek literature. A fact more firmly established than any other in the ancient history of Greece is that the Ionians learnt the alphabet from the Phenicians. The Ionians always called their letters Phenician letters[2], and the very name of Alphabet was a Phenician word. We can well understand that the Phenicians should have taught the Ionians in Asia Minor a knowledge of the alphabet, partly for commercial purposes, i.e. for making contracts, partly for enabling them to use those useful little sheets, called *Periplus*, or *Circumnavigations*, which at that time were as precious to sailors as maps were to the adventurous seamen of the middle ages. But from that to a written literature, in our sense of the word, there is still a wide step. It is well known that the Germans, particularly in the North, had their Runes for inscriptions on tombs, goblets, public monuments, but not for literary purposes[3]. Even if a few Ionians at Miletus and other centres of political and commercial life acquired the art of

[1] On the early use of letters for public inscriptions, see Hayman, Journal of Philology, 1879, pp. 141, 142, 150; Hicks, Manual of Greek Historical Inscriptions, pp. 1 seqq.

[2] Herod. (v. 59) says: 'I saw Phenician letters on certain tripods in a temple of the Ismenian Apollo at Thebes in Bœotia, the most of them like the Ionian letters.'

[3] Munch, Die Nordisch Germanischen Völker, p. 240.

writing, where could they find writing materials? and, still more important, where could they find readers? The Ionians, when they began to write, had to be satisfied with a hide or pieces of leather, which they called *diphthera*, and until that was brought to the perfection of vellum or parchment, the occupation of an author cannot have been very agreeable [1].

So far as we know at present the Ionians began to write about the middle of the sixth century B.C.; and, whatever may have been said to the contrary, Wolf's *dictum* stills holds good that with them the beginning of a written literature was the same as the beginning of prose writing.

Writing at that time was an effort, and such an effort was made for some great purpose only. Hence the first written skins were what we should call Murray's Handbooks, called *Periegesis* or *Periodos*, or, if treating of sea-voyages, *Periplus*, that is, guide-books, books to lead travellers round a country or round a town. Connected with these itineraries were the accounts of the foundations of cities, the *Ktisis*. Such books existed in Asia Minor during the sixth and fifth centuries, and their writers were called by a general term, *Logographi*, or λόγιοι or λογοποιοί[2], as opposed to ἀοιδοί, the poets. They were the forerunners of the Greek historians, and Herodotus (443 B.C.), the so-called father of history, made frequent use of their works.

---

[1] Herod. (v. 58) says: 'The Ionians from of old call βύβλος διφθέραι, because once, in default of the former, they used to employ the latter. And even down to my own time, many of the barbarians write on such diphtheræ.'

[2] Hekatæos and Kadmos of Miletos (520 B.C.), Charon of Lampsakos (504 B.C.), Xanthos the Lydian (463 B.C.), Pherekydes of Leros (480 B.C.), Hellanikos of Mitylene (450 B.C), &c.

The whole of this incipient literary activity belonged to Asia Minor. From 'Guides through towns and countries,' literature seems to have spread at an early time to Guides through life, or philosophical dicta, such as are ascribed to Anaximander the Ionian (610–547 B.C.[1]), and Pherekydes the Syrian (540 B.C.). These names carry us into the broad daylight of history, for Anaximander was the teacher of Anaximenes, Anaximenes of Anaxagoras, and Anaxagoras of Perikles. At that time writing was a recognised art, and its cultivation had been rendered possible chiefly through trade with Egypt and the importation of *papyros*. In the time of Æschylos (500 B.C.) the idea of writing had become so familiar that he could use it again and again in poetical metaphors[2], and there seems little reason why we should doubt that both Peisistratos (528 B.C.) and Polykrates of Samos (523 B.C.) were among the first collectors of Greek manuscripts.

In this manner the simple questions asked by Wolf helped to reduce the history of ancient Greek literature to some kind of order, particularly with reference to its first beginnings.

It would therefore seem but reasonable that the two first questions to be asked by the students of Sanskrit literature should have been :—

1. At what time did the people of India become acquainted with an alphabet ?

2. At what time did they first use such alphabet for literary purposes ?

Curiously enough, however, these questions remained in abeyance for a long time, and, as a

[1] Lewis, Astronomy, p. 92.

[2] See Hayman, Journal of Philology, 1879, p. 139.

consequence, it was impossible to introduce even the first elements of order into the chaos of ancient Sanskrit literature[1].

I can here state a few facts only. There are no inscriptions to be found anywhere in India before the middle of the third century B.C. These inscriptions are Buddhist, put up during the reign of Asoka, the grandson of *K*andragupta, who was the contemporary of Seleucus, and at whose court in Patalibothra Megasthenes lived as ambassador of Seleucus. Here, as you see, we are on historical ground. In fact, there is little doubt that Asoka, the king who put up these inscriptions in several parts of his vast kingdom, reigned from 259–222 B.C.

These inscriptions are written in two alphabets—one written from right to left, and clearly derived from an Aramæan, that is, a Semitic alphabet; the other written from left to right, and clearly an adaptation, and an artificial or systematic adaptation, of a Semitic alphabet to the requirements of an Indian language. That second alphabet became the source of all Indian alphabets, and of many alphabets carried chiefly by Buddhist teachers far beyond the limits of India, though it is possible that the earliest Tamil alphabet may have been directly derived from the same Semitic source which supplied both the *dextrorsum* and the *sinistrorsum* alphabets of India.

Here then we have the first fact, viz. that writing, even for monumental purposes, was unknown in India before the third century B.C.

But writing for commercial purposes was known

[1] See M. M., History of Ancient Sanskrit Literature, pp. 497 seqq., 'On the Introduction of Writing in India.'

in India before that time. Megasthenes was no doubt quite right when he said that the Indians did not know letters[1], that their laws were not written, and that they administered justice from memory. But Nearchus, the admiral of Alexander the Great, who sailed down the Indus (325 B.C.), and was therefore brought in contact with the merchants frequenting the maritime stations of India, was probably equally right in declaring that 'the Indians wrote letters on cotton that had been well beaten together.' These were no doubt commercial documents, contracts, it may be, with Phenician or Egyptian captains, and they would prove nothing as to the existence in India at that time of what we mean by a written literature. In fact, Nearchus himself affirms what Megasthenes said after him, namely that 'the laws of the sophists in India were not written.' If, at the same time, the Greek travellers in India speak of mile-stones, and of cattle marked by the Indians with various signs and also with numbers, all this would perfectly agree with what we know from other sources, that though the art of writing may have reached India before the time of Alexander's conquest, its employment for literary purposes cannot date from a much earlier time.

Here then we are brought face to face with a most startling fact. Writing was unknown in India before the fourth century before Christ, and yet we are asked to believe that the Vedic literature in its three well-defined periods, the Mantra, Brâhma*n*a, and Sûtra periods, goes back to at least a thousand years before our era.

---

[1] M. M., History of Ancient Sanskrit Literature, p. 515.

Now the Rig-veda alone, which contains a collection of ten books of hymns addressed to various deities, consists of 1017 (1028) poems, 10,580 verses, and about 153,826 words[1]. How were these poems composed—for they are composed in very perfect metre—and how, after having been composed, were they handed down from 1500 before Christ to 1500 after Christ, the time to which most of our best Sanskrit MSS. belong?

Entirely by memory. This may sound startling, but—what will sound still more startling, and yet is a fact that can easily be ascertained by anybody who doubts it—at the present moment, if every MS. of the Rig-veda were lost, we should be able to recover the whole of it—from the memory of the *S*rotriyas in India. These native students learn the Veda by heart, and they learn it from the mouth of their Guru, never from a MS., still less from my printed edition,—and after a time they teach it again to their pupils.

I have had such students in my room at Oxford, who not only could repeat these hymns, but who repeated them with the proper accents (for the Vedic Sanskrit has accents like Greek), nay who, when looking through my printed edition of the Rig-veda, could point out a misprint without the slightest hesitation.

I can tell you more. There are hardly any various readings in our MSS. of the Rig-veda, but various schools in India have their own readings of certain passages, and they hand down those readings with great care. So, instead of collating MSS., as we do in Greek and Latin, I have asked some friends of

---

[1] M. M., Hibbert Lectures, p. 153.

mine to collate those Vedic students, who carry their own Rig-veda in their memory, and to let me have the various readings from these living authorities.

Here then we are not dealing with theories, but with facts, which anybody may verify. The whole of the Rig-veda, and a great deal more, still exists at the present moment in the oral tradition of a number of scholars who, if they liked, could write down every letter, and every accent, exactly as we find them in our old MSS.

Of course, this learning by heart is carried on under a strict discipline; it is, in fact, considered as a sacred duty. A native friend of mine, himself a very distinguished Vedic scholar, tells me that a boy, who is to be brought up as a student of the Rig-veda, has to spend about eight years in the house of his teacher. He has to learn ten books: first, the hymns of the Rig-veda; then a prose treatise on sacrifices, called the Brâhma*n*a; then the so-called Forest-book or Âra*n*yaka; then the rules on domestic ceremonies; and lastly, six treatises on pronunciation, grammar, etymology, metre, astronomy, and ceremonial.

These ten books it has been calculated contain nearly 30,000 lines, each line reckoned as thirty-two syllables.

A pupil studies every day, during the eight years of his theological apprenticeship, except on the holidays, which are called 'non-reading days.' There being 360 days in a lunar year, the eight years would give him 2880 days. Deduct from this 384 holidays, and you get 2496 working days during the eight years. If you divide the number of lines, 30,000, by the number of working days, you get about twelve lines to be learnt each day, though much time is taken up, in addition, for practising and rehearsing what has been learnt before.

Now this is the state of things at present, though I doubt whether it will last much longer, and I always impress on my friends in India, and therefore impress on those also who will soon be settled as Civil Servants in India, the duty of trying to learn all that can still be learnt from those living libraries. Much ancient Sanskrit lore will be lost for ever when that race of *S*rotriyas becomes extinct.

But now let us look back. About a thousand years ago a Chinese, of the name of I-tsing, a Buddhist, went to India to learn Sanskrit, in order to be able to translate some of the sacred books of his own religion, which were originally written in Sanskrit, into Chinese. He left China in 671, arrived at Tâmralipti in India in 673, and went to the great College and Monastery of Nâlanda, where he studied Sanskrit. He returned to China in 695, and died in 703[1].

In one of his works which we still possess in Chinese, he gives an account of what he saw in India, not only among his own co-religionists, the Buddhists, but likewise among the Brâhmans[2].

Of the Buddhist priests he says that after they have learnt to recite the five and the ten precepts, they are taught the 400 hymns of Mâ*tri*k*e*ta, and afterward the 150 hymns of the same poet. When they are able to recite these, they begin the study of

---

[1] See my article on the date of the Kâsikâ in the Indian Antiquary, 1880, p. 305.

[2] The translation of the most important passages in I-tsing's work was made for me by one of my Japanese pupils, K. Kasawara.

the Sûtras of their Sacred Canon. They also learn by heart the *G*âtakamâlâ[1], which gives an account of Buddha in former states of existence. Speaking of what he calls the islands of the Southern Sea, which he visited after leaving India, I-tsing says: 'There are more than ten islands in the South Sea. There both priests and laymen recite the *G*âtakamâlâ, as they recite the hymns mentioned before; but it has not yet been translated into Chinese.'

One of these stories, he proceeds to say, was versified by a king (*K*ié-zhih) and set to music, and was performed before the public with a band and dancing —evidently a Buddhist mystery play.

I-tsing then gives a short account of the system of education. Children, he says, learn the forty-nine letters and the 10,000 compound letters when they are six years old, and generally finish them in half a year. This corresponds to about 300 verses, each *s*loka of thirty-two syllables. It was originally taught by Mahe*s*vara. At eight years, children begin to learn the grammar of Pâ*n*ini, and know it after about eight months. It consists of 1000 *s*lokas, called Sûtras.

Then follows the list of roots (dhâtu) and the three appendices (khila), consisting again of 1000 *s*lokas. Boys begin the three appendices when they are ten years old, and finish them in three years.

When they have reached the age of fifteen, they begin to study a commentary on the grammar (Sûtra) and spend five years on learning it. And here I-tsing gives the following advice to his countrymen, many

[1] See Bunyiu Nanjio's Catalogue of the Chinese Tripi*t*aka, p. 372, where Âryasûra, who must have lived before 434 A.D., is mentioned as the author of the *G*âtakamâlâ.

of whom came to India to learn Sanskrit, but seem to have learnt it very imperfectly. 'If men of China,' he writes, 'go to India, wishing to study there, they should first of all learn these grammatical works, and then only other subjects; if not, they will merely waste their labour. These works should be learnt by heart. But this is suited for men of high quality only. . . . They should study hard day and night, without letting a moment pass for idle repose. They should be like Confucius, through whose hard study the binding of his Yih-king was three times cut asunder, being worn away; and like Sui-shih, who used to read a book repeatedly one hundred times.' Then follows a remark, more intelligible in Chinese than in English: 'The hairs of a bull are counted by thousands, the horn of a unicorn is only one.'

I-tsing then speaks of the high degree of perfection to which the memory of these students attained, both among Buddhists and heretics. 'Such men,' he says, 'could commit to memory the contents of two volumes learning them only once.'

And then turning to the *heretics*, or what we should call the orthodox Brahmans, he says: 'The Brâhma*n*as are regarded throughout the five divisions of India as the most respectable. They do not walk with the other three castes, and other mixed classes of people are still further dissociated from them. They revere their Scriptures, the four Vedas, containing about 100,000 verses. . . . The Vedas are handed down from mouth to mouth, not written on paper. There are in every generation some intelligent Brâhmans who can recite those 100,000 verses. . . . I myself saw such men.'

Here then we have an eye-witness who, in the

seventh century after Christ, visited India, learnt Sanskrit, and spent about twenty years in different monasteries—a man who had no theories of his own about oral tradition, but who, on the contrary, as coming from China, was quite familiar with the idea of a written, nay, of a printed literature:—and yet what does he say? 'The Vedas are not written on paper, but handed down from mouth to mouth.'

Now, I do not quite agree here with I-tsing. At all events, we must not conclude from what he says that there existed no Sanskrit MSS. at all at his time. We know they existed. We know that in the first century of our era Sanskrit MSS. were carried from India to China and translated there. Most likely therefore there were MSS. of the Veda also in existence. But I-tsing, for all that, was right in supposing that these MSS. were not allowed to be used by students, and that they had always to learn the Veda by heart and from the mouth of a properly qualified teacher. The very fact that in the later law-books severe punishments are threatened against persons who copy the Veda or learn it from a MS., shows that MSS. existed, and that their existence interfered seriously with the ancient privileges of the Brâhmans, as the only legitimate teachers of their sacred scriptures.

If now, after having heard this account of I-tsing, we go back for about another thousand years, we shall feel less sceptical in accepting the evidence which we find in the so-called Prâtisâkhyas, that is, collections of rules which, so far as we know at present, go back to the fifth century before our era, and which tell us almost exactly the same as what we can see in India at the present moment, namely that the education of children of the three twice-born castes, the Brâhma*n*as, Kshatriyas, and Vaisyas, consisted in their passing at least eight years in the house of a Guru, and learning by heart the ancient Vedic hymns.

The art of teaching had even at that early time been reduced to a perfect system, and at that time certainly there is not the slightest trace of anything, such as a book, or skin, or parchment, a sheet of paper, pen or ink, being known even by name to the people of India; while every expression connected with what we should call literature, points to a literature (we cannot help using that word) existing in memory only, and being handed down with the most scrupulous care by means of oral tradition.

I had to enter into these details because I know that, with our ideas of literature, it requires an effort to imagine the bare possibility of a large amount of poetry, and still more of prose, existing in any but a written form. And yet here too we only see what we see elsewhere, namely that man, before the great discoveries of civilisation were made, was able by greater individual efforts to achieve what to us, accustomed to easier contrivances, seems almost impossible. So-called savages were able to chip flints, to get fire by rubbing sticks of wood, which baffles our handiest workmen. Are we to suppose that, if they wished to preserve some songs which, as they believed, had once secured them the favour of their gods, had brought rain from heaven, or led them on to victory, they would have found no means of doing so? We have only to read such accounts as, for instance, Mr. William Wyatt Gill has given us in his 'Historical Sketches of Savage Life in Polynesia [1],' to see how

[1] Wellington, 1880.

anxious even savages are to preserve the records of their ancient heroes, kings, and gods, particularly when the dignity or nobility of certain families depends on these songs, or when they contain what might be called the title-deeds to large estates. And that the Vedic Indians were not the only savages of antiquity who discovered the means of preserving a large literature by means of oral tradition, we may learn from Cæsar[1], not a very credulous witness, who tells us that the 'Druids were said to know a large number of verses by heart; that some of them spent twenty years in learning them, and that they considered it wrong to commit them to writing'—exactly the same story which we hear in India.

We must return once more to the question of dates. We have traced the existence of the Veda, as handed down by oral tradition, from our days to the days of I-tsing in the seventh century after Christ, and again to the period of the Prâtisâkhyas, in the fifth century before Christ.

In that fifth century B.C. took place the rise of Buddhism, a religion built up on the ruins of the Vedic religion, and founded, so to say, on the denial of the divine authority ascribed to the Veda by all orthodox Brâhmans.

Whatever exists therefore of Vedic literature must be accommodated within the centuries preceding the rise of Buddhism, and if I tell you that there are three periods of Vedic literature to be accommodated, the third presupposing the second, and the second the first, and that even that first period presents us with

[1] De Bello Gall. vi. 14; History of Ancient Sanskrit Literature, p. 506.

a collection, and a systematic collection of Vedic hymns, I think you will agree with me that it is from no desire for an extreme antiquity, but simply from a respect for facts, that students of the Veda have come to the conclusion that these hymns, of which the MSS. do not carry us back beyond the fifteenth century after Christ, took their origin in the fifteenth century before Christ.

One fact I must mention once more, because I think it may carry conviction even against the stoutest scepticism.

I mentioned that the earliest inscriptions discovered in India belong to the reign of King Asoka, the grandson of *K*andragupta, who reigned from 259–222 before Christ. What is the language of those inscriptions? Is it the Sanskrit of the Vedic hymns? Certainly not. Is it the later Sanskrit of the Brâhma*n*as and Sûtras? Certainly not. These inscriptions are written in the local dialects as then spoken in India, and these local dialects differ from the grammatical Sanskrit about as much as Italian does from Latin.

What follows from this? First, that the archaic Sanskrit of the Veda had ceased to be spoken before the third century B.C. Secondly, that even the later grammatical Sanskrit was no longer spoken and understood by the people at large; that Sanskrit therefore had ceased, nay, we may say, had long ceased to be the spoken language of the country when Buddhism arose, and that therefore the youth and manhood of the ancient Vedic language lie far beyond the period that gave birth to the teaching of Buddha, who, though he may have known Sanskrit, and even Vedic Sanskrit, insisted again and again on the duty that his disciples should preach his doctrines in the language of the people whom they wished to benefit.

And now, when the time allotted to me is nearly at an end, I find, as it always happens, that I have not been able to say one half of what I hoped to say as to the lessons to be learnt by us in India, even with regard to this one branch of human knowledge only, the study of the origin of religion. I hope, however, I may have succeeded in showing you the entirely new aspect which the old problem of the *theogony*, or the origin and growth of the Devas or gods, assumes from the light thrown upon it by the Veda. Instead of positive theories, we now have positive facts, such as you look for in vain anywhere else; and though there is still a considerable interval between the Devas of the Veda, even in their highest form, and such concepts as Zeus, Apollon, and Athene, yet the chief riddle is solved, and we know now at last what stuff the gods of the ancient world were made of.

But this theogonic process is but one side of the ancient Vedic religion, and there are two other sides of at least the same importance and of even a deeper interest to us.

There are in fact three religions in the Veda, or, if I may say so, three naves in one great temple, reared, as it were, before our eyes by poets, prophets, and philosophers. Here, too, we can watch the work and the workmen. We have not to deal with hard formulas only, with unintelligible ceremonies, or petrified fetishes. We can see how the human mind arrives by a perfectly rational process at all its later irrationalities. This is what distinguishes the Veda from all other Sacred Books. Much, no doubt, in the Veda also, and in the Vedic ceremonial, is already old and unintelligible, hard and petrified. But in many cases the development of names and concepts, their transition from the natural to the supernatural, from the individual to the general, is still going on, and it is for that very reason that we find it so difficult, nay almost impossible, to translate the growing thoughts of the Veda into the full-grown and more than full-grown language of our time.

Let us take one of the oldest words for god in the Veda, such as deva, the Latin *deus*. The dictionaries tell you that deva means god and gods, and so, no doubt, it does. But if we always translated deva in the Vedic hymns by god, we should not be translating, but completely transforming the thoughts of the Vedic poets. I do not mean only that *our* idea of God is totally different from the idea that was intended to be expressed by deva; but even the Greek and Roman concept of gods would be totally inadequate to convey the thoughts imbedded in the Vedic deva. Deva meant originally bright, and nothing else. Meaning bright, it was constantly used of the sky, the stars, the sun, the dawn, the day, the spring, the rivers, the earth; and when a poet wished to speak of all of these by one and the same word—by what we should call a general term—he called them all Devas. When that had been done, Deva did no longer mean 'the Bright ones,' but the name comprehended all the qualities which the sky and the sun and the dawn shared in common, excluding only those that were peculiar to each.

Here you see how, by the simplest process, the Devas, the bright ones, might become and did become the Devas, the heavenly, the kind, the powerful, the invisible, the immortal—and, in the end, something very like the θεοί (or *dii*) of Greeks and Romans.

In this way one Beyond, the Beyond of Nature, was built up in the ancient religion of the Veda, and peopled with Devas, and Asuras, and Vasus, and Âdityas, all names for the bright solar, celestial, diurnal, and vernal powers of nature, without altogether excluding, however, even the dark and unfriendly powers, those of the night, of the dark clouds, or of winter, capable of mischief, but always destined in the end to succumb to the valour and strength of their bright antagonists.

We now come to the second nave of the Vedic temple, the second *Beyond* that was dimly perceived, and grasped and named by the ancient Rishis, namely the world of the Departed Spirits.

There was in India, as elsewhere, another very early faith, springing up naturally in the hearts of the people, that their fathers and mothers, when they departed this life, departed to a Beyond, wherever it might be, either in the East from whence all the bright Devas seemed to come, or more commonly in the West, the land to which they seemed to go, called in the Veda the realm of Yama or the setting sun. The idea that beings which once had been, could ever cease to be, had not yet entered their minds; and from the belief that their fathers existed somewhere, though they could see them no more, there arose the belief in another Beyond, and the germs of another religion.

Nor was the actual power of the fathers quite imperceptible or extinct even after their death. Their presence continued to be felt in the ancient laws and customs of the family, most of which rested on their will and their authority. While their fathers were alive and strong, their will was law; and when, after their death, doubts or disputes arose on points of law or custom, it was but natural that the memory and the authority of the fathers should be appealed to to settle such points—that the law should still be their will.

Thus Manu says (IV. 178): 'On the path on which his fathers and grandfathers have walked, on that path of good men let him walk, and he will not go wrong.'

In the same manner then in which, out of the bright powers of nature, the Devas or gods had arisen, there arose out of predicates shared in common by the departed, such as pitris, fathers, preta, gone away, another general concept, what we should call *Manes*, the kind ones, *Ancestors, Shades, Spirits* or *Ghosts*, whose worship was nowhere more fully developed than in India. That common name, Pitris or *Fathers*, gradually attracted towards itself all that the fathers shared in common. It came to mean not only fathers, but invisible, kind, powerful, immortal, heavenly beings, and we can watch in the Veda, better perhaps than anywhere else, the inevitable, yet most touching metamorphosis of ancient thought,—the love of the child for father and mother becoming transfigured into an instinctive belief in the immortality of the soul.

It is strange, and really more than strange, that not only should this important and prominent side of the ancient religion of the Hindus have been ignored, but that of late its very existence should have been doubted. I feel obliged, therefore, to add a few words in support of what I have said just now of the supreme importance of this belief in and this worship of ancestral spirits in India from the most ancient to the most modern times. Mr. Herbert Spencer, who has done so much in calling attention to ancestor-worship as a natural ingredient of religion among all savage nations, declares in the most emphatic manner[1], 'that he has seen it implied, that he has heard it in conversation, and that he now has it before him in print, that no Indo-European or Semitic nation, so far as we know, seems to have made a religion of the worship of the dead.' I do not doubt his words, but I think that on so important a point, Mr. Herbert Spencer ought to have named his authorities. It seems to me almost impossible that anybody who has ever opened a book on India should have made such a statement. There are hymns in the Rig-veda addressed to the Fathers. There are full descriptions of the worship due to the Fathers in the Brâhma*n*as and Sûtras. The epic poems, the law books, the Purâ*n*as, all are brimful of allusions to ancestral offerings. The whole social fabric of India, with its laws of inheritance and marriage[2], rests on a belief in the Manes,—and yet we are told that no Indo-European nation seems to have made a religion of the worship of the dead.

The Persians had their Fravashis, the Greeks their *εἴδωλα*, or rather their *θεοὶ πατρῷοι* and their *δαίμονες*,

> *ἐσθλοὶ, ἐπιχθόνιοι, φύλακες θνητῶν ἀνθρώπων·*
> *οἵ ῥα φυλάσσουσίν τε δίκας καὶ σχέτλια ἔργα,*
> *ἠέρα ἑσσάμενοι πάντη φοιτῶντες ἐπ' αἶαν,*
> *πλουτοδόται* (Hesiodi Opera et Dies, vv. 122–126);

---

[1] Principles of Sociology, p. 313.

[2] 'The Hindu Law of Inheritance is based upon the Hindu religion, and we must be cautious that in administering Hindu law we do not, by acting upon our notions derived from English law, inadvertently wound or offend the religious feelings of those who may be affected by our decisions.' Bengal Law Reports, 103.

while among the Romans the *Lares familiares* and the *Divi Manes* were worshipped more zealously than any other gods [1]. Manu goes so far as to tell us in one place (III. 203): 'An oblation by Brâhmans to their ancestors transcends an oblation to the deities;' and yet we are told that no Indo-European nation seems to have made a religion of the worship of the dead.

Such things ought really not to be, if there is to be any progress in historical research, and I cannot help thinking that what Mr. Herbert Spencer meant was probably no more than that some scholars did not admit that the worship of the dead formed the whole of the religion of any of the Indo-European nations. That, no doubt, is perfectly true, but it would be equally true, I believe, of almost any other religion. And on this point again the students of anthropology will learn more, I believe, from the Veda than from any other book.

In the Veda the Pit*r*is, or fathers, are invoked together with the Devas, or gods, but they are not confounded with them. The Devas never become Pit*r*is, and though such adjectives as deva are sometimes applied to the Pit*r*is, and they are raised to the rank of the older classes of Devas (Manu III. 192, 284, Yâ*g*ñavalkya I. 268), it is easy to see that the Pit*r*is and Devas had each their independent origin, and that they represent two totally distinct phases of the human mind in the creation of its objects of worship. This is a lesson which ought never to be forgotten.

We read in the Rig-veda, VI. 52, 4: 'May the rising Dawns protect me, may the flowing Rivers

[1] Cicero, De Leg. II. 9, 22, 'Deorum manium jura sancta sunto; nos leto datos divos habento.'

protect me, may the firm Mountains protect me, may the Fathers protect me at this invocation of the gods.' Here nothing can be clearer than the separate existence of the Fathers, apart from the Dawns, the Rivers, and the Mountains, though they are included in one common Devahûti, or invocation of the gods.

We must distinguish, however, from the very first, between two classes, or rather between two concepts of Fathers, the one comprising the distant, half-forgotten, and almost mythical ancestors of certain families or of what would have been to the poets of the Veda, the whole human race, the other consisting of the fathers who had but lately departed, and who were still, as it were, personally remembered and revered.

The old ancestors in general approach more nearly to the gods. They are often represented as having gone to the abode of Yama, the ruler of the departed, and to live there in company with some of the Devas (Rig-veda VII. 76, 4, devânâ*m* sadhamâda*h*; Rig-veda X. 16, 1, devânâ*m* vasanî*h*).

We sometimes read of the great-grandfathers being in heaven, the grandfathers in the sky, the fathers on the earth, the first in company with the Âdityas, the second with the Rudras, the last with the Vasus. All these are individual poetical conceptions[1].

Yama himself is sometimes invoked as if he were one of the Fathers, the first of mortals that died or that trod the path of the Fathers (the pit*ri*yâ*n*a, X. 2, 7) leading to the common sunset in the West[2].

---

[1] See Atharva-veda XVIII. 2, 49.

[2] Rig-veda X. 14, 1–2. He is called Vaivasvata, the solar (X. 58, 1), and even the son of Vivasvat (X. 14, 5). In a later phase

Still his real Deva-like nature is never completely lost, and, as the god of the setting sun, he is indeed the leader of the Fathers, but not one of the Fathers himself[1].

Many of the benefits which men enjoyed on earth were referred to the Fathers, as having first been procured and first enjoyed by them. They performed the first sacrifices, and secured the benefits arising from them. Even the great events in nature, such as the rising of the sun, the light of the day and the darkness of the night, were sometimes referred to them, and they were praised for having broken open the dark stable of the morning and having brought out the cows, that is, the days (X. 68, 11)[2]. They were even praised for having adorned the night with stars, while in later writings the stars are said to be the lights of the good people who have entered into heaven[3]. Similar ideas, we know, prevailed among the ancient Persians, Greeks, and Romans. The Fathers are called in the Veda truthful (satyá), wise (suvidátra), righteous (*ri*távat), poets (kaví), leaders (pathik*rí*t), and one of their most frequent epithets is somya, delighting in Soma, Soma being the ancient intoxicating beverage of the Vedic *Ri*shis, which was believed to bestow immortality[4], but which had been lost, or at all events had become

---

of religious thought Yama is conceived as the first man (Atharva-veda XVIII. 3, 13, as compared with Rig-veda X. 14, 1).

[1] Rig-veda X. 14.

[2] In the Avesta many of these things are done by Ahura Mazda with the help of the Fravashis.

[3] See *S*atapatha Brâhma*n*a I. 9, 3, 10; VI. 5, 4, 8.

[4] Rig-veda VIII. 48, 3: 'We drank Soma, we became immortal, we went to the light, we found the gods;' VIII. 48, 12.

difficult to obtain by the Aryans, after their migration into the Punjâb[1].

The families of the Bh*ri*gus, the Aṅgiras, the Atharvans[2] all have their Pit*ri*s or Fathers, who are invoked to sit down on the grass and to accept the offerings placed there for them. Even the name of Pit*ri*ya*g*ña, sacrifice of the Fathers, occurs already in the hymns of the Rig-veda[3].

The following is one of the hymns of the Rig-veda by which those ancient Fathers were invited to come to their sacrifice (Rig-veda X. 15)[4]:—

1. 'May the Soma-loving Fathers, the lowest, the highest, and the middle, arise. May the gentle and righteous Fathers who have come to life (again), protect us in these invocations!

2. 'May this salutation be for the Fathers to-day, for those who have departed before or after; whether they now dwell in the sky above the earth, or among the blessed people.

3. 'I invited the wise Fathers . . . . may they come hither quickly, and sitting on the grass readily partake of the poured-out draught!

4. 'Come hither to us with your help, you Fathers who sit on the grass! We have prepared these libations for you, accept them! Come hither with your most blessed protection, and give us health and wealth without fail!

5. 'The Soma-loving Fathers have been called hither to their dear viands which are placed on the grass. Let them approach, let them listen, let them bless, let them protect us!

---

[1] Rig-veda IX. 97, 39. [2] Ibid. X. 14, 6. [3] Ibid. X. 16, 10.

[4] A translation considerably differing from my own is given by Sarvâdhikâri in his Tagore Lectures for 1880, p. 34.

6. 'Bending your knee and sitting on my right accept all this sacrifice. Do not hurt us, O Fathers, for any wrong that we may have committed against you, men as we are.

7. 'When you sit down on the lap of the red dawns, grant wealth to the generous mortal! O Fathers, give of your treasure to the sons of this man here, and bestow vigour here on us!

8. 'May Yama, as a friend with friends, consume the offerings according to his wish, united with those old Soma-loving Fathers of ours, the Vasish*th*as, who arranged the Soma draught.

9. 'Come hither, O Agni, with those wise and truthful Fathers who like to sit down near the hearth, who thirsted when yearning for the gods, who knew the sacrifice, and who were strong in praise with their songs.

10. 'Come, O Agni, with those ancient fathers who like to sit down near the hearth, who for ever praise the gods, the truthful, who eat and drink our oblations, making company with Indra and the gods.

11. 'O Fathers, you who have been consumed by Agni, come here, sit down on your seats, you kind guides! Eat of the offerings which we have placed on the turf, and then grant us wealth and strong offspring!

12. 'O Agni, O *G*âtavedas[1], at our request thou hast carried the offerings, having first rendered them sweet. Thou gavest them to the Fathers, and they fed on their share. Eat also, O god, the proffered oblations!

13. 'The Fathers who are here, and the Fathers who are not here, those whom we know, and those

[1] Cf. Max Müller, Rig-veda, transl. vol. i. p. 24.

whom we know not, thou, *G*âtavedas, knowest how many they are, accept the well-made sacrifice with the sacrifical portions!

14. 'To those who, whether burnt by fire or not burnt by fire, rejoice in their share in the midst of heaven, grant thou, O King, that their body may take that life which they wish for[1]!'

Distinct from the worship offered to these primitive ancestors, is the reverence which from an early time was felt to be due by children to their departed father, soon also to their grandfather, and great-grandfather. The ceremonies in which these more personal feelings found expression were of a more domestic character, and allowed therefore of greater local variety.

It would be quite impossible to give here even an abstract only of the minute regulations which have been preserved to us in the Brâhma*n*as, the *S*rauta, G*ri*hya, and Sâmayâ*k*ârika Sûtras, the Law-books, and a mass of latter manuals on the performance of endless rites, all intended to honour the Departed. Such are the minute prescriptions as to times and seasons, as to altars and offerings, as to the number and shape of the sacrificial vessels, as to the proper postures of the sacrificers, and the different arrangements of the vessels, that it is extremely difficult to catch hold of what we really care for, namely, the thoughts and intentions of those who first devised all these intricacies. Much has been written on this class of sacrifices by European scholars also, beginning with Colebrooke's excellent essays on 'The Religious Ceremonies of the Hindus,' first published in

[1] Note K.

the Asiatic Researches, vol. v, Calcutta, 1798. But when we ask the simple question, What was the thought from whence all this outward ceremonial sprang, and what was the natural craving of the human heart which it seemed to satisfy, we hardly get an intelligible answer anywhere. It is true that *S*râddhas continue to be performed all over India to the present day, but we know how widely the modern ceremonial has diverged from the rules laid down in the old *S*âstras, and it is quite clear from the descriptions given to us by recent travellers that no one can understand the purport even of these survivals of the old ceremonial, unless he understands Sanskrit and can read the old Sûtras. We are indeed told in full detail how the cakes were made which the Spirits were supposed to eat, how many stalks of grass were to be used on which they had to be offered, how long each stalk ought to be, and in what direction it should be held. All the things which teach us nothing are explained to us in abundance, but the few things which the true scholar really cares for are passed over, as if they had no interest to us at all, and have to be discovered under heaps of rubbish.

In order to gain a little light, I think we ought to distinguish between—

1. The daily ancestral sacrifice, the Pit*ri*ya*gñ*a, as one of the five Great Sacrifices (Mahâya*gñ*as);

2. The monthly ancestral sacrifice, the Pi*nd*a-pit*ri*-ya*gñ*a, as part of the New and Full-moon sacrifice;

3. The funeral ceremonies on the death of a householder;

4. The Agapes, or feasts of love and charity, commonly called *S*râddhas, at which food and other charitable gifts were bestowed on deserving persons

in memory of the deceased ancestors. The name of *S*râddha belongs properly to this last class only, but it has been transferred to the second and third class of sacrifices also, because *S*râddha formed an important part in them.

The daily Pit*ri*ya*gñ*a or Ancestor-worship is one of the five sacrifices, sometimes called the Great Sacrifices[1], which every married man ought to perform day by day. They are mentioned in the G*ri*hya-sûtras (Â*s*v. III. 1), as Devaya*gñ*a, for the Devas, Bhûtaya*gñ*a, for animals &c., Pit*ri*ya*gñ*a, for the Fathers, Brahmaya*gñ*a, for Brahman, i.e. study of the Veda, and Manushyaya*gñ*a, for men, i.e. hospitality, &c.

Manu (III. 70) tells us the same, namely, that a married man has five great religious duties to perform :—

1. The Brahma-sacrifice, i.e. the studying and teaching of the Veda (sometimes called Ahuta).

2. The Pit*ri*-sacrifice, i.e. the offering of cakes and water to the Manes (sometimes called Prâ*s*ita).

3. The Deva-sacrifice, i.e. the offering of oblations to the Gods (sometimes called Huta).

4. The Bhûta-sacrifice, i.e. the giving of food to living creatures (sometimes called Prahuta).

5. The Manushya-sacrifice, i.e. the receiving of guests with hospitality (sometimes called Brâhmya huta[2]).

The performance of this daily Pit*ri*ya*gñ*a seems to

---

[1] *S*atapatha Brâhma*n*a XI. 5, 6, 1; Taitt. Âr. II. 11, 10; Â*s*valâyana G*ri*hya-sûtras III. 1, 1; Pâraskara G*ri*hya-sûtras II. 9, 1; Âpastamba, Dharma-sûtras, translated by Bühler, pp. 47 seq.

[2] In the *S*âṅkhâyana G*ri*hya (I. 5) four Pâka-ya*gñ*as are mentioned, called Huta, ahuta, prahuta, prâ*s*ita.

have been extremely simple. The householder had to put his sacred cord on the right shoulder, to say 'Svadhâ to the Fathers,' and to throw the remains of certain offerings towards the South[1].

The human impulse to this sacrifice, if sacrifice it can be called, is clear enough. The five 'great sacrifices' comprehended in early times the whole duty of man from day to day. They were connected with his daily meal[2]. When this meal was preparing, and before he could touch it himself, he was to offer something to the Gods, a Vaisvadeva offering[3], in which the chief deities were Agni, fire, Soma the Visve Devas, Dhanvantari, a kind of Aesculapius, Kuhû and Anumati (phases of the moon), Pra*g*âpati, lord of creatures, Dyâvâ-p*ri*thivî, Heaven and Earth, and Svish*t*ak*ri*t, the fire on the hearth.

After having thus satisfied the Gods in the four quarters, the householder had to throw some oblations into the open air, which were intended for animals, and in some cases for invisible beings, ghosts and such like. Then he was to remember the Departed, the Pit*ri*s, with some offerings; but even after having done this he was not yet to begin his own repast, unless he had also given something to strangers (atithis).

When all this had been fulfilled, and when, besides, the householder, as we should say, had said his daily prayers, or repeated what he had learnt of the Veda, then and then only was he in harmony with the world that surrounded him, the five Great Sacrifices had been performed by him, and he was free from all the sins arising from a thoughtless and selfish life.

---

[1] Âsv. G*ri*hya-sûtras I. 3, 10.
[2] Manu III. 117–118.
[3] Manu III. 85.

This Pit*ri*yag*ñ*a, as one of the five daily sacrifices, is described in the Brâhma*n*as, the G*ri*hya and Sâmayâ*k*ârika Sûtras, and, of course, in the legal Sa*m*hitâs. Rajendralâl Mitra[1] informs us that 'orthodox Brâhmans to this day profess to observe all these five ceremonies, but that in reality only the offerings to the gods and manes are strictly observed, while the reading is completed by the repetition of the Gâyatrî only, and charity and feeding of animals are casual and uncertain.'

Quite different from this simple daily ancestral offering is the Pit*ri*yag*ñ*a or Pi*nd*a-pit*ri*yag*ñ*a, which forms part of many of the statutable sacrifices, and, first of all, of the New and Full-Moon sacrifice. Here again the human motive is intelligible enough. It was the contemplation of the regular course of nature, the discovery of order in the coming and going of the heavenly bodies, the growing confidence in some ruling power of the world which lifted man's thoughts from his daily work to higher regions, and filled his heart with a desire to approach these higher powers with praise, thanksgiving, and offerings. And it was at such moments as the waning of the moon that his thoughts would most naturally turn to those whose life had waned, whose bright faces were no longer visible on earth, his fathers or ancestors. Therefore at the very beginning of the New-Moon sacrifice, we are told in the Brâhma*n*as[2] and in the *S*rauta-sûtras, that a Pit*ri*yag*ñ*a, a sacrifice to the Fathers, has to be performed. A *K*aru

[1] Taittirîyâra*n*yaka, Preface, p. 23.

[2] Mâsi mâsi vo'*s*anam iti *s*rute*h*; Gobhilîya G*ri*hya-sûtras, p. 1055.

or pie had to be prepared in the Dakshi*n*âgni, the southern fire, and the offerings, consisting of water and round cakes (pi*nd*as), were specially dedicated to father, grandfather, and great-grandfather, while the wife of the sacrificer, if she wished for a son, was allowed to eat one of the cakes [1].

Similar ancestral offerings took place during other sacrifices too, of which the New and Full-Moon sacrifices form the general type.

It may be quite true that these two kinds of ancestral sacrifices have the same object and share the same name, but their character is different; and if, as has often been the case, they are mixed up together, we lose the most important lessons which a study of the ancient ceremonial should teach us. I cannot describe the difference between these two Pit*ri*ya*gñ*as more decisively than by pointing out that the former was performed by the father of a family, or, if we may say so, by a layman, the latter by a regular priest, or a class of priests, selected by the sacrificer to act in his behalf. As the Hindus themselves would put it, the former is a g*ri*hya, a domestic, the latter a *s*rauta, a priestly ceremony [2].

We now come to a third class of ceremonies which are likewise domestic and personal, but which differ

---

[1] See Pi*nd*apit*ri*ya*gñ*a, von Dr. O. Donner, 1870. The restriction to three ancestors, father, grandfather, and great-grandfather, occurs in the Vâ*g*asaneyi-sa*m*hitâ, XIX. 36–37.

[2] There is, however, great variety in these matters, according to different *s*âkhâs. Thus, according to the Gobhila-*s*âkhâ, the Pi*nd*a Pit*ri*ya*gñ*a is to be considered as smârta, not as *s*rauta (pi*nd*a-pit*ri*ya*gñ*a*h* khalv asma*kkh*âkhâyâ*m* nâsti); while others maintain that an agnimat should perform the smârta, a *s*rautâgnimat the *s*rauta Pit*ri*ya*gñ*a; see Gobhilîya G*ri*hya-sûtras, p. 671. On page 667 we read: anagner amâvasyâ*s*raddhâ, nânvâhâryam ity âdara*n*iyam.

from the two preceding ceremonies by their occasional character, I mean the funeral, as distinct from the ancestral ceremonies. In one respect these funeral ceremonies may represent an earlier phase of worship than the daily and monthly ancestral sacrifices. They lead up to them, and, as it were, prepare the departed for their future dignity as Pit*ri*s or Ancestors. On the other hand, the conception of Ancestors in general must have existed before any departed person could have been raised to that rank, and I therefore preferred to describe the ancestral sacrifices first.

Nor need I enter here very fully into the character of the special funeral ceremonies of India. I described them in a special paper, 'On Sepulture and Sacrificial Customs in the Veda,' nearly thirty years ago[1]. Their spirit is the same as that of the funeral ceremonies of Greeks, Romans, Slavonic, and Teutonic nations, and the coincidences between them all are often most surprising.

In Vedic times the people in India both burnt and buried their dead, and they did this with a certain solemnity, and, after a time, according to fixed rules. Their ideas about the status of the departed, after their body had been burnt and their ashes buried, varied considerably, but in the main they seem to have believed in a life to come, not very different from our life on earth, and in the power of the departed to confer blessings on their descendants. It soon therefore became the interest of the survivors to secure the favour of their departed friends by observances and offerings which, at first,

[1] Über Todtenbestattung und Opfergebräuche im Veda, in Zeitschrift der Deutschen Morgenländischen Gesellschaft, vol. ix, 1856.

were the spontaneous manifestation of human feelings, but which soon became traditional, technical, in fact, ritual.

On the day on which the corpse had been burnt, the relatives (samânodakas) bathed and poured out a handfull of water to the deceased, pronouncing his name and that of his family [1]. At sunset they returned home, and, as was but natural, they were told to cook nothing during the first night, and to observe certain rules during the next day up to ten days, according to the character of the deceased. These were days of mourning, or, as they were afterwards called, days of impurity, when the mourners withdrew from contact with the world, and shrank by a natural impulse from the ordinary occupations and pleasures of life [2].

Then followed the collecting of the ashes on the 11th, 13th or 15th day of the dark half of the moon. On returning from thence they bathed, and then offered what was called a *S*râddha to the departed.

This word *S*râddha, which meets us here for the first time, is full of interesting lessons, if only properly understood. First of all it should be noted that it is absent, not only from the hymns, but, so far as we know at present, even from the ancient Brâhma*n*as. It seems therefore a word of a more modern origin. There is a passage in Âpastamba's Dharma-sûtras which betrays, on the part of the author, a consciousness of the more modern origin of the *S*râddhas [3]:—

---

[1] Â*s*valâyana G*ri*hya-sûtras IV. 4, 10. [2] Manu V. 64–65.

[3] Bühler, Âpastamba, Sacred Books of the East, vol. ii. p. 138; also *S*râddhâkalpa, p. 890. Though the *S*râddha is prescribed in the Gobhilîya G*ri*hya-sûtras, IV. 4, 2–3, it is not described there, but in a separate treatise, the *S*râddha-kalpa.

'Formerly men and gods lived together in this world. Then the gods in reward of their sacrifices went to heaven, but men were left behind. Those men who perform sacrifices in the same manner as the gods did, dwelt (after death) with the gods and Brahman in heaven. Now (seeing men left behind) Manu revealed this ceremony which is designated by the word *S*râddha.'

Srâddha has assumed many[1] meanings, and Manu[2], for instance, uses it almost synonymously with pit*ri*-ya*gñ*a. But its original meaning seems to have been 'that which is given with *s*raddhâ or faith,' i.e. charity bestowed on deserving persons, and, more particularly, on Brâhma*n*as. The gift was called *s*râddha, but the act itself also was called by the same name. The word is best explained by Nârâya*n*a in his commentary on the G*ri*hya-sûtras of Â*s*valâyana (IV. 7), '*S*râddha is that which is given in faith to Brâhmans for the sake of the Fathers[3].'

Such charitable gifts flowed most naturally and abundantly at the time of a man's death, or whenever his memory was revived by happy or unhappy events in a family, and hence *S*râddha has become the general name for ever so many sacred acts com-

---

[1] As meaning the food, *s*râddha occurs in *s*râddhabhu*g* and similar words. As meaning the sacrificial act, it is explained, yatraita*k* *kh*raddhayâ dîyate tad eva karma *s*râddha*s*abdâbhidheyam. Pretam pit*rîm*s *k*a nirdi*s*ya bho*g*ya*m* yat priyam âtmana*h* *s*raddhayâ dîyate yatra ta*k* *kh*râddham parikîrtitam. Gobhilîya G*ri*hya-sûtras, p. 892. We also read *s*raddhânvita*h* *s*râddha*m* kurvîta, 'let a man perform the *s*râddha with faith;' Gobhilîya G*ri*hya-sûtras, p. 1053.

[2] Manu III. 82.

[3] Pit*r*în uddi*s*ya yad dîyate brâhma*n*ebhya*h* *s*raddhayâ ta*k* *kh*râddham.

memorative of the departed. We hear of *S*râddhas not only at funerals, but at joyous events also, when presents were bestowed in the name of the family, and therefore in the name of the ancestors also, on all who had a right to that distinction.

It is a mistake therefore to look upon *S*râddhas simply as offerings of water or cakes to the Fathers. An offering to the Fathers was, no doubt, a symbolic part of each *S*râddha, but its more important character was charity bestowed in memory of the Fathers.

This, in time, gave rise to much abuse, like the alms bestowed on the Church during the Middle Ages. But in the beginning the motive was excellent. It was simply a wish to benefit others, arising from the conviction, felt more strongly in the presence of death than at any other time, that as we can carry nothing out of this world, we ought to do as much good as possible in the world with our worldly goods. At *S*râddhas the Brâhma*n*as were said to represent the sacrificial fire into which the gifts should be thrown[1]. If we translate here Brâhma*n*as by priests, we can easily understand why there should have been in later times so strong a feeling against *S*râddhas. But priest is a very bad rendering of Brâhma*n*a. The Brâhma*n*as were, socially and intellectually, a class of men of high breeding. They were a recognised and, no doubt, a most essential element in the ancient society of India. As they lived for others, and were excluded from most of the lucrative pursuits of life, it was a social, and it soon became a religious duty, that they should be supported by the community at large. Great care was taken that

---

[1] Âpastamba II. 16, 3, Brâhma*n*âs tv âhavanîyârthe.

the recipients of such bounty as was bestowed at *S*râddhas should be strangers, neither friends nor enemies, and in no way related to the family. Thus Âpastamba says[1]: 'The food eaten (at a *S*râddha) by persons related to the giver is a gift offered to goblins. It reaches neither the Manes nor the Gods.' A man who tried to curry favour by bestowing *S*râddhika gifts, was called by an opprobrious name, a *S*râddha-mitra[2].

Without denying therefore that in later times the system of *S*râddhas may have degenerated, I think we can perceive that it sprang from a pure source, and, what for our present purpose is even more important, from an intelligible source.

Let us now return to the passage in the G*ri*hya-sûtras of Â*s*valâyana, where we met for the first time with the name of *S*râddha[3]. It was the *S*râddha to be given for the sake of the Departed, after his ashes had been collected in an urn and buried. This *S*râddha is called ekoddish*t*a[4], or, as we should say, personal. It was meant for one person only, not for the three ancestors, nor for all the ancestors. Its object was in fact to raise the departed to the rank of a Pit*ri*, and this had to be achieved by *S*râddha offerings continued during a whole year. This at least is the general, and, most likely, the original rule. Âpastamba says that the *S*râddha for a deceased relative should be performed every day during the year, and that after that a monthly *S*râddha only should be performed or none at all, that is, no more

---

[1] L. c. p. 142. [2] Manu III. 138, 140.

[3] Â*s*v. G*ri*hya-sûtras IV. 5, 8.

[4] It is described as a vik*ri*ti of the Pârva*n*a-*s*râddha in Gobhilîya G*ri*hya-sûtras, p. 1011.

personal *S*râddha [1], because the departed shares henceforth in the regular Pârva*n*a-*s*râddhas [2]. *S*âṅkhâyana says the same [3], namely that the personal *S*râddha lasts for a year, and that then 'the Fourth' is dropped, i.e. the great-grandfather was dropped, the grandfather became the great-grandfather, the father the grandfather, while the lately Departed occupied the father's place among the three principal Pit*ri*s [4]. This was called the Sapi*nd*îkara*n*a, i.e. the elevating of the departed to the rank of an ancestor.

There are here, as elsewhere, many exceptions. Gobhila allows six months instead of a year, or even a Tripaksha [5], i.e. three half-months; and lastly, any auspicious event (v*ri*ddhi) may become the occasion of the Sapi*nd*îkara*n*a [6].

The full number of *S*râddhas necessary for the Sapi*nd*ana is sometimes given as sixteen, viz. the first, then one in each of the twelve months, then two semestral ones, and lastly the Sapi*nd*ana. But here too much variety is allowed, though, if the Sapi*nd*ana takes place before the end of the year, the number of sixteen *S*râddhas has still to be made up [7].

---

[1] One of the differences between the acts before and after the Sapi*nd*îkara*n*a is noted by Sâlaṅkâyana:—Sapi*nd*îkara*n*am yâvad *ri*gudarbhai*h* pit*ri*kriyâ Sapi*nd*îkara*n*âd ûrdhva*m* dvigu*n*air vidhivad bhavet. Gobhilîya G*ri*hya-sûtras, p. 930.

[2] Gobhilîya G*ri*hya-sûtras, p. 1023.

[3] G*ri*hya-sûtras, ed. Oldenberg, p. 83.

[4] A pratyâbdikam ekoddish*t*am on the anniversary of the deceased is mentioned by Gobhilîya, l. c. p. 1011.

[5] Gobhilîya G*ri*hya-sûtras, p. 1039.

[6] *S*âṅkh. G*ri*hya, p. 83; Gobh. G*ri*hya, p. 1024. According to some authorities the ekoddish*t*a is called nava, new, during ten days; navami*s*ra, mixed, for six months; and purâ*n*a, old, afterwards. Gobhilîya G*ri*hya-sûtras, p. 1020.

[7] Gobhilîya, l. c. p. 1032.

When the *S*râddha is offered on account of an auspicious event, such as a birth or a marriage, the fathers invoked are not the father, grandfather, and great-grandfather, who are sometimes called asru-mukha, with tearful faces, but the ancestors before them, and they are called nândîmukha, or joyful[1].

Colebrooke[2], to whom we owe an excellent description of what a *S*râddha is in modern times, took evidently the same view. 'The first set of funeral ceremonies,' he writes, 'is adapted to effect, by means of oblations, the re-imbodying of the soul of the deceased, after burning his corpse. The apparent scope of the second set is to raise his shade from this world, where it would else, according to the notions of the Hindus, continue to roam among demons and evil spirits, up to heaven, and then deify him, as it were, among the manes of departed ancestors. For this end, a *S*râddha should regularly be offered to the deceased on the day after the mourning expires; twelve other *S*râddhas *singly* to the deceased in twelve successive months; similar obsequies at the end of the third fortnight, and also in the sixth month, and in the twelfth; and the oblation called Sapi*nd*ana on the first anniversary of his decease[3]. At this Sapi*nd*ana *S*râddha, which is the last of the ekoddish*t*a srâddhas, four funeral cakes are offered to the deceased and his three ancestors,

[1] Gobhilîya, l. c. p. 1047. [2] Life and Essays, ii. p. 195.

[3] Colebrooke adds that in most provinces the periods for these sixteen ceremonies, and for the concluding obsequies entitled Sapi*nd*ana, are anticipated, and the whole is completed on the second or third day; after which they are again performed at the proper times, but in honour of the whole set of progenitors instead of the deceased singly. It is this which Dr. Donner, in his learned paper on the Pi*nd*apit*ri*yag*ñ*a (p. 11), takes as the general rule.

that consecrated to the deceased being divided into three portions and mixed with the other three cakes. The portion retained is often offered to the deceased, and the act of union and fellowship becomes complete[1].'

When this system of *S*râddhas had once been started, it seems to have spread very rapidly. We soon hear of the monthly *S*râddha, not only in memory of one person lately deceased, but as part of the Pit*ri*ya*gñ*a, and as obligatory, not only on householders (agnimat), but on other persons also, and, not only on the three upper castes, but even, without hymns, on *S*ûdras[2], and as to be performed, not only on the day of New-Moon, but on other days also[3], whenever there was an opportunity. Gobhila seems to look upon the Pi*nd*apit*ri*ya*gñ*a as itself a *S*râddha[4], and the commentator holds that, even if there are no pi*nd*as or cakes, the Brâhmans ought still to be fed. This *S*râddha, however, is distinguished from the other, the true *S*râddha, called Anvâhârya, which follows it[5], and which is properly known by the name of Pârva*n*a *S*râddha.

The same difficulties which confront us when we try to form a clear conception of the character of the various ancestral ceremonies, were felt by the Brâh-

[1] See this subject most exhaustively treated, particularly in its bearings on the law of inheritance, in Rajkumar Sarvâdhikâri's Tagore Law Lectures for 1880, p. 93.

[2] Gobhilîya G*ri*hya-sûtras, p. 892.

[3] L. c. p. 897.

[4] See p. 666, and p. 1008. G*ri*hyakâra*h* pi*nd*apit*ri*ya*gñ*asya *s*râddhatvam âha.

[5] Gobhila IV. 4, 3, itarad anvâhâryam. But the commentators add, anagner amâvasyâ*s*râddham, nânvâhâryam. According to Gobhila there ought to be the Vai*s*vadeva offering and the Bali offering at the end of each Pârva*n*a-*s*râddha; see Gobhilîya G*ri*hya-sûtras, p. 1005, but no Vai*s*vadeva at an ekoddish*t*a *s*râddha, l. c. p. 1020.

mans themselves, as may be seen from the long discussions in the commentary on the *S*râddha-kalpa [1] and from the abusive language used by *K*andrakânta Tarkâlaṅkâra against Raghunandana. The question with them assumes the form of what is pradhâna (primary) and what is aṅga (secondary) in these sacrifices, and the final result arrived at is that sometimes the offering of cakes is pradhâna, as in the Pi*nd*apit*ri*ya*gñ*a, sometimes the feeding of Brâhmans only, as in the Nitya-*s*râddha, sometimes both, as in the Sapi*nd*îkara*n*a.

We may safely say, therefore, that not a day passed in the life of the ancient people of India on which they were not reminded of their ancestors, both near and distant, and showed their respect for them, partly by symbolic offerings to the Manes, partly by charitable gifts to deserving persons, chiefly Brâhmans. These offertories varied from the simplest, such as milk and fruits, to the costliest, such as gold and jewels. The feasts given to those who were invited to officiate or assist at a *S*râddha seem in some cases to have been very sumptuous [2], and what is very important, the eating of meat, which in later times was strictly forbidden in many sects, must, when the Sûtras were written, have been fully recognised at these feasts, even to the killing and eating of a cow [3].

This shows that these *S*râddhas, though possibly of later date than the Pit*ri*ya*gñ*as, belong nevertheless to a very early phase of Indian life. And though

---

[1] L. c. pp. 1005–1010; Nirnayasindhu, p. 270.

[2] See Burnell, The Law of Partition, p. 31.

[3] Kalau tâvad gavâlambho mâ*m*sadâna*m* *k*a *s*râddhe nishiddham, Gobhilena tu madhyamâsh*t*akâyâ*m* vâstukarma*n*i *k*a gavâlambho vihita*h*, mâ*m*sa*k*aru*s* *k*ânvash*t*akya*s*râddhe; Gobhilîya G*ri*hya-sûtra, ed. *K*andrakânta Tarkâlaṅkâra, Vi*gñ*apti, p. 8.

much may have been changed in the outward form of these ancient ancestral sacrifices, their original solemn character has remained unchanged. Even at present, when the worship of the ancient Devas is ridiculed by many who still take part in it, the worship of the ancestors and the offering of *S*râddhas have maintained much of their old sacred character. They have sometimes been compared to the 'communion' in the Christian Church, and it is certainly true that many natives speak of their funeral and ancestral ceremonies with a hushed voice and with real reverence. They alone seem still to impart to their life on earth a deeper significance and a higher prospect. I could go even a step further and express my belief, that the absence of such services for the dead and of ancestral commemorations is a real loss in our own religion. Almost every religion recognises them as tokens of a loving memory offered to a father, to a mother, or even to a child, and though in many countries they may have proved a source of superstition, there runs through them all a deep well of living human faith that ought never to be allowed to perish. The early Christian Church had to sanction the ancient prayers for the Souls of the Departed, and in more Southern countries the services on All Saints' and on All Souls' Day continue to satisfy a craving of the human heart which must be satisfied in every religion. We, in the North, shrink from these open manifestations of grief, but our hearts know often a deeper bitterness; nay, there would seem to be a higher truth than we at first imagine in the belief of the ancients that the souls of our beloved ones leave us no rest, unless they are appeased by daily prayers, or, better still, by daily acts of goodness in remembrance of them [1].

[1] Note L.

But there is still another Beyond that found expression in the ancient religion of India. Besides the Devas or Gods, and besides the Pit*ri*s or Fathers, there was a third world, without which the ancient religion of India could not have become what we see it in the Veda. That third Beyond was what the poets of the Veda call the *Ri*ta, and which I believe meant originally no more than 'the straight line.' It is applied to the straight line of the sun in its daily course, to the straight line followed by day and night, to the straight line that regulates the seasons, to the straight line which, in spite of many momentary deviations, was discovered to run through the whole realm of nature. We call that *Ri*ta, that straight, direct, or right line, when we apply it in a more general sense, *the Law of Nature;* and when we apply it to the moral world, we try to express the same idea again by speaking of the *Moral Law,* the law on which our life is founded, the eternal Law of Right and Reason, or, it may be, 'that which makes for righteousness' both within us and without [1].

And thus, as a thoughtful look on nature led to the first perception of bright gods, and in the end of a God of light, as love of our parents was transfigured into piety and a belief in immortality, a recognition of the straight lines in the world without, and in the world within, was raised into the highest faith, a faith in a law that underlies everything, a law in which we may trust, whatever befall, a law which speaks within us with the divine voice of conscience, and tells us 'this is *ri*ta,' 'this is right,' 'this is true,' whatever the statutes of our ancestors, or even the voices of our bright gods, may say to the contrary.

[1] See Hibbert Lectures, new ed. pp. 243–255.

These three Beyonds are the three revelations of antiquity; and it is due almost entirely to the discovery of the Veda that we, in this nineteenth century of ours, have been allowed to watch again these early phases of thought and religion, which had passed away long before the beginnings of other literatures[1]. In the Veda an ancient city has been laid bare before our eyes which, in the history of all other religions, is filled up with rubbish, and built over by new architects. Some of the earliest and most instructive scenes of our distant childhood have risen once more above the horizon of our memory which, until thirty or forty years ago, seemed to have vanished for ever.

Only a few words more to indicate at least how this religious growth in India contained at the same time the germs of Indian philosophy. Philosophy in India is, what it ought to be, not the denial, but the fulfilment of religion; it is the highest religion, and the oldest name of the oldest system of philosophy in India is Vedânta, that is, the end, the goal, the highest object of the Veda.

Let us return once more to that ancient theologian who lived in the fifth century B. C., and who told us that, even before his time, all the gods had been discovered to be but three gods, the gods of the *Earth*, the gods of the *Air*, and the gods of the *Sky*, invoked under various names. The same writer tells us that in reality there is but *one* God, but he does not call

---

[1] In Chinese we find that the same three aspects of religion and their intimate relationship were recognised, as, for instance, when Confucius says to the Prince of Sung: 'Honour the sky (worship of Devas), reverence the Manes (worship of Pitris); if you do this, sun and moon will keep their appointed time (*Rita*).' Happel, Altchinesische Reichsreligion, p. 11.

him the Lord, or the Highest God, the Creator, Ruler and Preserver of all things, but he calls him Âtman, THE SELF. The one Âtman or Self, he says, is praised in many ways owing to the greatness of the godhead. And he then goes on to say: 'The other gods are but so many members of the one Âtman, Self, and thus it has been said that the poets compose their praises according to the multiplicity of the natures of the beings whom they praise.'

It is true, no doubt, that this is the language of a philosophical theologian, not of an ancient poet. Yet these philosophical reflections belong to the fifth century before our era, if not to an earlier date; and the first germs of such thoughts may be discovered in some of the Vedic hymns also. I have quoted already from the hymns such passages as[1]—'They speak of Mitra, Varu*n*a, Agni; then he is the heavenly bird Garutmat; *that which is and is one* the poets call in various ways; they speak of Yama, Agni, Mâtari*s*van.'

In another hymn, in which the sun is likened to a bird, we read: 'Wise poets represent by their words the bird who is one, in many ways[2].'

All this is still tinged with mythology; but there are other passages from which a purer light beams upon us, as when one poet asks[3]:

'Who saw him when he was first born, when he who has no bones bore him who has bones? Where was the breath, the blood, the Self of the world? Who went to ask this from any that knew it?'

Here, too, the expression is still helpless, but

---

[1] Rig-veda I. 164, 46; Hibbert Lectures, p. 311.

[2] Rig-veda X. 114, 5; Hibbert Lectures, p. 313.

[3] Rig-veda I. 164, 4.

though the flesh is weak, the spirit is very willing. The expression 'He who has bones' is meant for that which has assumed consistency and form, the Visible, as opposed to that which has no bones, no body, no form, the Invisible, while 'breath, blood, and self of the world' are but so many attempts at finding names and concepts for what is by necessity inconceivable, and therefore unnameable.

In the second period of Vedic literature, in the so-called Brâhma*n*as, and more particularly in what is called the Upanishads, or the Vedânta portion, these thoughts advance to perfect clearness and definiteness. Here the development of religious thought, which took its beginning in the hymns, attains to its fulfilment. The circle becomes complete. Instead of comprehending the One by many names, the many names are now comprehended to be the One. The old names are openly discarded; even such titles as Pra*g*âpati, lord of creatures, Visvakarman, maker of all things, Dhât*ri*, creator, are put aside as inadequate. The name now used is an expression of nothing but the purest and highest subjectiveness,—it is Âtman, the Self, far more abstract than our Ego,—the Self of all things, the Self of all the old mythological gods—for they were not *mere* names, but names intended for something—lastly, the Self in which each individual self must find rest, must come to himself, must find his own true Self.

You may remember that I spoke to you in my first lecture of a boy who insisted on being sacrificed by his father, and who, when he came to Yama, the ruler of the departed, was granted three boons, and who then requested, as his third boon, that Yama should tell him what became of man after death.

That dialogue forms part of one of the Upanishads, it belongs to the Vedânta, the end of the Veda, the highest aim of the Veda. I shall read you a few extracts from it.

Yama, the King of the Departed, says:

'Men who are fools, dwelling in ignorance, though wise in their own sight, and puffed up with vain knowledge, go round and round, staggering to and fro, like blind led by the blind.

'The future never rises before the eyes of the careless child, deluded by the delusions of wealth. *This* is the world, he thinks; there is no other; thus he falls again and again under my sway (the sway of death).

'The wise, who by means of meditating on his *Self*, recognises the Old (the old man within) who is difficult to see, who has entered into darkness, who is hidden in the cave, who dwells in the abyss, as God, he indeed leaves joy and sorrow far behind.

'That Self, the Knower, is not born, it dies not; it came from nothing, it never became anything. The Old man is unborn, from everlasting to everlasting; he is not killed, though the body be killed.

'That Self is smaller than small, greater than great; hidden in the heart of the creature. A man who has no more desires and no more griefs, sees the majesty of the Self by the grace of the creator.

'Though sitting still, he walks far; though lying down, he goes everywhere. Who save myself is able to know that God, who rejoices, and rejoices not?

'That Self cannot be gained by the Veda; nor by the understanding, nor by much learning. He whom the Self chooses, by him alone the Self can be gained.

'The Self chooses him as his own. But he who

has not first turned away from his wickedness, who is not calm and subdued, or whose mind is not at rest, he can never obtain the Self, even by knowledge.

'No mortal lives by the breath that goes up and by the breath that goes down. We live by another, in whom both repose.

'Well then, I shall tell thee this mystery, the eternal word (Brahman), and what happens to the *Self*, after reaching death.

'Some are born again, as living beings, others enter into stocks and stones, according to their work, and according to their knowledge.

'But he, the Highest Person, who wakes in us while we are asleep, shaping one lovely sight after another, he indeed is called the Light, he is called Brahman, he alone is called the Immortal. All worlds are founded on it, and no one goes beyond. *This is that.*

'As the one fire, after it has entered the world, though one, becomes different according to what it burns, thus the One Self within all things, becomes different, according to whatever it enters, but it exists also apart.

'As the sun, the eye of the world, is not contaminated by the external impurities seen by the eye, thus the One Self within all things is never contaminated by the sufferings of the world, being himself apart.

'There is one eternal thinker, thinking non-eternal thoughts; he, though one, fulfils the desires of many. The wise who perceive Him within their Self, to them belongs eternal life, eternal peace [1].

---

[1] *Τὸ δὲ φρόνημα τοῦ πνεύματος ζωὴ καὶ εἰρήνη.* See also Ruskin, Sesame, p. 63.

'Whatever there is, the whole world, when gone forth (from Brahman), trembles in his breath. That Brahman is a great terror, like a drawn sword. Those who know it, become immortal.

'He (Brahman) cannot be reached by speech, by mind, or by the eye. He cannot be apprehended, except by him who says, *He is.*

'When all desires that dwell in the heart cease, then the mortal becomes immortal, and obtains Brahman.

'When all the fetters of the heart here on earth are broken, when all that binds us to this life is undone, then the mortal becomes immortal:—here my teaching ends.'

This is what is called Vedânta, the Veda-end, the end of the Veda, and this is the religion or the philosophy, whichever you like to call it, that has lived on from about 500 B.C. to the present day. If the people of India can be said to have now any system of religion at all,—apart from their ancestral sacrifices and their *S*râddhas, and apart from mere caste-observances,—it is to be found in the Vedânta philosophy, the leading tenets of which are known to some extent in every village[1]. That great revival of religion, which was inaugurated some fifty years ago by Ram-Mohun Roy, and is now known as the Brahma-Samâ*g*, under the leadership of my noble friend Keshub Chunder Sen, was chiefly founded on the Upanishads, and was Vedântic in spirit. There is, in fact, an unbroken continuity between the most modern and the most ancient phases of Hindu thought, extending over more than three thousand years.

---

[1] Major Jacob, Manual of Hindu Pantheism, Preface.

To the present day India acknowledgedness. who authority in matters of religion, ceremonial, at rest, and law than the *Veda*, and so long as India is nothing will extinguish that ancient spirit of and dântism which is breathed by every Hindu from earliest youth, and pervades in various forms the prayers even of the idolater, the speculations of the philosopher, and the proverbs of the beggar.

For purely practical reasons therefore,—I mean for the very practical object of knowing something of the secret springs which determine the character, the thoughts and deeds, of the lowest as well as of the highest amongst the people in India,—an acquaintance with their religion, which is founded on the Veda, and with their philosophy, which is founded on the Vedânta, is highly desirable.

It is easy to make light of this, and to ask, as some statesmen have asked, even in Europe, What has religion, or what has philosophy, to do with politics? In India, in spite of all appearances to the contrary, and notwithstanding the indifference on religious matters so often paraded before the world by the Indians themselves, religion, and philosophy too, are great powers still. Read the account that has lately been published of two native statesmen, the administrators of two first-class states in Saurâsh*t*ra, Junâgadh and Bhavnagar, Gokulaji and Gaurisankara[1], and you

---

[1] Life and Letters of Gokulaji Sampattirâma Zâlâ and his views of the Vedânta, by Manassukharâma Sûryarâma Tripâ*th*î. Bombay, 1881.

As a young man Gokulaji, the son of a good family, learnt Persian and Sanskrit. His chief interest in life, in the midst of a most successful political career, was the 'Vedânta.' A little insight, we are told, into this knowledge turned his heart to higher objects, promising him freedom from grief, and blessedness,

whether the Vedânta is still a moral and practical power in India or not.

But I claim even more for the Vedânta, and I recommend its study, not only to the Candidates for the Indian Civil Service, but to all true students of philosophy. It will bring before them a view of life, different from all other views of life which are placed before us in the History of Philosophy. You saw how behind all the Devas or gods, the authors of the Upanishads discovered the Âtman or Self. Of that Self they predicated three things only, that it is, that it perceives, and that it enjoys eternal bliss. All other predicates were negative: it is not this, it is not that—it is beyond anything that we can conceive or name.

But that Self, that Highest Self, the Paramâtman, could be discovered after a severe moral and intellectual discipline only, and those who had not yet discovered it, were allowed to worship lower gods, and to employ more poetical names to satisfy their human wants. Those who knew the other gods to be but names or persons—*personae* or masks, in the true sense of the word—pratîkas, as they call them in Sanskrit—knew also that those who worshipped these names or persons, worshipped in truth the Highest

---

the highest aim of all. This was the turning-point of his inner life. When the celebrated Vedânti anchorite, Râma Bâvâ, visited Junâgadh, Gokulaji became his pupil. When another anchorite, Paramahansa Sa*kk*idânanda, passed through Junâgadh on a pilgrimage to Girnar, Gokulaji was regularly initiated in the secrets of the Vedânta. He soon became highly proficient in it, and through the whole course of his life, whether in power or in disgrace, his belief in the doctrines of the Vedânta supported him, and made him, in the opinion of English statesmen, the model of what a native statesman ought to be.

Self, though ignorantly. This is a most characteristic feature in the religious history of India. Even in the Bhagavadgîtâ, a rather popular and exoteric exposition of Vedantic doctrines, the Supreme Lord or Bhagavat himself is introduced as saying: 'Even those who worship idols, worship me[1].'

But that was not all. As behind the names of Agni, Indra, and Pra*g*âpati, and behind all the mythology of nature, the ancient sages of India had discovered the Âtman—let us call it the objective Self—they perceived also behind the veil of the body, behind the senses, behind the mind, and behind our reason (in fact behind the mythology of the soul, which we often call psychology), another Âtman, or the subjective Self. That Self, too, was to be discovered by a severe moral and intellectual discipline only, and those who wished to find it, who wished to know, not themselves, but their Self, had to cut far deeper than the senses, or the mind, or the reason, or the ordinary Ego. All these too were Devas, bright apparitions—mere names—yet names meant for something. Much that was most dear, that had seemed for a time their

---

[1] Professor Kuenen discovers a similar idea in the words placed in the mouth of Jehovah by the prophet Malachi, i. 14: 'For I am a great King, and my name is feared among the heathen.' 'The reference,' he says, 'is distinctly to the adoration already offered to Yahweh by the people, whenever they serve their own gods with true reverence and honest zeal. Even in Deuteronomy the adoration of these other gods by the nations is represented as a dispensation of Yahweh. Malachi goes a step further, and accepts their worship as a tribute which in reality falls to Yahweh,—to Him, the Only True. Thus the opposition between Yahweh and the other gods, and afterwards between the one true God and the imaginary gods, makes room here for the still higher conception that the adoration of Yahweh is the essence and the truth of all religion.' Hibbert Lectures, p. 181.

very self, had to be surrendered, before they could find the Self of Selves, the Old Man, the Looker-on, a subject independent of all personality, an existence independent of all life.

When that point had been reached, then the highest knowledge began to dawn, the Self within (the Pratyagâtman) was drawn towards the Highest Self (the Paramâtman), it found its true self in the Highest Self, and the oneness of the subjective with the objective Self was recognised as underlying all reality, as the dim dream of religion,—as the pure light of philosophy.

This fundamental idea is worked out with systematic completeness in the Vedânta philosophy, and no one who can appreciate the lessons contained in Berkeley's philosophy, will read the Upanishads and the Brahma-sûtras and their commentaries without feeling a richer and a wiser man.

I admit that it requires patience, discrimination, and a certain amount of self-denial before we can discover the grains of solid gold in the dark mines of Eastern philosophy. It is far easier and far more amusing for shallow critics to point out what is absurd and ridiculous in the religion and philosophy of the ancient world than for the earnest student to discover truth and wisdom under strange disguises. Some progress however has been made, even during the short span of life that we can remember. The Sacred Books of the East are no longer a mere butt for the invectives of missionaries or the sarcasms of philosophers. They have at last been recognised as historical documents, aye, as the most ancient documents in the history of the human mind, and as palæontological records of an evolution that begins to elicit wider and deeper sympathies than the nebular formation of the planet on which we dwell for a season, or the organic development of that chrysalis which we call man.

If you think that I exaggerate, let me read you in conclusion what one of the greatest philosophical critics—and certainly not a man given to admiring the thoughts of others—says of the Vedânta, and more particularly of the Upanishads. Schopenhauer writes:

'In the whole world there is no study so beneficial and so elevating as that of the Upanishads. It has been the solace of my life—it will be the solace of my death [1].'

I have thus tried, so far as it was possible in one course of lectures, to give you some idea of ancient India, of its ancient literature, and, more particularly, of its ancient religion. My object was, not merely to place names and facts before you, these you can find in many published books, but, if possible, to make you see and feel the general human interests that are involved in that ancient chapter of the history of the human race. I wished that the Veda and its religion and philosophy should not only seem to you curious or strange, but that you should feel that there was in them something that concerns ourselves, something of our own intellectual growth, some recollections, as it were, of our own childhood, or at least of the childhood of our own race. I feel convinced that, placed as we are

---

[1] Sacred Books of the East, vol. i, The Upanishads, translated by M. M.; Introduction, p. lxi.

here in this life, we have lessons to learn from the Veda, quite as important as the lessons we learn at school from Homer and Virgil, and lessons from the Vedânta quite as instructive as the systems of Plato or Spinoza.

I do not mean to say that everybody who wishes to know how the human race came to be what it is, how language came to be what it is, how religion came to be what it is, how manners, customs, laws, and forms of government came to be what they are, how we ourselves came to be what we are, must learn Sanskrit, and must study Vedic Sanskrit. But I *do* believe that not to know what a study of Sanskrit, and particularly a study of the Veda, has already done for illuminating the darkest passages in the history of the human mind, of that mind on which we ourselves are feeding and living, is a misfortune, or, at all events, a loss, just as I should count it a loss to have passed through life without knowing something, however little, of the geological formation of the earth, or of the sun, and the moon, and the stars,—and of the thought, or the will, or the law, that govern their movements.

NOTES AND ILLUSTRATIONS.

NOTE A, p. 9.

ON THE TREASURES FOUND ON THE OXUS AND AT MYKENAE.

The treasure found on the north bank of the Oxus in 1877, and described by General Cunningham in the Journal of the Asiatic Society of Bengal in 1881, contains coins from Darius down to Antiochus the Great and Euthydemus of Bactria. The treasure seems therefore to have been buried on the bank of the river at the time when Euthydemus marched against Antiochus, who invaded Bactria in 208 B.C. Euthydemus was defeated, and the treasure, whether belonging to him or to one of his nobles, was left untouched till the other day. There can be no doubt as to the Persian character of many of the coins, figures, and ornaments discovered on the bank of the Oxus, and we must suppose therefore that they were spoils carried away from Persia, and kept for a time in Bactria by the victorious generals of Alexander.

Now of all the hypotheses that have been put forward with regard to the treasure found at Mykenae, or at least some portion of it, that of Professor Forchhammer has always seemed to me the most plausible. According to his view, some of the works of art discovered at Mykenae should be considered as part of the spoils that fell to Mykenae, as her legitimate share in the booty of the Persian camp. The Persian, or, if you like, Assyrian character of some of the things discovered in the tombs of Mykenae admits of no doubt. The representation of the king in his chariot, with the charioteer, hunting the stag, is clearly Assyrian or Persian. The dress of the figures on some of the seals is decidedly Assyrian or Persian. Now the same style of art meets us again in the various works of art found on the Oxus. We have the king in his two-wheeled chariot, standing behind his charioteer, in the silver Daric (Pl. xii, 6, 7), and in the gold relic (Pl. xii, 8). We have the peculiar Persian trowsers, the sarabâra (sarâwil), in the gold statue

(Pl. xii, 1), and again in the silver statuette (Pl. xi). Besides this, we have (Pl. xv, 6) the stag in gold, corresponding to the stag in silver-lead (Pl. 172, Mykenae). We have the figure of a man in bronze (Pl. xix, 4), and of a king in gold (Pl. xii, 1), both reminding us of the figure of a man found at Mykenae (Pl. 86), and we have the small pigeon (Pl. xv, 3) which might have come off from one of the figures found at Mykenae (Pl. 106, and 179).

All this would become intelligible, if we might trace the treasures found on the Oxus and the treasures found at Mykenae back to the same source—namely, to booty found by the Greeks in the Persian camp, and to booty carried off by Macedonian generals from the palaces of Darius.

This would not explain the origin of all the treasure found in the tombs of Mykenae, but it would give a clue to some of them, and thus impart a new interest to Dr. Schliemann's discoveries. (I have quoted the numbers of the Mykenae plates from the Collection of the original photographs presented to me by Dr. Schliemann.)

NOTE B, p. 25.

ON THE NAME OF THE CAT AND THE CAT'S EYE.

Our domestic cat came to us from Egypt[1], where it had been tamed by a long process of kindness, or, it may be, of worship[2]. In no classical writer, Greek or Roman, do we find the cat as a domestic animal before the third century A.D. It is first mentioned by Caesarius, the physician, brother of Gregory, the theologian of Nazianzus, who died 369 A.D. He speaks of κάτται ἔνδρυμοι. About the same time Palladius (De re rustica, IV, 9, 4), writes: 'Contra talpas prodest catos (cattos) frequenter habere in mediis carduetis (artichoke-gardens). Mustelas habent plerique mansuetas; aliqui foramina earum rubrica et succo agrestis cucumeris impleverunt. Nonnulli juxta cubilia talparum plures cavernas aperiunt, ut illae territae fugiant solis admissu. Plerique laqueos in aditu earum setis pendentibus ponunt.' Hehn supposes that *talpa* here means mouse. But whether it means mouse or mole, it is clear that when Palladius wrote (fourth century A.D.), tame mustelae were still more common than cats, whether called *cati* or *catti*.

Evagrius scholasticus (Hist. Eccl. 17, 23), about 600 A.D., speaks of κάττα[3] as the common name of αἴλουρος, here meant, therefore, for cat. He says: αἴλουρον ἣν κάτταν ἡ συνήθεια λέγει.

And Isidorus, his contemporary, expresses himself in the same sense when saying (12, 2, 38), 'hunc (murionem) vulgus *catum* a captura vocant.'

If we admit, in the absence of evidence to the contrary effect, that the tame cat came from Egypt to Greece and Italy

---

[1] Wagner, zu Schrebers Säugethiere, Suppl. ii, p. 536.

[2] See Hehn, Kulturpflanzen und Hausthiere, p. 398. It was the *Felis maniculata* Ruepp., see Hartmann, Zeitschrift für Aegypt. Sprache, 1864, p. 11.

[3] Catta in Martialis, 13, 69, seems to be a kind of bird.

in the fourth century A.D., and that the shrewd little animal was called by the Romans *cătus*, everything else becomes intelligible.

In the ruins of Pompeii, where the bones of horses, dogs, and goats have been found, no bones of cats have hitherto been discovered, and the pictures there which were supposed to be intended for cats, are now proved to be at all events not pictures of the tame cat[1].

In the language of Roumania no traces exist of the word *catus*, probably because at the time when that Romanic dialect became settled in Dacia, *catus* did not yet exist as a Latin word[2].

Mice were very troublesome no doubt to Greeks and Romans, but they fought against them, and against lizards and snakes also, not by cats, but by the γαλέη or γαλῆ, the ἴκτις, and the αἰέλουρος or αἴλουρος. We must not suppose that the names of these animals were used by the ancients with anything like zoological accuracy. So much only is certain that, before the fourth century B.C., none of them, when applied to animals outside Egypt[3], should be taken for our *Felis domesticus*, while Cuvier[4] maintains that in Egypt the cat-mummies, from the most ancient times, are anatomically the same as our tame cat.

My excellent friend, the late Professor Rolleston, whom I miss more than I can say, in a paper 'On Domestic Cats, ancient and modern,' published in the Journal of Anatomy and Physiology, 1868, pp. 47–61, came to the conclusion that when the ancient Greeks, such as Aristotle, Aristophanes, &c., spoke of γαλῆ, except in Egypt, they generally meant the *Mustela foina*, the white-breasted marten, called also beech-marten or stone-marten, sometimes the *Mustela furo*, the ferret, and the *Viverra genneta*, the genet, but never the polecat, *Mustela putorius*. What distinguishes the γαλῆ is that it destroys mice, snakes, and birds, that it steals the eggs of birds, and

[1] Hehn, l. c., p. 402.

[2] Hehn, l. c., p. 531.

[3] Herodotus, when speaking of the cat in Egypt, applies the Greek name of αἴλουρος to it; in the Sibylline Oracles, Prooem., v. 60, it is called γαλῆ; αἰσχύνθητε γαλᾶς καὶ κνώδαλα θειοποιοῦντες.

[4] Annales du Muséum, An. xi (1802), p. 234; Ossemens fossiles, Discours Préliminaire, pp. lxii–lxiii, ed. 1821; Rolleston, l. c., p. 50.

is offensive by its smell. The *γαλῆ ἀγρία* or *ἴκτις* shares these qualities, but it is larger and, what is important, fond of honey. Neither ferret (*Mustela furo*) nor weasel (*Mustela vulgaris*) will touch honey.

The cat, our *Felis domesticus*, may in extreme cases be brought to kill snakes, but it will not steal eggs, nor eat honey, nor go into holes, like the *γαλῆ* or the *Mustela*.

The most useful talent of killing mice was shared by *γαλῆ*, *mustela*, weasel, and cat; and when we say, cat and mouse, the Greeks said Μῦς *καὶ γαλῆ*, the Romans *Mus et mustela*.

When the Greeks came to know the tame Egyptian cat, they transferred to it the old names of *γαλῆ* and *αἴλουρος*. Most likely *κάττος* was the imitation of an Egyptian word, and when Kallimachos, writing in Egypt (third century B.C.), speaks of the *αἴλουρος*, his commentator was no doubt right in saying, *τὸν ἰδίως λεγόμενον κάττον*.

In the Greek fables, down to Babrius, *αἴλουρος* need never be taken for a tame cat, but for a weasel, marten, or possibly a wild cat[1].

The Romans did not transfer the name of *Mustela*[2] to the cat, but by a kind of popular etymology, changed *cattus* into *căttus*, and these two names, *κάττα* and *catus*, found their way afterwards into nearly all the languages of Europe[3].

In Germany the arrival of the cat[4] must have been sufficiently early to account for the adoption of cats, instead of weasels (O.H.G. *wisula*, or *wisale*), as drawing the chariot of the goddess Freya[5], unless we admit that here too the cat

---

[1] Hehn, l. c., p. 402, against Keller, Über die Geschichte der griech. Fabel, p. 392.

[2] The following are the different English names, all corresponding to some kind of *Mustela* :—

Mustela foina = white-breasted marten.
Mustela martes = yellow-breasted marten.
Mustela putorius = polecat.
Mustela furo = ferret.
Mustela vulgaris = weasel.
Mustela erminea = stoat.

[3] O.H.G. chazza; M.H.G. katze; A.S. cat; O.N. köttr; Fr. chat, chatte; Prov. cat, cata; Span. gato, gata; Ital. gatto, gatta; Mod. Gr. *γάτα, κατζί*; Ir. cat; Gael. cat; Welsh câth; Russ. kot", koška; Pol. kot, kotka; Boh. kot, kotě; Lith. katé; Finn. katti; Lapp. katto; Turk. kedy; Arm. citto.

[4] Hehn, l.c., p. 405.

[5] Grimm, Deutsche Mythologie, p. 634.

intended was originally the wild-cat, particularly as its place is often taken by the gold-bristled boar and the falcon [1].

We now come to the question, whether the cat was known at an early time in India. The two principal words in Sanskrit for cat are mârgâra and vidâla.

Mârgâra means the cleaner, the cat being well known for its cleanliness. The wild-cat is called aranya-mârgâra, the forest-cat (Pañkatantra, p. 165, l. 14).

Manu (XI, 131) places mârgâra by the side of the nakula, the ichneumon, and in the Pañkatantra (p. 110, l. 23) we read that there is a natural enmity between cats and dogs (sârameya-mârgârânâm) and between ichneumons and serpents (nakula-sarpânâm). This instinctive enmity between certain animals was so well known that Pânini gave a rule (II, 4, 9) according to which compounds may be formed of the names of such animals. But among these compounds we find in Pânini neither cat and dog, nor cat and mouse. Pânini knew the wild-cat, the vidâla (VI, 2, 72), but not the tame cat, the enemy of dogs and mice. Nay, even Patañgali, the author of the Mahâbhâshya, does not yet mention the cat among the animals exhibiting an instinctive hatred of other animals (II, 4, 9). He gives in the Mahâbhâshya instances (II, 4, 12, 2) of such instinctive enmities, as kâkolûkam, crows and owls, svasrigâlam, dogs and jackals (even sramana-brâhmanam, mendicants and Brâhmans), but not cat and dog, or cat and mouse. The later Kâsikâ, on the contrary, gives mârgâramûshakam, cat and mouse, as the very first instance of II, 4, 9.

Again (IV, 2, 104), the animals mentioned by Patañgali for a similar purpose are ahi-nakulikâh, serpents and ichneumons, and svâvarâhikâh, dogs and boars, but not cat and dog, nor cat and mouse.

In the Chinese translation of the story of Bedd Gelert, made by Fa Hian about 412 A.D., the animals that hate each other instinctively are the snake and the nakula, the little bird and the hawk, the Sramana and Brâhmana, the stepmother and the child of another wife [2].

A strong confirmation of the comparatively late date of the

---

[1] Radolph, Die Göttergestalt der Frigg, 1875, p. 37.

[2] See S. Beal, in the Academy, 1882, p. 331.

cat, as the enemy of mice, in India is furnished by the Pañ*k*atantra. Here we read (V, 109)[1], 'A mouse, though born in the house, must be killed, because it does mischief. A cat is asked for from elsewhere, and paid for, because it is useful.'

But in the Arabic translation (Guidi's Codd. F. and V.), instead of the cat we find the falcon; in the *Directorium* the nisus, or sparrow-hawk; in the Stephanites the ἱέραξ, and in the old Spanish translation, the *azor*.

It might have been supposed at first that as the cat occurred in the Pañ*k*atantra, the Arabic translation had changed the cat into a falcon. But no. The old Syriac version, which is older than our Pañ*k*atantra, has: 'Mice, though bred in the house, are killed on account of their mischievousness, but falcons are caught on account of their usefulness, and carried on the hand.'

This leaves no doubt that in the original the simile was taken from the mice and the falcon, and that the somewhat lame simile of the cat and the mice is of later date.

The second name for cat in Sanskrit is vi*d*âla or bi*d*âla. In the Vâ*g*asaneyi-sa*m*hitâ (XXIV, 31) v*ri*shada*m*sa is explained by vi*d*âla, and kept quite distinct from nakula (XXIV, 32), which occurs in the Atharva-veda (IV, 139, 5) as an animal hostile to serpents. Manu also (XI, 159) clearly distinguishes vi*d*âla from nakula, and his vana-vi*d*âla is most likely meant for the wild-cat. Pâ*n*ini must have known the word, for in XVI, 2, 72 he gives a rule for the accent of the compound bhikshâ-vi*d*âla.

It is difficult to analyse this word. I thought at first that it might be connected with vidala (bidala, in the Ait. Âr. III, 1, 2, 6) which means cut in half, split in the middle, which would be a very appropriate term for a cat's eye. But this would leave the lingual *d* unaccounted for. In the U*n*âdi-sûtras (I, 117) it is derived from vi*d*, to shout, with the suffix âla. This suffix shows a certain analogy with âlîya in mâr*g*âlîya, another name for cat.

The question then arises, whether from vi*d*âla a derivative vai*d*âlya might have been formed, and whether this word

---

[1] Selected Essays, i, p. 556.

could have given rise to the Greek *αἴλουρος* or *αἰέλουρος*, instead of *αἰόλος* and *οὐρά*, as commonly supposed. We should have to admit a parallel form vai*d*ârya, and then a transition of *ορρος* into *ουρος*, allowing at the same time the possibility that the word came into Greek, not as a common Aryan word, but as a foreign name for a foreign animal.

And this suggests a new question. Vai*d*ûrya and vaidûrya, the very form that would best correspond to the Greek *αἴλουρος*, means in Sanskrit the cat's eye. The cat is called ma*n*ivai*d*ûryalo*k*ana, i.e. having eyes like the Vai*d*ûrya jewel. It is true that so ancient a grammarian as Pâ*n*ini (IV, 3, 84) derives vai*d*ûrya from vidûra, 'very distant,' and that accordingly it is often spelt with a dental d. But this seems an afterthought. The transition of vai*d*ârya into vai*d*ûrya is not impossible, even in Sanskrit, if we remember such parallel forms as dûra and davîyas, sthûla, sthavîyas, &c. If then vai*d*ûrya was connected with vi*d*âla, cat, and meant originally a cat's eye, it is strange, to say no more, that the Prakrit form veluriya should, as Pott pointed out, appear in Greek as *βήρυλλος*, again a foreign name for a foreign jewel, i.e. for the beryl. It is true no doubt that, scientifically speaking, the cat's eye and the beryl differ, but in some cases, as Professor Fischer informs me, the colour of the beryl is like that of the eyes of a cat, though it never has that peculiar waving lustre which is perceived in all real cat's-eye minerals, when they have been cut convexly.

Vai*d*ûrya is also used as the name of the country or the mountain where the vai*d*ûrya mineral is found. At the time of Varâhamihira (B*ri*hat-sa*m*hitâ, XIV, 14), in the sixth century, the mines of beryl stone were said to be in the South of India. But in the commentary on the U*n*adi-sûtras (II, 20) we hear of Vidûra as the name of Bâlavâya, being either a mountain or a town, from whence the best Vai*d*ûrya stones are said to come. In the commentary on Pâ*n*ini also (VI, 2, 77) this Bâlavâya is mentioned as the name of a mountain.

It was objected by Kâtyâyana that Pâ*n*ini's rule (Pâ*n*. IV, 3, 84), according to which vai*d*ûrya is formed from Vidûra, must be wrong, because the Vai*d*ûrya jewel does not come from Vidûra, but from Bâlavâya, and is only cut or polished at Vidûra. We are not concerned here with the manner in which Patañgali tries to solve this dilemma, but with the dilemma itself, that is, with the fact that in Kâtyâyana's, or, at all events, in Patañgali's time Vaidûrya stones were known to come from the mountain Bâlavâya, not from Vidûra. We know nothing else about this Bâlavâya mountain, but Burnouf, by a very bold combination, tried many years ago to identify the name of the Bolor or Balur-tâgh [1] with the Vaidûrya mountain, the mountain supplying the Vaidûrya jewels. This would indicate new points of contact between the East and the West, which however it seems premature to follow up. Even the coincidences and similarities touched upon in this note are by no means firmly established, and I have only put them together because, if we should come to the conclusion that there is no historical relationship between vidâla, vaidûrya, αἴλουρος, βήρυλλος, and Belur-tâgh [2], we should, at all events, have learnt the useful lesson that the chapter of accidents is sometimes larger than we suppose.

Page 33. Professor Cowell calls my attention to the fact that Sir William Jones was thirty-seven years of age when he sailed for India, and that he received the honour of knighthood in March 1783, on his appointment as Judge of the Supreme Court of Judicature at Fort William, at Bengal. See 'Works of Sir William Jones, with the Life of the Author, by Lord Teignmouth,' vol. i, p. 402.

---

[1] Professor Weber adopts Pott's etymology of βήρυλλος, and Burnouf's derivation of Belur-tâgh from vaidûrya (see Omina und Portenta, p. 326), though he thinks it might be inverted. At a later time (Ind. Stud. xiii, 370) he prefers to think of Bâlavâya as connected with Belur-tâgh. See also, Die Indischen Mineralien, von Dr. R. Garbe, p. 85.

[2] The Bolor, the very existence of which had been denied, has lately been re-established as the real name of a real mountain by Robert Shaw. He found that the name was applied by the Kirghis to the district of Kitral. General Cunningham states that the same name, Palor, Balors, Balornts, is applied to the city of Iskardo. See Le Muséon, vol. i, p. 358. Hiouen-thsang also (i, 273) describes the kingdom of Pololo (Bolor) as rich in precious metals.

NOTE C, p. 49.

ON VILLAGE ESTATES.

As Colonel Sleeman's 'Rambles of an Indian Official' are not easily accessible, I give some more extracts from them bearing on village communities as he knew them. In the tenth chapter of the first volume he writes:—

'Nine-tenths of the immediate cultivators of the soil in India are little farmers, who hold a lease for one or more years, as the case may be, of their lands, which they cultivate with their own stock. One of these cultivators, with a good plough and bullocks, and a good character, can always get good lands on moderate terms from holders of villages. Those cultivators are, I think, the best who learn to depend upon their stock and character for favourable terms, hold themselves free to change their holdings when their leases expire, and pretend not to any hereditary right of property in the soil. The lands are, I think, best cultivated, and the society best constituted in India, when the holders of *Estates of Villages* have a feeling of permanent interest in them, an assurance of an hereditary right of property which is liable only to the payment of a moderate government demand, descends undivided by the law of primogeniture, and is unaffected by the common law, which prescribes the equal subdivision among children of landed as well as other private property among the Hindus and Mohammedans, and where the immediate cultivators hold the lands they till by no other law than of common specific contract.

'When I speak of villages, I mean the holders of lands that belong to villages. The whole face of India is parcelled out into estates of villages. The village communities are composed of those who hold and cultivate the land, the established village-servants[1], priest[2], blacksmith[3], carpenter[4], account-

---

[1] Grâma-bhrita.

[2] Grâma-yâgin or grâma-yâgaka, a despised office.

[3] Grâma-karmâra.

[4] Grâma-taksha, Pân. V, 4, 95.

ant[1], washerman[2] (whose wife is *ex officio* the midwife of the little village community), potter[3], watchman[4], barber[5], shoemaker, etc. In some parts of Central and Southern India, the Garpugree[6] who charms away hail-storms from the crops, and the Bhoomka[7] who charms away tigers from the people and their cattle, are added to the number of village-servants. To these may be added the little banker or agricultural capitalist, the shopkeeper, the brazier, the confectioner, the iron-monger, the weaver, the dyer, the astronomer, or astrologer[8] who points out to the people the lucky day for every earthly undertaking, and the prescribed times for all religious ceremonies and observances[9].

'In some villages the whole of the lands are parcelled out among cultivating proprietors, and are liable to eternal subdivision by the law of inheritance, which gives to each one the same share.

'In others, the whole of the lands are parcelled out among

---

[1] Grâma-lekhaka.

[2] Grâma-ra*g*aka.

[3] Grâma-kulâla, Pâ*n*. VI, 2, 62, com.

[4] Grâma-pâla.

[5] Grâma-nâpita, Pâ*n*. VI, 2, 62, com.; also called grâma*n*ı*h*.

[6] Mr. Platts, whom I consulted on these names, writes to me: 'I have now no doubt that the word is gar-paga*r*î (the accent being on pag); and that its correct form is गरपगड़ी, or rather गरपकड़ी, the क of which is changed to ग, and the ड़ *r* to र r; both of which are common changes in the Dakkhinî.

'The etymology will therefore be:

'gar° = gār = S. करका. pagar° = paka*r*° (root of paka*r*nā) = Prâk*r*it पक्कड़(इ), from Sanskrit प्रकृष्, rt. कृष् with प्र. î = S. ई (इन्).'

[7] Bhûmika.

[8] Grâma-*g*yotisha.

[9] Some other village officials mentioned in Sanskrit works are:—

Grâma-goduh, the man who milks the cows; Pâ*n*. Ga*n*apâ*th*a, 218.

Grâma-ghâtin, the village butcher, grâmasthabahulokaposha*n*ârtham pasughâtaka*h*.

Grâma-preshya, the village messenger, rather despised.

Grâma-ghoshin, the village cryer.

According to Nâgesa (Pâ*n*. I, 1, 48, ed. Ballantyne, p. 559) the five most common artisans in a village are the kulâla, potter, karmâra, smith, vardhaki, carpenter, nâpita, barber, and ra*g*aka, washerman or dyer. A village possessing them is called grâma*h* pa*ñk*akârukî. See Kielhorn, Kâtyâyana and Patañjali, p. 32, note: 'Avarata*h* can only mean "less in number." One calls a village a Brahman-village, although some of its inhabitants belong to other castes, because the number of Brahmans who live in it is greater than the number of inhabitants belonging to other castes.'

cultivators, who hold them on a specific lease for limited periods, from a proprietor who holds the whole collectively under government, at a rate of rent fixed either permanently or for limited periods.

'These are the two extremes. There are but few villages in which all the cultivators are considered as proprietors, at least but few in our Nerbudda territories; and these will almost invariably be found of a caste of Brahmans or a caste of Rajputs, descended from a common ancestor, to whom the estate was originally given in rent-free tenure, or at a quit rent, by the existing government, either for his prayers as a priest, or his services as a soldier. Subsequent governments, which resumed unceremoniously the estates of others, were deterred from resuming these by a dread of the curses of the one[1] and the swords of the others.

'Such communities of cultivating proprietors are of two kinds, those among whom the lands are parcelled out, each member holding his share as a distinct estate, and being individually responsible for the payment of the share of the government demand assessed upon it; and those among whom the lands are not parcelled out, but the profits divided as among co-partners of an estate held jointly. They, in either case, nominate one of their members to collect and pay the government demand; or government appoints a man for this duty, either as a salaried servant, or as a lessee, with authority to levy from the cultivating proprietors a certain sum over and above what is demandable from him.

'The communities in which the cultivators are considered merely as leaseholders, are far more numerous—indeed the greater part of the village communities in this part of India are of this description; and where the communities are of a mixed character, the cultivating proprietors are considered to have merely a right of occupancy, and are liable to have their lands assessed at the same rate as others holding the same sort of lands, and often pay a higher rate with which others are not encumbered.

'But this is not general: it is as much the interest of the

---

[1] See Vasishtha XVII, 86.

proprietor to have good cultivating tenants, as it is of the tenants to have good proprietors; and it is felt to be the interest of both to adjust their terms amicably among themselves without a reference to a third and superior party, which is always costly and commonly ruinous.'

For more minute details of the systems of land tenure in these village estates, see Sir H. Maine's 'Village Communities in the East and West; Six Lectures delivered at Oxford,' 1871.

Page 55, l. 19, add: The earliest witness is Su-we, a relative of Fan-chen, king of Siam, who between 222 and 227 A.D. sailed round the whole of India, till he reached the mouth of the Indus, and then explored the country. After his return to Siam, he received four Yueh-chi horses, sent by a king of India as a present to the king of Siam and his ambassador. At the time when these horses arrived in Siam (it took them four years to travel there), there was staying at the Court of Siam an ambassador of the emperor of China, Khang-thai, and this is the account he received of the kingdom of India: 'It is a kingdom in which the religion of Buddha flourishes. The inhabitants are straightforward, and honest, and the soil is very fertile. The king is called Meu-lun, and his capital is surrounded by walls,' &c. This was in about 231 A.D. In 605 we hear again of the emperor Yang-ti sending an ambassador, Fei-tu, to India, and this is what among other things he points out as peculiar to the Hindus: 'They believe in solemn oaths.' (See Stanislas Julien, Journal Asiatique, 1847, Août, pp. 98, 105.)

Page 56, l. 9, add: Again in the thirteenth century, Shems-ed-din Abu Abdallah quotes the following judgment of Bedi ezr Zenân: 'The Indians are innumerable, like grains of sand, free from all deceit and violence. They fear neither death nor life.' (See Mehren, Manuel de la Cosmographie du moyen âge, traduction de l'ouvrage de Shems-ed-din Abou Abdallah de Damas, Paris, Leroux, 1874, p. 391.)

NOTE D, p. 70.

TEXTS ON VENIAL UNTRUTHS.

Gautama V, 24: Kruddha h*ri*sh*t*a bhîtârtalubdha bâla sthavira mû*dh*a mattonmattavâkyâny an*ri*tâny apâtakâni.

Vasish*th*a XVI, 35; Mahâbh. VIII, 3436:

Vivâhakâle ratisamprayoge
prâ*n*âtyaye sarvadhanâpahâre
viprasya *k*ârthe hy an*ri*ta*m* vadeta,
pa*ñk*ân*ri*tâny âhur apâtakâni.

If a man speak an untruth at the time of marriage, during dalliance, when his life is in danger, or the loss of his whole property (is threatened), and also for the sake of a Brâhma*n*a, it has been declared that these five untruths are not mortal sins.

Gautama XXIII, 29: Vivâhamaithunanarmârtasa*m*yogeshv adosham eke 'n*ri*tam.

Some declare that an untruth spoken at the time of marriage, during dalliance, in jest or while one suffers severe pain, is venial.

Vish*n*u VIII, 15: Var*n*inâ*m* yatra badhas tatrân*ri*tena.

Whenever the death of a member of any of the four castes (would be occasioned by true evidence, they are free from blame) if they give false evidence.

Manu VIII, 103: Tadvadan dharmato 'rtheshu *g*ânann apy-anyathâ nara*h*,
Na svargâ*k k*yavate lokâd daivî*m* vâ*k*am vadanti tâm.
*S*ûdravi*t*kshatraviprâ*n*â*m* yatrartoktau bhaved badha*h*,
Tatra vaktavyam an*ri*ta*m* tad dhi satyâd vi*s*ishyate.

In some cases a giver of false evidence from a pious motive, even though he know the truth, shall not lose a seat in heaven; such evidence wise men call the speech of the gods.

Whenever the death of a man, either of the servile, the commercial, the military, or the sacerdotal class, would be occasioned by true evidence, falsehood may be spoken; it is even preferable to truth.

Comm. Tathâ Gautama*h*, Nân*ri*tavadane dosho ya*gg*îvana*m* *k*et tadadhîna*m*, na tu pâpîyaso *g*îvanam iti.

Mahâbh. I, 3412: Na narmayukta*m* va*k*ana*m* hinasti
Na strîshu râ*g*an na vivâhakâle,
Prâ*n*âtyaye sarvadhanâpahâre
Pa*ñk*ân*ri*tâny âhur apâtakâni.

Mahâbh. III, 13844: Prâ*n*ântike vivâhe *k*a vaktavyam an*ri*tam bhavet,
An*ri*tena bhavet satya*m* satyenaivân*ri*tam bhavet.

Mahâbh. VII, 8741: Sa bhavâ*ms* trâtu no dro*n*ât, satyâ*g* *g*yâyo 'n*ri*ta*m* va*k*a*h*,
An*ri*ta*m* *g*îvitasyârthe vadan na sp*ris*yate 'n*ri*tai*h*.
Kâminîshu vivâheshu gavâm bhakte tathaiva *k*a
Brâhma*n*âbhyupapattau *k*a an*ri*te nâsti pâtakam.

Manu (IV, 138) quotes what he calls a primeval rule, namely, 'Say what is true and say what is pleasant, but do not say what is true and unpleasant, nor what is pleasant and not true.'

In the Vish*n*u-purâ*n*a (Wilson's translation, p. 312) the same mixed lesson of truthfulness and worldly wisdom is repeated: 'Let a wise man ever speak the truth when it is agreeable, and when the truth would inflict pain let him hold his peace. Let him not utter that which, though acceptable, would be detrimental; for it were better to speak that which would be salutary, although it should give exceeding offence. A considerate man will always cultivate, in act, thought, and speech, that which is good for living beings, both in this world and in the next.'

Page 81, note 1. That the Mahâbhârata was publicly read in the seventh century A.D., we learn from Bâ*n*a; see Journal of Royal Asiatic Society, Bombay, vol. x, p. 87, note.

NOTE E, p. 86.

THE YUEH-CHI (YUEH-K').

The conquests of Alexander, though they seem to have left a very slight impression in India, so much so that the very name of Alexander is never mentioned in Sanskrit literature, supplied the first impulse to great commotions in Asia, which at last reacted most powerfully and fatally on India. The kingdoms of Bactria, Syria, and Egypt were essentially the outcome of Alexander's Oriental policy. Egypt and Syria, we know, fell after a time a prey to Roman conquest. But the Greek kingdom of Bactria came in contact with a different class of enemies, and was destroyed by the Tochâri (the Ta-hia in Chinese[1]), a Turanian race, who, after having made themselves masters of that position, advanced westward against the kingdom of Parthia, founded 250 B.C. by Arsaces I. Artabanus, the king of Parthia, fell fighting against the Tochâri, but his son Mithradates II (124 B.C.) repelled their inroads, and thereby drove an enormous wave of half-nomad warriors towards Kábul, and thence to India.

Chang Kien, who was sent by the Emperor Wu-ti as ambassador to the Yueh-chi, tells us that these Yueh-chi (also called Yueh-ti, the 'Εφθαλῖται of Greeks) had been driven at that time out of their old seats by the Hiung-nu, and had poured into Bactria, then occupied by the Tochâri (Τόχαροι of Strabo), and called Ta-hia, or Tocharia (now Tokharistán).

Chang Kien, who was sent by the Emperor Wu-ti to induce the Yueh-chi to make war against the Hiung-nu, met with them on the banks of the Tu-kwai-shui (Surkhâb), their

[1] The Δάαι are supposed to appear again as Dacians, and Grimm would have wished to connect them with Dânavas, evil spirits, and in the end with the Danes. All this is as yet mere vapour, though there may be some light behind it. Most of these identifications rest on little more than similarity of sound.

northern boundary being the Oxus (Kwai-shui). This must have been between the years 139–126 B.C., though rather towards the end of that time. The Yueh-chi are described as of a pink and white complexion, and as accustomed to shoot from horse-back. They were then 7000 li north of India. Their country was bounded on the South by the districts lately conquered by the Ta-hia (Tochâri) and on the West by Ansik, i. e. Parthia. They were herdsmen and nomads, and resembled the Hiung-nu in manners and customs. Driven out of their seats by the Hiung-nu, they fell on the Tochâri from the West, and defeated them[1]. They then followed the course of the Surkhâb, and founded a royal residence on its Northern bank. Some of them took refuge in Little Tibet (Khiang or Kanka), and were called the Lesser Yueh-chi.

To the South-east of the Tochâri lay Shen-tuh, i. e. India, and when Chang Kien was with the Tochâri, he saw articles of trade brought to their country from India. India was reckoned to be some thousand li to the South-east of Ta-hia (Bactria). The country was said to be cultivated, and the manners and customs of its inhabitants were very similar to those of the Tochâri. The climate was damp and hot, and the people made use of elephants in war. It lay near a great river[2].

So far our information about the Yueh-chi and their distant relation to India rests on Sze-ma Tsien, who was born in 163 B.C.[3]

If now we proceed to the Annals of the After (or Eastern) Han Dynasty (A.D. 25–220), or to the Annals of the Sui Dynasty (A.D. 589–618), we find some more information about the same subject, for which I am chiefly indebted to Professor Legge[4].

The Annals of the After Han Dynasty were written down

---

[1] Their capital was Lam-shi-*k*eng, *Δάραψα*. Kingsmill, Intercourse of China with Eastern Turkestan, Journal of the Royal Asiatic Society, 1882, p. 82, note.

[2] North-Eastern India is called Tîn-yût, apparently Sthânesvara; Kingsmill, l. c., p. 83, note.

[3] Kingsmill, l. c., p. 74.

[4] Lassen, Indische Alterthumskunde, vol. ii, p. 352 seq.

by Han Yô, who was killed in 445 A.D., and we there find the following account of Tien-chu, that is, India. It is said to be called also 身毒, Ken-toku or Shin-doku. Its situation is described as many thousand li South-east of the Yueh-chi. The customs of the people are said to be the same as those of the Yueh-chi. Its climate is damp and hot. The country is near to the great rivers. The people fight riding on elephants, and they are weaker than the Yueh-chi. They practise the religion of Futo, i.e. Buddha, and refrain from killing, and this forms their custom.

The whole region extends from a state of the Yueh-chi called Kôfu, i.e. Kâbul, to the West Sea in a South-western direction, and it reaches Eastward another state called Han-ki.

Then the Han annalist, speaking of the time of that Dynasty, 25–220 A.D., continues:

There are in Ken-toku separate castles which are counted by hundreds, and in each castle there is a chief[1].

There are also separate states which are counted by tens[2]; and in each state there is a King. Although there is a little difference, yet all of them are called Ken-toku or Shin-doku.

At that time (under the Eastern Han Dynasty) they all belonged to the Yueh-chi, who had killed the kings, and appointed generals to govern the people.

This seems to have happened about one hundred years after Chang Kien's embassy, or 20 B.C. At that time the five tribes of the Yueh-chi were united under Kieou-tsieu-kio, who then assumed the title of Kouei-shuang (it may be Gushan or *Κοϸϸανος* of the coins[3]). He conquered the Kings of Pota and Kipin, and then invaded Tien-chu or India.

The products of the country are elephants, rhinoceros, tortoise-shell, gold, silver, copper, iron, lead, and tin. The people have rare things, which are found in the country of Tai Chin

---

[1] This agrees well with the description of the royal castles or fortresses given in the early Law-books or Dharma-sûtras.

[2] The Dasagrâmîs of Pâṇini.

[3] Oldenberg, Ueber der Datirung der ältern indischen Münz- und Inschriften-reihen, p. 297. Thomas, Journal of the Royal Asiatic Society, 1877, p. 18, gives a coin of Heraos, Sakakorranos, where the expression Ἡράου τυραννοῦντος makes it evident that *Κοϸϸανος* has nothing to do with *Κοίρανος*.

or Great Chin, because they have communication with those of the Great Chin westward. There are also among the products of India fine linen, good rugs or mats made of wool and fur, several kinds of incense, stone honey, black pepper, ginger, and black salt.

In the time of the Emperor Hwa (89–105) they often sent messengers to China and presented something, as if it were their tribute. But afterwards those of the Western regions rebelled (against the Emperor of China), and interrupted their communication, until the second year of the period Yen-hsi (159) in the reign of the Emperor Kwan (147–167).

In the fourth year of the same period (161) the foreign people incessantly came from outside of the wall of a castle on the border at a place called Jitsu-nan.

This is an independent and, if we make allowance for Chinese modes of thought and expression, a perfectly trustworthy account of the state of things in India from the first century before to about the third century after Christ.

NOTE F, p. 89.

LETTERS ON BUDDHISM.

A Conference on Buddhism was held in June 1882 at Sion College, to discuss the real or apparent coincidences between the religions of Buddha and Christ. Being unable to assist in person, I addressed the following letters to the Secretary, which were read at the meeting and published afterwards.

I.

'I regret that it is quite out of my power to be present at the discussion on Thursday. May I venture, however, to say that a discussion on Buddhism in general seems to me almost an impossibility. The name of Buddhism is applied to religious opinions not only of the most varying, but of a decidedly opposite character held by people on the highest and the lowest stages of civilisation, divided into endless sects, nay, founded on two distinct codes of canonical writings. I hardly know any proposition that could be made with regard to Buddhism in general. *Divide et impera!* is the only way that can lead to a mutual understanding on the fundamental principles of Buddha's doctrine, and considering the special qualifications of those who will address your meeting, I should think that an account of what Buddhism is at the present moment in Ceylon, both with the learned and unlearned classes, would be far more interesting and useful than a general discussion on Buddhism. I shall mention the subject to two Buddhist priests who have been reading Sanskrit with me for several years, but their Buddhism is so different from the Buddhism now practised in Ceylon that they would hardly recognise it as their own religion.

'Excuse these hurried remarks, and believe me,

'Yours faithfully,

'F. MAX MÜLLER.'

II.

'I can have no objection to your reading my letter at your conference, and after receiving your second letter, I feel all the more sorry that I am unable to attend in person, not that I have much faith in *public* discussions, it being so very difficult to be quite frank and truthful when you are listened to by hundreds of people, and when success and applause seem for the moment more important than the establishment of facts and the recognition of truth. But I admire the fearless spirit in which you invite public discussion on a subject which has become a kind of bugbear to so many people. I fully sympathise with you, and I think I can say of myself that I have all my life worked in the same spirit that speaks from your letter, so much so that if any of your friends could prove to me what they seem to have said to you, namely, 'that Christianity was but an inferior copy of a greater original,' I should bow and accept the greater original. That there are startling coincidences between Buddhism and Christianity cannot be denied, and it must likewise be admitted that Buddhism existed at least 400 years before Christianity. I go even further, and should feel extremely grateful if anybody would point out to me the historical channels through which Buddhism had influenced early Christianity. I have been looking for such channels all my life, but hitherto I have found none. What I have found is that for some of the most startling coincidences there are historical antecedents on both sides, and if we once know those antecedents, the coincidences become far less startling. If I do find in certain Buddhist works doctrines identically the same as in Christianity, so far from being frightened, I feel delighted, for surely truth is not the less true because it is believed by the majority of the human race.

'I believe we have made some progress during the last thirty years. I still remember the time when all heathen religions were looked upon as the work of the Devil. We know now that they are stages in a growth, and in a growth not determined by an accidental environment only, but by an original purpose, a purpose to be realised in the history of the human race as a whole. Even missionaries have begun to approach the heathen in a new and better spirit. They look for what may safely be preserved in the religion of their pupils, and on that common ground they try to erect a purer faith and a better worship, instead of attempting to destroy the sacred foundations of religion which, I believe, exist, or at least existed, in every human heart. See on this subject the wise remarks of the Bishop of Lahore (French), as quoted in the *Liberal*, July 23, 1882.

'I send you a report which I have just issued on The Sacred Books of the East, translated by various Oriental scholars, and edited by myself. My object in publishing these translations is exactly the same as yours, namely, to give to those who are interested in the history of religion, facts, instead of theories.

'I had spent nearly the whole of my life in publishing the text and commentary of *one* of the Sacred Books of the East, the Veda, or more correctly the Rig-veda, the most ancient monument of Eastern religion, the root of all the later religious growth of India, in a certain sense, the key also to Buddhism, inasmuch as that religion starts with a denial of the sacred authority of the Veda. The publication of that work has produced a complete revolution, not only in our own views of the origin and growth of ancient religion, but in the religious life of the Hindus themselves, and this not so much on the surface as in its deepest foundations.

'When I saw how little there was left to me of active life, I invited the co-operation of my friends and colleagues to make, at all events, a beginning in the publication of trustworthy translations of all the more important among the Sacred Books of the East. From the enclosed report you will see that Buddhism in its various phases has received its full share of attention, and that some of its canonical books may now be studied by those who do not read Sanskrit, Pâli, or Chinese.

'Yours very faithfully,

'F. Max Müller.'

NOTE G, p. 93.

THE RENAISSANCE OF SANSKRIT LITERATURE.

Samvat Era.

One of the chief objections that will no doubt be raised against my belief in a literary interregnum, lasting from the first century B.C. to at least the third century A.D., is the famous Samvat era of 56 B.C.[1], dating from what used to be called the Augustan age of India, the glorious reign of Vikramâditya, the destroyer of the *S*akas and other Mle*kk*has, and the great patron of Sanskrit literature, at whose court the Nine Gems, Dhanvantari, Kshapa*n*aka, Amarasi*m*ha, *S*añku, Vetâlabha*tt*a, Gha*t*a-karpara, Kâlidâsa, Varâhamihira, and Vararu*k*i were supposed to have flourished[2].

It has long been an open secret, however, among all who are interested in Indian coins and inscriptions, that there is absolutely no documentary evidence whatever for the existence of such a king Vikramâditya in the first century B.C. But the puzzle has always been, how the belief in such a king, living in the first century B.C., and in all his wonderful achievements, could have arisen, and this puzzle has at last been solved, I believe, by what I may be allowed to call the architectonical genius of Mr. Fergusson[3].

---

[1] I spell Samvat instead of Sa*m*vat, because it has become almost an Anglo-Indian word, and I use 56 B.C. throughout as its initial year, though it begins in 57. See Indian Antiquary, xi, p. 271.

[2] These names are quoted from the *G*yotirvidâbhara*n*a (16th cent.). This verse seems, however, to be inserted there from elsewhere, and we find it quoted elsewhere as a kind of *versus memorialis*; see Hæberlin's Anthology, p. 1; Bhao Daji, Journal of the Royal Asiatic Society, Bombay, 1860, p. 26. It is hardly right to say that the only work which pretends to notice the contemporaneous existence of the Nine Gems, at the court of Vikrama, is the *G*yotirvidâbhara*n*a. The Nine Gems at the court of Vikrama, and the name of at least one of them, Amara-deva, occur in an inscription, dated 949 A.D. Asiatic Researches, i, p. 284. See, however, Weber, Z. D. M. G. xxii, p. 709.

[3] Journal of the Royal Asiatic Society, 1880. On the *S*aka, Samvat, and Gupta Eras; a Supplement to his Paper on Indian Chronology, 1870.

I do not mean to say that all difficulties which beset that period of Indian chronology have been removed by him, but I cannot help thinking that in the main his solution will turn out to be correct. Mr. Fergusson tries to prove that what is called the era of Vikramâditya, 56 B.C., was a date arrived at by taking the date of the great battle of Korur[1], in which Vikramâditya, i.e. Harsha of U*gg*ayinî, finally defeated the Mle*kk*has, 544 A.D.[2], and by throwing back the beginning of the new era 6 × 100 (or 10 × 60) before that date, i.e. 56 B.C. By a similar process, i.e. by adding 10 × 100 years, another chronological era, called the Harsha era[3], was fixed at 456 B.C., though it never seems to have come into actual use.

---

[1] This battle of Korur is described by Albiruni in his account of the *S*aka era:

'The *S*aka era,' he writes, 'called by the Indian *S*aka-kâla, is posterior to that of Vikrama Âditya by 135 years. *S*aka is the name of a prince who reigned over the countries situated between the Indus[*] and the sea. His residence was in the centre of the empire, in the country named Âryâvarta. The Indians represent him as born in another class than that of the *S*âkyas; some pretend that he was a *S*ûdra and a native of the town of Mansura (Bahman-abad). There are even some who say that he was not of the Indian race, and that he was born in Western countries. The people had much to suffer from his despotism until they received aid from the East. Vikramâditya marched against him, put his army to flight, and killed him in the territory of Korour, situated between Multan and the castle of Luny (in the Panjâb?). This epoch became celebrated by the joy which the peoples felt at *S*aka's death, and it was selected for an era, principally by astronomers. On the other hand, Vikramâditya received the title of *S*rî, on account of the honour which he had acquired.' But Albiruni adds that the date of the reign of this Vikramâditya does not allow us to identify him with the prince of the same name who ruled in Malva. This battle of Korur may be the same as that of Multan, mentioned by Târanâtha, '*S*rî Harsha abolished the teaching of the Mle*kk*has by massacring them at Multan.' Asaṅga and Vasubandhu were his contemporaries (900 p. B.N.); his predecessor was called Gambhîrapaksha, his successor *S*îla. Ind. Ant. 1875, p. 365.

[2] See Journal of the Royal Asiatic Society, 1880, p. 273. The same date, 466 *S*aka = 544 A.D., is mentioned in the *S*atruñgaya Mâhâtmya as the beginning of Vikramâditya's reign; Kern, Preface, p. 15, on the authority of Wilford. Bühler, however, calls the *S*atruñgaya Mâhâtmya 'a wretched forgery of the 12th or 14th century.' It has been edited by Professor Weber.

[3] Journal of the Royal Asiatic Society, 1880, p. 275. Reinaud, Mémoire sur l'Inde, p. 136. It is strange that Albiruni should not have guessed the real state of the case, when he was told by a native that Harsha lived 400 years

---

[*] Bhao Daji, Journal of the Royal Asiatic Society of Bombay, viii, p. 242, 1864. Reinaud, Mémoire sur l'Inde, 1849, p. 79.

This certainly seems very plausible[1]. We could thus understand why much that was said originally of the Vikramâditya of the sixth century A.D. was reflected on the purely nominal Vikramâditya of the Vikrama era, 56 B.C., the inventor of the era being projected 600 years before his actual reign, a period when there is really no monumental, numismatic, or historical evidence of the existence of any such king.

It has been said that there is as yet no other evidence for this battle of Korur (Kurukshetra?) besides Albiruni's statement. But Albiruni does not invent battles. He tells us what he was told, and he may sometimes have misunderstood what he was told. But in our case the chronological side of the argument is too strong to be set aside by mere general suspicions and surmises, though, no doubt, it would have to yield to contemporaneous evidence which should make a great battle against foreign invaders at that time and in that place impossible. Besides, the statements of Târânâtha as to Harsha's victory near Multan, though no doubt very modern, cannot be due to mere accident.

Others had guessed at such a solution before Mr. Fergusson, but what I admire in him is his pluck, and the clearness with which he puts forward his theories. Nothing, I feel sure, has injured Sanskrit studies so much as the want of a certain amount of scientific manliness and straightforwardness on the part of scholars who never venture to say Yes or No, and who always involve a crowd of reasons for and against in a cloud of words difficult to construe. Mr. Fergusson, whether he is right or wrong, at all events puts down his foot firmly and sticks to his colours as long as he can. There is an immense advantage in this. If he is wrong, he can be knocked down, and no one is likely to defend again

before Vikrama; but that, according to the Almanack of Kasmira, Harsha ought to be placed 664 years later, i.e. 608 A.D. The number of years may not be quite right, but what really took place is clearly indicated.

[1] Many years ago Holtzmann (Über den griech. Ursprung des indischen Thierkreises, p. 19) remarked, 'to assign to Vikramâditya the first year of his era might be quite as great a mistake as we should commit in placing Pope Gregory XIII in the year 1 of the Gregorian calendar, or even Julius Cæsar in the first year of the Julian period to which his name has been given, i.e. in the year 4713 B.C.' See Weber, Sanskrit Literature, p. 202.

what he has been unable to uphold. If he is right, there can be no mistake as to where he has planted his standard, and others may safely push forward beyond the point which he has reached.

Thus in the case before us, his position is clearly defined. The era of Vikrama, he holds, was not invented before the sixth century A. D. It cannot therefore occur in any historical document before that date, and the whole theory would collapse if one single coin or stone could be produced dated (contemporaneously) 543 of the Samvat of Vikrama. Other scholars would probably say that we know too little as yet of the history of the six centuries from 56 B.C. to 544 A.D. to enable us to speak with so much certainty on this point. True, but Mr. Fergusson speaks with perfect certainty on what, from his view of the case, would be an impossibility. And what is the result? Scholars do not like the defiant position which he assumes, and they try everything to upset it, and thus the truth will be discovered far sooner than by any amount of learned humming and hawing.

The contest has been going on for some time. Dr. Bhao Daji[1] arrived at the conclusion that 'not a single inscription or copper-plate grant is dated in the Vikrama Samvat before the eleventh century of the Christian era, and that the Vikrama Samvat was brought into use on the revival of *G*ainism and the establishment of the Anhilpura dynasty in Gujerat.' Mr. Fergusson[2] thought at first that the Vikrama era was invented in the age of Bho*g*a of Dhârâ (A.D. 993), or rather by the revived Châlukyas (A.D. 1003). This, however, was going too far. General Cunningham in his Archæological Reports, vol. ii, p. 266, denies indeed the possibility of any inscription being dated in the Samvat era in 747, and reads in consequence the date of one of Tod's inscriptions, not 747 — 56 = 691, but 747 + 78 = 825/6. Afterwards, however, on p. 68, he speaks of an inscription dated 811, which he interprets in the Vikrama era, i. e. 754/5 A. D., and which he quotes as the earliest inscription he is aware of, dated in that mediæval era[3]. Sir Walter Elliot

[1] Journal of the Royal Asiatic Society, Bombay, viii, p. 242 note.
[2] Journal of the Royal Asiatic Society, 1870, p. 132.
[3] There is no contradiction in this, as Mr. Fergusson seems to think (Journal

published translations of some Châlukya inscriptions in 1836 (J. R. A. S. 1837, p. 14), in which the incipient substitution of the Vikrama for the *S*aka era is alluded to[1]. Of course, nothing short of a contemporaneous document dated less than 600 of the Vikrama era would really upset Mr. Fergusson's theory, and such a date has, as yet, not been met with.

My learned friend, Professor Bühler, who still holds to the belief that the Vikrama era, which begins 56 B. C., was really established by a king of that name who lived before the beginning of the Christian era, has for years been engaged in the study of Indian inscriptions, and has of course been most anxious to produce at least one inscription dated contemporaneously in any year before 600 of Vikrama, or 544 A. D. He could easily prove that Bhao Daji's limit was much too late, as there is the Samângadh plate, the date of which in the Vikrama era comes to 754 A. D.[2] He also pointed out the Pâ*th*an inscriptions of Samvat 802 (746 A. D.), recording the accession of Vanarâ*g*a, though here Mr. Burges expressed some doubts as to its genuineness. Anyhow the fact remained that a scholar who had probably seen more inscriptions than any other, could not produce a single case where the Vikrama era was used before 754 A. D., that is, 810 years after its supposed introduction[3]. I should have expected therefore that Professor Bühler would have hesitated, when he suddenly came on the Kâvî inscription which gives the date 430 for its grantor *G*ayabha*t*a, before accepting it as a Vikrama date. Under other circumstances his arguments might have carried conviction, but when this is the only case of a Vikrama date before 600, the circumstantial evidence on which he relies requires, surely, careful reconsideration. If *G*ayabha*t*a is the father of Dada II, and if Dada's dates range from *S*aka 380 to 417 (A. D. 459–498), no doubt

---

of the Royal Asiatic Society, 1880, pp. 271, 272); but what seems strange is that on other occasions General Cunningham should translate Sam. 5 as B. C. 52. See Archæological Survey, iii, 31.

[1] 'Tribhuvana Malla (1182 A. D.) rubbed out the *S*aka, and instituted the Vikrama aera in its stead.' Journal of the Royal Asiatic Society, 1837, p. 14; 1880, p. 278. Journal of the Royal Asiatic Society, Bombay, ix, p. 316.

[2] Journal of the Royal Asiatic Society, Bombay, ii, p. 371 seq.

[3] Professor Bühler informs me that he now possesses an inscription, dated Samvat 794 = A. D. 737/8.

the date assigned to his father, viz. 486, cannot be *S*aka (A. D. 564). But does it follow therefore that it is Vikrama 486, i.e. 430 A. D.? Is it likely that the father would use one era, and the son another? Besides, the date in the inscription is injured, and even if the date were right, there would be considerable doubt whether the Ashâ*dh*a *S*udi could have fallen on a Sunday in 430 A. D. Heartily as I should welcome any evidence that would settle this interesting point either way, I cannot think that this one date[1] of *G*ayabha*t*a will settle it. What has to be proved is that an era, invented by a great king in 56 B.C., remained dormant for 600 years at least. This will require very plausible arguments, and the strongest monumental evidence.

Date of Vikramâditya Harsha of U*gg*ayinî.

Let us now see how, according to Dr. Bhao Daji[2] and Mr. Fergusson[3], the real date of Vikramâditya, the inventor of the Vikrama era, can be determined. During the whole of Hiouen-thsang's travels in India, *S*îlâditya (Harshavardhana Kumârarâ*g*a) was on the throne of Kânyakub*g*a, as supreme ruler in the north of India[4]. The date of these travels, according to Chinese chronology, is from 629–645. In about 640, or during his second stay at Nâlanda, Hiouen-thsang had a vision that king *S*îlâditya would die in ten years. This, apart from all visions, would place the king's death in 650 A. D. When Hiouen-thsang took leave of king *S*îlâditya, he had reigned thirty years, and was holding his sixth quinquennial assembly (called Mokshamahâparishad, or Pa*ñk*aparishad). The beginning of his reign must therefore be fixed at 610, its end about 650. He was by caste a Vai*s*ya[5].

---

[1] Professor Bühler's remark (Indian Antiquary, 1876, p. 152) has not escaped me; but here again the reading of the figures is very doubtful, see Fleet, Indian Antiquary, 1876, p. 68, and Professor Bühler himself admits now that there is no Samvat date on that plate.

[2] Journal of the Royal Asiatic Society, Bombay, 1860, p. 225; 1868, p. 249.

[3] Journal of the Royal Asiatic Society, 1870, p. 85.

[4] Dr. Edkins (Athenæum, 1880, July 3, p. 8) informs us that the same emperor who received Hiouen-thsang, received with equal favour the Syrian Christians, Alopen and his companions, in A. D. 639.

[5] Hiouen-thsang, i, p. 111. Vai*s*ya is sometimes changed into Vaidya.

The Chinese historian Ma Tuan-lin gives slightly different dates, for he speaks of an embassy sent to Magadha in 648[1] which found king *S*îlâditya dead, and his minister O-lo-na-shan (A-la-na-chun) ruling in his stead. So small a difference, however, in Indian chronology is really to be considered as a confirmation rather than as a difficulty; and so is Ma Tuan-lin's account of the wars between *S*îlâditya and his great opponent Pulake*s*in[2] of Kalyâ*n*a (whom he does not name), which he places in 618–627[3].

The father of this *S*îlâditya was Prabhâkara (or Prabhâkara-vardhana), and his elder brother, Râ*g*yavardhana[4]. Both had been reigning before *S*îlâditya.

The elder brother had been defeated and killed by *S*a*s*âṅka (moon) of Kar*n*asuvar*n*a[5], an enemy of the Buddhists[6], and it was then that *S*îlâditya was proclaimed king, though he declined the title of Mahârâ*g*a, preferring that of Kumâra-râ*g*a. In six years he conquered the 'five Indies,' but peace was not restored during thirty years. Being a strict Buddhist, he forbad the eating of meat. His minister was Po-ni (Bha*nd*i). This account of *S*îlâditya of Kânyakub*g*a, the supreme ruler of Northern India, and his two predecessors, coming from an eye-witness, the Chinese pilgrim Hiouen-thsang, is confirmed by a well-known Sanskrit author Bâ*n*a, in his Harsha*k*arita. This text was discovered by Dr. F. Hall, and its great importance pointed out in his preface to the

---

[1] Journal of the Royal Asiatic Society, 1870, p. 85; Journal of the Royal Asiatic Society, Bombay, vi, p. 69. Julien, Mélanges de Géographie Asiatique, p. 164, gives 646 as the date of the departure of the embassy, Na-fo-ti-a-la-na-chun as the name of the minister, and *S*rîkumâra as king of Eastern India, probably Bhâskara-varman, Kumâra.

[2] The inscriptions are supposed to give a different date for Pulake*s*in, the rival of Harsha. Bhao Daji, Journal of the Royal Asiatic Society, Bombay, viii, p. 250; and Journal of the Royal Asiatic Society, 1870, pp. 92–95. See, however, Fergusson, Indian Antiquary, 1873, p. 94, and Fleet, in Indian Antiquary, 1876, p. 67.

[3] See Stan. Julien, l. c. p. 162.

[4] Hiouen-thsang, i, p. 112.

[5] Hiouen-thsang, i, p. 112.

[6] L. c., ii, p. 250. He was the same who destroyed the Bodhi-tree 'dans ces derniers temps,' l. c., ii, p. 463, but different from Sâhasâṅka, whose life was written by Mahe*s*vara, and by the later Harsha; see Hall, Vâsavadattâ, pref. p. 18.

Vâsavadattâ. It has since been published at Calcutta. In this work, again the work of an eye-witness, the same Harsha or Harshavardhana *S*îlâditya is represented as the son of Pratâpa*s*îla and Ya*s*ovatî, his elder brother being Râ*g*yavardhana[1]. Prabhâkaravardhana is said to have been a worshipper of the sun, while his father Pushpabhûti had been a worshipper of *S*iva. Prabhâkaravardhana's spiritual guide was called Mâdhavagupta, his astrologer Târaka, his physician Sushe*n*a[2]. Both he and his brother had been educated by Bha*nd*i. Their sister, Râ*g*ya*s*rî, was married to Grahavarman, who was killed by the king of Mâlava[3] on the same day that Prabhâkara was defeated. This king of Mâlava was afterwards slain by Râ*g*yavardhana, and when Râ*g*yavardhana succumbed to Gupta, king of Gau*d*a, Harsha (Harsha Deva or Harsha Malla) succeeded. While Bha*nd*i defeated the Mâlavas, and Râ*g*ya*s*rî was recovered, Harsha made an alliance with Bhâskaravarman of Prâg*g*yotisha, the same as Bhâskaravarman, the king of Kâmarûpa, whom Hiouen-thsang visited, his title being Kumâra (Hiouen-thsang, iii, 77), like that of Harsha[4].

The duration of the reigns of Râ*g*yavardhana and Prabhâkara is not given, but as it is stated that about 640 *S*îlâditya had reigned thirty years, and that, about sixty years before that time, the throne was occupied by *S*îlâditya Pratâpa*s*îla, Mr. Fergusson proposes to fix the end of

---

[1] See Dr. Fitz-Edward Hall's important Introduction to his edition of Vâsavadattâ, p. 17, note. Harshavardhana, mentioned in the inscriptions, was vanquished by Pulakesin II, Satyâsraya, whose reign began in 609 A.D. (Ind. Ant. 1873, p. 94), while his great grandson reigned 700–705, according to inscriptions. See Journal of the R. Asiatic Society of Bombay, Jan. 1851, pp. 205, 207, 211; Oct. 1854, p. 5. Bhao Daji, On Kâlidâsa, p. 2.

[2] The author of the Romaka-siddhânta is called *S*rishena, but its date, 505 A.D., is too early to allow us to identify Sushe*n*a and *S*rishe*n*a.

[3] A son of the king of Mâlava was a guest at Harsha's court (Vâsavad. pref. 12), and a hostage (p. 50).

[4] It is to be hoped that the researches carried on with so much success by M. A. Barth and M. A. Bergaigne will bring to light some contemporaneous sovereigns in the inscriptions of Kambo*g*a. Unfortunately the inscriptions hitherto deciphered are deficient at the very time which interests us most, namely, the seventh century (Journal Asiatique, 1882, p. 188). But the many names, ending in varman, the name of Narendra, and the title of Kumâra (for, I think, it is a title on p. 227, l. 11) all give the impression that the sovereignty of the kings of Kâmarûpa may have extended to the valley of the Irâvatî.

*S*îlâditya Pratâpa*s*îla's reign in 580, which leaves about thirty years, 580–610 for Prabhâkaravardhana and Râ*g*yavardhana. *S*îlâditya Pratâpa*s*îla ruled fifty years, 530–580[1], and was preceded by Vikramâditya (at *S*râvastî[2]), whose reign would accordingly have ended in 530. From what Hiouen-thsang tells us of Vikrama's treatment of the Buddhist Manoratha[3], the king seems for a time to have favoured the Brahmans, while his successor *S*îlâditya favoured Vasubandhu and the Buddhists, though it is easy to see that, during most of these reigns, all sects enjoyed equal freedom and peace. One king is a Buddhist, the next a Brahmanist. Sometimes the same king favours both systems, or favours one at one time, the other at another. We hear of fathers turning Buddhists, and their children remaining Brahmanists[4], and if there are any feuds between the rival sects, they are settled by intellectual rather than by physical force.

Now this proposal to assign thirty years to the reigns of Prabhâkaravardhana and Râ*g*yavardhana, seems to me to create unnecessary difficulties. Hiouen-thsang says no more than that sixty years before 640 the throne was occupied by *S*îlâditya. If we assign to *S*îlâditya a reign from 550 to 600, it would have been equally true to say that *S*îlâditya reigned sixty years before 640. There would then remain ten years for the reigns of Prabhâkaravardhana and Râ*g*yavardhana, both of whom died a violent death, and we should have the battle of Korur and the starting point of the Vikrama era, as well as the appointment of Mât*ri*gupta to the throne of Ka*s*mîra, well within the reign of Vikramâditya, his reign extending to 550 A.D. 'Sixty years' is probably meant for the B*ri*haspati cycle.

---

[1] Ferishtah, who calls him Bho*g*a, assigns fifty years to him. Journal of the Royal Asiatic Society, 1880, p. 278 note.

[2] Hiouen-thsang, ii, p. 115.

[3] Manorhita, which would only be Mano'rhita, seems to be meant for Manoratha (Jou-i, in Chinese), see Hiouen-thsang, i, p. 405.

[4] M.M., Introduction to the Science of Religion, p. 173. Journal Asiatique, 1882, p. 163.

This may be seen from the following table:—

— 550. **Vikramâditya Harsha** of U*gg*ayinî.

531–579. Khosru Nushirvân and Barzôi.

544. Battle of Korur, 600 after 56 B.C., era of Vikrama.

Siddhasena Sûri, a *G*ain, helps in reckoning the era.

544. Mât*ri*gupta, ruler of Kasmîra, contemporary of Bhart*ri*men*th*a.

Kâlidâsa, contemporary of Dignâga, Vasubandhu, and Asaṅga.

" mentioned with Bhâravi in inscript. 634 A.D.

" his Setukâvya praised by Da*nd*in (6th cent.)

" quotes Bhâsa, Saumilla.

Varâha-mihira, died 587.

" quotes Aryabha*t*a, born 476.

" " Romaka-siddhânta by Srîshe*n*a, 505, based on Lâ*t*a, Vasish*th*a, Vi*g*ayanandin, &c.

" " Paulisa-siddhânta by Paulus al Yunâni.

" " Vasish*th*a-siddhânta by Vish*n*u*k*andra.

" " Saura-siddhânta.

" " Paitâmaha-siddhânta; also Satya Bhadanta, Bâdarâya*n*a, &c.

Amara-si*m*ha, translated into Chinese 561–566.

*G*ish*n*u, father of Brahmagupta (born 598).

Dignâga, criticised by Uddyotakara, who is mentioned by Subandhu, who is mentioned by Bâ*n*a.

Manoratha, teacher of Vasubandhu, disgraced, 900 p. B. N.?

550–600. ***S*îlâditya Pratâpa*s*îla** (Mâlava), called Bho*g*a by Ferishtah.

Vasubandhu, restored, Pandit at Nâlanda, brother of Asaṅga; died before 569.

Prabhâkaravardhana.

Mâdhavagupta, Târaka, Sushe*n*a, at his Court.

Râ*g*yavardhana (eldest son).

Defeats king of Mâlava.

Is defeated by *S*a*s*âṅka of Kar*n*asuvar*n*a, an enemy of Buddha, or Gupta of Gau*d*a.

Fei-tu, Chinese ambassador, 605.

610–650. ***S*îlâditya Harshavardhana** (younger son), called Kumârarâ*g*a, a Vai*s*ya.

His sister, Râ*g*ya*s*rî, wife of Grahavarman who was killed by king of Mâlava.

His minister Bha*nd*i (Po-ni).

Alliance with Bhâskara-varman, Kumâra of Prâ*gg*yotisha (Kâmarûpa).

Wars with Pulakesin II of Mahârâsh*t*ra, temp. Hiouen-thsang (618–625, Ma Tuan-lin).

Defeated by Pulakesin II, Satyâ*s*raya, who began to reign 609.

Chinese embassy to Magadha, leaves 648, arrives after *S*îl.'s death.

Visited by Hiouen-thsang, 629–645; by Alopen, 639.

Dandin, Dasakumârakarita, Kâvyâdarsa, old.
Subandhu, Vâsavadattâ, quoted by Bâna.
" " quotes Uddyotakara, Dharmakîrti, pupil of Asaṅga.
Bâna, Harshakarita, Kâdambarî, Kandikâstotra, Ratnâvalî (Dhâvaka?) Pârvatîparinayanâtaka (ed. Bombay).
Mayûra, Mayûra-sataka.
Mânatuṅga Sûri, Bhaktâmara-stotra.
Nârâyana.
Âdhyarâga.
Bhartrihari, died 650 (I-tsing).
Gayâditya (Kâsikâ), died 660 (I-tsing).
Brahmagupta, born 598.

Though some of the links in this chronological system are still doubtful, the belief in the existence of a Vikramâditya in the first century B.C. may now be accounted for, while his real existence in the sixth century admits of little doubt.

The Saka Era.

There is, however, another era, commonly called the Saka era, which, though it does not bear immediately on our subject, viz. the Renaissance of Sanskrit Literature, cannot well be passed over. And this for two reasons. First, because that era, beginning in 78 A.D., has often been supposed to mark the end of the Northern Invasion of India, and has been fixed upon by several scholars as the beginning of a revival of native government and native literature in India. Secondly, because here too we have to note a brilliant conjecture of Mr. Fergusson[1] which, if I cannot as yet accept it as readily as the former, seems to me nevertheless to contain a very considerable amount of truth. It gives me particular pleasure to acknowledge the high merit of Mr. Fergusson's chronological combinations, because I have on other occasions expressed my dissent from some of his theories with equal frankness. Surely *hanc veniam petimusque damusque vicissim*, and what would become of our studies if, from personal or any other considerations, we should ever shrink from speaking our

[1] See his two articles 'On Indian Chronology,' 1870, and 'On the Saka, Samvat, and Gupta Eras,' 1880, in the Journal of the Royal Asiatic Society.

mind? Mr. Fergusson, without pretending to any knowledge of Sanskrit, has certainly seen two points which Sanskrit scholars had failed to see, namely, that the *S*aka era is older than the Vikrama era in India, so far as monumental evidence is concerned, and that, far from marking the end of the reign of the *S*akas in India, it most likely dates from about the time of the inauguration of Kanishka, the *S*aka king, as lord paramount of India.

On the first point there seems little room for doubt; on the second, the question is whether Kanishka's inauguration really coincides with 78 A.D., or whether the era was fixed theoretically, like the Samvat era, and somewhere near the actual beginning of his reign. The facts established by Mr. Fergusson possess a very considerable historical significance, as showing that, like the knowledge of the alphabet and of coinage, the idea of chronology also, in our sense of the word, came to the Indians from without; in the first instance, from the Greeks, but, in its more practical application, from the *S*akas. The first traces of chronologically dated documents occur in the A*s*oka inscriptions, and then again in the inscriptions of Kanishka. Both kings give simply the years of their reign, without looking forward to the future or wishing to become founders of historical eras. Kanishka, as if to leave no doubt on the foreign influences which led him to make these inscriptions, uses Greek letters in addition to his own, and adds the Greek names of the months[1].

This is all perfectly natural and historically intelligible. There was no chronological or astronomical theory at the bottom of these dates. All that happened was that, while during the reign of Kanishka, we have in inscriptions the expression 'in the ninth year of the great king Kanishka' (mahârâ*g*asya Kanishkasya sa*m*vatsare[2] navame), we find in the inscriptions of his successors the number of the years carried on, so that, for instance, 'in the eighty-third year of

---

[1] We read in the Bahâwalpur Inscription: Maharā*g*assa Ra*g*adira*g*assa Devaputassa Kanishkassa, sa*m*vatsare ekadase Sam II. Daisisassa masassa divase attaviseti 28. This is meant for the Greek month Daisios. Journal of the Royal Asiatic Society, 1870, p. 500.

[2] Sometimes shortened to sa*m*vatsa, sa*m*vat, sa*m*va, and sam.

Vâsudeva' (mahârâ*g*asya Vâsudevasya sam 83), does not mean in the eighty-third year of Vâsudeva's reign, but in the 83 Samvatsara (counting from Kanishka's anointment) of Vâsudeva.

Date of Kanishka.

The question then arises whether Kanishka, the great *S*aka king, could be considered as the unconscious founder of the *S*aka era, i.e. whether his own consecration could have taken place so late as 78 A.D.

Mr. Fergusson has shown that the occurrence of Roman consular coins in the tope at Manikyala, which is believed to have been built by Kanishka, would prove no more than that that building cannot be earlier than 43 B.C., but would decide nothing as to how much later it may be, while the state of the Roman denarii, as compared with the coins of Kanishka, found side by side, would almost amount to a proof that these Roman coins must have had a long course of wear and tear, before they were deposited in that Tope. Mr. Fergusson's next argument, though not irresistible, is certainly ingenious. Taking his stand on the numismatic fact that the coins of Gondophares, who reigned in the North-west provinces of India, are anterior to those of Kanishka [1], he argues that those who invented the legend of St. Thomas' visit to Gondophares [2], must have been aware that Gondophares lived after Christ's death, and that therefore the numismatically later Kanishka could not have lived in the century B.C., and date the years of his reign from the Vikramâditya Samvat, 56 B.C. [3]

The next argument, namely, that in the Ahin Posh Tope, near Jellalabad, excavated by Mr. W. Simpson, new coins of Kadphises, Kanishka, and Huvishka were found, together with Roman coins of Domitian, Trajan, and the Empress Sabina, the wife of Hadrian, would prove, no doubt, that the Tope could not have been erected before 120 A.D., but the fact

---

[1] Prinsep's Essays, ed. Thomas, vol. ii, p. 214.

[2] Eusebius, Hist. Eccles. i, 13; Socrates, Hist. Eccles. i, 19.

[3] The name of Gondophares, as a king of India, may have become known in the West through his coins, which contain his name clearly written in Greek letters.

that Huvishka, if we reckon his dates from the *S*aka era, 78 A.D., would have lived 78+48=126 A.D., and thus have been an actual contemporary of the Empress Sabina, is no more than noteworthy, until it can be proved that Huvishka himself built the Tope.

The same applies to the find of Vâsudeva coins in the Ali Musjid Tope. Even if, on architectural evidence, this Tope could not be earlier than the second or third century A.D., it would still have to be proved that it was built by Vâsudeva.

There is a passage in Albiruni which throws light on the practical working of the eras in his own time, and likewise on the manner in which they had been built up. Albiruni says that the capture of Somnath by Mahmud of Gazni, January, 1026, was placed by the Hindus in the year 947 of the *S*aka era. This gives us 1026−947=78/9 A.D. for the beginning of the *S*aka era, and he then goes on to tell us, how they arrived at that date. They first put 242 years, that is, 4 × 60 years + 2 years as allowance for Loka-kâla, thus arriving at 78/9+242=320 A.D., as the first year of what by some scholars has been called the Gupta era (319 A.D.). They then added 606 years, that is, six centuries, and six years as allowance for Loka-kâla, and again ninety-nine years, which had elapsed of the seventh century, and this gave them the real *S*aka date, namely 242+606+99=947, which, with 78/9 years of *S*aka, corresponds to 1025/6 A.D.

But we are now met by the same question which had to be answered with regard to the Vikrama era, namely, how did people begin to believe that the *S*aka era marked the destruction of the *S*aka kings, if it really marked their recognition all over India. Dr. Bhao Daji was, I believe, the first to point out that this idea of the *S*aka era beginning with the destruction of the *S*akas, does not crop up before the eighth century A.D.[1] Âryabha*t*a (born 476) knows as yet neither the Vikrama nor the *S*aka era, and when the *S*aka era is mentioned for the first time by Varâhamihira[2], it is simply called *S*aka-bhûpa-kâla or *S*akendra-kâla, the time of the

[1] Journal of the Royal Asiatic Society, Bombay, viii, 242.

[2] Colebrooke, Life and Essays, iii, p. 428.

*S*aka king or kings. Brahmagupta (born 598) was quoted by Colebrooke as having used the expression *S*akan*ri*pânte, which a scholiast of Bhâskara explained as meaning 'at the end [of the life or reign] of Vikramâditya, who slew a people of barbarians named *S*akas.' Whatever the commentator may have said, Brahmagupta's era is that of 78 A.D., and his expression *S*akan*ri*pânte was probably the same as *S*âka, and never intended by him to mean 'at the end of the *S*aka kings[1].'

Legends about the *S*akâri.

My own suspicion, I shall call it no more, is that the misunderstanding in taking the *S*aka king for the enemy and conqueror of the *S*akas arose from the name *S*akâri. This was taken by later writers, who had no knowledge whatever of what we call history, in the obvious sense of enemy (ari) of *S*akas, while originally it may have been only another name for *S*aka, namely *S*akâra, fem. *S*akârî, scil. (ga*n*anâ)[2].

Another explanation also is possible. *S*akâra, we know, is a name given to barbarians, and we are told that they were so called, because they could not distinguish the three Sanskrit sibilants, but pronounced them all alike as *s*a. The dialect spoken by these *S*akâras, or *S*a-sayers, was actually called *S*âkârî, and we are told in the Sâhitya-darpa*n*a (§ 432, v. 4) that it should be employed (in plays) by *S*akâras, *S*akas, and others; and so we find it, for instance, in the M*rikkh*aka*t*ika. This is certainly curious, but I must confess that, in spite of the actual use of such a dialect in the plays, the explanation of *S*akâra, as meaning *S*a-sayer, sounds to me too much like many of the later artificial etymologies of Sanskrit grammarians, and I prefer to consider *S*akâra or *S*âkâra as a derivative of *S*aka, used originally in the sense of a descendant of the *S*akas[3]. Pâ*n*ini, it is true, does not seem to know the *S*akas and the

---

[1] On anta, at the end of words, see Jacobi, Die Epen Kâlidâsa's, pp. 142, 156. In Bhao Daji's article on Kâlidâsa, p. 27, we find *s*akan*ri*pâlât, i. e. 'counting from the *S*aka king,' not *s*akan*ri*pântât.

[2] See Junagadh Inscription, guptasya kâlâga*n*anâm vidhâya.

[3] In the Prâk*ri*ta-sarvasva (Cod. Bodl. 412), the five principal Prak*ri*t dialects (vibhâshâs) seem to be called: *S*âkarî, *K*â*n*dâlî, *S*âvarî, Âbhîrikî, and *S*âkkî.

*S*aka kings[1], but he gives a rule that there is a patronymic suffix âra, by which, for instance, from godhâ he forms Gaudhâra[2], and by which from *S*aka might be formed *S*âkâra. Curiously enough, he restricts the use of that suffix to the Northerners, and it is perfectly true, that it is not a very common suffix. It is quite possible, therefore, though I do not wish to say more, that the later grammarians, meeting with the *S*âkârî dialect, explained it as the dialect of the *S*akâras, that is, the dialect of those who pronounced all sibilants as *s*, while it was used originally in the sense of the dialect of the *S*akas and their descendants. If so, it would be equally possible that the *S*âkâra era, or the *S*âkârî era, meant originally no more than the era of the *S*akas and their descendants, and was misinterpreted at a later time, into the era of the enemy of the *S*akas. There is a curious analogy in *s*ulbâri, originally a Sanskrit adaptation of sulphur, but explained as 'enemy of *s*ulba,' which *s*ulba is supposed to mean copper. See Petersb. Wörterbuch, s. v.

We now return to the question whether the *S*aka era, 78 A.D., can be identified with the inauguration of king Kanishka, the great *S*aka king, whose coins and inscriptions we possess, and who is celebrated for having convoked the great Council of Northern Buddhists in Ka*s*mîra, about 400 p. B. N. I confess I feel doubtful on that point, and I always thought it possible that while the years of Kanishka's reign were purely historical, the years of the *S*aka era, though beginning about the same time, may, like the Vikrama era, have been fixed originally by chronological computation. Even Professor Oldenberg who, independent of Mr. Fergusson, has started exactly the same theory[3],—and Mr. Fergusson could not have wished for a more useful ally,—has not quite convinced me on that point, though the difference between us is of little consequence.

---

[1] *S*âkapârthiva in ii, 1, 69, 8, has a totally different meaning, and is explained as *s*âkabhog*î* pârthiva*h*.

[2] Patañ*g*ali adds *g*â*d*âra*h*, pâ*nd*âra*h*. Ethnical names in âra are frequent, though their etymology is not always clear, e. g. gandhâra, tukhâra, etc.

[3] See his essay 'Über Datirung der älteren indischen Münz- und Inschriftenreihen.'

Professor Oldenberg, in support of his theory, appeals to the inscription of Bâdâmi, where we read, 'When 500 years had elapsed since the anointment of the *S*aka king[1],' and the other inscriptions, where the *S*aka era is simply called 'the year of the time of the *S*aka king[2].' He shows how the time between the first permanent occupation of India by the Yueh-chi, about 24 B.C., and the coronation of Kanishka, 78 A.D., is well filled by sovereigns whose historical character is established by their coins, the Σωτὴρ μέγας, the Sy Hermaios; then Kozulo Kadphises, Kozola-kadaphes, and Ooemo-Kadphises. In this manner he arrives at the conclusion that an era, beginning 78 A.D., if referring to any historical sovereign, could only have been the era of king Kanishka, and that in this date we have as useful and trustworthy a milestone in the history of India as in the dates of A*s*oka, 259–222 B.C., of *K*andragupta, 315–291 B.C., and of *S*îlâditya, the contemporary of Hiouen-thsang. Kanishka is followed by Huvishka, Huvishka by Vâsudeva, or, as they are called on their own coins, Kanerki, Ooerki, and Bazodeo; and the last of them, if we may trust to numismatic evidence, reigned to about 178 A.D., i.e. to the time when the Chinese chronicles tell us 'that the foreign people incessantly came from outside of the wall of a castle on the border at a place called Jitsu-nan.'

What happened in India after the expulsion of the *S*aka kings, at the end of the Indian Völkerwanderung, we hardly know. The Hindus themselves look upon the period immediately following as a blank, or as a time of utter confusion, until new Brahmanic dynasties arose again, such as, for instance, the Guptas, and the rulers of Valabhî, who employ different eras beginning 190 and 319 A.D.

I subjoin a few extracts from the Gârgî sa*m*hitâ[3], an astro-

---

[1] Burgess, Archæological Survey of Western India, vol. ii, p. 273; Oldenberg, l. c., pp. 292–293. (*S*akanr*i*patirâ*gy*âbhishekasa*m*vatsareshv atikrânteshu pa*ñk*asu *s*ateshu; and *S*akanr*i*pakâlasa*m*vatsare).

[2] Eggeling, Indian Antiquary, 1874, p. 305.

[3] Professor Kern assigns it to about 50 B.C. But as it prophesies the destruction of the *S*akas, it can hardly be earlier than about 200 A.D.; probably it is later. If the Gârgî sa*m*hitâ is the work of Garga, we must remember that Garga knew the sixty names of the B*r*ihaspati cycle (Nirnaya-sindhu,

nomical work, probably of the second or third century A.D. After speaking of the Kings of Pâtaliputra (mentioning Sâlisûka, the fourth successor of Asoka, by name), the author adds 'that then the viciously valiant Greeks, after reducing Sâketa (Oude)[1], the Pañkâla-country, and Mathurâ, will reach Kusumadhvaga, that is, the royal residence of Pâtaliputra, and that then all provinces will be in disorder.' This may refer to the Bactrian conquests in India, which would thus seem to have extended as far as Oude, Mathurâ, and Pâtaliputra.

Then follows a complaint about low-caste people (vrishalas) assuming the garb of hermits, which may refer to the rule of an Asoka and his Buddhistic successors. Even Kandragupta is called a vrishala.

The rule of the Greeks, we are then told, will come to an end in Madhyadesa, owing to discord among themselves, and then will follow seven kings, and, in the end, the reign of the Sakas. When that is destroyed, the earth will be empty[2].

These are very vague prophecies, yet sufficiently definite to enable us to say that they could not have been uttered before the last of the events to which they refer, that is, not before the destruction of the supremacy of the Saka kings in India at the beginning of the third century A.D.

On the other hand, as the Gârgî samhitâ is quoted by Varâhamihira, who wrote in the first half of the sixth century, its prophecies may claim more of a truly historical character than the similar prophecies which we meet with in the later Purânas. They remind me, in fact, of the prophecies, the so-called Vyâkaranas, which we find in the writings of the Northern Buddhists, and which may be assigned to about the same period.

There are several such prophecies, for instance, in the Lankâvatâra-sûtra, one of the nine Dharmas[3]. The minimum date

---

p. 1), while Gargi adjusted the Nakshatras and the zodiacal signs, see p. 325, n. 2.

[1] Cf. Mahâbhâshya, iii, 2, 11, arunad Yavanah Sâketam.

[2] See Kern's Preface to his edition of Varâhamihira's Brihat-samhitâ, pp. 36–39.

[3] This Sûtra attacks Sânkhya, Vaiseshika, Lokâyatika, and Hînayâna doctrines, and establishes two Vigñânas, the mano-vigñâna and the âlaya-vigñâna in addition to the usual six vigñânas.

this Sûtra is established through its Chinese translations. The first, by Gu*n*abhadra, was made in 443 A.D.; the second by Bodhiru*k*i, in 513 A.D.; the third by *S*ikshânanda in 700–704 A.D. In Gu*n*abhadra's translation, however, the introductory and the two concluding chapters are wanting, but they are given in the other translations. The introductory chapter treats of Râva*n*a, the lord of Laṅkâ, inviting Buddha to preach. The first of the two concluding chapters is called the Dhâra*n*î-adhyâya, the second the Gâthâ-saṅgraha. This Gâthâ-saṅgraha occupies about one-fourth of the whole work, and some of the Gâthâs occur also in the earlier chapters.

It is in this Gâthâ-saṅgraha that the following prophecies, placed in the mouth of Buddha Vira*g*as [1], not of *S*âkyamuni, occur:

Vyâsa*h* Ka*n*âda *Ri*shabha*h* Kapila*h* *S*âkyanâyaka*h*
Nirv*ri*te(r)mama pa*s**k*ât tu bhavishyanty evamâdaya*h*.
Mayi nirv*ri*te varsha*s*ate Vyâso vai Bhâratas tathâ
Pâ*nd*avâ*h* Kauravâ Râma*h* pa*s**k*ât sauro bhavishyati.
Mauryâ Nandâ*s* *k*a Guptâ*s* *k*a tato Mle*kkh*â n*ri*pâdhamâ*h*
Mle*kkh*ânte *s*âstra*s*a*m*kshobha*h* *s*âstrânte *k*a kalir yugam.
Kaliyugânte lokai*s* *k*a saddharmo hi na bhâshita*h*
Evamâdyâny atîtâni *k*akravad bhramati *g*agat.

The text is very incorrect, and it would be useless to give more extracts without having access to better documents. All I wished to point out here is that these prophecies have a peculiarly Buddhistic character, and that what they prophesy is probably what was known to have happened before the beginning of the fifth century A.D. [2]

---

[1] The son of Pra*g*âpati*h*, Vasumati*h*, of the race of Kâtyâyana, born at *K*ampâ.

[2] The following may serve as curious specimens:—

Pâ*n*ini*m* *s*abdanetâram Akshapâdo B*ri*haspati*h*
Lokâyatapra*n*etâro brahmagarbho bhavishyati.
Kâtyâyana*h* sûtrakartâ Ya*gñ*avalkas tathaiva *k*a
Pudruka (Buddhaka, MS. C.) *g*yotishâdyâni bhavishyanti kalau yuge.
Vâlmîko Mayûrâksha*s* *k*a Kau*t*ilya Â*s*valâyana*h*
*Ri*shayas *k*a mahâbhâgâ bhavishyanti anâgate.
Siddhârtha*h* *S*âkyatanayo bhûtânta*h* pa*ñk*a*k*û*d*aka*h*,
Vâsali arthamedhâvi pa*s**k*ât kâle bhavishyati.

The Saka Era called the Sâlivâhana Era.

Though I have throughout called the era which begins 78 A.D. the *S*aka era, or the *S*âka, I cannot admit that it is wrong to call it the *S*âlivâhana era, or speak of it, as Dr. Kern does, as the era which *Anglice,* but not in Sanskrit, is called *S*âlivâhana era.

At the end of the Muhûrtaga*n*apati (ed. Bombay), for instance, we read श्रीनृपशालिवाहनशके १७८५, which is A.D. 1863. This, however, it may be said, is only the editor's writing. But at the end of the Muhûrtamârta*nd*a we find the following verses[1]:

श्रीमत्कौशिकपावनो हरिपदद्वंद्वार्पितात्मा हरिस्तज्जोऽनंत इलासुरोचितगुणो नारायणस्तत्सुतः । ख्यातं देवगिरेः शिवालयमुदक् तस्मादुदक् टापरग्रामस्तद्वसतिर्मुहूर्तभुवनोन्मार्तंडमत्राकरोत् ॥[2]

'Hari, the glory of the noble Kau*s*ikas, gave his soul to (the worship of) the feet of Hari. His son Ananta possessed all the virtues fit for Brâhmans. His son was Nârâya*n*a. There is north of Devagiri the famous temple of *S*iva (the Commentator says purâ*n*aprasiddha*m* *s*ivâlaya*m* dhus*r*ine*s*a-*s*ivâlayam iti prasiddha*m* *g*yotirliṅgasthânam asti). North of it there is the village *T*âpara. Nârâya*n*a, who dwelt there, composed there the Muhûrtabhuvanonmârta*nd*a, i.e. "the sun throwing light on the world of hours."

यः षष्ट्यायुतशत १६० वृत्तबद्धमेनं मार्तंडं पठति नरः स विश्वपूज्यः ।
बह्वायुःसुखधनपुत्रमित्रभृत्यान्संप्राप्नोत्यविकलधीश्च तीर्थसिद्धिं ॥ २ ॥

'The man who reads this Mârta*nd*a, composed of 160 verses, is to be revered by all; he obtains long life, happiness, wealth, sons, friends, slaves; with sound mind he obtains the perfection of knowledge.'

---

[1] See Cat. Bodl. No. 787.

[2] The metre requires bhuvanonmârta*nd*a, at least it requires a long syllable at the end of bhuvana. The Bombay edition reads bhuvano mârta*nd*a, which gives no sense. The MS. Bodl. gives bhuvanonmârta*nd*a, and this the Commentator explains as, teshâm uddyotako mârta*nd*a iva mârta*nd*as, tathâ tam.

त्र्यंकेंद्रप्रमिते वर्षे शालिवाहनजन्मतः ।
कृतस्तपसि मार्तंडोऽयमलं जयतूद्गतः ॥ ३ ॥

'In the year 1493 from the birth of *S*âlivâhana was this Mârta*nd*a (the sun) composed in the month Mâgha. May this risen sun be fully successful.'

Now this date is A. D. 1571, and it is repeated at the end in the following words: Sukhanidhipurushârthakshmâ 1493 samâbhi*h* parimite *s*akakâle, i.e. *S*aka 1493, A.D. 1571.

The Vikramâditya Period of Literature.

These preliminary disquisitions [1] were necessary before we could approach the question which concerns us more immediately, namely, the real date of Kâlidâsa, and of the literature more or less contemporaneous with him.

If Vikramâditya, during whose reign the era of 56 B.C. was invented, lived in the sixth century after, instead of the first century before Christ, we now ask the question whether Kâlidâsa and his friends also may not have lived at the same time [2]? We see Kâlidâsa's name and that of Bhâravi, the author of the Kirâtâr*g*unîya, quoted in an inscription which was formerly supposed to date from the year *S*aka 506 (585 A.D.), but has lately been proved to date from the year *S*aka 556 (637 A.D.) [3]. This gives us a limit on one side, and we may

---

[1] I discussed the whole of this chronological and literary problem with Bhao Daji in 1863, and though in general I still hold the opinions which I then expressed, and some of which were published by him at the time, I have modified them on several points, and wish even now that what I put forward here should be considered as tentative only, and subject to correction.

[2] It seems almost impossible to give the opinions held by various Sanskrit scholars on the date of Kâlidâsa, or on the dates of certain works ascribed to Kâlidâsa, on account of their constantly varying opinions and the vague language in which they are expressed. Those who desire information on this point, may consult Professor Weber's Sanskrit Literature. That accomplished scholar seems to put Kâlidâsa's three plays between the second and fourth centuries B.C., the period of the Gupta princes, *K*andragupta, &c., see l.c., p. 204 note; but I am not quite certain that this is his real opinion.

[3] See Bhao Daji, Journal of the Royal Asiatic Society, Bombay, ix, p. 315; Fleet, Indian Antiquary, vii, p. 209; and Bhandarkar, Journal of the Royal Asiatic Society, Bombay, xiv, p. 24. I owe this reference to Professor Bühler.

even say that by that time both Kâlidâsa and Bhâravi had probably become famous in India. Let us now see whether we can fix some kind of limit on the other side.

Vasubandhu.

Hiouen-thsang[1] tells us that Vasubandhu, the pupil of Manorhita (Monoratha), was a contemporary of Vikramâditya of *S*râvastî (probably his northern residence). This Vasubandhu was a very famous Buddhist writer, whose date can be fixed with tolerable certainty, not only by the testimony of Hiouen-thsang, whose travels in India are separated by two or three generations only from Vasubandhu, but by the literary history of the Buddhists also. It may be quite true that the dates assigned by Chinese or Tibetan writers to certain Bodhisattvas and Arhats are not always trustworthy. But when we find the works of great Buddhist authorities so arranged that the later presuppose the earlier ones, we may place a certain amount of confidence in such statements.

Thus I-tsing tells us that Mât*rik*eta (Mother-child), who in his youth worshipped Mahe*s*vara, became later in life a follower of Buddha and composed 400 hymns, and afterwards 150 hymns.

These 150 hymns, he continues, were admired by Asaṅga and Vasubandhu.

---

[1] According to Hiouen-thsang (ii, 115) the Bodhisattva Vasubandhu composed his Abhidharmakosha-sâstra in the Great Monastery near Peshawer (Purushapura), and he tells us that there was a tablet there to commemorate the fact. His teacher Manorhita (Manoratha) also lived in the same monastery, and wrote there his famous Vibhâshâ-sâstra. Manorhita was the contemporary of king Vikramâditya of *S*râvastî, and lost the favour of the king. The king convoked an assembly of *S*âstrikas and *S*rama*n*as, in which the latter were defeated, which seems to mean that Vikramâditya withdrew his favour from the Buddhists and encouraged the followers of the old Brahmanic religion.

When Vikramâditya had died, Vasubandhu wished to revenge his master Manorhita, and in an assembly convoked by the new king, he defeated the *S*rama*n*as, that is, he regained the favour of king *S*îlâditya for himself and his co-religionists. Hiouen-thsang says in another place that *S*îlâditya, who occupied the throne sixty years before his time (640 − 60 = 580), was full of respect for 'the *three precious* ones.' See also Bhao Daji, On Kâlidâsa, p. 225.

The Bodhisattva *G*ina[1] added one stanza to each of the 150 hymns, so that they became 300 hymns, called the Mixed Hymns.

*S*âkyadeva of the Deer-park again added one stanza to each, so that they became 450 hymns, called the Noble Mixed Hymns.

This gives us the following succession:—

(1) Mât*rik*eta,
(2) Asaṅga and Vasubandhu (pupil of Saṅghabhadra),
(3) *G*ina,
(4) *S*âkyadeva.

We must now have recourse to another work, Târânâtha's History of Buddhism. This is no doubt a very modern compilation, and in many cases quite untrustworthy. Still it may come in as confirmatory evidence[2].

Târânâtha (p. 118) tells us that Vasubandhu was born one year after his brother Asaṅga had become a priest. Their father was a Brâhman. Vasubandhu went to Ka*s*mîra, and became a pupil of Saṅghabhadra, studying under him the Vibhâshâ, the *S*âstras of the eighteen schools, the six Tîrthya theories, and other works. After returning to Magadha he at first rejected the doctrine propounded by his brother Asaṅga in the Yogâ*k*âryabhûmi-*s*âstra. But when his brother had sent two of his pupils who recited the Akshayamati-(sûtra) and the Da*s*abhûmika-sûtra to Vasubandhu, he became convinced and converted. Vasubandhu then became his brother's pupil[3]. This brother Asaṅga, in order to expiate sin, had been commanded to teach the Mahâyâna with commentaries, and to repeat the Ush*n*îsha-vi*g*aya-vidyâ a hundred thousand times. Vasubandhu, after he had become his brother's pupil, recited many books, the Guhyapati-vidyâ among the rest, and obtained Samâdhi. He was so learned that he could repeat

---

[1] See Hiouen-thsang, iii, p. 106. Was he the author of the Hetuvidyâ-*s*âstra, and the teacher of the Yogâ*k*ârya-bhûmi*s*âstra of Maitreya?

[2] Târânâtha finished his history in 1608, when he was only thirty years of age. The Tibetan text was published from four MSS., by Wassiljew, who added a Russian translation, which was translated into German by Schiefner, and published at St. Petersburg in 1869.

[3] Akshayamati also is mentioned as his teacher.

500 Sûtras (300,000 slokas), besides 49 collections made by Ratnakû*t*a, the Avata*m*saka, Samayaratna, *S*atasâhasrika-pra*g*ñâpâramitâ, with 500 great and small Mahâyâna-sûtras, 500 Dhâra*n*îs, &c.

Vasubandhu became Pa*nd*ita in Nâlanda, travelled about in Gaura and O*d*ivi*s*a, and died in Nepal.

Many works, chiefly commentaries, are ascribed to him, his best known composition being the Abhidharma-kosha, which, with his commentary, he sent to Saṅghabhadra, his old teacher in Ka*s*mîra [1].

All we wish to utilise in these statements of Târânâtha is the relation of teacher and pupil between

Saṅghabhadra
|
Vasubandhu,

and between

the brothers Asaṅga and Vasubandhu.

We now proceed to consult another Tibetan work, the Life of Bhagavat Buddha by Ratnadharmarâ*g*a. It is more modern even than Târânâtha's work, having been composed in 1734, and we possess an abstract only of it, published by Schiefner in 1848, in the *Mémoires de l'Académie de St. Pétersbourg*. Here we read in the last chapter, that, four hundred years after the death of Buddha, Kanishka will be born, the king of *G*âlandhara, and will be taught by the Arhat Sudar*s*ana. During his reign a third collection of Buddhist sacred writings is to take place in Ka*s*mîra, in the Ear-ornament (ku*nd*ala-vana?) Vihâra, there being assembled five hundred Arhats under Pâr*s*va, and five hundred Bodhisattvas under Vasumitra. There existed at that time eighteen sects. There lived also the Â*k*ârya Nâgâr*g*una, who was received by Râhulabhadra, and who, having lived sixty years and taught the Middle-system (Mâdhyamika), went to Sukhâvatî. His disciples were *S*âkyamitra (Si*m*hala), Âryadeva, Nâgabodhi (?), Buddhapâlita. Âryadeva's pupils were *S*ûra, *S*ântideva, and Dharmatrâta.

---

[1] On works ascribed to Vasubandhu, see Târânâtha, p. 122.

This gives us:—

Kanishka = Pârsva and Vasumitra
Nâgârguna (received by Râhulabhadra)

Sâkyamitra, Ârya-deva, Nâgabodhi, Buddhapâlita

Sûra, Sântideva, Dharmatrâta.

After this, the Tibetan chronicler adds that nine hundred years after the death of Buddha, Ârya Asaṅga and Vasubandhu appeared.

Ârya Asaṅga is said to have been brought by Maitreya to Tushita, where he was taught by Agita, and supported the Mahâyâna doctrine.

Vasubandhu was brought by Ârya Asaṅga to Tushita to see Maitreya. He had been a pupil of Vinayabhadra (Saṅghabhadra?) in Kasmîra, and of Akshayamati in Nâlanda.

Then follow their pupils;

(1) Ârya Asaṅga's pupils were:—

Sthiramati in Abhidharma, favoured by Târâ (Kien-hoei, see H. Ths. iii, 46, 164).

Dignâga in Pramâna, favoured by Mañgusrî.

Dharmakîrti in logic. The two last quoted by Subandhu, in his Vâsavadattâ, p. 235.

(2) Vasubandhu's pupils were:—

Vimokshasena in the Pâramitâs,

Gunaprabha (bhadra?) in Vinaya (H. Ths. iii, 125),

Âryadeva, a Brahman,

A Chinese Master of the Tripitaka[1] (Hiouen-thsang?),

Gunamati (H. Ths. iii, 46, 164),

Yasomitra[2], the prince.

Without looking upon these statements as firmly established historical facts, we may at least try to find out how far they fit with what we know from elsewhere.

---

[1] This, according to Julien, Mélanges de Géographie, p. 189, is the recognised name of Hiouen-thsang, viz. San-thsang-fa-sse, Tripitakâkârya. During his travels in India he called himself Mokshadeva, or Mahâyânadeva (Hiouen-thsang, i, p. 248; Journal of the Royal Asiatic Society, 1882, p. 95).

[2] Yasomitra, author of the Abhidharmakoshavyâkhyâ sphutârthâ, quotes Gunamati and his disciple Vasumitra (not the author of the Mahâvibhâshâ).

We had placed Vikramâditya in the first half of the sixth century, about 100 years before Hiouen-thsang. If then we remember that Kanishka's birth is placed 400 years[1] and Asaṅga 900 years after Buddha's death (see also Wassiljew, Buddhismus, p. 52), we find an interval of 500 years between Kanishka and Asaṅga. And if we are right in placing Kanishka's coronation 78 A. D., we should get for Asaṅga and Vasubandhu about the second half of the sixth century, that is, nearly the same date at which we arrived before on the evidence supplied by Hiouen-thsang.

This is something, and we now proceed to consider another fact which was first brought to our notice by one of the most ingenious Sanskrit scholars, whose death has proved a real misfortune to the progress of native scholarship in India, Dr. Bhao Daji. In a paper, read in 1860 before the Asiatic Society of Bombay, he wrote: 'Mallinâtha, in commenting on the 14th verse of the Meghadûta, incidentally notices that

---

[1] This is a very common date for Kanishka with the Northern Buddhists, whether of his birth or of his coronation, may sometimes seem doubtful (Hiouen-thsang, ii, 172). If we take 78, the beginning of the *S*aka era, as the date of Kanishka's coronation (abhisheka), the initial date of Buddha's Nirvâ*n*a would have to be placed, not as a real event, but for the purpose of chronological calculation only, at about 322 B.C. Pârsva and Vasumitra would belong to the same period as Kanishka.

According to the same chronological system, Asoka is placed 100 years after Buddha's Nirvâ*n*a (Hiouen-thsang, ii, p. 170), i.e. 222 B.C., and this, if I am right in my rectification of the chronology of the Southern Buddhists, is the real date of his death (Dhammapada, Introd. p. xxxix).

Again, the king of Himatala, who defeats the Krityas, who are enemies of Buddhism, is placed 600 after B.N., i.e. 278 A.D. (Hiouen-thsang, ii, p. 179).

Hiouen-thsang is fully aware of the existence of three different eras. He says that some place the Nirvâ*n*a 1200 years ago (about 560 B.C.), others 1500 years ago (about 860 B.C.), but, he adds, some assert that more than 900 and less than 1000 years have now elapsed since Buddha's Nirvâ*n*a. These were no doubt the authorities who placed Kanishka 400 years after the Nirvâ*n*a, and Hiouen-thsang himself, about 960 years after Buddha (Hiouen-thsang, i, p. 131). Wassiljew (Buddhismus, p. 52) states from Tibetan sources that after the death of Gambhîrapaksha (p. 282, n.), the patron of Asaṅga (900 post B.N.) *S*rîharsha was the most powerful king in the west of India, and was succeeded by his son *S*îla. It is curious to observe that in Tibetan literature Buddha's birth is supposed to have happened not long before the birth of Confucius (Journal of the Royal Asiatic Society of Bombay, 1882, p. 100). It might be well to distinguish the Southern Buddhist era by p. B.S. from the Northern Buddhist era, p. B.N.

Dignâgâkârya and Nikula were contemporaries of Kâlidâsa, the former his adversary, and the latter a fellow and bosom friend[1].' Whatever we may think of the pointed allusion which Mallinâtha discovers in Kâlidâsa's own words to Nikula and Dignâga—and I confess that I believe he is right—there can be little doubt that Mallinâtha must have known of both Nikula and Dignâga as contemporaries of Kâlidâsa, before he could have ventured on his explanation[2]. Dignâga is not a very common name, and if we know from our former evidence that Dignâga was a pupil of Asaṅga's, and that Asaṅga was a contemporary of Vikramâditya, we shall probably now feel more confident in placing Kâlidâsa in the middle of the sixth century.

It might be objected, no doubt, that Dignâga was a Buddhist, and that a worshipper of *S*iva, like Kâlidâsa, was not likely to have any personal relations with a heretic, such as Dignâga. The more we know, however, of the intellectual and social state of India at the time when Kâlidâsa lived, the less weight shall we ascribe to such an objection. Believers in Buddha and believers in the Veda lived together at that time very much as Protestants and Roman Catholics do at the present day, fighting when there is an opportunity or necessity for it, but otherwise sharing the same air as fellow creatures. We are told that Mânatuṅga, though a *G*aina, was admitted to the court of Harsha on the same terms as Bâ*n*a and Mayûra. I see no reason therefore why Dignâga should not have met Kâlidâsa at the court of Vikramâditya, or why he should not be the very Dignâga who is famous as a writer on Nyâya. We know that Vasubandhu, the brother of Asaṅga, was a student of the Nyâya philosophy, and published the posthumous work of Saṅghabhadra, the Nyâyânusâra*s*âstra (H. Ths. i, 108). The Bodhisattva *G*ina, who succeeded Asaṅga (see before, p. 303), composed the Nyâya-dvâra-

[1] The same discovery was made subsequently, but independently, by Professor Weber, Zeitschrift der D. M. G. xxii, p. 726. See also Shankar P. Pandit's preface to the Raghuva*ms*a, p. 68.

[2] Mallinâtha is placed by Dr. Bhao Daji in the fourteenth century, see On Kâlidâsa, p. 22; see also Bhandarkar, preface to Mâlatimâdhava, p. xii, and Journal of the Royal Asiatic Society, Bombay, ix, p. 321.

târaka (H. Ths. i, 188 [1]), and Hiouen-thsang himself, though a Buddhist, studied logic under a Brâhma*n*a (H. Ths. i, 187). I see no reason therefore why Dignâga, the pupil of Asaṅga in Pramâ*n*a, i. e. logic, should not be the author of a work on Nyâya, which, as Professor Cowell has shown in his important preface to the Kusumâ*ñg*ali, was criticised by Uddyotakara, the author of the Nyâya-vârttika [2].

We placed Dignâga, as the pupil of Asaṅga, in the middle of the sixth century. Uddyotakara, his critic, is quoted by Subandhu (Vâsavadattâ, p. 235 [3]), and, curiously enough, together with Dharmakîrti [4], a pupil of Asaṅga's, who, like Asaṅga, was the great authority on logic among the Buddhists. Subandhu, again, is quoted by Bâ*n*a, and Bâ*n*a was the contemporary of Hiouen-thsang. All this agrees, and fits so naturally that we can hardly attribute it all to mere accident.

At one time I thought that there were certain dates of the Chinese translations of Sanskrit texts which made it impossible to assign to Asaṅga and Vasubandhu so late a date. The fact is that two works which are ascribed to Vasubandhu, the *S*atasâstra (No. 1188), and the Bodhi-*k*ittotpâdana-*s*âstra (No. 1218), are supposed to have been translated by Kumâra*g*îva, i.e. about 404 A.D. The earliest translations of his other works belong

---

[1] The Nyâya-dvâra-târaka-*s*âstra is ascribed to the Bodhisattva Dharmapâla, Hiouen-thsang, i, p. 191.

[2] Subandhu in his Vâsavadattâ recurs several times to the eclipse that has come over the Mîmâ*m*sâ and Nyâya through the teaching of the Buddhists. See also Weber, Streifen i, p. 379.

[3] See Hall, Vâsavadattâ, preface, p. 9 note, as corrected by Cowell, in his preface to the Kusumâ*ñg*ali.

[4] Dr. Burnell, who had great faith in Târânâtha's History of Indian Buddhism, wrote in the preface to the Sâmavidhâna-brâhma*n*a, p. vi: 'Târânâtha states that Kumâralîla (i. e. Kumârila) lived at the same time as Dharmakîrti, the great Buddhist writer on Nyâya. Some of his works still exist in Tibetan translations in the Tanjur, and he is quoted by name in the Sarvadarsanasaṅgraha as an authority on Buddhism. Now Dharmakîrti is stated by the Tibetans to have lived in the time of Sroṅ-tsan-gam-po, king of Yârlang, who was born 617 A.D., and reigned from 629–698 A.D. About this date there can be no doubt, for the king married a Chinese princess, whose date is certain. As Hiouen-thsang left India in 645 A.D., and there is no mention in his work of the great and dangerous Brahman enemy of the Buddhists, Kumârila cannot have lived before that date, and for many reasons he cannot have been later than 700 A.D.'

all to the sixth century, though, as they are assigned to Bodhiruki, to the beginning of it. This is strange, though not impossible. But what shall we say of translations of Vasubandhu by Kumâragîva? There must be some mistake here. In the case of the Sata-sâstra (Pai-lun), most likely the work is wrongly attributed to Vasubandhu, for Hiouen-thsang (i, 99) ascribes it to Deva, while, in another place (i, 191), the Sata-sâstra-vaipulya, is ascribed to Dharmapâla. As to the Bodhikittotpâda, the difficulty remains, and cannot at present be solved, though I see that this work is sometimes ascribed to Maitreya. However that may be, the evidence in support of making Vasubandhu a contemporary of Vikramâditya and Sîlâditya is too strong to be surrendered, and for the present it is the Chinese evidence which will have to yield[1].

I shall mention now a few more of the undesigned coincidences which support our placing the revival of Buddhist literature under the auspices of Asaṅga and Vasubandhu in the time of Vikramâditya and Sîlâditya in the course of the sixth century.

We have Vasubandhu's Abhidharmakosha, which was explained by Gunamati and his pupil Vasumitra, both of whom are quoted by the commentator Yasomitra, who is himself a pupil of Vasubandhu[2].

Another pupil of Vasubandhu's was Gunaprabha of Parvata. His pupil was Mitrasena, and it was Mitrasena (eighty years old) who taught Hiouen-thsang (i, 109) the Tattvasatya-sâstra (by Gunaprabha, i, 106) and the Abhidharma-gñâna-prasthâna-sâstra (ascribed to Kâtyâyana, i, 102, 109, 330; or to Kâtyâyanî-putra, 300, p. B. N.) We saw that Vasubandhu had been for a time a pupil of Saṅghabhadra's, and that he became afterwards converted by his brother Asaṅga. This

---

[1] Mr. Bunyiu Nanjio informs me that in the preface to the Chinese translation of the Pâi-lun (Sata-sâstra) the text is ascribed to Deva, who lived about 800 p. B.N., the commentary to Vasu, the translation to Kumâragîva. The Bodhihridayotpâda-sâstra is ascribed to Vasubandhu, and its translation to Kumâragîva. But in the Khai-yuen-lu (A.D. 730) the text is assigned to either Maitreya or Vasubandhu. Again, in the list of the twenty-three Indian Patriarchs (Cat. No. 1340) Vasubandhu is the twentieth. There were three more after him, and they all are supposed to have been known in China in 472 A. D.

[2] Schiefner, Lebensbeschreibung, p. 310.

seems to have been a conversion from the Hînayâna to the Mahâyâna, for Saṅghabhadra lived and died in a monastery attached to the Hînayâna (H. Ths. i, 107), while Asaṅga belonged to the Mahâyâna.

Now one of Asaṅga's pupils was the famous *S*îlabhadra (called Dharmakosha), an old man when Hiouen-thsang came to see him (i, 144) and to study the Yoga*s*âstra under him. *S*îlabhadra, being too old, appointed his pupil, *G*ayasena (of Surâsh*t*ra) to teach Hiouen-thsang (i, 212, 215). Afterwards when a Brâhman of the Lokâyata sect challenged *S*îlabhadra and the monks of his monastery (Nâlanda), Hiouen-thsang disputed with him and defeated him, showing a profound knowledge of the Sâṅkhya and the Vai*s*eshika systems (i, 225). He afterwards composed a treatise against the Hînayâna, which was highly praised by *S*îlabhadra.

Another link between Hiouen-thsang and Asaṅga is Sthitamati[1]. He too was a pupil of Asaṅga, and the teacher[2] of *G*ayasena, who, as we have seen, was the teacher of Hiouen-thsang.

One more link in our chain of arguments is supplied by one of *S*îlabhadra's teachers. At the time of Hiouen-thsang's visit to Nâlanda, about 637–639, we know that *S*îlabhadra was old, say seventy years. When he was thirty years of age his master, Dharmapâla, employed him for the first time to dispute against the heretics, say 600 A.D. Now we are told by I-tsing that Dharmapâla was the contemporary of Bhart*ri*hari, and that Bhart*ri*hari died 650 A.D., which, chronologically at all events, would harmonise very well. We may take notice also that Dharmapâla[3] was a contemporary of

---

[1] Schiefner, Lebensbeschreibung, p. 80.

[2] Hiouen-thsang, i, 212. Sthitamati (An-hoei-pou-sa) is different from Sthiramati (Kien-hoei). Gu*n*amati and Sthiramati are always mentioned together (Hiouen-thsang, iii, 46; 164), and Gu*n*amati was the teacher of Vasumitra, both having written on Vasubandhu's Abhidharmakosha.

[3] Works ascribed to a Dharmapâla, whose name is translated 護法 Hu-fâ, lit. guardian of the law. See Eitel, p. 32 b.

No. 1174. 'Âlambanapratyayadhyâna-*s*âstra-vyâkhyâ' (A.D. 710, by I-tsing).
[This is a commentary on the Bodhisattva *G*ina's *s*âstra.]

„ 1197. Vidyâmâtrasiddhi(-*s*âstra) (A.D. 659, by Hiouen-thsang).
[This is a commentary on Vasubandhu's thirty verses.]

Bhavaviveka (H. Ths. iii, 112), though Bhavaviveka may have been considerably his senior [1].

- Asanga
  - Sthitamati
    - *G*ayasena
      - Hiouen-thsang
  - *S*îlabhadra
    - *G*ayasena
      - Hiouen-thsang.

- Sanghabhadra
  - Vasubandhu
    - Yasomitra, (quotes *G*u*n*amati and Vasumitra)
    - Gu*n*aprabha
      - Mitrasena
        - Hiouen-thsang.

- Bhavaviveka (iii, 112).
  - Dharmapâla and Bhart*ri*hari, died 650 A.D.
    - *S*îlabhadra.

It seems not unlikely, in fact, that the teachers whose names Hiouen-thsang mentions as famous in his time (iii, 46), were men whom he might either have known himself, such as *S*îlabhadra, or whose memory was still quite fresh at Nâlanda at the time of his visit. Several of these names are the same which I-tsing, who was at Nâlanda in 673, or about thirty-six years later, mentions as recent, distinguishing them from the oldest and the middle teachers on one side, and the teachers still living on the other.

HIOUEN-THSANG (iii, 46). 637–639 A.D.	I-TSING. 673 A.D.
Dharmapâla (*S*abdavidyâsa*m*yukta-*s*âstra).	Dharmapâla.
*K*andrapâla.	
Gu*n*amati (teacher of Vasumitra).	Gu*n*amati.

No. 1198. *S*ata*s*âstravaipulya-vyâkhyâ (A.D. 650, by H. T.)
[This is a commentary on Deva's *s*âstra.]

„ 1210. Vidyâmâtrasiddhi(-*s*âstra) (A.D. 710, by I-tsing).
[This is similar to No. 1197.]

[1] The following list of Hiouen-thsang's teachers is given from Tibetan sources (Journal of the Royal Asiatic Society of Bombay, 1882, p. 96): Dântabhadra or -deva (*S*îlabhadra ?), Ârya Sanga (Asanga), Vasumitra (pupil of Gu*n*amati), Dharmarakshita, Vinaya-bhadra (Sanghabhadra ?), Dântasena (*G*ayasena ?). Buddha, Ânanda, and Maitreya also are mentioned.

Sthiramati.	Sthiramati.
Prabhâmitra.	
*G*inamitra.	*G*ina (Nyâyadvâratâraka *s*âstra).
*G*ñâna*k*andra.	
*S*îghrabuddha.	
*S*îlabhadra (Dharmakosha).	*S*îlabhadra.

I-tsing mentions besides, as of recent date: Dharmaya*s*as (Fa-hian ?), Si*m*ha*k*andra (one of Hiouen-thsang's fellow students, i, 261), Pra*g*ñâgupta (a follower of the Hînayâna, i, 220), Paramaprabha, and Gu*n*aprabha (pupil of Devasena, i, 106), some of whom may possibly be identified with Hiouen-thsang's names. As teachers of an early age I-tsing mentions all those whom we have placed in the sixth century A. D., viz. Sanghabhadra (vidyâmâtra), Asanga (Yoga), Vasubandhu, and Bhavaviveka.

As old teachers he enumerates, Nâgâr*g*una (*S*ûnya), Deva (pupil of Nâgâr*g*una), and A*s*vaghosha[1].

Among those whom he had known personally, he mentions, Pra*g*ñâ*k*andra (in the monastery Si-ra-chu at Surat), Ratnasi*m*ha (in Nâlanda), Divâkaramitra (in Eastern India), Tathâgatagarbha (in Southern India), and *S*âkyakîrti (in Si-ri-fa-sai).

Pravarasena, King of Ka*s*mîra.

Uncertain as some of these facts may be, their harmony serves nevertheless to produce some confidence that we are on *terra firma*, and not altogether on the quicksand of Indian tradition. Nor is this all. There are still some other supports which may serve to strengthen our position, and the date which we have assigned to Kâlidâsa and his patron Vikramâditya Harsha of U*gg*ayinî. Most of the facts which have still to be considered, were first pointed out by the late Dr. Bhao Daji, now twenty years ago, and I then expressed to him my

[1] The lives of these three teachers are stated to have been translated by Kumâra*g*îva, about 405 A.D. The life of Vasubandhu was translated by Paramârtha, 557-589 A.D. See Bunyiu Nanjio's Catalogue, Nos. 1460-1463.

general agreement with his arguments, revolutionary as they sounded at that time to most Sanskrit scholars [1].

Dr. Bhao Daji thought that the great Vikramâditya, the founder of the Vikrama era, was for a certain time the contemporary of Pravarasena, the king of Kasmîra. We read in the Râgataranginî (Book III, verses 102–252) of the two sons of Sreshthasena, Hiranya and Toramâna, ruling Kasmîra together for a time, till Hiranya, jealous of his brother, threw him into prison. Toramâna's wife Añganâ, the daughter of Vagrendra of the family of Ikshvâku, gave birth to a son, Pravarasena; but after the death of his father Toramâna, and of his uncle Hiranya, Pravarasena was unable, it seems, to assert his indirect claims to the throne of Kasmîra. Under these circumstances Vikramâditya, called Harsha, the king ruling at Uggayinî, the destroyer of Sakas, and recognised as Emperor (ekakkhatras kakravartî) of India, appointed an eminent poet, who had come to seek service at his court, Mâtrigupta by name, to the throne of Kasmîra. Mâtrigupta ruled Kasmîra till the death of his patron Vikramâditya. He then retired to Vârânasî as a Yati, while Pravarasena succeeded to the throne of Kasmîra. He became so powerful a ruler that he had actually to reinstate the son of Vikramâditya, Sîlâditya Pratâpasîla, on the throne of Uggayinî.

Dr. Bhao Daji started the bold theory that this Mâtrigupta, who was for a time ruler of Kasmîra, was the great poet Kâlidâsa, and he informs us that there always has been a tradition that Vikramâditya was so pleased with Kâlidâsa that he bestowed on this poet half of his territories [2]. Without confessing myself convinced, I must say that his arguments in support of this view are at all events very able.

First, as to the name, we know that names in the literary history of India are often titles and honorific appellations

---

[1] See Journal of the Bombay Branch of the Royal Asiatic Society, 1868, pp. 249, 251. May I venture to suggest that the friends and admirers of Dr. Bhao Daji owe it to themselves and to the memory of their eminent countryman to collect his essays and to publish them, together with a sketch of his life, and a description of his valuable collection of MSS., coins, and other antiquities! [See Bhao Daji, Journal of the Royal Asiatic Society, Bombay, 1860, p. 220.]

[2] Bhao Daji, l. c., p. 228.

rather than proper names, and that even in proper names, if they have a meaning, the same meaning may be expressed in different ways. The Trikâ*nd*a-sesha gives Raghukara, Medhârudra, and Ko*t*i*g*it as synonyms of Kâlidâsa. Kâlidâsa means 'the servant of the goddess Kâlî,' and if instead of Kâlidâsa we were to find Kâlîgupta, i. e. protected by Kâlî, we should probably hesitate but little to accept this as a synonym of Kâlidâsa. Kâlî, however, is one of the goddesses called Mât*ri* or Mothers[1], and therefore Mât*ri*gupta conveys the same meaning as Kâlîgupta or Kâlidâsa.

Dr. Bhao Daji then asks, Who is Mât*ri*gupta? He must have been a great poet, yet we never meet with his name, except here in the History of Kasmîra[2].

Secondly, the author of that history mentions other poets, even Bhavabhûti, who is evidently more modern than Kâlidâsa, but he never mentions Kâlidâsa.

Thirdly, we are told that Pravarasena, when restored to his kingdom, and Kâlidâsa, when retiring to Benares, parted as friends. Now, there is in existence a poem in Prâkrit, called the Setu-kâvya, the Bridge-poem, with a Sanskrit commentary, in which it is said that the poem was composed by Kâlidâsa at the request of Pravarasena[3]. Vidyânâtha, in his work on poetry, the Pratâpa-rudra (end of twelfth century), quotes an Âryâ verse from the Setu-kâvya, calling it a Mahâprabandha, while Da*nd*in (in the sixth century) praises the same poem in his Kâvyâdarsa as an ocean of beautiful sentences, though written in Prâkrit. Lastly, Râmâsrama, the com-

---

[1] The name of Mât*ri* occurs in the royal family of Kasmira, Toramâ*n*a being the son of Mât*ri*dâsa, a grandson of Mât*ri*kula, perhaps the same as Mât*ri*vishnu (Bhao Daji, On Kâlidâsa, p. 220). Might not therefore Mât*ri*gupta have belonged to Toramâna's family, and have sought refuge at the court of Vikramâditya after Toramâ*n*a's fall? And might not Vikramâditya have appointed him to succeed to the throne of Kasmira on account of his relationship with the old royal family?

[2] Dr. Bhao Daji discovered a commentary on *S*akuntalâ by Râghava Bha*t*a, son of P*ri*thvîdhara of Visvesvarapattana (Benares), in which Mât*ri*gupta is quoted with reference to the characteristics of dramatic composition. He met in the same commentary with *s*lokas worthy, as he says, of Kâlidâsa, and with one from the Hayagrîvabadha, a play written by Bhart*ri*bha*tt*a or Bhart*ri*me*nth*a, during the short reign of Mât*ri*gupta.

[3] Published by S. and P. Goldschmidt, Râva*n*avaha oder Setubandha, 1880.

mentator on Sundara's Vârânasî-Darpana, speaks of Kâlidâsa, who wrote the Setu-kâvya. Pravarasena again is known to have constructed a famous bridge of boats across the Vitastâ (Hydaspes) on which the capital of Kasmîra was then situated (Râgat. iii, 354), and it was in connection with this event that Kâlidâsa is supposed to have written his Bridge-poem. This, at least, we may gather from a verse of the poet Bâna, the contemporary of Hiouen-thsang, who says (Harshakarita, p. 1):

> Kîrtih Pravarasenasya prayâtâ kumudoggvalâ
> Sâgarasya param pâram kapiseneva setunâ [1],
> Nirgatâsu na vâ kasya [2] Kâlidâsasya sûktishu
> Prîtir madhurasârdrâsu mañgarîshv iva gâyate?

'The glory of Pravarasena, bright as the white lotus, went forth to the other shore of the ocean by means of his bridge, like (Râma's) army of monkeys (which crossed over to Ceylon on a bridge). Or who does not feel delight in the beautiful lines sent forth by Kâlidâsa, as in clusters of flowers moist with sugar?'

This, if it proves nothing else, fixes at all events the fame of Kâlidâsa for the beginning of the seventh century, and likewise his connection with Kasmîra and its king Pravarasena [3].

---

[1] See Beames, Indian Antiquary, 1873, p. 2406.

[2] Nisargasûravamsasya, ed. Calcutta.

[3] It is but right to state that Dr. Bhao Daji himself brought forward some objections against his identification of Mâtrigupta and Kâlidâsa. 'Kâlidâsa,' he remarks, 'was a Sârasvata Brahman, a worshipper of Siva and Pârvatî, while Mâtrigupta, as ruler of Kasmîra, appears from the Râgataraṅginî to have conciliated the Buddhists and Gains by prohibiting the destruction of living beings. He also pleased the Vaishnavas by constructing a temple to Vishnu, and the deities invoked in the Setu-kâvya are first Vishnu and then Siva.' (See Bhao Daji, Abstract of a paper on Kâlidâsa, p. 8.) Now this, I confess, would disturb me least; on the contrary, it would to my mind seem to reflect the true character of the time. Mâtriketa, like Mâtrigupta, began as a worshipper of Siva, and then became a famous Buddhist poet. Lalitâditya erected statues to Vishnu and Buddha. (See before, p. 307.) What troubles me most, as I wrote to Dr. Bhao Daji in 1861, is that 'Mâtrigupta is spoken of in the Râgataraṅginî as a poet, and yet never identified with the famous author of Sakuntalâ. Is it possible that Kalhana Pandita, who is so well acquainted with literary history, should have told the extraordinary career of Mâtrigupta without giving a hint that this poet, raised to the throne of Kasmîra, was the famous Kâlidâsa?' I also pointed out to him that the two verses which he had

Fourthly, Dr. Bhao Daji tries to connect this Pravarasena, the king of Kasmîra, and the friend, if not the successor of Kâlidâsa, with the king who ruled in Kasmîra, and was an old man at the time of Hiouen-thsang's visit to that country. We read that 'when Hiouen-thsang arrived at the capital of Kasmîra, he stopped in a convent, called Gayendra-vihâra, which had been built by the father-in-law of the king.' According to the Râgatarangini (iii, 355), the genealogy of the kings of Kasmîra was:

Vagrendra

|

About 500[1], Toramâna and Angana, her brother Gayendra

|

Pravarasena.

It is stated in the Râgatarangini that Gayendra raised an edifice known by the name of Vihâra of Srî Gayendra and of the great Buddha, 'the very edifice, no doubt, in which Hiouen-thsang was received as the guest of the king.' Hiouen-thsang mentions besides another house where he spent a night, and calls it the 'house of happiness.' Now, according to the Râgatarangini there was in the same town a house called 'Amrita-bhuvana, i.e. the abode of immortal or heavenly bliss,' for the use of foreign mendicants, built by the great-grandmother of Pravarasena.

All this is very welcome evidence to support the statements contained in Hiouen-thsang's travels. No doubt, he passed through the capital of Kasmîra, he may have slept in the very houses which are described in the chronicle of Kasmîra. But the king who received him could not have been Pravarasena. Hiouen-thsang never mentions his name, and nothing is said in the text of Gayendra, the builder of the Gayendra-vihâra, being the maternal uncle of the then reigning king. There is a note in Julien's translation, '*ce couvent avait été*

---

given from the Harshakaritra, and which seemed to join Pravarasena and Kâlidâsa, do not follow each other immediately, as published by Dr. F. Hall (Vâsavadattâ, Preface, p. 14), while in the Calcutta edition the various reading nisargasûravamsasya seems to point to the Raghuvamsa rather than to the Setubandha.

[1] Bhao Daji, Journal of the Royal Asiatic Society, Bombay, viii, p. 249.

construit par le beau-père du roi (Note de l'auteur chinois).' This does not necessarily mean that *G*ayendra was the father-in-law of the then reigning king, but only of the king living at his time. Nor had *G*ayendra, so far as we know, ever been the father-in-law of Pravarasena, but his maternal uncle.

But, however that may be, Hiouen-thsang, so far as we know at present, returned to China in 645. Pravarasena, if he ascended the throne of Kasmîra after the death of Vikramâditya, may be supposed to have begun his reign about 550, and even if he reigned sixty years, that would only bring us to 610 A.D. How then could he be brought together with Hiouen-thsang and his visit to India in 629–645?

Here, therefore, I can no longer follow Dr. Bhao Daji who, in order to escape from this difficulty, wishes to put Hiouen-thsang's visit sixty years earlier. We have only to give up what after all is a mere conjecture, that Pravarasena was the king of Kasmîra who received Hiouen-thsang, and all the rest of our chronological arrangement holds good. I know, of course, that Dr. Bhao Daji has other reasons also for wishing to place *S*îlâditya, the friend of Hiouen-thsang, in the middle of the sixth century [1], but these will have to be discussed independently, and after a new and careful examination of the dates of the Chalukya dynasty.

Hiouen-thsang's travels in India are contemporaneous with the Hejrâh (622 A.D.), and the first spreading of Mohammedanism, and, curiously enough, the historian Bedia-ad-dîn tells us that the first year of the Hejrâh coincided with the thirtieth year of Beckermadul, i. e. Vikramâditya of Kasmîra [2], and that Baladut, i. e. Balâditya, was contemporaneous with Yezdijerd. Instead of Pravarasena, therefore, Balâditya would have been the most likely host of Hiouen-thsang in Kasmîra, and 622 A. D. would represent the thirtieth year of his great predecessor Vikramâditya, while Pravarasena would retain his date of about 550, the time between him and Vikramâditya,

---

[1] Journal of the Royal Asiatic Society, Bombay, viii, p. 250.

[2] See Wilson, Asiatic Researches, xv, pp. 41, 42; Fergusson, Journal of the Royal Asiatic Society, 1870, p. 97.

who began to reign 590, being filled by Yudhishṭhira, Narendrâditya, and his brother Raṇâditya [1].

It cannot here be my intention to give new outlines for the whole history of mediæval Sanskrit literature, but considering how chaotic the state of that history has hitherto been, it may be useful to mention at least a few more facts which seem to fit easily into the system here devised, and thus may serve to confirm what otherwise, from the nature of the case, can only be considered for the present as a provisional programme.

Early Astronomers.

Some of the earliest works of the Renaissance period of Sanskrit literature of which it is possible to fix the date are the works of astronomers. Some of the knowledge conveyed by them is presupposed by Kâlidâsa and his contemporaries, and we therefore expect that these astronomical writings should be of an earlier date than the period of Vikramâditya, while on the other hand, if our view of the Turanian Interregnum, (100 B.C.—300 A.D.) is right, they should not be earlier than the third century A.D.

'The founder of astronomical and mathematical science in India,' as Lassen called him, was Âryabhaṭa, or Âryabhaṭa the

---

[1] If Mr. Fergusson is right in stating that copper plates assign to Dhruvasena of Valabhî the dates 628 and 640, reckoned according to the Valabhî era (310 + 318 = 628; 322 + 318 = 640), he may also be right in identifying Dhruvasena with Dhruvapaṭu, the nephew of Śîlâditya of Mâlava, and son-in-law of Śîlâditya of Kânyakubga, the patron of Hiouen-thsang. See Hiouen-thsang, i, 206; iii, 162. Journal of the Royal Asiatic Society, 1870, p. 90. The Valabhî and Gupta dates, however, are very doubtful, because the era is doubtful from which they are reckoned. Dr. Bühler has published a Valabhî grant (Ind. Ant. 1877, p. 91) in which the grantee is the monastery of Srî Bappapâda (see Indian Antiquary, 1878, p. 80), built by the Âkârya Bhadanta Sthiramati. He has also pointed out that this must be the monastery described by Hiouen-thsang (iii, p. 164) as at a little distance from Valabhî, erected by the Arhat Âkâra, and then inhabited by the Bodhisattvas Sthiramati and Guṇamati. If then any additions to the Vihâra had been made by Sthiramati, at the time when the grant was made, the grant could not have been made very long before Hiouen-thsang's visit to India. Yet the grant is dated Sam 269! This, with 190, would give only 459 A.D., while with 319 (see p. 294), it would give 589 A.D., at all events a possible date, if Hiouen-thsang and I-tsing are to be trusted.

elder (V*ri*ddhâryabha*t*a), who is quoted by Varâhamihira, Brahmagupta, Bha*tt*otpala, and Bhâskarâ*k*ârya, and who was born, as he tells us himself, in A.D. 476 [1]. He was the author of what is called the Âryabha*t*îya Sûtra [2], consisting (1) of the ten verses of the Dasagîtikâ, and the 108 verses of the Âryâsh*t*asata, the latter divided into three Pâdas, (2) the Ga*n*itapâda, (3) Kâlakriyâpâda, and (4) Golapâda [3]. He seems to have written no more, but he will always remain famous as having boldly pronounced in favour of the revolution of the earth on its axis, and on the true cause of solar and lunar eclipses [4]. This was known hitherto from a quotation from Âryabha*t*a by P*ri*thûdaka, 'the sphere of the stars is stationary, and the earth, making a revolution, produces the daily rising and setting of the sun.' We have it now in the very words of Âryabha*t*a [5]: 'As a person in a vessel, while moving forward, sees an immovable object moving backward, in the same manner do the stars, though immovable, seem to move (daily). At Laṅkâ (i.e. at a situation of no geographical latitude) they go straight to the West (i.e. at a line that cuts the horizon at right angles, or, what is the same, parallel to the prime vertical at Laṅkâ).'

Here then we have the oldest scientific Indian astronomer, clearly fixed as born at Pâ*t*aliputra at the end of the fifth and the beginning of the sixth century A.D., and the fact that Âryabha*t*a quotes no predecessors [6] tends to show that there were none to quote.

We next come to Varâhamihira, the son and pupil of Âdityadâsa, a native of U*gg*ayinî, born at Kâpitthaka in Avantî. He wrote several works. First, the Kara*n*a [7], commonly known under the name of Pa*ñk*asiddhântikâ,

---

[1] Bhao Daji, On the age of Âryabha*t*a, &c., pp. 5, 14.

[2] Different from this is what Dr. Bhao Daji calls the Mahâryasiddhânta, containing about 600 to 612 verses, ascribed to a junior Âryabha*t*a.

[3] The Âryabha*t*îya, with the commentary of Paramâdîsvara (Bha*t*adîpikâ), edited by Dr. H. Kern, Leiden, 1874.

[4] Colebrooke, Miscellaneous Essays, vol. ii, p. 392.

[5] Âryabha*t*îya, ed. Kern, p. 76 (Golapâda, verse 9).

[6] Dr. Bhao Daji mentions one doubtful allusion to the Brahma-siddhânta, l. c., p. 15.

[7] Kara*n*as adopt the Yuga era, Siddhântas the *S*aka era. Kern, pref. p. 24.

because founded on the five Siddhântas[1]. Secondly, a Horâ-sâstra, divided into a *G*âtaka, a Yâtrika, and a Vivâha-pa*t*ala, all these existing in two forms, long or short. Lastly, the B*ri*hat-sa*m*hitâ. He generally wrote in the Âryâ metre, a metre which, as Professor Kern pointed out, has a certain chronological character[2]. We know that he died *S*aka 509, A.D. 587[3], and, as far as chronology is concerned, he may well take rank as one of the Nine Gems, and a contemporary of Kâlidâsa.

He quotes his predecessor Âryabha*t*a, and adopts the epoch of the Romaka-siddhânta, which, according to Dr. Bhao Daji, dates from A.D. 505[4], though Albiruni assigns this date to Varâhamihira's Pa*ñk*asiddhântikâ[5]. Varâhamihira also notices the Paulisa[6], Vâsish*th*a[7], Saura, and Paitâmaha Siddhântas, all of which must therefore belong to the sixth century.

The beginning of the sphere being determined by ζ Piscium refers the Siddhântas to the same century (Rig-veda, vol. iv, p. xiv).

The next great mathematician, Brahmagupta, wrote his Brâhma Sphu*t*a-siddhânta when he was thirty years of age, in A.D. 628. His father is called *G*ish*n*u, and it is just possible he may have been the *G*ish*n*u mentioned as a contemporary of Kâlidâsa[8].

We may add, though they belong to a later period, the dates of Bha*tt*otpala, the commentator of Varâhamihira, as fixed at 967, and that of Bhâskara Â*k*ârya, the author of the Siddhântasiroma*n*i, who was born 1114[9].

---

[1] A MS. of this work was discovered by Dr. Bühler (Report, 1874, p. 11), who gives the curious verse in which the movement of the earth is refuted.

[2] Bhao Daji, l. c., p. 16; also Shankar P. Pandit, Mâlatîmâdhava, pref. p. 27.

[3] See Bhao Daji, On the Age and Authenticity of the work of Âryabha*t*a, Varâhamihira, Brahmagupta, Bha*tt*otpala and Bhâskarâ*k*ârya, p. 15.

[4] Romaka can only be a name for Roman, and Romaka-vishaya (Varâhamihira, Kern's pref. p. 57), for the Roman Empire. The Romaka-siddhânta is ascribed by Brahmagupta to *S*rishena, who bases his calculations on those of Lâ*t*a, Vasish*th*a, Vi*g*ayanandin, and Âryabha*t*a.

[5] See Bhao Daji, l. c., p. 16; Journal Asiatique, 1844, p. 285.

[6] Composed by Paulus al Yunâni, according to Albiruni, and based on Paulus Alexandrinus, according to Bhao Daji, who also identifies the Yavanesvara Asphu*g*idhva*g*a with Speusippus, while Kern (pref. p. 48) suggests Aphrodisius.

[7] Ascribed to Vish*n*u*k*andra. Vish*n*ugupta, who is quoted by Varâhamihira, is identified with *K*â*n*akya by Utpala.

[8] See Bhao Daji, l. c., p. 28.

[9] One of his ancestors, as Dr. Bhao Daji remarks, Bhâskara-bha*tt*a, received

What is important for our purposes is the Greek influence clearly perceptible in these astronomical compositions, and again in the poetical literature of the Indian Renaissance. If we confine our remarks to one subject, namely, the adoption of the Greek zodiac in India, the evidence is so irresistible that it might seem almost a waste of time to restate it, if it were not for the fact that some very eminent scholars, particularly in India, still try to escape from the consequences of that discovery[1]. I shall therefore state the case once more, briefly, but I hope, clearly, and I trust that the rising generation of Sanskrit scholars in India will no longer allow their patriotism to interfere with their judgment, remembering the words of Garga[2]:

'The Yavanas (Greeks) are indeed Mle*kkh*as, but amongst them this science (astronomy) is firmly established. Hence they are honoured, as though they were *Ri*shis; how much more then an astrologer who is a twice-born man[3]!'

The Names and Pictorial Representations of the Twelve Zodiacal Divisions.

It is most likely that the division of the heavens into twelve equal portions was first made by Chaldæan or Babylonian astronomers. Letronne, Ideler, Lassen agree on that point, and they likewise agree in admitting that the knowledge of this division of the heavens into twelve equal portions or dodecameries reached the Greeks from Babylonia (about 700 B.C.?)

Whether the Babylonians possessed names and pictorial representations for these dodecameries, and whether these too were borrowed by the Greeks, is more doubtful. But what is quite certain is this,

That to the time of Eudoxos, 380 B.C., the Greeks, though they had twelve divisions (introduced by Kleostratos

---

the title of Vidyâpati from Bhoga, king of Dhârâ, 1042 A.D. See also Weber, Sanskrit Literature, p. 261.

1 See Shankar P. Pandit's preface to his edition of the Raghuva*m*sa.

2 Kern, pref. p. 35; see also B*ri*hat-sa*m*hitâ, ii, 15.

3 Mle*kkh*â hi Yavanâs, teshu samyak *s*âstram ida*m* sthitam,
*Ri*shivat te 'pi pûgyante, kim puna*r* daivavid dvi*g*a*h*.

of Tenedos, 496 B.C.), had but eleven signs, the two divisions, now represented by scorpion and balance, being represented by one sign only, the scorpion with its claws stretching across two divisions. Even Aratus and Hipparchus, 150 B.C., do not know the Balance as a separate sign, and it is first mentioned by Geminus and Varro, about the beginning of the first century B.C.

Hence the important criterion by which Letronne destroyed the presumed fabulous antiquity of Egyptian and other zodiacal representations, viz. 'in whatever monument or book the Balance occurs as a separate sign (ζῴδιον), that book or monument cannot be earlier than the first century B.C.;' and, we may add, the astronomy of that country, whether Egypt or India, must have been directly or indirectly under the influence of Greece.

The earliest Sanskrit astronomer, as far as we know at present, who mentions the names of the twelve divisions of the Greek zodiac is Âryabha*t*a (Golapâda, v. 1)[1]. There never was any authority for saying that 'the twelve zodiacal pictures' occur in Anquetil Duperron's translation of the Maitrâya*n*î Upanishad (Weber, Ind. Stud. i, p. 278), for we only find there 'duodecim bordy (signa) solis,' which are the Âdityas in the original. It is different with a statement of Colebrooke's, who (Life and Essays, vol. ii, p. 215) quoted a passage from Baudhâyana in which the names of some of the Greek zodiacal signs occur. It is true that he took the passage, not from Baudhâyana direct, but from an astronomical writer, Divâkarabha*tt*a. Nevertheless, the fact seems true. In the Baudhâyana-sûtras (see Sâya*n*a's commentary in MS. India Office Library, p. 13 a) we read: 'Meshav*ri*shabhau sauro vasanta*h*, mînameshau vâ[2].' This,

---

[1] The occurrence of the zodiacal signs in the Râmâya*n*a (i, 19; ii, 15, ed. Schlegel) has been often discussed. See also Urvasî, ed. Bollensen, p. 70. 14.

[2] MS. 288, India Office Library, p. 13 a: अथात ऋतूनामेव मीमांसा ॥ वसंते ब्राह्मणोऽग्नीनादधीत ग्रीष्मे राजन्यः शरदि वैश्यो वर्षासु रथकार इति ॥ आपस्तंबस्तु हेमंते वा शरदि वैश्यस्य शिशिरः सार्ववर्णिक इत्याह ।५.३.१८–२०॥ अथो खलु यदेवैनं यज्ञोपनमेदथादधीत सैवास्यर्द्धिरिति ॥ अत्र वसंतादयः सौराश्चांद्राश्चेति द्विधा भवंति ॥ मेषवृषभौ सौरो वसंतः । मीनमेषौ

though differing from Colebrooke's quotation, is evidently the passage meant, and, unless it belonged originally to an old commentary, would certainly prove a knowledge, not only of the twelve divisions, but of their Greek names, at the time when the Baudhâyana-kalpa-sûtras were finally settled. This point, however, requires further elucidation.

Next to Âryabhaṭa, the oldest astronomer who, so far as we know, shows an acquaintance with the names and pictorial representations of the zodiacal divisions is Satya.

This Satya Bhadatta (or Bhadanta, i.e. the Buddhist, see Cat. Bodl. p. 509) is quoted by Varâhamihira, and is therefore older than Varâhamihira, who died 587 A.D.

Satya, as quoted by Utpala in his Commentary on Varâhamihira's B*ri*ha*gg*âtaka, says (MS. Bodl. Walker 165, p. 6^b):

मेषो वृषभो वीणागदाधरं मिथुनमंभसि कुलीरः ।
सिंहः शैले कन्या नौकास्था दीपसस्यकरा ॥ १ ॥
पुरुषस्तुलाधरो वृश्चिकोऽथ धन्वी नरो हयांत्यार्धः ।
मकरार्धे मृगपूर्वे कुंभी पुरुषश्च मीनमत्स्यौ ॥ २ ॥[1]

वा ॥ मृगा(मेषा)दिराशिद्वयभानुभोगात्षड् ऋतवः स्युः शिशिरो वसंत इति वचनात्। अत्र यावदादित्यो मीनमेषयोस्तिष्ठति तावत्कालो वसंतः। एवं वृषभादिद्वंद्वेषु क्रमाद्ग्रीष्मवर्षाशरद्धेमंतशिशिराः॥ एवं चांद्रा ऋतवश्चांद्रमासाभ्यां भवंति। चांद्रमासाश्च चैत्रादिसंज्ञकाः। चैत्रसंज्ञा च सवितरि मेषराशिस्थिते सति यो दर्श आगच्छति तदवसाननिबंधना। एवं वृषभस्थे सवितरि यो दर्श आगच्छति तदवसाननिबंधना वैशाखसंज्ञा। एतावुभौ चांद्रौ चैत्रवैशाखौ चांद्रो वसंतः। एवमुत्तरत्रापि द्रष्टव्यं। तथा च ज्योतिःशास्त्रे। मेषादिस्थे सवितरि यो मासः प्रपूर्यते चांद्रः। चैत्रादिसंज्ञक इति। एवं च सौरचांद्रयोरेव मासयोर्यज्ञांगत्वं न नाक्षत्रादीनां। मुखं वा एतत्संवत्सरस्य यच्चित्रापौर्णमास इति श्रुतेः। अथवा फाल्गुनश्चैत्रो वसंतः। मुखं वा एतत्संवत्सरस्य यत्फाल्गुनीपूर्णमास इति श्रुतेः। एवं च सौरचांद्रभेदभिन्नं वसंतद्वयमुपसंगृहीतं भवति। फाल्गुने मासि सवितुर्मीनराश्यनुप्रवेशसंभवात्। उभयमपि श्रूयते। चंद्रमाः षड्होता स ऋतून्कल्पयातीति। अनेन चंद्रमस ऋतुकल्पनमुक्तं। दिग्भ्राज ऋतून्करोतीति च। दिग्भ्राज इति निषंगः। अनेन सूर्यस्य ऋतुकल्पनमुक्तं। अनेन सौरचांद्रवसंतयोर्विकल्पः। एवं पक्षांतरेष्वपि ॥

[1] Taking the first verse as an Âryâ, 12 + 18 + 12 + 15, I had to read mesho instead of go, the reading of the MS. The second verse is a Gîti, 12 + 18 + 12 + 18.

'The ram[1], the bull[2], a pair[3], one holding a lyre, the other a club, in the water a crab[4], a lion[5] on a mountain, a girl[6] standing in a ship holding in her hand a lamp and corn, a man[7] holding a balance, a scorpion[8], then a man[9] with a bow, and his hinder part a horse, half of a Makara[10] in front a beast, a man[11] with a pot, a fish[12] and a fish.'

It will be seen that this description of the signs by Satya contains none of those indications by which Lassen (ii, p. 1127) endeavoured to prove that the Indian pictorial representations were not borrowed from Greece, but from Babylon. He might indeed object to 'the pair, one holding a lyre, the other a club,' instead of the Greek twins, but in all other respects the Indian representatives of the twelve divisions are accurate copies of the Greek representatives, such as we find them after the first century, B.C.

Another astronomer, likewise quoted by Varâhamihira and therefore supposed to be anterior to him, is Bâdarâyana[1] (Kern, pref. p. 29). He too describes the pictorial representations of the twelve divisions, and at the same time their relation to the different parts of the body of Brahman or the Creator:

मेषः शिरोऽथ वदनं वृषभो विधातुः
वक्षो भवेन्नृमिथुनं हृदयं कुलीरः ।
सिंहस्तथोदरमथो युवतिः कटिश्च ।
वस्तिस्तुलाभृदथ मेहनमष्टमः स्यात् ॥ १ ॥
धन्वी चास्योरुयुगं मकरो जानुद्वयं भवति ।
जंघाद्वितयं कुंभः पादौ मत्स्यद्वयं चेति ॥ २ ॥[2]

'The ram[1] is the head, the face of the creator is the bull[2], the breast would be the man-pair[3], the heart the crab[4], the lion[5] the stomach, the maid[6] the hip, the balance-bearer[7] the belly,

[1] Both Satya and Bâdarâyana are mentioned in the *G*yotirvid-âbharana as contemporaries of Vikramâditya. See Shankar P. Pandit, Raghuvamsa, pref. p. 44.

[2] The metre of the first verse is Vasantatilaka, of the second Upagîti, if we supply two syllables by reading *kaitasyeti* or something like this.

the eighth (scorpion)[8] the membrum, the archer[9] his pair of thighs, the Makara[10] his pair of knees, the pot[11] [1] his pair of legs, the fish[12] pair his two feet.'

This distribution of the zodiacal signs among the different members of the body of Brahman has been considered a modern invention. It occurs, however, in Varâhamihira's B*ri*ha*gg*âtaka, where the members of Kâla, Time, are given in the same succession:

कालांगानि वरांगमाननमुरो हृत्क्रोडवासोभृतः ।
वस्तिर्व्यंजनमूरुजानुयुगले जंघे ततोऽङ्घ्रिद्वयं ॥ ४ ॥

'The members of Kâla are the head, the face, the chest, the heart, the stomach, the hip, the belly and the membrum, the two thighs and knees, the two legs, and the pair of feet.'

Other writers who knew the zodiacal signs are Yavane*s*vara[2] and Gârgi (B*ri*ha*gg*âtaka, MS. Bodl. Walker 165, p. 6[a]), but as their age is more difficult to fix, their statements as given by Utpala in his commentary to the B*ri*ha*gg*âtaka need not here be quoted. The verses of Varâhamihira himself, in which he describes the representatives of the twelve zodiacal divisions, have been often referred to by Whish[3], Lassen[4], and others. They are:

मत्स्यौ घटी नृमिथुनं सगदं सवीणं ।
चापी नरोऽश्वजघनो मकरो मृगास्यः ।
तौली ससस्यदहना प्लवगा च कन्या ।
शेषाः स्वनामसदृशाः स्वचराश्च सर्वे ॥ ५ ॥

'Two fishes, a man with a waterpot, a pair of men, one

---

[1] Here the pot instead of the pot-bearer would favour Lassen's argument.

[2] Yavanesvara in translating the old Nakshatra division into the modern zodiacal division assigned 2¼ Nakshatra to each zodiacal division. Gârgi did the same and identified Mesha (Aries) with A*s*vinî, Bhara*n*î, and one quarter of K*ri*ttikâ. Tathâ *k*a Yavanesvara*h*, dve dve sapâde bhavanam matam bheti. Tathâ *k*a Gârgi*h*, A*s*vinî bhara*n*î mesha*h* k*ri*ttikâpâdam eva *k*a, &c. See also Raghunandana, *G*yotistattva, p. 1.

[3] Whish states that they are taken from the Horâsâstra; see Transactions of the Literary Society of Madras, Part I, London, 1827, pp. 63–77.

[4] Zeitschrift für die Kunde des Morgenlandes, iv, 302.

with a club, the other with a lyre, a man carrying a bow, ending in a horse, a Makara with the face of a wild beast, a man with a balance, a maid in a boat, carrying corn and a lamp; the rest are like what their names say, and they all are placed in their own element,' (i.e. the fishes in the water, &c.)

Much more important, however, than this is another verse, in which Varâhamihira gives the actual Greek names of the zodiacal divisions in their Sanskrit corruptions. I give it from the B*ri*ha*gg*âtaka (MS. Bodl. Walker 165, p. 11):

क्रियतावुरिजितुमकुलीरलेयपार्थेजुककौर्प्याख्याः ।
तौक्षिक आकोकेरो हृद्रोगश्चांत्यभं चेत्थं ॥ ८ ॥

क्रियो मेषः *κριός*,
तावुरिर्वृषः *ταῦρος*,
जितुमो मिथुनं *δίδυμος*,
कुलीरः कर्कटः, Sanskrit word retained, though karka*t*a*h* would have better corresponded to *καρκίνος*,
लेयः सिंहः *λέων*,
पार्थेः कन्या *παρθένος* (पार्थोन, comm.),

जुकस्तुला *ζυγόν*,
कौर्पो वृश्चिकः *σκορπίος*,
तौक्षिको धन्वी *τοξικός*,
आकोकेरो मकरः *αἰγόκερως*,
हृद्रोगः कुंभः *ὑδροχόος* (not हृद्रोगः),
इत्थं मीनः *ἰχθύς*.

This knowledge of Greek astronomy and even of Greek astronomical terminology came to India not later than the fifth century. If then we find clear traces of it in the poetry of Kâlidâsa and his contemporaries, our proposal to place the renaissance of Sanskrit poetry in the sixth century will receive a new support. That Kâlidâsa, both in his Raghuva*ms*a and in his Kumâra-sambhava, shows a familiarity with Greek astronomy, particularly as embodied in the Horâsâstra, was clearly shown by Dr. Jacobi (Monatsberichte der Preuss. Academie, 1873, p. 544), who dwelt strongly on the word *g*âmitra (*διάμετρον*), used by Kâlidâsa in the Kumâra-sambhava (vii, 1), as one of the many words borrowed by Sanskrit astronomers from Greek. Shankar P. Pandit, in his preface to the Raghuva*ms*a, has tried to invalidate the conclusions to be drawn from such evidence, but without effect. He might indeed have quoted Kâlidâsa's belief in Râhu swallowing the moon (Raghuv. xii, 28), as pre-Âryabha*t*ean; but in the very same poem (xiv, 40) Kâlidâsa shows his knowledge of Âryabha*t*a's astronomy, by saying, 'For what in reality is only the shadow of the Earth, is regarded by the people as an impurity of the pure Moon.' Shankar Pándurang Pandit himself points out several passages clearly proving the poet's acquaintance 'with the judicial astrology based on the zodiac,' but he declines to discuss 'the very large question of how much the Indians borrowed or lent' (p. 37), and suggests, that even if the Indians borrowed from the Greeks, 'they might have done so two or three centuries before the Christian era' (p. 43). They might, no doubt; but is there any allusion to a native scientific astronomer at that early date?

Amarasi*m*ha.

Having proceeded so far, we may try at least whether one or two more of the other so-called 'Nine Gems,' or, as we should say, the Nine Classics of the Renaissance, can have a place assigned to them in the chronological scheme which we have elaborated so far. And first of all Amara or Amarasi*m*ha.

We owe to General Cunningham[1] a very ingenious attempt to fix the age of this famous lexicographer. He shows that the Buddhist temple at Buddha-Gayâ is the same which was seen by Hiouen-thsang, and which did not yet exist at the time of Fa-hian. It must therefore have been built, he thinks, between 414 and 642. An inscription found by Mr. Wilmot and translated by Wilkins in 1785 (Asiatic Researches, vol. i, p. 284) ascribes the building of the temple at Buddha-Gayâ to Amaradeva, one of the Nine Gems at the court of Vikramâditya. This is certainly curious. But the date of the inscription is Samvat 1015 (949 A.D.), and unfortunately we have not the original to test the accuracy of the translation. Still, so far as it goes, Amarasi*m*ha's date, as one of the Nine Gems of Vikramâditya, in the middle of the sixth century, would well agree with this Amaradeva, one of the

[1] Kern, B*r*ihatsa*m*hitâ, pref. p. 19.

Nine Gems of Vikramâditya, and the builder of a temple at Buddha-Gayâ.

It should be added that Stanislas Julien quotes a Chinese translation of the Amara-kosha, called Fân-wâï-kwo-yu, or Kü-shö-lun-yin-yuen-sh', by Gu*n*arata, a native of U*gg*ayinî, who lived under the Emperor Wou-ti of the Tcheou dynasty (561–566), though he does not know whether it is still in existence [1].

Vetâlame*nth*a.

Another name among the Nine Gems is Vetâlabha*tt*a, the author of the Nîtipradîpa, published in Hæberlin's Anthology (p. 528). Dr. Bhao Daji has identified him with Vetâlame*nth*a, and maintains that he is mentioned in the Râ*g*atarangi*n*î as a contemporary of Vikramâditya, but without giving chapter or verse [2].

Bhart*ri*me*nth*a is spoken of very highly by Râ*g*a*s*ekhara (14th cent.) in his Bâlarâmâya*n*a (ed. Calc. p. 9), where Vâlmîki, Bhart*ri*me*nth*a, Bhavabhûti, and Râ*g*a*s*ekhara himself seem placed much on the same level.

Mankha (1150 A.D.) informs us that his style resembled that of Subandhu, Bâ*n*a, and Bhâravi, being full of puns (Bühler, Journal of the Royal Asiatic Society of Bombay, 1877, p. 42).

Dr. Bhao Daji is inclined to take Bhart*ri*me*nth*a for Bhart*ri*bha*tt*a, and this again for Bhart*ri*hari, but there is no proof for this [3].

There is a poet called Bhart*ri*me*nth*a, the author of a poem (Bühler, Detailed Report, p. 42) the Hayagrîva-vadha, who was royally rewarded by Mât*ri*gupta (Râ*g*at. iii, 260); but I cannot find a Vetâlame*nth*a [4].

I do not like to attempt any more of the 'Nine Gems,' because I could only repeat the more or less vague conjectures of other scholars as to the probable date and character

---

[1] Journal Asiatique, 1847, Août, p. 87.

[2] Journal of the Royal Asiatic Society of Bombay, 1862, p. 218.

[3] Bhao Daji, l. c., p. 218.

[4] Professor Weber suggests that Vetâlabha*tt*a may be the author of the Vetâlapa*ñk*avi*m*sati, Z. D. M. G. xxii, p. 723.

of Dhanvantari[1], Kshapa*n*aka[2], *S*aṅku[3], Gha*t*akarpara, and Vararu*k*i. Having, however, found Hiouen-thsang's memoirs so useful a sheet-anchor for some of the floating literature of the sixth and seventh centuries, I add a few more cases in which the Chinese traveller seems to me to have supplied some useful hints as to the dates of certain names famous in Sanskrit literature.

Bâ*n*a and Mayûra.

We saw that Bâ*n*a, the author of the Harsha*k*arita, passed some time at the court of *S*îlâditya, the king of Kânyakub*g*a, the patron of Hiouen-thsang. He was a Vâtsyâyana, the son of *K*itrabhânu[4]. We therefore can fix the date of Bâ*n*a and his literary productions, such as the Kâdambarî, and possibly the Ratnâvalî[5] (ascribed, like the Nâgânanda, to Harsha), in the first half of the seventh century. Now Bâ*n*a tells us himself in his Harsha*k*arita that he counted Bhadra, Nârâya*n*a[6], Î*s*âna, and Mayûraka among his friends. In fact, Bâ*n*a and Mayûra are generally mentioned together, and we are told that Mayûra was the son-in-law of Bâ*n*a. Râ*g*asekhara[7], as quoted in the *S*ârṅgadhara-paddhati, speaks of Bâ*n*a and Mayûra as living at the Court

---

[1] Quoted by Da*n*d*in in the Dasakumâra*k*arita as a famous physician.

[2] Might this be Bhart*ri*hari?

[3] This cannot be *S*aṅku, the son of Mayûra, quoted by *S*ârṅgadhara (Cat. Bodl. 124, 125), nor *S*aṅkuka (Bühler, Journal of the Royal Asiatic Society, Bombay, 1877, p. 42).

[4] Hall, Vâsavadattâ, preface. Bhao Daji, Journal of the Royal Asiatic Society, Bombay, 1860.

[5] See Bühler, Indian Antiquary, ii, p. 127; and Ind. Studien, xiv, p. 407. 'All Kasmîra MSS. of the Kâvyaprakâsa read Bâ*n*a, not Dhâvaka. In the *S*âradâ alphabet the two words may easily be confounded.' Hall, Vâsavadattâ, pref. p. 15.

[6] The Ve*n*isa*m*hâra is ascribed to a Bha*tt*a Nârâya*n*a, and the date of this poet is referred by Grill, in his edition of the Ve*n*isa*m*hâra, to the sixth century. But, according to Rajendralal Mitra (Journal of the Asiatic Society, Bengal, 1864, p. 326) Bha*tt*a Nârâya*n*a, the author of the Ve*n*isa*m*hâra, was one of the Brahmans who came to the Court of Âdi*s*ûra, A.D. 1072?

[7] Hall, l. c., p. 20. Râ*g*asekhara wrote this Prabandhakosha in 1347. Indian Antiquary, 1872, p. 113 note.

of *S*rîharsha, again the patron, we should think, of Hiouen-thsang [1].

The story [2] told of Bâ*n*a and Mayûra is that Mayûra was a Pandit living at U*gg*ayinî, honoured by the older Bho*g*a. His son-in-law was Bâ*n*a, who was likewise very learned, and they soon began to squabble with each other. The king therefore sent them to Ka*s*mîra, which seems at that time to have been celebrated for its learning, and told them to have it settled there which of them possessed greater learning. The award seems to have been slightly in favour of Bâ*n*a. When they had returned to Bho*g*a's capital, Mayûra, the father-in-law, once listened to a quarrel between Bâ*n*a and his wife, and called his daughter a *Kand*î, a scold. Thereupon the daughter cursed him, and he became a leper. In order to be freed from his leprosy, Mayûra wrote the Mayûra-*s*ataka [3] in praise of the sun, and having been cured became a great favourite with Bho*g*a. Bâ*n*a, being jealous, had his own hands and feet cut off, and then praised *Kand*ikâ [4], asking her to restore his limbs. This also was accomplished. Then the *G*ainas, anxious to show that their holy men could perform as great a miracle, produced Mânatuṅga Sûri, who allowed himself to be fettered with forty-two chains, and by composing the Bhaktâmara-stotra, in forty-two verses, freed himself from them.

If then Bâ*n*a, Mayûra, and possibly Mânatuṅga [5] lived early

---

[1] The other Harsha, the son of Hîra, and sometimes called the nephew of Mammaṭa, is reported to have written, besides the Naishadhîya, the Sthairya-vi*k*ârana, the Vi*g*aya-pra*s*asti, the Kha*nd*ana-kha*nd*a-khâdya, the Gau*d*orvîsa-kula-pra*s*asti, the Ar*n*ava-var*n*ana, the *Khand*apra*s*asti, the *S*iva*s*aktisiddhi, and the Nava-sâhasâṅka-*k*arita: see Hall, Vâsavadattâ, pref. p. 18; Bibliography, p. 160; P. N. Pûrnaiya, Indian Antiquary, 1874, p. 29; Cat. Bodl. p. 124ᵇ; Bühler, Journal of the Royal Asiatic Society, Bombay, 1875, p. 279.

[2] See Bühler, on Chandikâsatakam of Bâ*n*abha*tt*a, in Indian Antiquary, April, 1872. The story is told by the *G*aina commentator on the Bhaktâmarastotra.

[3] The Mayûra-*s*ataka (sûrya-sataka), in *S*ardûla-vikrî*d*ita metre, was published by Ya*gñ*esvar *S*âstrî.

[4] The *Kand*ikâ-stotra, in *S*ardûla-vikrî*d*ita metre, consists of 102 verses.

[5] Called also Mâtaṅga, as in the verse of Râ*g*asekhara, 'Aho prabhâvo vâgdevyâ yan Mâtaṅgadivâkara*h* *S*rîharshasyâbhavat sabhya*h* samo Bâ*n*amayûrayo*h*.' Cf. Hall, Vâsavadattâ, pref. p. 21. This surely proves that all three were favourites of Harsha (whatever Mahesa Chandra Nyâyaratna in his edition

in the seventh century at the Court of Harsha(vardhana), the works and the writers whom Bâ*n*a quotes must be referred to a still earlier period. Such are:

*K*aura, i. e. *K*aurîsuratapa*ñk*â*s*ikâ, see Bühler, Ind. Stud. xiv, p. 406.

Subandhu, author of the Vâsavadattâ.

Bha*tt*âra-Hari*k*andra.

*S*âlivâhana or Sâtavâhana, the author of an Anthology (Gâthâkosha[1]).

Bhâsa[2], a dramatic writer.

Kâlidâsa, whose date, as the author of the Setukâvya, is fixed by that of king Pravarasena, and as the author of the Meghadûta by that of Dignâga.

The author of the B*ri*hatkathâ, Gu*n*â*dh*ya[3], and Â*dh*yarâ*g*a, or Âdyarâ*g*a, of whom we know nothing, for he cannot be meant for Kavirâ*g*a, the author of the Râghavapâ*nd*avîya, who himself quotes both Subandhu and Bâ*n*abha*tt*a as his equals in the art of poetry[4].

As to Subandhu, the contemporary of Bâ*n*a and Mayûra, it is possible that he may have lived even somewhat earlier. Bâ*n*a quotes him, not he Bâ*n*a, and in several places[5] when the three are mentioned together, Subandhu's name comes first, though, of course, this may be an accident only. Like

---

of the Kâvyaprakâsa, Vi*gñ*âpana, p. 19, may say to the contrary); for the meaning is that the power of Sarasvatî is so great that even a *G*aina could become a favourite of king Harsha, like Bâ*n*a and Mayûra, i. e. as if he were their equal.

[1] See Bühler, Indian Antiquary, 1873, p. 106. Hema*k*andra gives Hâla as a synonym of Sâtavâhana.

[2] Kâlidâsa, in the well-known passage in the introduction to the Mâlavikâgnimitra, quotes Bhâsa and Saumilla, as his predecessors in dramatic composition. The name of Dhâvaka, as the real author of Harsha's Nâgânanda, is supposed to be due to a wrong reading.

[3] See p. 357.

[4] Râgh. i, 41. Kavirâ*g*a's patron was Râ*g*â Kâmadeva of the Kâdamba family, at *G*ayantîpura, in the Southern Marhatta country (see Fleet, Indian Antiquary, x, p. 249). If the Mu*ñg*a, whom he refers to, is the uncle of Bho*g*a of Dhârâ, his date must, of course, be later. Hall, Vâsavadattâ, pref. p. 19, places *G*ayantîpura among the Khasiya hills in Eastern Bengal; Weber, Ind. Streifen, i, p. 371, in the East, according to the scholiast.

[5] Kavirâ*g*a mentions Subandhu before Bâ*n*a, so does Râ*g*asekhara (Vâsavadattâ, Hall, pref. p. 21), and Bho*g*a in the Sarasvatî-ka*nth*âbhara*n*a.

Bâna and Dandin, Subandhu quotes Gunâdhya, the author of the Brihatkathâ (in Bhûtabhâshâ), and he seems familiar with Upanishads, Bhârata, Râmâyana, Harivamsa, Purânas[1], the Khandovikiti, Nakshatravidyâ, Nyâyasthiti, Uddyotakara, Bauddhasangati[2], Alankâra (Dharmakîrti), Mallanâga's (Vâtsyâyana's) Kâmasûtra[3], &c.

Dandin.

Dandin, again, the author of the Dasakumârakarita and of the Kâvyâdarsa may be earlier than Bâna, but he can hardly be placed before Kâlidâsa. Nor did Colebrooke ever say this. He writes, 'Dandin, this distinguished poet, famous above all other Indian bards for the sweetness of his language, and therefore ranked by Kâlidâsa himself (if tradition may be credited) next to the fathers of Indian poetry, Vâlmîki and Vyâsa[4].' But it is well known that Dandin quotes Kâlidâsa's Prâkrit poem, the Setubandhu (i, 34), and the utmost therefore that could be conceded to tradition would be that Dandin was a contemporary of Kâlidâsa, who wrote the Setubandhu (Dasamukhabadha) for Pravarasena, the king of Kasmîra.

Bhavabhûti.

Having had to fix some of the dates of the kings of Kasmîra who were brought in contact with Vikramâditya and his successors, we may determine the date of Bhavabhûti and some later writers, mentioned in the history of that country.

We saw that Vikramâditya of Kasmîra came to the throne in 592 A.D., and that his successor, Bâlâditya, may have been

---

[1] There is a reference by name to one at least of the Purânas in Bâna's Kadambarî, ed. Calcutta, p. 83, namely, the Vâyu-purâna; see Bhartrihari, ed. Telang, p. viii.

[2] Is this the Buddhasamgîti-sûtra (Cat. No. 401) which was translated by Dharmaraksha between 265–316? There is also (Cat. No. 1298) the Mahâyâna-bodhisattva-vidyâ-sangîti-sâstra, ascribed to Dharmayasas (the commentator of the Vâsavadattâ mentions Dharmakîrti), and translated by Fâ-hu (Dharmaraksha?) and others.

[3] Hall, pref. p. 11; Catal. Bodl. p. 218.

[4] Colebrooke's Life and Essays, iii, p. 154.

the contemporary of Hiouen-thsang. With him the Gonardîya (or Gonandîya) dynasty came to an end, and a new dynasty began with Durlabhavardhana, the husband of Anaṅgalekhâ. After Durlabhavardhana follows Durlabhaka Pratâpâditya, and he is succeeded by *K*andrâpî*d*a, who was murdered and succeeded by his brother Târâpî*d*a (Va*g*râditya).

Here we have to note a synchronistic event, namely, an embassy, mentioned by Chinese historians, as having been sent in the years 713 and 720 to king *K*entolopili, who must be *K*andrâpî*d*a. Târâpî*d*a having been murdered, his brother Muktâpî*d*a, known as Lalitâditya, succeeded to the throne of Ka*s*mîra, and acquired the supreme sovereignty of India. Here again we receive a certain confirmation from Chinese history, for the Mutopi, to whom an embassy under Foe-li-to was sent during the reign of the Chinese emperor Hiouen-tsung 713–755, was probably Muktâpî*d*a, i.e. Lalitâditya. His minister was *S*aktivarman[1].

It would carry us too far were we to examine the exact dates of these kings from Vikramâditya to Lalitâditya, which will have to be settled hereafter on the evidence of coins and inscriptions rather than on the statements of the Râ*g*atarangi*n*î. I doubt even whether the number of years assigned to some of these kings refers to the years during which they reigned, and not to the years of their lives. Reigns of 42, 35 (or 13), 36, and 50 years, following each other as in the case of Vikramâditya, Bâlâditya, Durlabhavardhana, and Pratâpâditya are very unusual. For our present purpose, however, we may be satisfied with the *terminus a quo*, namely, Vikramâditya 592–634, and the *terminus ad quem*, namely, Lalitâditya, whose reign, we are assured, began 700, leaving the intervening reigns to be determined by future archæological evidence[2].

---

[1] See Indian Antiquary, 1873, p. 106. It was during his reign that Va*g*rabodhi, a learned Â*k*ârya of Mâlava, and his pupil Amogha-va*g*ra arrived in China and introduced Tantrik doctrines (Journal of the Royal Asiatic Society, Bombay, 1882, p. 93).

[2] Bühler, Brief von Kaschmir, Sept. 16, 1875, and his Report on Ka*s*mir, Journal of the Royal Asiatic Society of Bombay, 1877, p. 42, where a correction of twenty-five years is recommended.

One of the earliest victories of Lalitâditya was that over Yasovarman, king of Kânyakubga, and this Yasovarman, as the Râgataraṅginî informs us, was the patron of Bhavabhûti, Vâkpati[1], and Râgyasrî.

Here then we are again on literary ground. Bhavabhûti was a native of the Vidarbhas, the modern Berars, but he may well have lived at the Court of Yasovarman in Kânyakubga. Vâkpati is known as the author of a Prâkrit poem (discovered by Dr. Bühler, and now in course of publication), the Gaudabaha, celebrating Yasovarman's victory over a Gauda king, and in that poem he speaks highly of Bhavabhûti. If then we place Bhavabhûti in the first half of the eighth century, he is at a proper distance from Kâlidâsa, and we can understand at the same time why Bâna, who lived under Harshavardhana, 610–650, should have left out Bhavabhûti's name in the list of poets at the beginning of his Harshakarita[2].

After the glorious reign of Lalitâditya we have Kuvalâyâpîda, reigning one year, 736–737, then Vagrâditya (also called Vappîyaka and Lalitâditya) 737–744, Prithivyâpîda 744–748, Saṅgrâmâpîda 748–755. Then follows Gayâpîda (755–786), and his reign supplies us again with some literary facts, though of a date too late for our immediate purpose. We are told that the king himself studied Sanskrit under Kshîra, who has been supposed to be the same as the commentator of the Amarakosha[3]. He re-established the Mahâbhâshya[4] (of

---

[1] King Yasovarman of Kânyakubga and Vâkpatirâga, author of the Gaudabaha, are mentioned in the Tapâgakha Pattâvalî as living about Samvat 800, i.e. 744 A.D. This is not very far from the date we have assigned to his contemporary, Lalitâditya, particularly if we were to adopt the correction in the chronology of the Râgataraṅginî, proposed by Cunningham and Bühler, who places Lalitâditya 725 A.D.

[2] All this has been very ably discussed by R. G. Bhandarkar, in the preface to his edition of the Mâlatîmâdhava, 1876.

[3] Râgat. iv, 485 seq. Kshîra, the commentator of Amara, quotes from Kâlidâsa (cf. Shankar P. Pandit, Raghuvamsa, pref. p. 77). Professor Aufrecht, however (Zeitschrift der D. M. G., 1874), places the commentator Kshîra between the eleventh and twelfth centuries, chiefly because he quotes the Sabdânusâsana, ascribed to Bhoga or Bhogarâga. Bühler mentions a Kshîra as the author of an Avyayavritti and Dhâtutaraṅginî, and he calls him '*Gayâpîda's* teacher.'

[4] Helarâga, the author of a commentary on Bhartrihari's Vâkyapadîya,

Patañgali?), and there lived at his Court the following literary men:—Thakriya, Bhatta, Dâmodaragupta[1], Manoratha, Sankhadatta, Kâtaka, Sandhimat, and Vâmana.

KINGS OF KASMÎRA.

A.D.	Sreshthasena.		Vagrendra.
About 500	Hiranya and Toramâna.		Angana (her brother, Gayendra).
544–550	Mâtrigupta, patronises Bhartrimentha.	550	Pravarasena. Kâlidâsa's Setukâvya, praised by Dandin and Bâna.
531–579	Khosru Nushirvân.		
			Yudhishthira and Padmavatî.
			Narendrâditya.
			Ranâditya and Ranârambhâ.
622	Hejrah.	592–634	Vikramâditya.
632	Yezdijerd.		Bâlâditya, cont. Hiouen-thsang (?).
			Durlabhavardhana Anangalekhâ.
			Durlabhaka Pratâpâditya (Karkota dynasty).
			Kandrâpîda (713 and 720, Chinese embassy).
			Târâpîda Vagrâditya.
	Yasovarman of Kânyakubga defeated by Lalitâditya, patronises Bhavabhûti.	700–736	Muktâpîda Lalitâditya Pratâpâditya. His minister Saktisvâmin. (713–755, Chinese embassy.)
		736–37	Kuvalayâpîda.
	Vâkpati.	737–44	Vagrâditya.
		744–48	Prithivyâpîda.
		748–55	Sangrâmâpîda.
		755–86	Gayâpîda, patronises Kshîra, Vâmana, introduces Mahâbhâshya.
		788	Birth of Sankarâkârya.

Gainas, Siddhasena, Mânatunga.

I had hoped that the study of the Gaina literature, since it was taken up in good earnest by Dr. Jacobi and others, would

---

descended from Lakshmana, the minister of Muktâpîda, i. e. Lalitâditya. See Indian Antiquary, 1874, p. 285.

[1] The Hânumân-nâtaka is ascribed to a Dâmodara-misra.

have yielded some useful results in support of our chronology of the Renaissance period of Sanskrit literature. It has thrown, no doubt, considerable light on the religious state of India at the time when *S*âkyamuni started his reform by the side of other reformers, such as Vardhamâna Mahâvîra *G*ñâtaputra[1], the founder of *G*ainism, Pûra*n*a Kâ*s*yapa, Maskarin Go*s*âliputra, Sañ*g*ayin Vaira*tt*î-putra, A*g*ita Ke*s*akambala, Kakuda Kâtyâyana[2], and others. The date of Vardhamâna's Nirvâ*n*a, 526 B.C., shows him to have been, or to have been believed to have been, a contemporary of *S*âkyamuni, and if his era is liable to the same kind of correction as the Ceylonese era of Buddha, 543 B.C., we should have the true date of the founder of *G*ainism, 460 B.C., by the side of the corrected date of Buddha, 477 B.C.[3]

Leaving, however, the early period, we ask at what time the sacred canon of the *G*ainas was fixed and written down, and here the answers vary, though within narrow limits. Devarddhiga*n*i[4] Kshamâ*s*rama*n*a, to whom the work of writing down the sacred canon is ascribed by tradition, lived 980 after Vardhamâna's Nirvâ*n*a, i.e. 454 A.D. (or, if corrected, 520 A.D.). He did for *G*ainism what Buddhaghosha had done about thirty years before for Buddhism[5].

At the very same time, 980 A.V., we are told that Bhadrabâhu's Kalpasûtra was re-arranged in nine vâ*k*anâs or lectures, and was read in the hall of Dhruvasena, king of Ânandapura, to console him after the death of his son Senaṅga*g*a[6].

One more statement should here be mentioned, which was first made by Bhao Daji (Kâlidâsa, p. 25), and has since been repeated by others, viz. that '*G*aina records mention Siddhasena

---

[1] Kalpasûtra, ed. Jacobi, Introduction, p. 6.

[2] Burnouf, Introduction, p. 162; Indian Antiquary, Nov. 1879.

[3] See Jacobi, l.c., p. 6.

[4] Also called Devavâ*k*aka, pupil of Dûshaga*n*i; cf. Indian Antiquary, xi, p. 247.

[5] Jacobi, l.c., p. 16.

[6] Other dates of this event are 993 A.V. and 1080 A.V. See Jacobi, l.c., p. 24. The last date 1080, if corrected, would give us 620 A.D., and thus bring Dhruvasena of Ânandapura together with Dhruvabha*t*a of Valabhi, provided Dr. Bühler's conjecture as to the era of the Valabhi grant (Indian Antiquary, 1878, p. 80) be correct. See before, p. 318, note.

Sûri, a learned *G*aina priest, as the spiritual adviser of Vikramâditya[1].' Professor Jacobi (Kalpasûtra, pref. p. 14) added: 'Siddhasena is a *G*aina author, who is said to have made the arrangement of the Samvat era for king Vikramâditya[2].'

Now Sena (*S*rî-she*n*a) is mentioned by Brahmagupta and Albiruni[3] as the author of the Romaka-siddhânta, one of the five siddhântas used by Varâhamihira. S*ri*ta-sena or *S*rutisena is quoted as one of the astronomers of Vikramârka, in the *G*yotirvidâbhara*n*a. The question therefore arises whether all these names belong to one and the same Sena, called Siddhasena (the blessed Sena) by the *G*ainas, and *S*rî-she*n*a by the Brâhmans, and whether the calculation of the Vikrama era, as 600 before 544 A.D., the date of the battle of Korur, is actually the work of this *G*aina astronomer. We find a certain confirmation in the Pa*tt*âvalîs of which Dr. Klatt has lately given extracts in the Indian Antiquary, xi, p. 245. Here we read in the Kharataraga*kh*a Pa*tt*âvalî that at the time of Si*m*hagiri there lived Pâdaliptâ*k*ârya, V*ri*ddhavâdisûri, and his pupil Siddhasena-divâkara, who received the Dîkshâ name of Kumuda*k*andra, and that the latter converted Vikramâditya. The same story is repeated in the Pa*tt*âvalî of the Tapâga*kh*a, where we read that Ârya-mangu, V*ri*ddhavâdin, Pâdalipta, and Siddhasena-divâkara lived at the same time, and that the last, the author of the Kalyâ*n*amandirastava, converted Vikramâditya. The date assigned to Siddhasena is 470 after Vardhamâna's Nirvâ*n*a, which would be exactly the beginning of the Vikrama era 56 B.C., but cannot be used for historical purposes.

The same Pa*tt*âvalîs confirm also the accounts of Mânatunga which we discussed before. We find in the Kharataraga*kh*a Pa*tt*âvalî, under No. 23, Mânatunga, author of the Bhaktâmara and Bhayahara stotras, and in the Tapâga*kh*a Pa*tt*âvalî, under No. 20, Mânatunga (mâlave*s*vara-

---

[1] See Hall, Bibliography, p. 166. In the Journal of the Royal Asiatic Society, Bombay, x, p. 130, Dr. Bhao Daji quotes the Prabandha *K*intâma*n*i and other works in support of the statement that Siddhasena Divâkara and Kâlidâsa were contemporaries of Vikrama.

[2] Siddhasena is quoted by Varâhamihira, B*ri*hagg. 7, 7.

[3] Kern, B*ri*hatsa*m*hitâ, pref. p. 47.

*k*aulukyavayarasi*m*hadevâmâtya*h*), who by means of his Bhaktâmarastavana converted the king who had been beguiled by the sorceries of Bâ*n*a and Mayûra at Vârâ*n*asî, and convinced Nâgarâ*g*a by means of his Bhayaharastavana. He also composed a stavana, beginning 'Bhattibhara.' The date assigned, somewhat before 980, i.e. before Devarddhiga*n*i (454 or 520 A.D.), is again systematic rather than historical. It should be borne in mind that all these statements taken from *G*aina authorities are either of very modern or of very doubtful date. Nevertheless there is some hope that, under certain restrictions, the *G*aina literature also may help to the elucidation of Indian chronology.

I-tsing.

I entertain, in fact, a strong hope that a continued study of the *G*aina and Buddhist books will bring out some more facts throwing light on the parallel stream of Brahmanic literature, which by itself is without any landmarks, and seemingly flowing from nowhere to nowhere. We shall soon possess a catalogue of the whole Buddhist Tripi*t*aka in its Chinese translation, giving us the dates of each translator, whether Hindu or Chinese, and thus enabling us, if we may trust the Chinese chroniclers, to fix at all events the lowest date of the Sanskrit originals. We owe a great deal already to information contained in the travels of Chinese pilgrims in India, particularly of Fa-hian, 400–415 A.D., of Hwui Seng and Sung Yun, 518 A.D., and of Hiouen-thsang, 629–645, in helping us to determine a period of literary and religious activity in India extending from about 400 to 700 A.D., the very period of what we may now call the Renaissance of Sanskrit Literature. I shall add here a short abstract of some quite unexpected information on the literary state of India in the seventh century, which I lately discovered in the works of the Chinese pilgrim, I-tsing.

The Kâsikâ.

There is a famous commentary on Pâ*n*ini's grammar, called the Kâsikâ V*ri*tti*h*[1].

[1] Kâsikâ, a Commentary on Pâ*n*ini's Grammatical Aphorisms, by Pandit

Professor Boehtlingk, in the introduction to his edition of Pâ*n*ini's Grammar (p. liv), referred the Kâ*s*ikâ V*ri*tti to about the eighth century, on the supposition that Vâmana, the author of the Kâ*s*ikâ, could be proved to be the same as the Vâmana who is mentioned in the Chronicle of Ka*s*mîra (iv, 496). The evidence on which that careful scholar relied was as follows:—Kahla*n*a Pa*nd*ita, the author of the Râ*g*atarangi*n*î, is evidently anxious to do full justice to *G*ayâpî*d*a, who, after the battle of Pushkaletra, recovered the throne of his father, and became a patron of literature. He mentions, therefore, in full detail his exertions for the restoration of grammatical studies in Ka*s*mîra, and particularly the interest he took in a new edition, as we should call it, of Pata*ñg*ali's Mahâbhâshya. He then passes on to give the names of other learned men living at his Court, such as Kshîra (author of Dhâtutarangi*n*î, according to Bühler), Dâmodaragupta, Manoratha, *S*ankhadatta, *K*âtaka, Sandhimat, and Vâmana. This Vâmana was supposed to be the author of the Kâ*s*ikâ. But if this Vâmana had been the author of the Kâ*s*ikâ—that is to say, of a complete commentary on Pâ*n*ini's Grammar—would not Kalha*n*a have mentioned him as connected with the revival of grammatical learning in Ka*s*mîra, instead of putting his name casually at the end of a string of other names?

It ought to be stated that Professor Boehtlingk has himself surrendered this conjecture. There is another conjecture, first started by Wilson (Asiatic Researches, xv, p. 55), that the Vâmana here mentioned at the Court of *G*ayâpî*d*a was the author of a set of poetical Sûtras and of a V*ri*tti or gloss upon them. Dr. Cappeller argues against this in the introduction to his edition of Vâmana's Kâvyâlankâra-v*ri*tti (Jena, 1875). Vâmana, he says, the author both of the text and of the gloss of this work, quotes *S*ûdraka, the author of the M*rikkh*aka*t*ika; Kâlidâsa, the author of the *S*akuntalâ, Urva*s*î, Mâlavika, Meghadûta, Kumârasambhava, and Raghuva*ms*a; Amaru, Bhavabhûti, Mâgha, the Hariprabodha, the Nâmamâlâ, Kâmandakanîti, Vi*s*âkhila, and Kavirâ*g*a. Now if this Kavirâ*g*a

---

Vâmana and *G*ayâditya. Edited by Pa*nd*it Bâla*s*âstrî, Professor of Hindu Law in the Sanskrit College, Benares. (Benares, 1876, 1878.)

is intended for the author of the Râghavapâ*nd*avîya, who is supposed to have lived later than the tenth century, this would be sufficient to place Vâmana at least after 1000 A. D., while *G*ayâpî*d*a, his supposed patron, died in 776 (or 786) A. D.

All depends here on the date of Kavirâ*g*a, who may after all not be so late as Dr. Cappeller supposes.

After having assigned Vâmana, the author of the Kâvyâlankâra, to the twelfth century, Dr. Cappeller proceeds to identify this late Vâmana with Vâmana, the author of the Kâ*s*ikâ V*ri*tti. His arguments, however, are hardly convincing. He relies chiefly on a statement of Bâla*s*âstrin, in the introduction to his edition of the Kâ*s*ikâ, where that learned scholar speaks of a third Vâmana, a poet, who wrote the Lokottaralalita, in Mahârâsh*t*ra, and places him in *S*aka 1595, i. e. 1673 A. D., adding that the grammarian Vâmana lived 500 years earlier, i. e. 1173 A. D. If Professor Weber states that Bâla*s*âstrin assigns the grammarian Vâmana to the thirteenth century (Hist. of Sansk. Lit. p. 226), this must refer to some other paper which has escaped my notice. Bâla*s*âstrin, however, gives no evidence in support of his statement, nor does he, so far as I am aware, ever hint at Vâmana, the grammarian, being the same as Vâmana, the rhetorician.

Professor Goldstücker, in a similar manner—that is, without producing sufficient evidence—referred Vâmana, the grammarian, to the same recent period as the Siddhânta-kaumudî, Nâge*s*a, Purushottama, and other grammarians (Goldstücker, Pâ*n*ini, p. 89)—therefore to a period later at all events than the thirteenth century.

Before we proceed further, it will be necessary to determine, first, whether Vâmana was the only author of the Kâ*s*ikâ. Colebrooke (Sanskrit Grammar, p. 9) spoke of the Kâ*s*ikâ as the work of *G*ayâditya, or Vâmana *G*ayâditya. Bâla*s*âstrin, the editor of the Kâ*s*ikâ, thought likewise at first that Vâmana and *G*ayâditya, who are mentioned as the authors, were one and the same person (Pa*n*dit, June 1878, p. 20, l. 9). He found, however, afterwards that Bha*tt*o*g*idîkshita, the author of the Siddhânta-kaumudî, clearly distinguishes between the opinions of *G*ayâditya and Vâmana (Sûtra v, 4, 42; ed. Tarkavâ*k*aspati, i, p. 727); and he might have learnt the same from

Professor Aufrecht's excellent edition of the Unâdi Sûtras (pref. p. xv, Sûtra i, 52). Bâlasâstrin afterwards assigned the first, second, fifth, and sixth books to Gayâditya, the rest to Vâmana, while in an ancient MS. of the Kâsikâ, discovered by Dr. Bühler in Kasmîra (Journal of the Bombay Branch of the R. A. S., 1877, p. 72), the first four adhyâyas are ascribed to Gayâditya, the last four to Vâmana. (See also Professor Kielhorn, Kâtyâyana and Patañgali, p. 12, note.) The evidence is therefore decidedly in favour of Vâmana and Gayâditya being two different persons and joint authors of the Kâsikâ.

In the preface to the sixth volume of my edition of the Rig-veda (p. xxix), I endeavoured to show that the statement made by Bhattogidîkshita in the Sabdakaustubha, and by the author of the Manoramâ, viz. that Vâmana, whose fame had been eclipsed by Vopadeva, had been brought forward again by Mâdhava, was to some extent confirmed by the commentary on the Rig-veda, Vopadeva being nowhere quoted by Mâdhava, while Vâmana is quoted at least once in the commentary on the Rig-veda, and more frequently in Sâyana's Dhâtuvritti. Bâlasâstrin concluded rightly that Vâmana must be older than Mâdhava, 1350 A. D., and older than Vopadeva, who lived in the twelfth century. I added that Sâyana quotes both Haradatta, the author of the Padamañgarî, an exposition of the Kâsikâ, and Nyâsakara, i. e. Ginendra, the author of the Nyâsa or Kâsikâ-vritti-pañgikâ. This last book is likewise quoted by the author of a commentary called the Kâvyakâmadhenu, probably the work of Vopadeva, so that the interval between the authors of the Kâsikâ and those who could quote from commentaries on their works must be extended accordingly.

This was the state of uncertainty in which the date of the Kâsikâ had to be left. 'It must be earlier than the twelfth century' (Burnell, Aindra School of Sanskrit Grammarians, p. 92); 'it is not a modern work' (Bühler, loc. cit., p. 73). Such were the last utterances of two of the most competent judges.

One other argument in favour of the comparatively early date of Vâmana and Gayâditya should not be passed over. It was produced by Bâlasâstrin, who showed that both were evidently *G*ainas, or, what is the same with him, Bauddhas. Like the Amarakosha, the Kâ*s*ikâ begins without any invocation or exposition of the character of the book, a custom always observed by orthodox writers. Secondly, the authors of the Kâ*s*ikâ actually alter the text of Pâ*n*ini, which no orthodox Brâhman would venture to do. In Sûtra iv, 2, 43, they insert sahâya, writing grâma*g*anabandhusahâyebhyas tal instead of Pâ*n*ini's grâma*g*anabandhubhyas tal. Thirdly, they quote instances referring to Buddhist literature, which, again, no respectable writer would do. When giving an instance of the use of the verb nî, in the Âtmanepada, meaning 'to be honoured' (Pâ*n*. I, 3, 36), they say, '*K*ârva leads, i.e. is honoured in the Lokâyata school.' This *K*ârva (*K*ârvâka?) is said to be a name of Buddha, and means here an heretical teacher, who is honoured in the Lokâyata school[1]. An orthodox writer would have quoted authorities from orthodox, never from nihilistic, schools. And Bâla*s*âstrin adds that there were other distinguished grammarians too at that time who were *G*ainas—for instance, the author of the Nyâsa, *G*inendrabuddhi[2]—but that their works were afterwards eclipsed by those of orthodox grammarians, such as Bha*tt*o*g*idîkshita, Haridîkshita, Nâge*s*abha*tt*a, &c.

After thus having established two points—viz. that Vâmana and *G*ayâditya were joint authors of the Kâ*s*ikâ, and that they were *G*ainas or Bauddhas—we return to the question as to their probable date. Meeting in Mr. Beal's Catalogue of the Buddhist Tripi*t*aka (p. 94) with the title of a work called Nan-hae-ki-kwei-chouen, being 'Records concerning Visits and Returns to the Southern Seas,' I consulted my friend and pupil Mr. Kasawara on the contents of the work. He informed me that it was written by I-tsing, one of the best-known Chinese pilgrims, who left Kwang-chau, in China, in the eleventh lunar month of the year 671 A.D., arrived at Tâmralipti, in India, after a long voyage, in the second month of 673, and started from that place for Nâlanda

[1] On Lokâyata as another name of the *K*ârvâka school, see Cowell, Sarvadarsana-sangraha, p. 2.

[2] 'Not later than the twelfth century, because quoted by Vopadeva,' Bühler, Indian Antiquary, 1878, p. 57.

in the fifth month of the same year. After the lapse of some years, he returned to Tâmralipti, and sailed to Si-ri-fa-sai, in the Southern Sea countries.

It seems that he wrote his book, 'The Accounts of Buddhist Practices sent, being entrusted to one who returns to China, from the Southern Sea Countries,' in Si-ri-fa-sai, for he generally compares the practices of India with those of the Southern Sea countries. His work consists of two volumes, containing four books and forty chapters. Though he does not mention how long he was in India, yet, as he refers to the usurper Queen, Tsak-tin-mo-hau, whose date is 690, we see that he must then have been absent from China twenty years, and have spent eighteen years in India. We may gather, in fact, from remarks occurring in his work that he was born about 635, that he left China in 671, arrived at Tâmralipti in 673, and was still absent in 690, at the time of the usurpation of Queen Tsak-tin-mo-hau. That usurpation lasted till 705, when the Tang dynasty was restored. It is stated elsewhere that I-tsing died in 713, seventy-nine years old, and that he had returned to China in 695.

In the thirty-fourth chapter of his work I-tsing treats of learning in the West, and chiefly of grammatical science, the *S*abdavidyâ, one of the five vidyâs or sciences. He gives the name Vyâkara*n*a, grammar, and then proceeds to speak of five works, generally called grammar in India.

I. The first is called elementary Siddhânta, and begins with siddhirastu. It was originally taught by Mahe*s*vara, and is learnt by heart by children when they are six years old. They learn it in six months.

Most likely this refers to the *S*iva Sûtras, granted by the favour of Mahe*s*vara. But, from the description given, this Siddhânta must have contained much more than the fourteen *S*iva Sûtras. 'There are forty-nine letters,' I-tsing writes, 'the compounds of which are divided into eighteen sections, and of which altogether more than 10,000 words are formed. These words are arranged in 300 *s*lokas, of thirty-two syllables each.'

II. The second grammatical work is called Sûtra, the foundation of all grammatical science. It is the work of Pâ*n*ini, and contains 1,000 *s*lokas. He was inspired by Mahe*s*vara, and is said to have been endowed with three eyes. Children begin to learn it when they are eight years old, and learn it in eight months.

III. Dhâtu. This consists of 1,000 *s*lokas, and treats of grammatical roots. Evidently a Dhâtupâ*th*a.

IV. Three so-called Khilas:—(1) Ash*t*adhâtu, consisting of 1,000 *s*lokas (on declension and conjugation); (2) Man-*k*a, consisting of 1,000 *s*lokas; (3) U*n*âdi, consisting of 1,000 *s*lokas.

Boys of ten years learn these parts of grammar, and finish them after three years.

The explanation of Khila as 'uncultivated pieces of land' is no doubt quite correct. We should say appendix or excursus instead. But it is difficult to say what I-tsing could have meant by the second Khila. Mr. Beal called my attention to a note of Stanislas Julien's in his index to Hiouen-thsang, where (vol. iii, p. 514) Men-tse-kia is evidently meant for the same word, and explained by Ma*nd*aka. Hiouen-thsang mentions Men-tse-kia (vol. i, p. 166) as one of two classes of words, the other class being the U*n*âdi. He tells us that Professor Spiegel approved of this interpretation, but I cannot find any place where Professor Spiegel has treated of ma*nd*aka and traced it back as a technical term to some corresponding sa*m*g*ñ*â of Sanskrit grammar. I found afterwards that in 1871 I had consulted my learned friend, Stanislas Julien, on the same subject, asking him whether Men-tse-kia could possibly be intended for Nirukta or Nigha*nt*u. He wrote on the first of December, 1871, 'Je regrette de vous dire que je ne suis pas en mesure de repondre parfaitement aux différentes questions de votre lettre. Dans ma Méthode de transcription (p. 221) le second mot de Men-tse-kia répresente *d*a dans pa*nd*aka et *dh*a dans virû*dh*aka, mais il y a loin de là à Nirukta.'

What I-tsing really says, according to Mr. Kasawara's translation, is:—'Ma*ñk*a treats of the formation of words by means of combining (a root and suffix, or suffixes). One of many names for tree, for instance, is v*ri*ksha in Sanskrit (that is to say, the word v*ri*ksha is made up of v*ri*ksh and a). Thus a name for a thing is formed by mixing the parts together, according to the rules of the book, which consists of more than twenty sentences (or feet of *s*loka). U*n*âdi is nearly the same, with a few differences, such as what is full in the one is mentioned in brief in the other, and *vice versa*.'

Mr. Kasawara informed me that Ma*ñk*a may be meant for ma*nd*a, possibly for ma*nd*aka, but I do not see that even this would help us much. Ma*nd* means to adorn, ma*nd*a is used for cream on milk, also for gruel, but all this, even if we admitted the meaning of mixing, would not yield us a technical name for the formation of words by means of joining a suffix with a root. At all events, I have never met with ma*nd*, or any of its derivatives, in that technical sense. I thought at one time that ma*nd*a might be meant for Mâ*nd*ûka, because the Mâ*nd*ukeyas were famous for their grammatical works (see M. M., History of Ancient Sanskrit Literature, p. 146), and one of these might possibly have been used by I-tsing when studying the K*ri*d-anta chapter. But I do not think this likely, even if, as I am told, the Chinese transliteration should admit of it.

We now proceed at once to No. V, which is called V*ri*tti Sûtra, a commentary on the foregoing Sûtra. We are told that 'it is the best among the many commentaries. It contains 18,000 *s*lokas, citing the words of the Sûtras, and explaining intricate matters very clearly. It exposes the laws of the universe and the precepts of heaven and man. Boys of fifteen begin to study this commentary, and understand it completely in five years. This commentary is the work of the learned *G*ayâditya, who was endowed with great ability. His literary talent was so excellent that he understood matters of literature hearing them once, and did not require to be told twice. He revered the three venerable ones, and performed all religious duties. Since his death it is nearly thirty years.'

If we take the lowest date for I-tsing's work, viz. 690 A.D. (because he mentions the usurpation which took place in that year), he would have been four years, as he says, in Si-ri-fa-sai, and thirteen in India, when he wrote the thirty-fourth chapter of his work; and there is no reason why he should not have known, and, if he cared, have been able to ascertain the exact date of the death of the author of one of the most famous grammars of that time, moreover a grammar which he recommends all true students, coming from China to India, to learn by heart. On the whole, his description of that grammar agrees well with the Kâsikâ V*ri*tti, and it is almost impossible to imagine that he should have fixed by accident or fraud on the real name of one of the authors of that grammar, *G*ayâditya. Unless the whole of I-tsing's work can be shown to be a spurious compilation, we are justified in assuming that he knew a commentary on Pâ*n*ini's Sûtras by *G*ayâditya, and that he believed *G*ayâditya to have died not later than 660 A.D.

I-tsing then continues: 'After having studied this commentary, the students learn composition in prose and in verse, and devote themselves to logical science (Hetuvidyâ) as well as to the Kosha (*S*abda-kosha, or Abhidharma-kosha ?).' After learning the Li-men-lun (Nyâyadvâra-târaka *s*âstra, ascribed to *G*ina or Dharmapâla) they draw inferences correctly (Anumâna), and after studying the Pan-shang-kwan (*G*âtaka-mâlâ) their talents become excellent. Then, being instructed by their teachers, and instructing others, they pass two or three years, generally in the monastery of Nâlanda in Central India, or in Valabhî in Western India. These two places are like *K*ing-ma, Shih-*k*siu, Lung-man, and *K*süé-li (the seats of learning in China). There eminent and accomplished men assemble like clouds, and discuss the possibility and impossibility of their opinions; and having been approved as to their excellence by the wise, having become famous for their pre-eminence far and wide, and having made themselves assured of the sharpness of their own abilities, they go thence to the Imperial Court to lay down before it the sharp words (of their intellect). There they present their schemes to show their (political) talent, being desirous to receive good appointments. When they are in the place of discussion, they prove their wonderful cleverness. When they are in the place of refutation, all their opponents become tongue-bound and own their shame. Then the sound of their fame makes the five mountains vibrate, and their renown flows, as it were, over the four borders. They then receive grants of land, and enjoy high rank, and their names, written in white, are celebrated high on the lofty gate. After this they can follow whatever occupation they like.'

Patañgali's Mahâbhâshya.

I-tsing then returns to the V*ri*tti Sûtra, i.e. the Kâ*s*ikâ V*ri*tti, and says: 'There is a commentary on it, entitled *Kûrni*, containing 24,000 *s*lokas. It is a work of the learned Patañgali, and explains clearly that commentary (V*ri*tti) by illustrating accurately its meaning, and inquiring into its small details. Advanced scholars learn it in three years, and the labour is similar to that of learning the *Kh*un-tshu and the Yih-king (in China).'

As *Kûrni* is a name for commentary, and Patañgali is actually called *Kûrnikrit*, the author of the *Kûrni*, there can be little doubt, if any, that I-tsing is here speaking of Patañgali's Mahâbhâshya. It does not follow, however, that he considered Patañgali's Mahâbhâshya as more recent than the Kâ*s*ikâ, though it is not impossible.

Bhartrihari.

I-tsing then continues: 'Next, there is the Bhart*ri*hari-discourse, a commentary on the foregoing *Kûrni*, the work of the great scholar Bhart*ri*hari. It contains 25,000 *s*lokas, which treat of the principles of human affairs and of grammatical science, and relates also the source of the rise and fall of many families. Bhart*ri*hari was intimately acquainted with (the principles of the doctrine of) "Only Knowledge" (vidyâmâtra), and well versed in logic (lit. in the reason, hetu and in the example, udâhara*n*a). This scholar was very famous throughout the five divisions of India, and his virtues were known everywhere. He believed deeply in the "Three Jewels," and meditated on the "Twofold Voidness." Having desired (to embrace) the excellent religion, he belonged to the priestly order, but, overcome by worldly desires, he returned again to the laity. Thus he seven times became a priest, and seven times returned to the laity. Unless one believes well in the truth of cause and effect, one cannot act like him. He wrote the following verse with self-reproach:

"Through attachment I returned to the laity,
Being free from desire I again wear the priestly cloaks.
Why do those two things play with me like a child?"

He was contemporaneous with Dharmapâla.'

This Dharmapâla was most likely the teacher of *S*îlabhadra, who was an old man when he received Hiouen-thsang at Nâlanda in 633. Dharmapâla's name is mentioned in connection with a grammatical work, the *S*abdavidyâ-sa*m*yukta *s*âstra (saṅgraha *s*âstra), and his time would therefore well agree with Bhart*ri*hari's time, supposing that, as I-tsing says, he died 650 A.D.

I-tsing goes on to tell some other stories about Bhart*ri*hari which make it not unlikely that he is speaking of Bhart*ri*hari, the author of the three *S*atakas on Kâma (love), Nîti (discipline), and Vairâgya (tranquillity). 'Once,' he says, 'Bhart*ri*hari was a priest, living in a monastery. Overcome by worldly desires, he was disposed to return to the laity. Yet he remained firm, and asked a student to get a carriage ready at the outside of the monastery. A man asked the cause. "It is," he replied, "the place where one performs meritorious actions, and it is designed for the dwelling of those who keep the moral precepts. Now passions already predominate within me, and I am incapable of following the excellent law. One such as I am should not intrude into an assembly of the priests from every quarter." Then he returned to be a lay devotee (upâsaka), and, wearing a white garment, continued to exalt the true religion in the monastery.'

'It is forty years since his death.'

'There is besides, the Vâkya-discourse (Vâkyapadîka), which contains 700 *s*lokas, and 7,000 (words) in its explanation. It is also Bhart*ri*hari's work, a treatise on observation and inference according to the scriptures.'

As the second work is the Vâkyapadîya, we can see in the first a commentary only on the Mahâbhâshya by Bhart*ri*hari, i.e. the Mahâbhâshya-vyâkhyâ [1]. We might think of the Kârikâs, which

[1] This work exists in the Dekhan, fragments at Berlin.

are mentioned by Târânâtha (pref. to Siddhânta-kaumudî, vol. ii, p. 2) as between Bhartrihari's commentary on the Mahâbhâshya and his Vâkyapadîya (also called Vâkyapradîpa), but they would probably have been described by a different name.

Here then we should have the famous Bhartrihari, so often described as the elder brother of king Vikramâditya in the first century B.C. as a Buddhist, a man tossed about between kâma and dharma, between the world and the monastery, a poet, a grammarian, a philosopher, the contemporary of Dharmapâla, known, it would seem, to some of the eminent men whom I-tsing visited in his travels through India, and reported to have died not more than forty years ago, say 650, that is, shortly after Hiouen-thsang's return to China. That there was a Buddhistic flavour about Bhartrihari's *S*atakas, has long been perceived; still, even those who did not believe in the Augustan Court of Vikramâditya and his brother Bhartrihari in the first century B.C., hardly ventured to do more than place him hesitatingly in the first or second century, instead of the seventh century A.D.

There is one more difficulty which we have to meet.

After having told us all this about Bhartrihari, I-tsing continues: 'Next, there is the Pina or Pida or Vina. It contains 3,000 verses of Bhartrihari, and 14,000 (words?) in its explanation by Dharmapâla, an author of treatises. It fathoms the deep secrets of heaven and earth, and treats of the philosophy of man. A person who has reached the study of this work (after having learnt gradually the foregoing works) is said to know grammatical science very well, and may be likened to one who has learnt the nine Kings and all the classics (in China). All those above mentioned are studied by both priests and laymen, otherwise they cannot be called well-informed.'

The text from which this translation was made, is very imperfect, and Mr. Kasawara wishes his rendering to be considered in many places as tentative only, hoping to publish a better one as soon as he has returned to Japan. I asked him, as a mere conjecture, whether it was possible that Pida could represent Bha*tt*i, and he thought it was just possible, but no more. It is clear that the book must have been a grammatical work, and the Bha*tt*ikâvya (or Râva*n*abadha) may be called a grammatical work. It is also well known that the authorship of that poem has frequently been assigned to Bhart*ri*hari. Among the various commentators, Kandarpa*k*akravartin calls the author Bhart*ri*hari, the book Bha*tt*i; Vidyâvinoda calls the author Bhart*ri*hari, the son of *S*rîdharasvâmin; Bharata Mallika calls him Bhart*ri*hari. The oldest manuscript calls the poet Bha*tt*i-brâhma*n*a, the son of *S*rîdharasvâmin of Va*l*abhî; the oldest commentator, *G*ayamangala, calls him Bha*tt*i, Harihara does the same, while Pu*nd*arîkâksha in his Kalâpadîpikâ speaks of him simply as Bha*tt*i [1]. Bhao Daji and Bhandarkar inform us that Bha*tt*i was believed by some to have been the son of Bhart*ri*hari, and to have lived under *S*rîdharasena of Va*l*abhî.

After all this, we can well understand that I-tsing should have been told that the Bha*tt*i was the work of Bhart*ri*hari, always supposing that Bha*tt*i could in Chinese have been represented by Pida. As to the date of the Bha*tt*ikâvya we know very little beyond the fact that its author lived under *S*rîdharasvâmin of Va*l*abhî. Lassen [2] identified this king with *S*rîdharasena of Va*l*abhî, the son of Guhasena, 530–545, but this too is a mere guess, and need not by itself invalidate I-tsing's statement.

I may add in conclusion the little we know of Bhart*ri*hari as a grammarian, from Brahmanic sources.

Tarkavâ*k*aspati, in his edition of the Siddhânta-kaumudî [3], reminds us very properly that Somadeva's Kathâsarit-sâgara is only an extract from the B*ri*hatkathâ, a work in 70,000 *S*lokas, supposed to have been composed by Kâtyâyana, and taught by him to Kâ*n*abhûti. He then tells the story of Vararu*k*i, called Kâtyâyana, and his fellow-pupils Vyâ*d*i and Pâ*n*ini. They were all three the disciples of Upavarsha. Pâ*n*ini, the least clever of them, having been vanquished in a disputation by the others, went to propitiate Mahâdeva, and, having been taught by him, composed a grammar in four parts

---

[1] See Proceedings of the Asiatic Society, Bengal, Aug. 1881.

[2] Ind. Alterthumskunde, iii, 512.

[3] See also *S*abdârtharatna by Târânâtha Tarkavâ*k*aspati, Calcutta, 1852, Bhûmikâ, p. 2; and Z. D. M. G. xiv, 566.

(the Sûtra-pâ*th*a, the Ga*n*apâ*th*a, the Dhâtupâ*th*a, and the Lingânu*s*âsana), which he afterwards proclaimed before Upavarsha. Vararu*k*i, recognising the excellency of that new grammar, composed the Vârttika by way of completing and briefly explaining it, while Vyâ*d*i composed a work, called Sangraha, consisting of 100,000 *S*lokas, intended to explain by arguments the principles of Pâ*n*ini's grammatical system. These works became so famous that the Aindra and other popular grammars of the time fell into disrepute and were lost.

It is added that Pâ*n*ini was the son of Dâkshî [1]; that Vararu*k*i was the son of a Brâhman Somadatta of Kau*s*âmbî and of Vasudattâ, and that, after composing the B*ri*hatkathâ, and other works, he became Minister of King Nanda; while Vyâ*d*i, the son of a Brahman Karambha, dwelt at Vetasa.

Tarkavâ*k*aspati then quotes another story, taken from the Vâkyapadîya, a work which he ascribes to Bhart*ri*hari, the elder brother of Vikramâditya. He first states himself that in the course of time the Sangraha by Vyâ*d*i became neglected, and Pâ*n*ini's work too had suffered considerable damage, when the Bhagavat Pata*ñg*ali resolved to compose the Mahâbhâshya, containing first the essence of the Sangraha, namely the Sûtras, Vârttikas, and the comment, and secondly the arguments laid down in the Sangraha [2].

But in this form also the system of Pâ*n*ini was again neglected, though one copy of the original grammatical work, made by Râva*n*a, was preserved in the South on the mountain *K*itrakû*t*a. This copy was carried off by some Rakshas, in the guise of a Brâhman, and given to Vasurâta, *K*andra and other teachers, and from them descended to their pupils, Bhart*ri*hari and others. Bhart*ri*hari explained the Mahâbhâshya, composed the explanatory Kârikâs, and also the Vâkyapadîya, sometimes called Vâkyapradîpa, consisting of three parts, the Brahma, Vâkya, and Padakâ*nd*a [3].

---

[1] See Pâ*n*. I, 1, 20, Kârikâ in Mahâbhâshya.

[2] This agrees well with Kielhorn's correct description of the character of the Mahâbhâshya, given in his essay Kâtyâyana and Pata*ñg*ali (1876), p. 7 seq.

[3] See Goldstücker, Pâ*n*ini, p. 237; Weber, Indische Studien, v, 159; Stenzler, ibid. p. 447; Kielhorn, Indian Antiquary, 1874, p. 285.

He then quotes from Bhart*ri*hari's Vâkyakâ*nd*a the following verses :

प्रायेण संक्षेपरुचीनल्पविद्यापरिग्रहान्।
संप्राप्य वैयाकरणान्संग्रहेऽस्तमुपगते ॥१॥
कृतेऽथ पतंजलिना गुरुणा तीर्थदर्शिना ।
सर्वेषां न्यायबीजानां महाभाष्ये निबंधने ॥२॥
अलब्ध[1]गाधे गांभीर्यादुत्तान इव सौष्ठवात्।
तस्मिन्नकृतबुद्धीनां नैवावास्थित निश्चयः ॥३॥
वैजिसौभवहर्यक्षैः शुष्कतर्कानुसारिभिः ।
आर्षे विप्लाविते ग्रंथे संग्रहप्रतिकंचुके ॥४॥
यः पतंजलिशिष्येभ्यो भ्रष्टो व्याकरणागमः ।
काले स दाक्षिणात्येषु ग्रंथमात्रे व्यवस्थितः ॥५॥
पर्वतादागमं लब्ध्वा भाष्यबीजानुसारिभिः ।
स नीतो बहुशाखत्वं चंद्राचार्यादिभिः पुनः ॥६॥
न्यायप्रस्थानमार्गांस्तानभ्यस्य स्वं च दर्शनं ।
प्रणीतो गुरुणास्माकमयमागमसंग्रहः ॥७॥

'When the Sangraha (of Vyâ*d*i) had been lost, having come down to grammarians who mostly preferred short manuals, and possessed but a small stock of knowledge,

'And when afterwards by the venerable and studious Patañ*g*ali the Mahâbhâshya had been composed, a work containing the original Sûtras (vî*g*a), and the argumentations,

'Unfathomable from its depth, and yet almost shallow from its perfect method[2]; then men of small minds were yet unable to understand it.

'And when this work of the *R*ishi, which contained the (substance of the) Sangraha, had been perverted by Vai*g*i, *S*aubhava, and Haryaksha, because (in attempting to explain it) they followed their own sterile reasoning only,

'The tradition of the grammar, which had fallen away from the disciples of Patañ*g*ali, existed in time as a text only (without being understood) among the people in the South[3].

---

[1] अलब्ध.

[2] Read paripâ*t*i, in the commentary.

[3] It is no doubt very easy to discredit the native traditions with respect to the early literary history of India. They are certainly not historical, in our sense

'But *K*andrâ*k*ârya and others (Vasurâta, etc.) received the tradition again from Parvata (the mountain *K*itrakû*t*a or Trikû*t*a?), and following the original Sûtras (vî*g*a) and the Bhâshya, they made it branch off into many schools[1].

'Then, after having studied the different lines on which the (grammatical) arguments rest and his own grammatical system also, the Guru (*K*andra or Vasurâta) brought to us this resumé of old grammars.'

We have now examined a considerable number of names, famous in Sanskrit literature, most, in fact, of the Mahâkavis and the Mahâkâvyas, and we have seen, I think, that not one of them could be referred to a date beyond the fifth century A.D. Kâlidâsa, formerly represented as the contemporary of Augustus, has become the contemporary of Justinian, and the very books which were most admired by Sanskrit students as specimens of ancient Indian poetry and wisdom, have found their natural and rightful place in the period of a literary renaissance, coinciding with a period of renewed literary activity in Persia, soon to be followed there, as later on in India, by the great Mohammedan conquests.

I have confined myself chiefly to what used to be called the art poetry of India, nor could I attempt to examine here the whole of our post-Vedic literature, partly for want of space, partly for want of knowledge.

There was no necessity, considering what our immediate object is, for going beyond the ninth century, for it is not likely that any literary works that can be referred to so late a date, would ever be claimed for the four blank centuries between 100 B.C. to 300 A.D.

---

of the word, but, on the other hand, they possess this merit that, as a rule, they are not invented with a purpose, or intended to support any preconceived system. What purpose, for instance, could the author of the Uttara-kâ*nd*a of the Râmâya*n*a (sect. 36, vv. 44 seq.) [this curious passage was pointed out by Muir, Sanskrit Texts, iv, p. 490] have had in saying that Hanumat, when he was studying grammar, studied it, Sa-sûtra-vritty-arthapadam mahârtha*m* sa-saṅgraham, that is, according to the commentary, 'the Mahâbhâshya (Pata*ñg*ali), containing the Sûtras, the commentary, and the Vârttikas, and the Saṅgraha (Vyâ*d*i),' thus making the Râmâya*n*a, at all events, more modern than Vyâ*d*i?

[1] See Kielhorn, Indian Antiquary, 1876, p. 245.

In the eighth century we enter already on the age of commentaries and glosses. We have *S*ankara, the great commentator of the Vedânta Sûtras, born in 788, and he was preceded by Govinda and Gau*d*apâda, to whom a commentary on the Sâṅkhya-kârikâ is ascribed. If we may accept Burnell's conjecture, Bhavasvâmin, the commentator of the Baudhâyana Sûtras, belonged to the same age, though I must confess that his arguments do not seem to me quite convincing[1].

Epic Poems.

Nor have I said anything of the two great epic poems, the Mahâbhârata and Râmâya*n*a, beyond noting their being mentioned by name among the popular literature of the sixth and seventh centuries. We want a great deal more of truly scholarlike work[2], and a great deal less of truly unscholarlike theories on the Mahâbhârata and Râmâya*n*a, before any clear light will dawn on the sources, the growth, and the final redaction of these Indian epic cycles. But whatever date may in the end be assigned to these poems, as we now have them, or to their first collection, or to their gradual augmentation, our views on the literary blank between 100 B.C. and 300 A.D. could hardly be affected thereby. Epic poetry, as we know, if it is popular, and not artificial, like that of Kâli-

---

[1] Burnell, Catalogue (1870), p. 13, says that Mâdhava quotes Bhâskara Misra's commentary on the Black Ya*g*ur-veda, and that the Pandits place him 400 years before Sâya*n*a. Bhâskara, again, quotes not only the Mânava-dharma-sâstra, and, what is more important, the last book of it (xii, 100), but also Bhavasvâmin, the commentator of the Baudhâyana Kalpa Sûtras, 'who may therefore have lived in the eighth century' (Cat. p. 26). It is well known that Sâya*n*a also wrote a commentary on Baudhâyana (Cat. Southern Division, Bombay, fasc. i, p. 8), and that in his Ya*gñ*atantra-sudhânidhi, which gives the Âdhvaryava as well as the Hautra and Audgâtra of the principal sacrifices, he chiefly follows Baudhâyana. He there calls himself the son of Mâya*n*ârya, and the brother (sahodara) of Mâdhavârya. See also Bühler, Sacred Books of the East, vol. xiv, p. xlii.

[2] Adolf Holtzmann, Agni, nach den Vorstellungen des Mahâbhârata, 1878; Arjuna, ein Beitrag zur Reconstruction des Mahâbhârata, 1879; Über das alte indische Epos, 1881; Über das Mahâbhârata. Weber, Über das Râmâya*n*a, 1870. K. T. Telang, Was the Râmâya*n*a copied from Homer? 1872; R. G. Bhandarkar, Considerations of the date of the Mahâbhârata, Journal of the Royal Asiatic Society, Bombay, x, p. 81 (1872).

dâsa, may live on among the people, when all other literary activity has ceased. It forms, so to say, the literary bread and water, without which no nation can long subsist. What we want to know is to what period the work of Vyâsa, the Diaskeuast, can be ascribed, how many such Vyâsas were employed in giving some kind of form to the enormous masses of floating epic poetry in India, and lastly, how much should be ascribed to their individual genius, particularly in the case of Vâlmîki, in what we now admire in the two great national epics of India, the Râmâya*n*a and Mahâbhârata [1]. I ought to add, that I do not think that hitherto any facts or arguments have been produced to justify us in admitting any Greek influences in the growth of epic poetry in India, still less any Christian influences in the production of that famous episode of the Mahâbhârata which is known under the name of the Bhagavadgîtâ Upanishads.

Popular Stories.

And what applies to epic poetry, applies also to what we call Folk-lore. No people is ever without popular stories, and no country was probably richer in them than India. It has lately become the fashion to ascribe all these popular stories in India to a Buddhistic source, nor can there be a doubt of the truth of Benfey's great discovery that the fables which we find collected in the Hitopade*s*a, the Pa*ñk*atantra, and similar works, belonging to the Renaissance period of Sanskrit literature, presuppose Buddhistic collections of them. But that is very different from saying that the Buddhists invented them. The Buddhists used them, improved them, added to them, but they invented them as little as the brothers Grimm invented 'Rumpelstiltzchen.' There is one Buddhist collection of so-called *G*âtaka-stories, in Sanskrit, the date of which can be fixed in the fourth century A. D. It is ascribed to Ârya*s*ûra; and another work of the same author is stated to have been translated in the year 434 A. D. We also know that the

[1] The occurrence of the name of Vyâsa and Vâlmîki in the Lankâvatâra is of interest, but the date of the chapter in which they occur is doubtful.

fame of these stories had reached Persia at the time of Khosru Nushirvan (531–579 A.D.), and that he sent Barzôî to India to bring them to his Court and translate them into Pahlavi[1]. But the original from which Barzôî translated has not yet been discovered, and the Brahmanic collections of fables which we possess, the Pañkatantra, Hitopadesa, etc., are of a later date.

The Kathâ-sarit-sâgara, again, by Somadeva, is as late as the beginning of the twelfth century, having been written to console Queen Sûryavatî, the mother of King Harsha of Kasmîra, on the death of her son who was killed 1101 A.D. It should be remembered, however, that Somadeva too did not invent, did not even claim to have invented, the tales collected in his 'Ocean of the Rivers of Stories,' and that their existence can probably be traced back to the time of Pânini.

As this is of importance with regard to certain historical or semi-historical statements contained in Somadeva's work, it may not be out of place here to explain why I consider some of them quite as trustworthy as, for instance, Kalhana's History of Kasmîra, so far as it bears on early times. It is easy to say that what Somadeva tells about Pânini and his friends is only a story. To me 'only a story' carries more weight than history made on purpose, such as we know Kalhana's history to have been. We must take Indian literature as it is, and try to make the best of it. And in doing this we must, as much as possible, divest ourselves of the idea that Hindu writers always wish to impose upon us, and to make everything as old as possible. First of all, these writers never thought of us 'outer barbarians,' in writing down what they knew, or what they imagined they knew, of their ancient history. Secondly, what we should call 'old,' would not seem at all old to them, to whom ten thousand years more or less is a mere nothing.

My impression is that Somadeva, when telling us about Pânini, Vyâdi, and Kâtyâyana, tells us simply what he knew,

---

[1] See Selected Essays, vol. i, p. 527.

and that what he knew came to him from tradition, which in India was more tenacious than anywhere else. We know, besides, thanks chiefly to the researches of Burnell and Bühler, that Somadeva was not left entirely to depend on tradition. He tells us that his book contains the essence of the Brihatkathâ, written originally in the Paisâkî dialect by Gunâdhya, and that it differs from its original in language only, and by its being more condensed[1]. The story of Gunâdhya is no doubt legendary too, but it need not therefore be considered as a pure invention, so far as Gunâdhya himself is concerned.

We are told that originally the stories of the seven Vidyâdhara Kakravartin's or Fairy Kings were told by Siva to Pârvatî. They were overheard by an attendant, Pushpadanta, who repeated them to his wife Gayâ. For this he was cursed by Pârvatî and condemned to be born as a man, and his brother Mâlyavat, who interceded for him, received the like sentence. Afterwards Pârvatî relented so far that she decreed that Pushpadanta's curse should end when he had met a Pisâka, called Kânabhûti, and told him the stories; while Mâlyavat should be free when he had heard the Brihatkathâs from the mouth of Kânabhûti, and spread them over the earth.

Pushpadanta, we are then told, was born as Vararuki Kâtyâyana, and became a great grammarian and Minister of Yogananda, the last of the Nandas. Having communicated the stories to the Pisâka Kânabhûti, he returned to his heaven.

Some time later Mâlyavat, who as Gunâdhya of Pratishthâna had become Minister of Sâtavâhana, went with his two pupils, Gunadeva and Nandideva, to the dwelling of Kânabhûti, and received from him the seven stories in the Paisâkî dialect. Then he wrote them down with his own blood in 100,000 Slokas each, and sent them to Sâtavâhana. Sâtavâhana, however, rejected them; upon which Gunâdhya burnt six of the stories. The seventh only was preserved, and Sâtavâhana, after studying it with the help of Gunadeva and

[1] See Bühler, Indian Antiquary, 1872, p. 302.

Nandideva, wrote the introduction to it, likewise in the Pai*s*â*k*î dialect.

Dr. Fitz-Edward Hall[1] was the first to show that this legend was not entirely a legend, for Dà*nd*in in his Kâvyâdar*s*a (I, 38), mentions a B*ri*hatkathâ written in a Bhûta (Pi*s*â*k*a) dialect; and Subandhu, the author of the Vâ*s*avadattâ, knows a B*ri*hatkathâ divided into Lambakas. Da*nd*in, we know, is at least as old as Bâ*n*a, the court-poet of Harshavardhana in the seventh century, while Vasubandhu must be older than Bâna, being praised by him in his Harsha*k*aritra.

Thus it may be accepted as a fact that a B*ri*hatkathâ in a Bhûta dialect, and divided, like Somadeva's work, into Lambas or Lambakas, existed at least before the seventh century of our era.

Nor is this all. Dr. Bühler, during his literary researches in Gujarât, discovered a work very similar to the Kathâsaritsâgara of Somadeva, namely, the B*ri*hatkathâ-ma*ñg*arî of Kshemendra Vyâsadâsa[2]. This Kshemendra wrote during the second and third quarters of the eleventh century, and he too seems to have based his own work on the Pai*s*â*k*î text of the B*ri*hatkathâ, ascribed to Gu*n*â*dh*ya. He says[3]: '*S*arva proclaimed it first; Kâ*n*abhûti heard it from the Ga*n*a (Pushpadanta-Vararu*k*i), and told it to Gu*n*â*dh*ya, who delivered it in turn to his pupils and to Sâtavâhana. The story which thus had come to be written in the Pi*s*â*k*a language gave trouble to the readers, and was for this reason rewritten in Sanskrit.' Although Somadeva was perhaps two or three generations later than Kshemendra, Dr. Bühler has shown that he could not have copied from Kshemendra, but that both must have used the same original in Pai*s*â*k*î or Prâkrit.

We thus arrive at the very unexpected result that the stories told by Somadeva in the twelfth century were known, at all events, before the seventh century, and, if we could accept the historical character of Sâtavâhana and Yogananda, of Kâ*n*abhûti and Vararu*k*i-Kâtyâyana, in the first century

---

[1] Vâ*s*avadattâ, pref. pp. 22–24; Bühler, l.c., p. 303.

[2] Journal of the Royal Asiatic Society of Bombay, 1877, p. 46.

[3] Bühler, Indian Antiquary, 1872, p. 307.

A. D., or even, it may be, before the end of the Nanda dynasty. Without as yet wishing, however, to make Kâtyâyana-Vararu*k*i, the original promulgator of the Seven Stories, the same person as Kâtyâyana Vararu*k*i, the author of the Vârttikas and the contemporary of Pâ*n*ini, we may at all events say this, that Somadeva's much-despised Kathâ-sarit-sâgara carries really as much historical weight as Kalha*n*a's Râ*g*ataraṅgi*n*î, the Chronicle of Kashmir, 1148–57. Kalha*n*a wrote in the middle of the twelfth century, and was therefore later than Somadeva. What his ideas of history were has been well shown by Dr. Bühler[1], who writes: 'An author who boasts that "his narrative resembles a medicine, and is useful for increasing and diminishing statements of previous writers regarding kings, place, and time," must always be sharply controlled, and deserves no credit whatever in those portions of his work where his narrative shows any suspicious figures or facts.'

Philosophical Sûtras.

A second class of literature which I have not touched upon consists of the philosophical Sûtras. These were and are still supposed by many scholars to belong to the centuries preceding our era. All I can say is, I know, as yet, of no sound arguments, still less of any facts in support of such assertions. Neither in the Pâli nor in the Sanskrit canon of the Buddhists have any references to or quotations from the six collections of philosophical Sûtras been discovered.

It is different with the philosophical systems themselves. The names of the three Vedas, possibly of four, such words also as Vedânta and Upanishad (upanisâ), and Yoga, occur in Pâli, but they do not prove the existence of our Vedânta or our Yoga Sûtras. In the Buddhist Sanskrit canonical books there are constant references to tîrthaka or heretical systems of philosophy. The names of the founders of six of these are mentioned again and again, but we hear nothing of literary works ascribed to Bâdarâya*n*a, the founder of the Uttara-mîmâ*m*sâ, of *G*aimini,

[1] Journal of the Royal Asiatic Society of Bombay, 1877, p. 58.

the founder of the Pûrva-mîmâmsâ, Kapila, the founder of the Sâṅkhya, Patañgali, the founder of the Yoga, Kaṇâda, the founder of the Vaiseshika, and Gotama, the founder of the Nyâya. The occurrence of the names of Kaṇâda, Kapila, Akshapâda and Brihaspati in the Laṅkâvatâra is curious, but requires verification. What is still more curious is that in the literary works which we have referred to the sixth, seventh, and eighth centuries no actual quotations from the Sûtras of the six Darsanas have yet been met with. It is true, that Varâhamihira mentions Kapila and Kaṇabhug[1], and that Bâṇa in his Harshakarita knows of Aupanishadas, Kâpilas, and Kâṇâdas[2], but even this does not establish the existence of the Sûtras, containing their doctrines. And yet we know now, thanks to Mr. K. B. Pathak (Ind. Ant. 1882, p. 174)[3], the date of Saṅkara Âkârya[4], to whom most, if not all of these Sûtras must have been known. He was born 788 A.D., and he must have lived to a considerable age, if he accomplished all that is ascribed to him. The date 3921 Kali, i.e. 820 A.D., cannot be intended for the date of his death, but is meant for that of his becoming a Muni, which we are told took place in his 32nd year (dvâtrimse).

The first tangible evidence of the existence of a systematic treatise on any of the six systems of India would really seem to be the Chinese translation of the Suvarṇa-saptati-sâstra, that is, the Sâṅkhya-kârikâ, with a commentary[5]. It is said by the Chinese translator to have been composed by the Rishi Kapila, a heretic, and to explain the twenty-five truths (tattvas[6]). Towards the end of the work it is stated that there were 60,000 gâthâs composed by

---

[1] Brihatsamhitâ, ed. Kern, pref. p. 29.

[2] Vâsavadattâ, ed. Hall, pref. p. 53.

[3] He quotes from a MS. the following list: *Siva* (Saṅkara), Vishṇu, Brahman, Vasishtha, *Sakti*, Parâsara, Vyâsa, *Suka*, Gauḍapâda, Govinda, *Saṅkara*. He also mentions Râmânuga as the pupil of Yâdavaprakâsa, and Madhva as pupil of Akyutapreksha.

[4] It is his descent from *Siva* which is alluded to in calling him *Saṅkarâkâryanavâvatâram*.

[5] I am informed by Mr. Kasawara that this commentary resembles the commentary of Gauḍapâda, but that the name of Gauḍapâda is not mentioned.

[6] See Sâṅkhya-sâra, ed. Hall, pref. pp. 6, 42.

Pa*ñk*a*s*ikha (Kâpileya), the pupil of Âsuri, the pupil of Kapila, and that afterwards a Brâhman, named Î*s*vara K*ri*sh*n*a, selected 70 gâthâs out of the 60,000. As this work was translated into Chinese by *K*an-ti, i. e. Paramârtha, during the *Kh*an dynasty, 557–589, we have proof positive that Î*s*vara K*ri*sh*n*a's work, such as we now possess it, and a commentary, belonged at least to the sixth century, and that the author, who has actually been identified with Kâlidâsa[1], may at all events have been a contemporary of the great poet.

But it follows by no means that what we call the Sâṅkhya Sûtras must have existed before that time. The metrical Kârikâ seems in this case older than the Sûtras, and where there are literal coincidences between the two, it has been shown that the metrical version is the more original[2].

With regard to the Vai*s*eshika also, we can prove the existence of at least one work, the Vai*s*eshika-nikâya-da*s*apadârtha-*s*âstra, composed by *G*ñâna*k*andra[3], previous to Hiouen-thsang's time, because he translated it into Chinese, and his translation is still in existence. In this case, however, the Sanskrit original has not yet been discovered.

It certainly would be going too far were we to conclude from the fact that Hiouen-thsang did not translate and did not even mention the authoritative Vai*s*eshika Sûtras by Ka*n*âda that therefore they did not exist at his time. Much less should I venture to apply this line of argument to the Sarvadar*s*ana-saṅgraha. Still we ought to take note of it. Hiouen-thsang evidently knew the Vedânta-philosophy, for he speaks of Aupanishadas, which can only be an older name of the followers of the Vedânta. He tells us that he studied Nyâya under a Brâhman, and he mentions several works on Nyâya, which were written by Buddhists:—

1. Nyâya-dvâra-târaka-*s*âstra by *G*ina Bodhisattva (i, 188) or Nâgâr*g*una (i, 102), explained by Dharmapâla (i, 191).

2. Nyâyânusâra-*s*âstra by Saṅghabhadra (i, 93; ii, 183; 227), edited by Vasubandhu (i, 108).

He mentions the Sâṅkhya and Vai*s*eshika systems by name

---

[1] See Sâṅkhya-sâra, ed. Hall, pref. p. 29.

[2] Hall, l. c., p. 11.

[3] See above, p. 312.

(i, 225), and relates how Gu*n*amati had defeated a famous student of the Sâṅkhya-philosophy, called Mâdhava (ii, 442).

It is difficult to say anything about the Yoga-philosophy, because that name was adopted by the Buddhists themselves. *G*ina Bodhisattva was a teacher of Yoga (iii, 110), and Hiouenthsang's chief object in going to India was to study there (i, 144) that very Yoga-philosophy which he had studied already in China from such books as the Saptada*s*a-bhûmi-*s*âstra (by Maitreya Bodhisattva, iii, 109), afterwards called Yogâ*k*ârya-bhûmi-*s*âstra (i, 13; 118). One of the books which he most carefully studied during his stay in India was the Yogâ*k*ârya-bhûmi-*s*âstra-kârikâ (i, 211).

If we turn to the literature of the *G*ainas, we find in the Kalpasûtra (ed. Jacobi, p. 35) only one system of philosophy mentioned, the Shash*t*i-tantra, and this is explained by the commentator (p. 101) as Kapilîya-*s*âstra, so called on account of the sixty padârthas[1]. In other passages, however, this Shash*t*i-tantra is mentioned by the side of the Kâpila, the system of Kapila, and it becomes extremely doubtful, therefore, whether the two were originally identical, or whether the Kâpila system is a later form of the Shash*t*i-tantra[2]. In the Anuyogadvâra-*s*âstra, quoted by Weber, the principal systems of philosophy mentioned are: Vai*s*eshika, Buddha*s*â*s*ana, Kâpila, Lokâyata, Shash*t*itantra, while in the later Sha*d*dar*s*ana-samu*kk*aya the author refers to the Sâṅkhya, Vai*s*eshika, Naiyâyika, *G*aiminîya, Bauddha, and *G*aina systems[3].

It is probably in the Sanskrit literature of the Buddhists that we find the earliest mention of these systems[4]. Thus we read in the Lalita-vistara, p. 179, that the young Bodhisattva had to study, besides many other subjects, the Sâṅkhya, the Yoga, the Vai*s*eshika, the Bârhaspatya, the

[1] See also Bhagavatî (ed. Weber), ii, pp. 246-648.

[2] According to Dr. Leumann, the Berlin MS. of the Nandisûtra leaves out Kâvila. The Calcutta edition has it, and the Aupapâtika-Sûtra (§ 76) mentions 'the followers of the Sâṅkhya and the Yoga-philosophy, and of Kâpila, &c.'

[3] Hall, Bibliography, p. 165. In Merutuṅga's Sha*dd*âr*s*anavi*k*âra the six systems discussed are: Gaina, Bauddha, Sâṅkhya, *G*aiminîya or Mîmâ*m*sâ, Aulûkya or Kâ*n*â*d*a, and Gautamîya. See Journal of Royal Asiatic Society of Bombay, ix, p. 147.

[4] See above, p. 17.

Hetuvidyâ [1], &c. But again, these are but titles of philosophical doctrines, and they cannot strictly be used to prove the existence of the six collections of Sûtras which at present are considered as the classical text-books of these systems. Similar names, as is well known, occur in the Upanishads and Brâhma*n*as, and the first germs of the later growth of philosophical thought may be discovered even in the hymns of the Veda. But all this does not concern us at present, and with regard to what does concern us, namely, the date of the six Dar*s*anas, as we now possess them, all we can say is that, as yet, nothing has been produced to prove that they were composed previous to 300 A.D.

Metrical Law-books.

There remains one more class of Sanskrit literature which will no doubt be appealed to by many Sanskrit scholars as being post-Vedic, and yet decidedly more ancient than the

---

[1] In *Ku* Fa-hu's translation (A.D. 308) the whole paragraph is left out. This does not, however, prove that it did not exist, as passages referring to subjects of no immediate interest to Buddhists, or, it may be, unintelligible to them, are sometimes passed over by the translators. In Divâkara's translation (A.D. 683) we find certain portions of this paragraph rendered into Chinese, but others likewise left out. Among the subjects in which the Bodhisattva excelled, are mentioned: 'Quick jumping, racing, wrestling (lañghite, prâk*k*alite), writing, seals, counting-numbers (lipi-mudrâ-ga*n*anâsañkhyâ), archery, riding, going on the water, cleverly managing horse and chariot, and (fishing with) a hook and line (sâlambhadhanurvede *g*avite, plavite, asvap*ri*sh*th*e, rathe, añku*s*agrahapâ*s*agrahe); Matma (?), gambling (akshakrî*d*â), physiognomy or expression of face (kâvya-vyâkara*n*e ?), drawing (granthara*k*ite rûpe), carving (rûpakarma*n*i), playing on musical instruments (vî*n*âyâm), singing and dancing (vâdyan*ri*tye), theatrical performance (gîtapa*th*ita âkhyâte), shampooing (sa*m*vâhite), changing several precious things, magic (ma*n*irâge vastrarâge mâyâk*ri*te), divining a dream (svapnâdhyâye), the marks of six kinds of animals (cows, horses, sheep, pigs, dogs, and fowls), and several mixed sorts of polite accomplishments (strîlakshа*n*e, purushalaksha*n*e, a*s*valaksha*n*e, hastilaksha*n*e, golaksha*n*e, *a*galaksha*n*e, mi*s*rita laksha*n*e); the *S*âstras of Keita (kai*t*abhe*s*vara-laksha*n*e), Ni-ken-dzu (Nirgha*n*tau), Pu-ra-na (Purâ*n*e), I-*k*i-ka-sha (Itihâse), I-da (Vede), Ni-ro-*k*i (Nirukte), Shik-sha (*s*ikshâyâm), Shi-ka (Sâñkhye ?), Bi-shi-ka (Vaiseshike), [could Kriyâkalpe be meant for *G*aiminîya ?] A-ta (arthavidyâyâm), king or kings (Bârhaspatye ?), A-bi-ri (?), all birds and beasts (m*ri*gapakshirute), the science of sound (*s*abdavidyâyâm ?), the science of cause (hetuvidyâyâm). All the polite accomplishments of men and gods he thoroughly understood.'

fourth century A.D., namely, the metrical Dharmaśâstras, and more particularly those of Manu and Yâgñavalkya.

It is generally supposed that Manu was a purely mythological name, that it meant measurer, and therefore law-giver, that it naturally became the name for moon, as the measurer of times and seasons, and lastly a recognised name for man in general, the measurer, the thinker. There is some truth in all this, but it is curious nevertheless that Manu, the law-giver, often discloses some personal traits of character even in the vague traditions which are related of him.

When we read in the Rig-veda, VIII, 30, of 'the thirty-three gods, the gods of Manu,' we ought no doubt to take Manu as a representative of man in general. Yet, the definite number of his gods, the Thirty-three, leaves an impression that even here an individual man, or rather an individual clan, was meant.

When we read in the Taittirîya-Samhitâ, II, 2, 10, 2, 'Whatever Manu said is medicine[1],' we have again a kind of suspicion that Manu must be more than a general name for mankind, and that the saying possibly refers to a sage whose utterances were remembered and recorded.

In the Brâhmanas, Manu, as saved from the Deluge[2], is no doubt a mythical character, but as the father of Nâbhânedishtha, and as laying down the law on inheritance (avavaditri), the historical element begins again to betray itself[3].

It has been supposed that even our Manu Svâyambhuva is sometimes referred to as a legal authority in very early times. There is a curious passage in the Nirukta (III, 4) in which Manu Svâyambhuva is quoted, and again on the very subject of inheritance. It is true the passage comes in rather incongruously, but unless we start with the *a priori* conviction that there can be nothing incongruous in an ancient Sanskrit author, we can hardly off-hand reject the passage as a forgery. The verse (sloka) quoted says: 'The share of sons, of boys and girls, is the same according to law, Manu Svâyambhuva said so in the beginning of the creation.'

---

[1] M. M., History of Ancient Sanskrit Literature, p. 89.

[2] Ibid. p. 425.

[3] Ibid. p. 423.

This seems indeed to imply the existence of a legal authority under the name of Manu Svâyambhuva, but though the wording strongly reminds us of the phraseology of our Manu, the doctrine is not his, unless we completely twist the meaning of Manu IX, 105, where it is said that the eldest brother takes possession of the patrimony, while the others live under him, as they lived under their father. This would hardly be the same thing as that all children take equal shares as heirs. The Nirukta goes on quoting the opinions of other teachers: 'Some say that daughters do not (inherit). Hence it is known that a male is an heir (dâyâda), not a female. Therefore they expose a female, not a male child. Females are given away, sold, and exposed, not males; though some say, males also, as we see in the case of *S*una*hs*epa.'

I pointed out (see p. 235) that Manu, a real Manu, seems to have had something to do with the first introduction of *S*râddhas, and in a passage of the *S*âṅkhâyana G*ri*hya Sûtras (II, 16) Manu's name is again quoted in support of the doctrine that at *S*râddhas, or, more accurately, at a sacrifice in which the Pit*ri*s are the deities, also at a Madhuparka and a Soma sacrifice, the killing of cattle is allowed. This is not only the teaching of Manu, but the very words, as here quoted by *S*âṅkhâyana, have been incorporated in our text of Manu (V, 41). There are many more such references to a Manu[1], as well as quotations, both in prose and in verse, occurring in the Dharmasûtras and embodying Manu's own peculiar doctrines, so that we can hardly doubt that there was, during the Brâhma*n*a and Sûtra periods, some real Manu, or some real clan claiming descent from Manu, and possessing some collection of legal saws.

It is well known also that the Mahâbhârata contains many verses ascribed to Manu, some of which form part of our Dharma*s*âstra, others do not.

But when we come to the question whether a metrical Mânava Dharma*s*âstra, or a Bh*ri*gu-sa*m*hitâ in twelve books, is ever appealed to either during Vedic times, or in early Buddhistic writings where there was so much opportunity for

---

[1] See Bühler, Sacred Books of the East, vol. xiv, pp. xvii–xx.

it, or even during the first centuries of the Renaissance period, our answer must be in the negative.

I am willing to admit that Bâ*n*a's mention in the Harsha*k*arita of Dharma*s*âstrins[1] and Paurâ*n*ikas proves the existence of certain Dharma*s*âstras and Purâ*n*as in the seventh century A.D. I may admit even that the fact of Varâhamihira quoting from Manu a number of *s*lokas, proves his knowledge of a Manu-Dharma*s*âstra, though certainly not of the one which we possess. But it is well known that what we call the Manu-sa*m*hitâ is in reality a Bh*ri*gu-sa*m*hitâ[2], and certainly the spirit of the lines quoted by Varâhamihira as coming from Manu, is very different from the spirit that pervades our Manu-sa*m*hitâ in its chapter on Women. Nor is it likely that these verses, a string of regular *s*lokas, were taken from the Mânava-dharma Sûtras, the character of which has lately been so well described by P. von Bradke in his careful essay, 'Über das Mânava G*ri*hya Sûtra.' They may be taken, however, from earlier editions of the Manu-sa*m*hitâ, which are often quoted under the names of V*ri*ddha and B*ri*ha*t* Manu[3].

And here it should be remembered that even V*ri*ddha Manu was acquainted with the Greek zodiacal signs, for in a passage, quoted in the commentary on the Gobhilîya G*ri*hya Sûtras, he speaks of the sun entering the sign of Kanyâ, i.e. Virgo[4].

From whatever source therefore these verses are taken, they would in no way prove the existence of our twelve books of Manu at the time of Varâhamihira. How much later than the fourth century A.D. our Manu-sa*m*hitâ may prove to be, I do not wish to discuss at present, as, I have no doubt, that this question will soon be treated by far abler hands, by Dr. Burnell and Professor Bühler in their promised translations of Manu. All I am concerned with is the absence of any proofs of its existence previous to 300 A.D.

---

[1] Hall, Vâsavadattâ, pref. 53.

[2] See Sâṅkhya-sâra, ed. Hall, pref. p. 8. Pa*ñk*a*s*ikha*h* sûtrakâra âsuri*s*ishya*h*. Kâpilam iti prasiddhis tu sampradâya-prav*ri*tte*h*, Bh*ri*guproktasa*m*hitâyâm iva Manusamâkhyâ.

[3] On V*ri*ddha and B*ri*ha*t*, see Sarvâdhikâri's Tagore Lectures, p. 168.

[4] Madhye vâ yadi vâpyante yatra Kanyâ*m* vra*g*ed ravi*h*
Sapaksha*h* sakala*h* *s*resh*th*a*h* *s*râddhashoda*s*akam prati.

NOTE H, p. 137.

TEXTS ON THE DELUGE.

The Varâha or Boar.

Taittirîya-Sa*m*hitâ VII, 1, 5, 1[1]:—

Ãpo vấ idám ágre salilám âsît, tásmin pra*g*ấpatir vâyúr bhutvấ*k*arat, sá imấm apa*s*yat, tấ*m* varâhó bhûtvấharat, tấ*m* vi*s*vákarmâ bhûtvấ vyamâr*t*.

Sấprathata, sấ p*ri*thivy abhavat, tát p*ri*thivyaí p*ri*thivítvá*m*. Tásyâm a*s*râmyat pra*g*ấpati*h*, sá devấn as*rig*ata, vásûn rudrấn âdityấn.

Té devấ*h* pra*g*ấpatim abruvan, prá *g*âyâmahâ íti. Sò 'bravît ‖1‖ yáthâhám yushmấ*m*s tápasấs*ri*kshy evá*m* tápasi pra*g*ánanam i*kkh*adhvam íti.

Tébhyo 'gním âyátanam prâya*kkh*ad, eténâyátanena *s*râmyatéti. Tè 'gnínâyátanenâ*s*râmyan, té sa*m*vatsará ékâ*m* gấm as*rig*anta, tấ*m* vásabhyo rudrébhya âdityébhya*h* prấya*kkh*an, etấ*m* rakshadhvam íti, tấ*m* vásavo rudrấ âdityấ arakshanta.

Taittirîya-Brâhma*n*a I, 1, 3, 5 seq.:—

Ãpo vấ idám ágre salilám âsît. Téna pra*g*ấpatir a*s*râmyat ‖5‖ Kathám idá*m* syâd íti. Sò 'pasyat pushkarapar*n*á*m* tísh*th*at. Sò 'manyata ásti vaí tát, yásminn idám ádhitish*th*atîti. Sá varâhó rûpá*m* k*ri*tvópanyàma*gg*at. Sá p*ri*thivî*m* adhá âr*kkh*at, tásyâ upahátyódama*gg*at. Tát pushkarapar*n*é 'prathayat. Yád áprathayat ‖6‖ tát p*ri*thivyaí p*ri*thivitvám. Ábhûd vấ idám íti, tád bhûmyai bhûmitvám.

*S*atapatha-Brâhma*n*a XIV, 1, 2, 11:—

Atha varâhavihatam, iyaty agre âsîd îtîyatî ha vâ iyam agre p*ri*thivy âsa prade*s*amâtrî. Tâm emûsha iti varâha

---

[1] See Colebrooke, Miscellaneous Essays, i, 75; Muir, Original Sanskrit Texts, i, p. 52.

u*gg*ag*h*âna so 'syâ*h* pati*h* pra*g*âpatis tenaivainam etanmithunena priye*n*a dhâmnâ samardhayati k*ri*tsna*m* karoti.

The Kûrma or Tortoise.

*S*atapatha-Brâhma*n*a VII, 5, 1, 5:—

Sa yat kûrmo nâma, etad vai rûpa*m* k*ri*tvâ pra*g*âpati*h* pra*g*â as*ri*gata yad as*rig*atâkarot tad yad akarot tasmât kûrma*h* ka*s*yapo vai kûrmas tasmâd âhu*h* sarvâ*h* pra*g*â*h* kâ*s*yapya iti ‖5‖. Sa ya*h* sa kûrmo 'sau sa âditya*h*.

Taittirîya-Âra*n*yaka I, 23, 1:—

Yo rasa*h* so 'pâm antarata*h* kûrma*m* bhûta*m* sarpanta*m* tam abravît, mama vai tvanmanasâ samabhût. Nety abravît, pûrvam evâham ihâsam iti. Tat purushasya purushatvam iti.

The Annual Deluge.

Plutarch De Solertia Animalium (ed. Reiske, 10, p. 37):—

Οἱ μὲν οὖν μυθολόγοι τῷ Δευκαλίωνί φασι περιστερὰν ἐκ τῆς λάρνακος ἀφιεμένην, δήλωμα γενέσθαι, χειμῶνος μὲν, εἴσω πάλιν ἐνδυομένην, εὐδίας δὲ, ἀποπτᾶσαν.

Page 153. The following passage from the Aitareya-Âra*n*yaka III, 1, 2, 2, shows that during a heavy rain people used to say that heaven and earth embraced each other: Tad utâpi yatraitad balavad anûdg*ri*b*n*an sandadhad ahorâtre varshati dyâvâp*ri*thivyau samadhâtâm ity utâpyâhu*h*. See Sacred Books of the East, vol. i, p. 249: ('The first half is the earth, the second half the heaven, their uniting the rain, the uniter Par*g*anya.) And so it is when it (Par*g*anya) rains thus strongly, without ceasing, day and night together, then they say also, "Heaven and earth have come together."'

NOTE I, p. 194.

ON PARGANYA IN GERMAN.

I am afraid that Slavonic scholars may think that I have represented the identity of Par*g*anya and the Lithuanian Perkuna as more certain than it really is. Though I have pointed out one difficulty, namely, the Lithuanian guttural tenuis k taking the place of a Sanskrit palatal media, I ought perhaps to have added that the transition of Perkuna into the Old Slav. Perunŭ is not free from difficulties either. G. Krek (Einleitung in die Slavische Literaturgeschichte, Gratz, 1874, p. 101) still keeps to the old derivation of Perunŭ (thunder) from a root pr, ferire, and looks upon the k as a phonetic intrusion, as in Lith. arklas=Old Slav. oralo. The name Perkuna, however, seems older than the forms without the k, for it occurs in the Lithuanian Dainos (Schleicher, Handbuch der Litauischen Sprache, vol. ii, p. 1 seq.). In Russian the name of Perun is mentioned by Nestor (about 1100 A.D.), while Perkunŭ still occurs in old Russian documents of the thirteenth century (Kerk, l. c., p. 101, n. 3). All this is difficult to explain; yet Slavonic scholars would hardly feel inclined to admit two different deities, one Perkunŭ, the other Perun. Here we must wait for further researches, particularly with reference to the phonetic laws of the Slavonic languages.

But if the identification of Par*g*anya with Perkuna is not quite free from doubt, this is much more the case with another identification of Par*g*anya with the Gothic faírguni, first suggested by Grimm in his Teutonic Mythology, and supported by him, as may be expected, with very powerful arguments. Faírguni in Gothic means mountain, and Grimm thinks that the chief mountains, being considered originally as the seat of the thunder-god, may after a time have been called by his name, as we speak of the St. Bernard, instead of the Mount of St. Bernard, and that, still later, the name of the chief mountain may have become the name for mountain in general. As relics of the proper name he points out *Fergunna*, an old name of the Erzgebirge, and *Virgunia*, the tract of wooded mountains between Ansbach and Ellwangen, etc. The name of the god, if it had been preserved in Gothic, would have been Faírguneis, and the existence of that name is confirmed by the Old Norse Fiörgyn, fem., gen. Fiörgynior, the goddess of the Earth, the mother of Thor, and by Fiörgynn, masc., gen. Fiörgyns, the father of Frigg, the wife of Oðin.

A young and talented scholar, Professor Zimmer, has lately supported the same view by some more and very ingenious arguments, in the Zeitschrift für Deutsches Alterthum, Neue Folge, vol. ii, p. 163 seq. According to him, the Northern nations formed a feminine deity *Fiörgyn* by the side of the masculine *Fiörgynn*. This *Fiörgyn*, as a feminine, was meant for the Earth, just as Par*g*anya's wife was P*ri*thivî, the Earth. *Ôðinn*, who took the place of *Týr* (Dyaus), and of the male *Fiörgynn* (Par*g*anya), was the husband of *Iörd*, the Earth, and became naturally the husband also of *Fiörgyn*, the Earth, while *Fiörgynn* himself became absorbed in *Thórr*. If therefore *Thórr* is called the first son of *Ôðinn*, this is the same as Par*g*anya being called the son of *Dyaus*, and if *Thórr* is called *Iarðar burr* and *Fiörgynjar burr*, this is the same as Par*g*anya being called the son of P*ri*thivî, though being her husband also.

Grimm in his German Dictionary, vol. i, p. 1052, thinks that Greeks and Romans, changing *f* into h, represented Fergunna or Fergunnia by Hercynia, and he traces in the end both *berg* and *burg* back to Par*g*anya.

NOTE K, p. 227.

ON THE PITRIS OR FATHERS.

In Manu the belief in the Pit*ri*s or Fathers and the rules for their worship have assumed a most complicated character, and there are many passages that might be quoted by those who hold that in India also a belief in the Fathers came first, and a belief in the Devas followed afterwards. There are other arguments too that might be used in support of such a theory, and I wonder they have not been used, though I do not think they can be upheld against the mass of evidence on the other side. The name of the oldest and greatest among the Devas, for instance, is not simply Dyaus, but Dyaush-pitâ, Heaven-Father, and there are several other names of the same character, not only in Sanskrit, but in Greek and Latin also. Does it not look as if Dyaus, the sky, had become personal and worshipful, only after he had been raised to the category of a Pit*ri*, a father, and that this predicate of Father must have been elaborated first, before it could have been used to comprehend Dyaus, the sky, Varu*n*a, and other Devas? This sounds plausible, nor do I deny that there may be some truth in it. But it is not the whole truth, and nothing, I believe, is so constant a source of error as this mistaking of some truth for the whole truth. The Vedic poets believed in Devas, gods, if we must so call them, literally, the bright ones; Pit*ri*s, fathers; and Manushyas, men, mortals[1]. Who came first and who came after is difficult to say, but as soon as the three were placed side by side, the Devas certainly stood highest, then followed the Pit*ri*s, and last came the mortals. Ancient thought did not go so far as to comprehend the three under one common concept, but it paved the way to it. The mortals, after passing through death, became Fathers, and the Fathers

[1] Atharva-veda X, 6, 32.

became the companions of the Devas. This answered for a time—it was some truth, but not the whole truth.

In Manu there is a decided advance beyond this point. The world, all that moves and rests, we are told (Manu III, 201), has been made by the Devas, but the Devas and Dânavas were born of the Pit*ri*s, and the Pit*ri*s of the *R*ishis. The *R*ishis were originally the poets of the Veda, where their number is given as seven, the Sapta *R*ishaya*h*[1]. How they came to be placed above the Devas, and above the Pit*ri*s, is difficult to understand; still so they are, at least at the time of Manu. He gives even their names and genealogy[2].

Manu Hairanyagarbha

His sons, the seven *R*ishis.						
Virâg	Marî*k*i	Atri	Kavi (Bh*ri*gu)	Aṅgiras	Pulastya	Vasish*th*a
Their sons, the Pit*ri*s.						
Somasads	Agnishvâttas	Barhishads	Somapas	Havishmats	Â*g*yapas	Sukalins
Their descendants.						
Sâdhyas	Devas	Daityas	Brâhma*n*as	Kshatriyas	Vaisyas	*S*ûdras

He then mentions the Pit*ri*s who belong exclusively to the Brâhma*n*as:

Agnidagdhas, Anagnidagdhas, Kâvyas, Barhishads, Agnishvâttas, Saumyas.

The first book of Manu tells us of seven Manus (I, 61). These were:

Svâyambhuva, Svâro*k*isha, Auttami, Tâmasa, Raivata, *K*âkshusha, Vaivasvata.

Svâyambhuva Manu is said by Kullûka to have been the grandson of Brahman or Svayambhû, and would therefore have to be taken as the son of Virâ*g* (I, 32). But in another place (I, 58) we read of Manu Svâyambhuva receiving the law from Brahman, and teaching the code to the Munis (*R*ishis), viz. Marî*k*i and the rest, including Bh*ri*gu. Again, our Manu Svâyambhuva tells us that he first created ten Pra*g*âpatis, viz.

Marî*k*i, Atri, Aṅgiras, Pulastya, Pulaha, Kratu, Pra*k*etas, Vasish*th*a, Bh*ri*gu, Nârada,

and that these created the seven Manus.

---

[1] Rig-veda IV, 42, 8.

[2] Manu III, 193 and 198.

These Manus are intimately connected with the theory of the Yugas and Kalpas.

(1) The K*ri*ta-Yuga . .	=	1,728,000 years
(2) The Tretâ-Yuga . .	=	1,296,000 years
(3) The Dvâpara-Yuga .	=	864,000 years
(4) The Kali-Yuga . .	=	432,000 years
A Mahâyuga . . .	=	4,320,000 years
		71
A Manu period . .	=	306,720,000 years
		14
		4,294,080,000 years
With fifteen intervals of 1,728,000 each .		25,920,000 years
		4,320,000,000 years,

which is one short day of Brahman.

In this way the tradition about the Fathers and the *Ri*shis and the Manus and Pra*g*âpatis goes on growing, different conceptions being mixed up together, each family or school adding their own legends, till in the Purâ*n*as the confusion exceeds all bounds, and the original germs of sense are smothered beneath a thick layer of mere nonsense.

NOTE L, p. 242.

ON *S*RÂDDHAS.

In the Nirnaya-sindhu the *S*râddhas are classified under twelve heads[1]:—

1. Nitya-*s*râddha; perpetual, obligatory, daily offerings to ancestors, without the Vai*s*vadeva offerings[2]. A man who is unable to offer anything else may perform this *s*râddha with water.

2. Naimittika-*s*râddha; occasional, as, for instance, the ekoddish*t*a, i. e. the *s*râddha intended for a person lately deceased, and not yet incorporated with the Pit*ri*s. This, too, is without the Vai*s*vadeva offering, and the number of Brâhma*n*as invited should be unequal.

3. Kâmya-*s*râddha; voluntary, or rather, offered for a special object.

4. V*ri*ddhi-*s*râddha; offered on occasions of rejoicing or prosperity, such as the birth of a son, etc.

5. Sapi*nd*ana-*s*râddha; performed when the recently departed is incorporated among the Pit*ri*s. For this *s*râddha four pâtras or vessels are required, full of sesame and scented water for argha, and the vessel of the recently deceased person is poured into the vessels of the Pit*ri*s, with the two verses 'ye samânâ*h*.' It is in one sense an ekoddish*t*a, and for the rest to be performed like the nitya-*s*râddha. It can be offered for a woman also[3].

6. Pârva*n*a-*s*râddha; performed on a parvan day, i. e. new moon, the eighth day, the fourteenth day, and full moon.

7. Gosh*th*î-*s*râddha; performed in a gosh*th*î (house of assembly), for the benefit of a number of learned men.

8. *S*uddhi-*s*râddha; performed for the expiation of some sin,

---

[1] See Colebrooke, Life and Essays, vol. ii, p. 196; Wilson, Vishnu-purâ*n*a, p. 314.

[2] Vishnu-purâ*n*a, p. 326.

[3] See Yâg*ñ*avalkya I, 252–253.

and including the feeding of Brâhma*n*as. It forms part of a prâya*s*kitta, or expiatory rite.

9. Karmâṅga-*s*râddha; forming part of some other ceremony, such as the Sa*m*skâras or sacraments at birth, etc.

10. Daiva-*s*râddha; offered for the sake of the Devas.

11. Yâtrâ-*s*râddha; performed by a person going on a journey, for his safe return.

12. Push*t*i-*s*râddha; performed for the sake of health and wealth; also called aupa*k*âyika.

The four principal *S*râddhas are the Pârva*n*a, Ekoddish*t*a, V*ri*ddhi, and *S*api*nd*ana *s*râddhas.

*S*râddhas may be performed in one's own house, or in some secluded and pure place. There are besides certain localities which are considered particularly favourable to the performance of the ancestral rites, and these naturally vary during different periods of Indian history. In the Mahâbhârata the following are mentioned as particularly sacred: Kurukshetra, Gayâ, Gaṅgâ, Sarasvatî, Prabhâsa, Pushkara. In the Âditya-purâ*n*a Gayâkshetra is described as five kro*s*as, Gayâ*s*iras as one kro*s*a, west of the great river as far as the mountain G*ri*dhre*s*vara, north of Brahmayûpa, as far as Dakshi*n*a-mânasa (?). Other localities are mentioned also as particularly unfavourable for the performance of *S*râddhas, and a careful study of these places, both favourable and unfavourable to the performance of *S*râddhas, would be very instructive as to the geographical horizon of successive generations.

The number of *S*râddhas to be performed each year by those who can afford it varies considerably, but ninety-six seems to be a generally received number. Mr. Bourguin, in his translation of the Dharmasindhu (Journal of the Royal Asiatic Society of Bombay, 1881, p. 22), enumerates them as follows:—'Twelve Amâ or new-moon rites; four Yuga and fourteen Manu rites (i.e. on the anniversary days of the beginnings of the fourteen Manvantaras and the four Yugas); twelve Krânti, corresponding to the twelve passages of the sun into the zodiacal mansions; twelve Dh*ri*ti, performed on the day of the month the sun and the moon are on the same side of either solstice, but of opposite direction; twelve Pâta, performed on the day of the month the sun and the moon are on opposite sides of either solstice and their declination is the same; fifteen Mahâlaya, great funeral rites and sacrifices performed at the end of the Hindu lunar year in the month of Bhâdrapada (which is the last month of the year of the era of Vikramâditya, but not of *S*âlivâhana, showing that Vikramâditya's era was once followed by all Hindus (?), as now even those who follow *S*âlivâhana's era still perform those rites according to Vikramâditya's calendar in the month of Bhâdrapada); five Ash*t*akas, performed on the eighth day of five months of the year; five Anvash*t*akas, performed on the ninth day of five months of the year; and five Pûrvedyu*h*, performed on the seventh day of five months of the year.' This is summed up in the following verse:

अमामनुयुगक्रांतिधृतिपातमहालयाः ।
अन्वष्टक्यं तु पूर्वेद्युः षण्णवत्यः प्रकीर्तिताः ॥

It should be remarked, however, as Colebrooke pointed out, that different authorities do not concur exactly in the number, or in the particular days, when the *S*râddhas should be solemnized.

Note to page 328. I have received the following note from Mr. Bunyiu Nanjio with reference to the Chinese translation of the Amara-kosha mentioned by Stanislas Julien. It shows how careful we ought to be in using the statements even of the very best Chinese scholars.

'I venture to say a few words on this statement of M. Stanislas Julien. According to the Khâi-yuen-lu (compiled A. D. 730), fasc. 7, fol. 6 a, the titles of the Chinese translation in question are—

'1. 翻 外 國 語 Fân-wâi-kwo-yu, lit. "translation-foreign ('outside')-country-word."

'2. 俱 舍 論 因 緣 事 *K*ü-shö-lun-yin-yuen-sh', lit. "Kosha-*s*âstra-hetu-pratyaya-vastu."

'3. 雜 事 Tsâ-sh', lit. "Sa*m*yukta-vastu."

'The two latter titles are given in a note under the first title.

The work is said to have been in seven fasciculi, and already missing in A. D. 730, when the Khâi-yuen-lu was compiled.

'From the second title, I can judge that the work might have been one which treated or explained the subject of the six kinds of cause (Hetu) and the four kinds of co-operating cause (pratyaya)—these being the subjects fully discussed in the second chapter of the Abhidharmakosha-*s*âstra, by Vasubandhu. But there is no trace in the three different titles of the *Amara*-kosha.

'The name of the translator may be Kulanâtha, instead of Gu*n*arata; because this name is translated 親 依 Tshin-i, lit. "intimate-relying," though it is transliterated *K*ü-nâ-lo-tho (*K*ü-lo-nâ-tho ?). See my Catalogue, col. 423 (Appendix II), No. 104.

'Kulanâtha (Gu*n*arata) or Paramârtha first worked at translations, A. D. 548–557, under the Liâṅ dynasty, A. D. 502–557; then A. D. 557–569, under the *Kh*an dynasty, A. D. 557–589. He did not, however, work during the reign of the Emperor Wou-ti, of the Tcheou (*K*eu) dynasty, who reigned A. D. 561–577 (not 566, when the name of the year was changed into a new one, which happened once more in 572). Anyhow it is strange that Julien mentions this Emperor, who belonged only to a secondary dynasty, contemporaneous with the *Kh*an, and was one of four famous sceptical Chinese rulers with regard to Buddhism.

'B. N.'

INDEX.